The Phenomenology of Husserl

CLASSICS IN PHENOMENOLOGY

Volume 1

General Editors

Burt Hopkins, *Seattle University*
Steven Crowell, *Rice University*

Consulting Editors

Damian Byers, *Darlinghurst, Australia*
Marcus Brainard, *Munich, Germany*
Ronald Bruzina, *University of Kentucky*
Patrick Burke, *Seattle University*
John Drabinski, *Grand Valley State University*
R.O. Elveton, *Carleton College*
Parvis Emad, *La Crosse, Wisconsin*
Kathleen Haney, *University of Houston, Downtown*
James Hart, *Indiana University*
James Mensch, *St. Francis Xavier University, Canada*
Algis Mickunas, *Ohio University*
Dermot Moran, *University College Dublin*
James Risser, *Seattle University*
Thomas Seebohm, *Bonn, Germany*
Thomas Sheehan, *Stanford University*

Copyright © 2000, Noesis Press, Ltd.

The Phenomenology of Husserl

Selected Critical Readings

SECOND EDITION

EDITED, TRANSLATED
AND WITH A NEW INTRODUCTION BY

R. O. Elveton

SEATTLE
Noesis Press, Ltd.

THE PHENOMENOLOGY OF HUSSERL. Copyright © 1970 by R. O. Elveton. All rights reserved, including the right to reproduce this book or portions thereof in any form. For information: www.noesispress.com. Manufactured in the United States of America.

Library of Congress Card Number: 00-104617
ISBN: 0-9701679-0-3

Acknowledgments

THE EDITOR wishes to acknowledge gratefully the editors and publishers of the following journals for their permission to use the article listed below:

Dr. G. Martin and the publishers of *Kant-Studien* for Oskar Becker's "*Die Philosophie Edmund Husserls,*" *Kant-Studien* 35 (1930), 119-150, and Eugen Fink's "*Die phänomenologische Philosophie Edmund Husserls in der gegenwärtigen Kritik,*" *Kant-Studien* 38 (1933), 319-383.

Dr. G. Shischkoff and the publishers of *Zeitschrift für philosophie Forschung* for Walter Biemel's "*Die entscheidenden Phases in Husserls Philosophie,*" *Zeitschrift* 13 (1959), 187-213, and Rudolf Boehm's "*Zum Begriff des 'Absoluten' bei Husserl*" *Zeitschrift* 13 (1959), 214-242.

J. C. B. Mohr (Paul Siebeck) for Hans Wagner's "*Kritische Bemerkungen zu Husserls Nachlass,*" *Philosophische Randschau* I (1953/54), 1-22 and 93-123, and Ludwig Landgrebe's "*Husserl Abschied vom Cartesianismus,*" *Philosophische Randschau* IX (1962).

For

Kevin and Rachel, Solveig and David, and

Saundra

Contents

Introduction to the Second Edition	xi
Introduction	3
The Philosophy of Edmund Husserl	
by Oskar Becker	38
The Phenomenological Philosophy of Edmund Husserl and Contemporary Criticism	
by Eugen Fink	70
The Decisive Phases in the Development of Husserl's Phenomenology	
by Walter Biemel	140
Husserl's Concept of the "Absolute"	
by Rudolf Boehm	164
Critical Observations Concerning Husserl's Posthumous Writings	
by Hans Wagner	192
Husserl's Departure from Cartesianism	
by Ludwig Landgrebe	243

The Phenomenology of Husserl

Introduction to the Second Edition

It is now over eighty-five years since Edmund Husserl published the first volume of his *Ideen zu einer reinen Phänomenologie und phänomenologischen Philosophie*,[1] the text in which Husserl announced the breakthrough to a transcendental phenomenology. While a fair amount of Modern Continental Philosophy has been recognized, and even assimilated, by Anglo-American philosophy, Husserl's work, seminal to the very evolution of Twentieth Century Continental thought, remains relatively unexplored by English-speaking philosophers.

In the philosophy of mind, currently one of the most active fields within the Anglo-American philosophical tradition, there is growing interest in the topics of consciousness, self-consciousness, intentionality, and methodologies for the study of consciousness. In the emerging disciplines of artificial intelligence and the cognitive sciences, disciplines that exercise substantial influence in philosophical discussions of the mind, allied topics are investigated, such as the nature of mental representations and structures of human cognition.

Husserl's phenomenology addresses these types of concerns explicitly. Structures of intentionality are central to Husserl's view of consciousness. Different forms of intentional structure are correlated with different realms of meaning. Husserl's radical program of reflective description appears to insure the centrality of self-consciousness. Transcendental phenomenology's systematic investigation of the way consciousness' experience of the world achieves an overall synthetic harmony indicates a concern for those global cognitive structures that provide a basis for a unified experience of the world. Why, then, does Husserl's thought tend to remain alien to the English-language discussion of these issues?

I

In at least one respect, the situation facing Husserl's thought today is comparable to the early reception of Husserl's phenomenological philosophy by his contemporaries and students, a reception documented in detail by the essays included in this collection. Indeed, philosophical dis-

Introduction to the Second Edition

cussion today is perhaps even less inclined to accept an avowed form of transcendental idealism than it was in Husserl's own time.[2]

Husserl's most celebrated student, Martin Heidegger, expresses this rejection of philosophical idealism in *Being and Time*. While his thought clearly remains indebted to Husserlian phenomenology and many of its central themes, the patent refusal of Heidegger in the early pages of *Being and Time* to secure a rigorous methodological access to the phenomena surrounding Dasein's being-in-the-world by invoking either Husserl's famous phenomenological reduction or a comparable strategy, clearly signals an all-important philosophical break between the two. The manifest thinness of methodological considerations in *Being and Time* contrasts vividly with the laborious attention paid to the issue of gaining proper access to the realm of transcendental phenomena that is the philosophical autograph of virtually all of Husserl's writings. It is quite likely that Heidegger believed that he had good reason to dispense with the elaborate mechanisms associated with Husserl's various epochés, not the least of which is the strongly "Cartesian" character of Husserl's standard formulation of the phenomenological reduction, a feature that Husserl himself found increasingly problematic and which is extensively discussed in the following essays.

Heidegger's rejection of Cartesian metaphysics and the "problem of the external world" is made explicit by the end of the first third of *Being and Time*. The "existence" of the world of objects is to be retained from the outset in Heidegger's version of phenomenology, rather than, in Husserlian fashion, being set aside. In maintaining that the true character of the beings that are encountered in Dasein's world are not the perceived objects with which Husserlian analysis is strongly concerned, but objects that fall within the scope of Dasein's daily concerns and use, Heidegger takes another step to distance himself from the attitude of theoretical withdrawal strongly characteristic of Husserl's phenomenological reduction, a withdrawal that substitutes a realm of "pure phenomena" for the "being" of Dasein's directly experienced world and its instrumental complexes.

When Heidegger does begin to move away from the Dasein-analysis of *Being and Time*, he does so with explicit reference to Husserl's transcendental phenomenology. Whereas Husserl is concerned with the transcendental life of consciousness, for Heidegger the ". . . phenomenological reduction means leading phenomenological vision back from the apprehension of being, whatever may be the character of that apprehension, to the understanding of the being of this being . . . Like every other scientific method, the phenomenological method grows and changes due to the progress made precisely with its help into the subjects under investigation."[3] The overt association of Heidegger's question of Being with Husserl's reduction is only slightly less distancing than Heidegger's

Introduction to the Second Edition

strategy in *Being and Time*. In both *Being and Time* and *The Basic Problems of Phenomenology*, Heidegger can call upon a pre-conceptual understanding of Being as a substantive and legitimating framework for his phenomenological investigations. Husserl clearly must direct his readers to a realm of phenomenological descriptions for which no prior orientation is possible and whose motivation, the identification of strictly certain foundations that are the basis of our experience, remains at least esoteric, if not deeply suspect. Equally significant is the growing prominence of the question of Being in Heidegger's work and the emerging, and finally decisive, shift away from the life of consciousness or Dasein as a foundation for Heideggerian phenomenological analysis.

Even Husserl's largely sympathetic reception in France also involved the rejection of his phenomenological idealism. Here the work of Sartre and Merleau-Ponty is central. Sartre's ontological dualism of the in-itself and for-itself managed to combine an ontologically realist interpretation of Husserlian intentionality while completely overturning Husserl's claim that the phenomenologically disclosed life of the transcendental ego constituted an autonomous, independent realm of being.

Merleau-Ponty's influential reinterpretation of Husserl's phenomenological reduction in the introduction to *The Phenomenology of Perception* suggested an additional variation on the effort to retain distinctively Husserlian insights while separating them from the philosophical idealism within which they appeared to be embedded. According to Merleau-Ponty, Husserl's reduction is an indispensable feature of all phenomenological philosophy. However, we must give up the claim that the reduction achieves an absolute perspective. It is better analyzed as a form of disengagement from consciousness' absorption in the world, a disengagement that allows us to uncover the presupposed background embedded in our experience of the world. Such disengagement can only be partial and must be continually re-enacted by the phenomenologist.[4]

II

Within the Anglo-American tradition, current discussions of consciousness, intentionality and the relationship of consciousness to its world are at one with these negative stances on the question of transcendental idealism. However, it is also apparent that these discussions are largely motivated by issues quite distinct from the questions that were of central importance to Husserl and his immediate Continental successors.

From the *Logical Investigations* onward, Husserl saw his phenomenological philosophy as both radically breaking away from the empirical sciences and as seeking to provide a foundation for them. The empirical

xiii

Introduction to the Second Edition

sciences, Husserl writes, are possessed by the "... enthusiasm afforded by the creative play of a theoretical technique, the discovery of theories, with which so much that is useful can be achieved and which fascinate the entire world." But this enthusiastic pursuit of theoretical inventiveness cannot itself substitute for a genuinely "radical self-responsibility," which, for Husserl, means the identification of truly all-encompassing and absolute principles in terms of which human rational judgment is to be properly comprehended and justified.[5]

Whatever final interpretation of Husserl's phenomenological reduction we adopt, one central aim of Husserl's methodology is painfully clear: taking up the attitude of the phenomenological reduction leads to a point of view that rejects viewing consciousness simply as an element within the causal nexus that makes up the natural world. The "natural attitude" situates consciousness within the context of causal relationships with other physical objects. The phenomenological reduction takes up a radically polemical stance toward this distinctive feature of the "natural attitude."

By contrast, much current work in the philosophy of mind is clearly installed within the "natural attitude" and draws its explanatory power and plausibility from its situatedness within the empirical sciences. Whatever the final story will turn out to be, consciousness and its intentional nature must be at least compatible with the causal texture of the physical world. However, and more optimally, consciousness' intentional relationship to the world of physical objects will itself be capable of being understood as a complex of causal processes. This is perhaps the ultimate aim of Fodor's work and the program of a "naturalized epistemology" urged by Quine and other central figures in the philosophy of mind.

In Husserl's view, the form of empirical inquiry represented by the natural sciences, though quite powerful and eminently successful, is naïve by virtue of its lacking an authoritatively established basis for its epistemological claims and cannot serve as a model for philosophical understanding. The usefulness of the sciences should not be accepted as a substitute for a truly autonomous grounding of all forms of human knowledge from a set of unassailable first principles. Acquainted as he was with the controversies of his day surrounding the foundations of logic, mathematics and modern physics,[6] it is quite understandable that Husserl should view the matter of "first principles" and the foundations of the individual sciences as central to his conception of philosophy's proper aims. However, current philosophy of mind finds itself unsympathetic to this dimension of Husserl's thought. "Ultimate" epistemological justification is unattainable. Philosophical reflection is critically indebted to the explanations afforded by the natural sciences and has no special claims to make over and against our best empirical theories. From this perspective,

Introduction to the Second Edition

inquiry into the nature of mind and its intentional structure is, therefore, necessarily empirical in character.

Husserl's rejection of such a stance would appear to allow little room for useful philosophical exchange between Husserlian phenomenology and the philosophy of mind. Hubert Dreyfus and others have argued that Husserl's view of the synthesizing activities that are characteristic of his theory of the constitution of consciousness' intentional objects are comparable to the rule-governed cognitive processes which define the symbol processing view of human cognition in the cognitive sciences. Whatever the merits of this argument, current discussions within the cognitive sciences regarding the plausibility of the symbol-processing, connectionist, dynamical systems and embodied mind paradigms of human cognitive processes appear to rest securely within the experimental methodologies of the empirical sciences. Whatever parallels might obtain between Husserl's phenomenology and present discussions in the cognitive sciences and philosophy of mind might not, from a Husserlian perspective, be richly illuminating.

Despite this difference, it is nevertheless important to call attention to the fact that, within current philosophy of mind itself, there is considerable recognition of the apparent irreducibility of the intentional structures of consciousness to a purely causal, scientific language. One can be convinced, as, for example, is the philosopher Colin McGinn,[7] that consciousness is indeed a product of natural, causal processes, and yet also be convinced that the distinctions that must be made between consciousness and non-conscious physical processes are conceptually unbridgeable. Categories employed to describe the one will be incompatible with those used to describe the other.

Insofar as such a view is not founded upon an appropriate critique of the natural sciences themselves, this option manifestly does not satisfy Husserl's program of strong philosophical justification. But one could argue that, in practice, McGinn's stance on the "phenomenological" separateness of consciousness from the natural order holds out the possibility that the Husserlian descriptions of the life of consciousness might provide useful, and, perhaps, even indispensable, resources for the analysis of intentionality.

McGinn's view clearly does not preclude the experimental modeling of conscious processes in physical media (artificial intelligence). However, by arguing that our best scientific theories may not be able to close the gap between what we understand consciousness to be and our understanding of the way in which the physical world works, McGinn encourages greater autonomy in principle in the analysis of what is properly distinctive regarding the structures of consciousness and intentionality,

Introduction to the Second Edition

autonomy for a type of analysis that is at least not overtly hostile to Husserl's efforts.

The recent work of John Searle,[8] pointing in the direction of the ontological distinctness of consciousness, is also consonant with Husserl's emphasis upon the autonomy of the life of consciousness. However, the emphases of both McGinn and Searle appear to be only broadly compatible with certain Husserlian themes, and fall considerably short of Husserl's detailed efforts to analyze the intentionality of perception, the intersubjectivity of world-constitution, the temporal structure of consciousness and the nature of the world-horizon itself.

III

In considering the rejection of idealism and the privileged role of scientific knowledge in the exploration of consciousness, we have discovered a considerable gap between contemporary discussions in the philosophy of mind and Husserlian phenomenology. While there appear to be no strong indications of a rapprochement between these distinct philosophical traditions, there is some indication that recently emerging reassessments of the analytical tradition itself might serve as one possible basis upon which to restructure discussion between them.

The work of Frege has been pivotal for the development of modern analytical philosophy and for the philosophy of mind. The early correspondence and agreement between Frege and Husserl concerning the analysis of logical and mathematical concepts and the threats posed by psychologism have been evaluated by philosophers within both traditions.[9] Setting aside the detailed questions that are proper to such an evaluation, both Husserl and Frege emerge as philosophers who, up to a point, increasingly shared a central focus, not only on the question of meaning, but upon the distinctness of considerations pertaining to the question of meaning from those directed toward the relationship of language and thought. It is on the basis of this alliance that Michael Dummett argues that, along with Frege, Husserl shares a founding role with respect to the beginnings of analytical philosophy.

Both Dummett, and, more recently, Michael Luntley, distinguish analytical philosophy, rooted in the analysis of language, from the "philosophy of thought." A necessary precondition for the emergence of the philosophy of thought is that it become "disentangled from philosophical psychology,"[10] a common step taken by both Frege and Husserl. For Dummett, the thesis concerning the centrality of meaning (a crucial tenet of the philosophy of thought) is discernible in both Frege and Husserl: in Frege's attending to symbolic, linguistic expressions as a

Introduction to the Second Edition

means of analyzing the content of thought, and in Husserl's generalizing the concept of meaning to include perceptual experience. Husserl's specifically phenomenological project, then, can be seen as an important contribution to the "philosophy of thought."

Without specifically alluding to Husserl, Luntley's recent work characterizes the philosophy of thought as a form of "intentional realism." Intentional realism is defined by two components, one of which is a "phenomenology component," a component that requires ". . . that a theory of content offer a description of the way in which content shapes our encounters with the world . . . Beliefs are not characterizable independently of that which they represent—the world—. . . possession of content amounts to possession of the world!"[11] Whether such a characterization would be of interest to Husserl would perhaps largely depend upon the descriptive analyses in question. However, the implied correlativity of acts of consciousness and intentional content is, as we shall see, consistent with the essentials of Husserl's position. But an additional feature of intentional realism as defined by the "philosophy of thought" outlined by Luntley would possibly be of greater interest.

Luntley contends that the philosophy of thought embraces the specifically Fregean principle that "semantics exhausts ontology." As an illustration of this principle, he argues that present theories about the nature of mental representations entail that "Semantics must be fitted into an ontology derived from science."[12] Luntley views such an assumption as unjustified and considers the Fregean principle regarding the privileged role of semantics as superior. Such an analysis seems to point more sympathetically in the direction of Husserl's view that intentionality is genuinely accessible only from a point of view that avoids viewing the mind as a complex of causal processes causally embedded within a physical environment.

What Luntley refers to as the "standard model" of mental content contains a form of representationalism that is exemplified by Jerry Fodor's representational theory of the mind. In Fodor's view, mental states possess semantic content and can additionally be characterized in purely syntactic terms. These two characterizations must indeed be correlated so that a piece of semantic content will be surrounded by an appropriate syntactic envelope. However, the syntax in question is chosen on the basis of its compatibility with physical, computational, models. Since syntactic structure, on Fodor's view, can be embedded within causal processes of the sort employed by digital computers, one primary merit of Fodor's hypothesis is that it is in agreement with present empirical, computer-as-mind research.

It is Luntley's view that this appealing model of mental states in fact unjustly constrains our theory of mental content (semantics) to the

Introduction to the Second Edition

structures of the requisite syntax. The philosophy of thought avoids such an assumption by freeing the analysis of mental content from this explicit ontological framework. "Frege's prioritizing of semantics over metaphysics means that the constitutive theory of content, in which we account for content in terms of our rationalizing explanations of behavior, has priority over the account of the mechanisms by which we think about the world. For Frege, there is such a thing as an investigation of our capacities for thought and talk that is not dependent on our scientific theories of the mechanisms that underpin those capacities. Furthermore, the constitutive account has a general priority over metaphysics. This means that, for Frege, the starting-point to philosophy is a description of our intentionality—how things are for us in our thought and experience shaped by thought. . . . Furthermore, the description offered is an a priori description. This enterprise needs to be undertaken before we can offer credible models of these abilities. We need to start with an accurate description of the phenomena to be modeled."[13]

Broadly construed, this perspective is congenial to Husserlian phenomenology in several respects.

The emphasis upon a descriptive program that centers upon the ways in which the world is experienced, as opposed to how the world is theorized about or referred to linguistically, is consonant with the stress Husserl placed upon accurate and theory-free descriptions of the life of world-experiencing consciousness.

The autonomy of this descriptive task in relation to the empirical sciences is also consistent with Husserl's rejection of the naiveté of the "natural attitude," which shares with the empirical sciences the unanalyzed belief in the factual givenness of consciousness as one entity among others. It is true that Husserl's reservations concerning the justifiability of the empirical sciences betray a more radical suspension of belief in the sciences than does Luntley's sketch of the philosophy of thought. Nevertheless, they seem to be united in rejecting an *a priori* legitimacy of empirical-scientific discourse with reference to the question of an adequate description of the intentionality of consciousness.

Finally, in rejecting a privileged role for language as the proper focus of philosophical analysis, we can observe some alignment of Husserl's rejection of the natural attitude with Frege's reservations regarding the perspicuity of ordinary language. Although Husserl views the natural attitude, the empirical sciences and the forms of linguistic expression correlated with them, as metaphysically tainted and Frege views ordinary language as hopelessly confused, their common aspiration to seek a vantage point for the description of consciousness that can be sharply distinguished from the framework of ordinary discourse appears to be another

Introduction to the Second Edition

potentially congenial element of the "philosophy of thought" and Husserl's phenomenology.

While such features betray a significant shift toward some of Husserl's concerns, one additional feature of Luntley's program for the philosophy of thought appears to be especially significant. This pertains to the possibility of a transcendental dimension for the philosophy of thought. This dimension encompasses an "a priori study of grammar," where grammar signifies the objective patterns of thought which may, or may not, be embedded in language. As Luntley states, "The study of grammar is the study of thought, and grammar exhausts metaphysics. In this sense, the philosophy of thought is foundational to the rest of philosophy."[14] In so far as these objective patterns of thought serve as a priori constitutive features of the mind's experience of its world, they are at least suggestive of Husserl's notion of the constitutive role of "transcendental" structures of consciousness.

IV

The reflections of Dummett and Luntley may hold out the possibility of a more receptive attitude toward Husserlian phenomenology in future discussions of topics in the philosophy of mind, language and thought within a tradition that hitherto has held Husserl at a distance. But it must be conceded that Husserl's philosophy itself provides a formidable challenge to such receptivity. As the essays included in this volume amply testify, Husserl's account of the nature of the relationship between the world and the world-constituting activities of transcendental consciousness appears to be far from transparent.

If the transcendental reduction is the threshold to Husserl's distinctive philosophy, we must ask just what this threshold entails. As at least a preliminary step towards this task, let us pick up a thread introduced earlier: the distance from Husserl's transcendental phenomenology announced in Heidegger's *Being and Time*.

We have noted that, for Heidegger, the very *problem* of the "existence of the external world" indicates a failure of Cartesian philosophy. Heidegger could well have viewed Husserl's "Cartesian Way" of introducing the transcendental reduction as committing a similar mistake. By speaking of the reduction as a "bracketing" of the natural attitude's belief in the existence of external objects, it is tempting to infer that what is left after the performance of this "reduction" is indeed simply a tag-end of the world, that piece of it that we call an individual consciousness. The problem is then posed concerning how the "reduced" consciousness can be eventually related once again to the world of existent things that were initially, and methodologically, excluded.[15]

In its methodological framework, *Being and Time* contrasts sharply with Husserlian phenomenology, a contrast which, perhaps, was critical for Heidegger's distancing himself from the entire Cartesian problematic. Although Heidegger's aims in *Being and Time* are arguably at least partly "transcendental," in place of a transcendental reduction there is simply an opening definition of "phenomenology" as the study of beings with respect to their Being. Yet this opening definition is to a great extent merely a prolegomenon to an analysis carried out with an immensely creative repertoire of a new philosophical language.

Much of the burden in Heidegger's analyses in *Being and Time* is carried by a rich and inventive vocabulary. A central premise of Heidegger's deployment of this new language is his concern that philosophical language itself has become heavily tainted with metaphysical notions, notions that are greatly misleading and inappropriate to the task of offering an adequate analysis of human Dasein. This concerted effort on Heidegger's part may to a significant extent represent his interpretation of the driving force behind Husserl's theory of the phenomenological reduction. What needs to be accomplished is a transformation of the categories within which the life of consciousness is to be understood. For Husserl, this radical shift in perspective is articulated as a change in point of view, a change which will force terms used to describe the life of consciousness to be understood in a new way. For Heidegger, it appears that this radical shift in perspective is partly articulated in a new vocabulary and by a descriptive procedure that simply stresses an intuitive grasp of the structures ("conditions for the possibility of") that are constitutive of the salient content of Dasein's being.

Heidegger's novel language in *Being and Time* attempts to be more adequate to the structures and experiences that are distinctive for human existence. As is well known, Heidegger's new vocabulary centers on the seamless relationship between Dasein and the world of instrumental complexes. The world is not primarily an object of disinterested perception, as is the case for Husserl's central phenomenological analyses of perceptual consciousness. It is the scene of Dasein's directed involvements. The world is radically open to Dasein's activities, and, as such, is subject to an analysis that is vigorously opposed to Descartes' program of radical doubt. The mutual openness of Dasein and world instantiates what Heidegger terms the "between," a space that encompasses both individual Dasein and the world.

Let us cautiously transpose Heidegger's concerns to Husserl's philosophical project. Husserl's central insight into the nature of intentionality involves the recognition that the very being of consciousness is

Introduction to the Second Edition

bound up with the worlds of transcendent and other intentional objects. In his own way, Husserl, too, is concerned to elaborate the nature of a "between." The phrase "transcendence in immanence" signifies that the "world" is not simply "out there." The world of transcendent objects is directly available to consciousness in and through those acts of consciousness which intend such objects as objects that *are* transcendent, as objects that are incompletely given and as objects nevertheless given directly with the meaning of their incompleteness and transcendent nature. In contrast, the natural attitude takes objects as given, construing them as simply being external to consciousness. The phenomenological attitude understands that this construal is inadequate. To view transcendent objects as simply there apart from activities of consciousness is to fail to recognize that the attribution of this very meaning is itself one important product of the transcendental life of consciousness.

In marked contrast to Heidegger, Husserl seeks to disclose the complex and harmoniously layered strata of consciousness' activities, "constitutive activities" that synthesize the manifolds of variations and that are responsible for the stability and endurance of the perceived world.

As Oskar Becker's essay, "The Philosophy of Edmund Husserl," (the first essay included in this collection) shows, Husserl's concern with such constitutive and synthetic activities remains constant from the early *Philosophy of Arithmetic* to the mature, post-*Ideas*, writings. Becker, who was especially interested in the philosophy of mathematics and the natural sciences, was Heidegger's student in Marburg, and, later, in Freiburg. His survey of Husserl's *Philosophy of Arithmetic* shows an early attempt to reconcile the "psychologism" of this work with the anti-psychologism of Husserl's *Logical Investigations*. Becker also usefully stresses the importance of "eidetic" analysis for Husserl, and claims that "eidetic" and "transcendental" analyses are autonomous and mutually consistent procedures. If defensible, this view permits phenomenology to first proceed "eidetically," possibly avoiding altogether the pitfalls associated with the Cartesian approach to phenomenology characteristic of both the *Ideas* and the late *Cartesian Meditations*. Such an option might also serve as a suggestive characterization of Heidegger's procedures in *Being and Time* and *Basic Problems of Phenomenology*. Heidegger's descriptions of the "world" in the former and his analyses of perception and intentionality in the latter, seem to be broadly analogous to Husserl's method of "eidetic insight." Thus, Heidegger notes that "To see something like such an intentional structure of production and interpret it in one's analysis without prepossession, to make it accessible and keep hold of it and adapt one's concept to what is thus held fast and seen—this is the sober sense of the much ventilated so-called phenomenological *Wesenshau*."[16]

Introduction to the Second Edition

Although the first stages of Husserl's philosophy can be characterized as developing a method of "essential insight," successive stages clearly show the increasing centrality of the phenomenological reduction in Husserl's thought. Walter Biemel's essay, "The Decisive Phases in the Development of Husserl's Philosophy," argues that the first volume of the *Ideas* remains definitive for Husserl's philosophical position. Biemel, the editor of both the Husserliana editions of the first and third volumes of the *Ideas* and the much later text of the *Crisis*, views Husserl's overall development as consistent and coherent, arguing that the late *Cartesian Meditations* can be considered as constituting Husserl's originally planned third volume of the earlier *Ideas*. Husserl's later discovery of "history" and his suggestive theory of the life-world do not disturb the foundations for phenomenology laid down in these middle-period works, but do signal an evolution of the concept of apodictic evidence from the model of mathematical knowledge to the model of an "enlightened knowledge of reason."

Eugen Fink's important essay, "The Phenomenological Philosophy of Edmund Husserl and Contemporary Criticism," makes several important observations about the intelligibility and rationale for the phenomenological reduction. Fink, a student of both Husserl and Heidegger, became, after Heidegger himself, one of Husserl's closest philosophical associates. The author of several important essays on Husserlian phenomenology and of larger philosophical works of a broadly phenomenological content,[17] Fink claims that ". . . every exposition of the phenomenological reduction is in a unique way *false*." The phenomenological reduction itself and the concepts central to the elaboration of phenomenology's central project of understanding "the origin of the world," necessarily stand outside of the framework of the non-phenomenological, "natural" attitude. Hence, they are comprehensible only from "within" the phenomenological perspective. Thus, terms such as "constitution," "noema" and "meaning" take on new content from within this perspective and are easily (even necessarily) misinterpreted. Thus, Husserl may be as deeply involved in a transformation of traditional language as was Heidegger.

If this is the case, then we must be doubly cautious regarding efforts to translate Husserl's statements regarding the intentional relationship between consciousness and objects into the current idioms of representational theories. Not only is representationalism in Luntley's sense suspect because of its empirical assumptions, but the very nature of consciousness' relationship to its objects must itself be recast outside of the customary language of "internal symbol" and "external object."

Mental representations can be interpreted as symbols that relate (possibly in a causal manner) to the objects they are said to symbolize and to which they refer. Within a representationalist framework, an act of perception will be construed as a perceived object causing the activation of a specific mental symbol for this object. Such a construal is similar to Husserl's characterization of "sign-theory." In construing something as being "symbol," Husserl indicates that ". . . we view something in consciousness as depicting or signifying something else. Having the one element in view, we are not directed toward it, but rather, through the vehicle of founded apprehension, to the object depicted or indicated. In truth, nothing at all like this takes place, either in perception or in simple acts of recollection or fantasy."[18] Transcendental phenomenology's account of such acts is significantly different.

Husserl argues that this manner of representing consciousness' relationship to its objects is itself the product of a certain attitude consciousness adopts toward itself: that of viewing consciousness simply as a part of the world. We can view the mind as containing mental representations, symbols and symbolic structures, which "refer," in some perhaps unspecified manner, to objects in the real world. The force of transcendental phenomenology's reduction is to attempt a radically different perspective. The reduction gives us access to ". . . an infinite realm of being of a new kind. . . ."[19] Corresponding to this realm of being of a new kind, we find Husserl referring to its all-embracing noetic-noematic structures, and to the objects of consciousness as ". . . solely. . . the intentional correlates of modes of consciousness of them."[20] We clearly misunderstand Husserl's language if we translate "noetic" and "noematic" as "sign" and "object signified." Noetic-noematic structures refer to the inextricable unity of, for example, "perception" and "perceived physical thing," a unity that does not collapse the one into the other but holds them essentially distinct. As Husserl notes, it is my perception of the physical object that undergoes changes just as I continue to perceive an object that does not change. At the same time, the essential correlativity of noesis and noema forces us to recognize the immediate (and non-symbolic) givenness of the transcendent physical object in and through those acts that intend it, therefore also admitting what might be termed an ontological "harmony" that holds between consciousness and its acts and the transcendent objects "constituted" by them.

The relationship in question between act and object is clearly not comparable to ". . . a relation between some kind of psychological occurrence—referred to as an inner experience—and another real, existing entity—referred to as an object—or of a psychophysical or comparably real connection that holds as a matter of objective fact between the one and the other."[21] Nor is Husserl's talk about consciousness' "constituting" of its intentional objects to be understood as an act of literal creation. It is not a "doing" or "making" in either the customary sense of these words or in the Heideggerian sense of Dasein's direct involvement with worldly entities.

xxiii

Introduction to the Second Edition

"Constitutive" activities on the part of consciousness appear to be more comparable to the establishment of a network of synthesizing and potentially disharmonious acts that serves to embed the intended object within a framework of "horizons" within which the reality of such objects can be judged.

Rudolph Boehm's essay, "Husserl's Concept of the 'Absolute,'" discusses Husserl's various explications of the relationship of the "absolute being" attributed by Husserl to transcendental consciousness and the world of "real," "transcendent" objects. Boehm, like his colleague, Walter Biemel, is a major contributor to the editorial achievements of the Husserl-Archives in Louvain. He is also a leading member of the second generation of German philosophers centrally interested in Husserl's phenomenology. In addition to serving as editor for Husserl's posthumous *Erste Philosophie I & II* and *Phänomenlogische Psychologie,* and the Husserliana edition of *Zur Phänomenlogie des Inneren Zeitbewusstseins,* he is the author of a series of philosophical essays that continue within the Husserlian tradition.[22] Rejecting a subjective idealism that simply identifies real objects with states of consciousness, Boehm notes that Husserl argued for a radical, ontological distinction between "absolute" consciousness and the "relative" being of transcendent objects. Within this framework, the reader of Husserl must come to terms with the transcendental character of the relationship between them. In Boehm's memorable formulation, ". . . *there is nothing without absolute consciousness, although there is also nothing with absolute consciousness alone.*" The identification of this transcendental dimension with the themes of intentionality, Husserl's criterion of evidence and theory of modes of "givenness," represents a delineation of mind and world that attempts to do justice to both the independent reality of "things," their direct givenness, and to the complex, synthesizing intentional activities of consciousness.

We also find Husserl insisting on the importance of structures of intersubjectivity and of the intentional structure of the "world-whole" that is present ". . . as the existing background of our whole natural life."[23] Such structures are deeply implicated in the synthesizing activities that make up consciousness' constitutive activity. The essay by Hans Wagner included in this collection, "Critical Observations Concerning Husserl's Posthumous Writings," considers Husserl's theory of intersubjectivity to be one of the more successful aspects of Husserlian phenomenology. Characterizing Husserl's attribution of absolute being to consciousness as a fateful error, Wagner argues that Husserl's reflections on intersubjectivity and the objectivity of the world contain, implicitly, a reliable analysis. Wagner's Kantian perspective also provides a useful contrast to Fink's

Introduction to the Second Edition

attempt to distinguish Husserlian phenomenology from Neo-Kantian positions.

These two themes of Husserlian phenomenology, the world and intersubjectivity, suggest rather directly the difficulty causal, representationalist schemes might have in offering an account of them. As an intentional "correlate," the world-whole does not appear to be reducible to a single causal relationship to a special object, or even to a sum of the causal effects of many objects. The "world-whole" functions in Husserl's thought as a mark of a "unitary *universe*" and hence as a structural feature reflecting an a priori, transcendental organization or structure rather than a collection of causal effects. Similarly, intersubjectivity does not simply refer to the causal interactions amongst individuals. For Husserl, the "constitution" of the other is another indispensable, structural feature of the "world-whole," and, as such, once again appears to transcend causal relatedness. It is *within* this framework that our "natural" and "representationalist" views must be situated: "Manifestly it is essentially necessary to the world constituted transcendentally in me (and similarly necessary to the world constituted in any community of monads that is imaginable by me) that it be a *world of men* and that, *in each particular man*, it be more or less perfectly constituted *intrapsychically* – in intentional processes and potential systems of intentionality, which, as 'psychic life,' are themselves already constituted as existing in the world."[24]

Given this contrast between those relationships that are taken to be "existing in the world," and those structures of intentionality that are the theme of transcendental phenomenology (for example, intersubjectivity and the "world as such"), we should be prepared to see Husserlian terminology pointing to a construal of intentionality not easily comparable to current representationalist theories of intentionality.

While it is important to recognize the explicit distance Husserl creates between the transcendental-phenomenological content of concepts such as "intentional object," the "object as such," "noetic-noematic correlation," and "transcendental subjectivity" and our natural representationalist terminology, the difficulty of directly expounding this content remains a challenge. The concluding essay in this volume, Ludwig Landgrebe's "Husserl's Departure from Cartesianism," shows in detail how the various elements of Husserl's philosophy can enter into, not only tension, but mutual incompatibility. Like Boehm, Landgrebe's philosophical work focuses upon the attempt to develop a critical evaluation of Husserl's phenomenology from a perspective within this tradition itself.[25] Landgrebe argues that Husserl's concern to establish the transcendental ego as a "field of experience" which can be surveyed by the phenomenologist is challenged by the very temporality of the transcendental ego. The all-important criterion of apodictic evidence must, as a consequence, become seriously modified, if not surrendered. And with this result, the Cartesianism of Husserl's phenomenology also becomes radically compromised. Landgrebe's delineation of these conflicts mirrors in a marvelously concise manner Husserl's own increasing preoccupation with, and awareness of, these very problems. Thus, the theory of intentionality that lies at the core of Husserl's philosophy becomes deeply enmeshed in a complex of factors whose problematic nature can adversely effect any attempt to give an account of this core.

Husserl's ongoing re-thinking of these central themes, their accessibility and their coherence, clearly witnesses to an effort to achieve greater clarity on his own part. In spite of the reluctance of Husserl's major philosophical successors to embrace many of the crucial details of his philosophical vision, his thought today can still serve as a resource for those wishing to evaluate the adequacy of current theories of intentionality. For beneath the complexities of Husserl's thought identified in the following essays, the philosophical movement known as "phenomenology" has found in Husserl's work a sustained inspiration and philosophical direction that continues to view the intentional structures of consciousness as a touchtone for the understanding of human experience, structures that are increasingly recognized as central in other philosophical traditions as well.

NOTES

1. Edmund Husserl, *Ideen zu einer Reinen Phänomenologie und phänomenologische Philosophie: Erstes Buch* (Den Haag: Martinus Nijhoff, 1950.)

2. It is worth reminding ourselves once again of Herbert Spiegelberg's observations about the opposition of North American philosophy to Husserl's thought in the 1950's. Spiegelberg notes the fateful ". . . intersection of Husserl's turning toward Cartesianism and to transcendental idealism with the American rejection of Descartes and the English revolt against Hegelian Idealism." See Herbert Spiegelberg, "Perspectivenwandel: Konstitution eines Husserlbildes" in H. L. Van Breda and J. Taminiaux, *Edmund Husserl: 1859-1959* (Den Haag: Martinus Nijhoff, 1959), p. 62.

3. Martin Heidegger, *The Basic Problems of Phenomenology,* (Bloomington: Indiana University Press, 1982), p. 21.

4. Maurice Merleau-Ponty, *The Phenomenology of Perception* (New York: Humanities Press, 1962), pp. xiii f.

5. Edmund Husserl, *Formale und Transzendentale Logik: Versuch einer Kritik der logischen Vernunft* (Den Haag: Martinus Nijhoff, 1974) (*Husserliana*, XVII), pp. 9f.

6. Questions central to the Heidegger of *Being and Time* as well.

Introduction to the Second Edition

7. See McGinn, *The Problem of Consciousness* (Cambridge: Blackwell) 1991.
8. See Searle, *The Rediscovery of the Mind* (Cambridge: MIT Press) 1991.
9. See J. N. Mohanty, *Husserl and Frege* (Bloomington: Indiana University Press), 1982, and Dagfinn Follesdal. "Husserl's Notion of Noema" in Dreyfuss, *Husserl, Intentionality and Cognitive Science* (Cambridge: MIT Press), 1982.
10. Michael Dummett, *Origins of Analytical Philosophy*, (Cambridge: Harvard University Press, 1993), p. 127.
11. Michael Luntley, *Contemporary Philosophy of Thought* (Cambridge: Blackwell Publishers, 1999), pp. 5, 11.
12. *Ibid.*, p. 12.
13. *Ibid.*, pp. 15f.
14. *Ibid.*, pp. 17f.
15. The point is clearly made in Jaakko Hintikka's essay, "The Phenomenological Dimension," in Smith and Smith, *The Cambridge Companion to Husserl* (Cambridge: Cambridge University Press, 1995).
16. Heidegger, *The Basic Problems of Phenomenology* (Bloomington: Indiana University Press, 1982), p. 114. Jacques Taminiaux notes Heidegger's fascination with Husserl's *Logical Investigations* and his positive evaluation of the "method" (prior to the formulation of the phenomenological reduction) exercised by Husserl in this work: "Above all, it is in the excellent way by which Husserl's analyses approach the question of Being that they earn Heidegger's praise for having given to philosophy its authenticity, 'empirical apriorism.'" "Heidegger and Husserl's *Logical Investigations*: In Remembrance of Heidegger's Last Seminar" in Jacques Taminiaux, *Dialectic and Difference: Modern Thought and the Sense of Human Limits* (Atlantic Highlands: Humanities Press International, Inc., 1990), p. 110.
17. Although much of Eugen Fink's work remains unavailable in English translation, a notable exception is Ronald Bruzina's translation of Fink's *Sixth Cartesian Meditation: The Idea of a Transcendental Theory of Method* (Bloomington: Indiana University Press, 1995). Bruzina's "Translator's Introduction" provides valuable historical context for Fink's elaborations of Husserl's phenomenological philosophy. Another recent addition to translations of Fink's work into English is the text of the *Heraclitus Seminar* (Evanston: Northwestern University Press, 1994), including both Fink's and Heidegger's contributions to their jointly conducted seminar, held in 1966-67 in Freiburg, on Heraclitus. In addition, mention must be made of Fink's *Sein, Wahrheit, Welt: Vor-Fragen zum Problem des Phänomen-Begriffs* (Den Haag: Martinus Nijhoff, 1958) and *Studien zur Phänomenologie 1930-1939* (Den Haag: Martinus Nijhoff, 1966).
18. Edmund Husserl, *Ideas*, op, cit. p. 79.
19. Edmund Husserl, *Cartesian Meditations* (The Hague: Martinus Nijhoff, 1960), p. 27.
20. *Ibid.*, p. 37.
21. *Ideen*, op. cit., p. 80.
22. See Rudolph Boehm, *Vom Gesichtspunkt der Phänomenologie: Husserl-Studien* (Den Haag: Martinus Nijhoff, 1968).
23. *Cartesian Meditations*, op. cit.
24. *Ibid.*, p 130.
25. Landgrebe's principal work is *Der Weg der Phänomenologie* (Gütersloh: Gütersloher Verlagshaus Gerd Mohn, 1963). An English translation of a collection of Landgrebe's essays dealing with Husserl's philosophy has been edited by Donn Welton. See *The Phenomenology of Edmund Husserl: Six Essays* (Ithaca: Cornell University Press, 1981.)

xxvii

Introduction

THIS ANTHOLOGY is a collection of essays dealing with the philosophy of Edmund Husserl. All of the articles have appeared previously in various German philosophical journals and are important contributions to a continuing discussion of Husserl's thought, which has hitherto remained inaccessible to the English-speaking student. The essays range from the earliest published analyses of Husserl's philosophy to more recent discussions stimulated by the publication of Husserl's posthumous works. The reader will find in these essays a careful documentation of the major turning points in the development of Husserl's phenomenology as well as detailed analyses of the crucial problems and themes that define its essential features. All of the essays appear here in translation for the first time.

The essays themselves require little additional comment. Since, however, major portions of Husserl's works presently available to the English-speaking student (such as the *Ideas* and the *Cartesian Meditations*) contain important reflections dealing with the problem of gaining proper access to transcendental phenomenology, and since the following essays repeatedly discuss and evaluate Husserl's notion of a *phenomenological reduction* and related issues, the reader may find a prefatory discussion of this notion to be helpful in understanding Husserl's phenomenological philosophy. Not only is this notion customarily employed to differentiate Husserl's phenomenology from other phenomenological philosophies, but, as Husserl himself was aware, it can also be the source of serious misunderstandings concerning the nature of this philosophy: hence it is no doubt worthy of a preliminary examination. On the basis of Husserl's posthumous writings, we can now recognize that the phenomenological reduction increasingly occupied Husserl's attention, both because of its continued necessity for a transcendental phenomenology and because of the difficulties Husserl himself acknowledges are bound up with the most wellknown formulations of his theory of the reductive method. Since Husserl claimed that the phenomenological reduction presents the only true access to a specifically phenomenological philosophy, much, if not all that we are to understand by such a philosophy will depend upon the proper understanding of this uniquely Husserlian theme.

Introduction

I

The difficulty which Husserl's contemporaries encountered in grasping Husserl's transition from the earlier phenomenology of mathematical and logical concepts to the later transcendental idealism of the *Ideas* has been often noted. The refusal of many of Husserl's students to accept either the theory of transcendental subjectivity advanced in the published portions of the *Ideas* or the notion of the phenomenological reduction with which this theory is related suggests a major reorientation in Husserl's thought, which quite naturally raises a question about the relationship of the earlier investigations into the structure of logical-mathematical activities to the later "pure" phenomenology of the *Ideas*.[1]

The question as to the *continuity* of Husserl's ideas is taken up several times in the following essays. The essay by Oskar Becker, one of the first attempts to deal with the development of Husserl's thought from its earliest to its later stages, emphasizes the continuity of Husserl's philosophy, thereby implying that Husserl's transition to a transcendental philosophy is not out of place. A similar theme is expressed in the later essay by Walter Biemel, which complements Becker's earlier discussion by using various letters and unpublished manuscripts that cast additional light upon the path taken by Husserl from the *Philosophy of Arithmetic* to the standpoint adopted in the *Ideas*. A detailed analysis of the relationship between the *Logical Investigations* and the *Ideas* is found in Eugen Fink's important essay, "The Phenomenological Philosophy of Edmund Husserl and Contemporary Criticism." These essays may speak for themselves about the issue of the continuity of Husserl's philosophical development. Nevertheless, it is correct to say that a major reformulation does occur between the publication of the *Logical Investigations* and the *Ideas*. Twenty years after their publication, Husserl characterized the *Logical Investigations* as "incomplete." A new point of departure is thus required for the further advance of phenomenological inquiry, for this "incompleteness" stems from a restricted position that must be subsequently surmounted by the breakthrough to a *transcendental* phenomenology.[2]

The transition from the earlier phenomenology of logical experience to the later development of transcendental phenomenology can be explained, at least in part, by the new requirement of *universality*.[3] In 1925 Husserl remarked that "the highest level of true clarity was by no means reached in the *Logical Investigations*. Only by advancing beyond the limited problem-sphere of the *Logical Investigations,* only by consistently extending these investigations to a problematic encompassing the totality of possible objects in general (or possible subjectivity in general) could an ultimate clarity of principle evolve."[4] But what is involved in such a

Introduction

task? At first glance, the question of universality does not appear to be very formidable. May we not simply extend the intentional analysis of individual acts of consciousness, an analysis which had already been undertaken for "logical" acts and their intentional correlates, to include acts of other types as well? Here "universality" (as Husserl himself appears to suggest in the above passage) would be coextensive with the continued increase of the scope of phenomenological inquiry to the point of including an intentional analysis of all possible acts and objects of consciousness, thus achieving the required "ultimate clarity of principle." Husserl is quite clear, however, that the kind of universality called for by a *transcendental* phenomenology cannot be achieved solely by such means The *Ideas* announces that this requisite dimension must be won "at one stroke" by the performance of the phenomenological reduction.

The reason for this demand is found in Husserl's analysis of the nature of intentional acts. Not only do individual intentional acts "intend" their respective objects, but they also cointend a *horizon* (ultimately, that of the "world"), which, although not consciously reflected upon, is nevertheless continually present and operative in all acts of consciousness. The phenomenological analysis of intentionality will remain incomplete as long as this cointended horizon remains outside the scope of phenomenological inquiry. This horizon is operative within experience as an "acceptance," and can be made the object of inquiry only if we reflectively suspend all acceptances that could serve as an intentional horizon-component, thereby assuring an unrestricted and transcendental character to phenomenological investigation. The primary task of the *Ideas* is to secure methodologically the possibility of an inquiry to expose the "ultimate" horizon: our acceptance of or "belief" in the world.

This inquiry will focus upon the life of the transcendental subject wherein the intentional activities of consciousness merge to form a unified life of consciousness whose "correlate" is the world as it is experienced. The phenomenological reduction secures access to this transcendental life of consciousness by overthrowing the naive belief in the world characteristic of the "natural attitude," that is, the unquestioning attitude of everyday consciousness with respect to its experience. The natural attitude is blind to those dimensions and horizons of experience that transcend and yet encompass particular "intentional" activities that are not thematically present in such activities. Only by achieving a radical and reflective distance from the inherent preoccupation of the natural attitude with the apparently insular solidarity and ready-made fixity of individual objects of experience, a preoccupation which effectively excludes the reflective reintegration of these objects with the deeper-lying strata of intentional implications that are essentially constitutive of every individual experience

Introduction

in the "world," can we become aware of the transcendental syntheses whereby a coherently ordered and harmonious world of experience is achieved. We "suspend" the preoccupations of the natural attitude, thereby freeing consciousness to reflect thematically upon the nonthematic ground of all experience. Once we have referred our experience of particular objects back to the life of experience within which they are embedded and from which they derive their constitutive function in our experience of the world, we shall have achieved, in principle, the reorientation of phenomenological inquiry that permits it to be characterized as "transcendental philosophy," that is, the inquiry into the essential ground of all experience that serves as the foundation for the ego-world correlation. "The term '*transcendental philosophy*' has become widespread since Kant. . . . It is the inquiry into the ultimate source of all knowledge-formations, the reflection of the knowing subject upon himself and his knowing life. . . . This source is entitled *myself,* together with my entire actual and possible life of knowledge. . . . The entire transcendental problematic revolves about . . . the relationship of this . . . ego and my life of consciousness to the world of which I am conscious and whose true being I know in my own knowledge-formations."[5] The reduction frees us for the systematic referral of our experience back to its ultimate ground; it does so by presenting us with a new reflective attitude within which the transcendental dimension of experience can be directly manifested. The very nature of this inquiry demands that it be a "radical" movement on the part of the knowing subject, for we can enter into this new attitude only by casting the *entire* "world" into the specifically phenomenological viewpoint in order to insure its thematic presence.

We thereby leave the problematic of the *Logical Investigations* and are compelled to take up what Husserl calls a *"radical transcendental subjectivism."* The earlier phenomenology of logical experience concerned certain kinds of intentional correlates and did not explicitly include analyses of those horizons which are constitutive of our experience of a *world.* This analysis falls short of phenomenology's new task because the world is not a single "intentional object" that could appear as the correlate of a single intentional act.[6]

Husserl's posthumously published works repeatedly raise the question of the proper access to transcendental subjectivity and phenomenology's specifically transcendental problematic. These works continually seek to achieve a more adequate formulation of what is involved by such a procedure. The following passage may serve as an example:

> At first it appears that the correct way to achieve this (i.e., the discovery of transcendental consciousness) would be as follows: we perform a reflective survey of our entire life of consciousness, and

Introduction

passing from one individual reflection to another, reduce it to the pure life of consciousness in such a way that each natural self-experience . . . when taken individually, is purified of everything that is non-subjective, thereby gaining its purely subjective content. . . . Nevertheless, this method of continual advance, which is exercised with the aim of being universally extended to include all those conscious experiences which can be reflectively singled out from our conscious life, is not, when applied to individual acts of consciousness, able to offer us the radically pure life of consciousness, pure in the transcendental sense.[7]

Our goal is pure transcendental subjectivity. This goal can be reached by moving into the phenomenological attitude: suspending all existential claims as to the objective existence of the object of experience in order to surmount the naiveté of the natural attitude and reflectively return to the life of consciousness as such. The procedure outlined in the above quotation, however, is "impure" in the transcendental sense. This impurity can be identified as the failure of this procedure to address itself to the "acceptance of the world," which still remains as the operative background that has not been phenomenologically thematized by the bracketing of each single intentional object. "Only those (objectivities) which were posited in acceptance *in* or *by* those acts, respectively, are bracketed, and only temporarily, in order to win the pure act-contents." Here the world is not raised to reflective presence. This procedure therefore still holds the world in uncritical acceptance. The reduced actcontents remain present to reflection "as *my* psychical act, the act of *this particular man*. . . . Hence every purely subjective element which I have obtained by a reflective process constantly carries with it (as something which has not been touched upon by this process) an objective *acceptance-component,*"[8] which is present here as an index of the worldly particularity of the reduced act-contents. We must make a clear distinction between two types of reflection: reflection that takes place "within a universally encompassing acceptance of the world," and the uniquely phenomenological type of reflection that directly subjects "the entire universe of my acceptances, everything which has hitherto been held by me and is still held by me as valid, to an *epoché* and to posit *ab ovo* something new in their place."[9]

This "something new" is once again the "world," but now it is to be accepted as a structured system of coherent and harmonious experience that includes, as its correlate, the evidence for a necessarily existent experienced world. This evidence, which receives its proper clarification only within the phenomenological attitude, provides the basis for our positing of the world in its reality. Hence transcendental reflection does not signify that the world is robbed of its proper meaning,[10] that it is

Introduction

somehow lost or "surrendered." Instead of denying the world in turning toward an elucidation of transcendental subjectivity, transcendental reflection, which comes into view with the performance of the phenomenological reduction, approaches the world in such a manner so that its true meaning is now capable of being disclosed. The world is at first given to us with complete self-evidence, but our conviction as to its existence is naive in that it fails to question itself about its ultimate origins. The phenomenological reduction questions this faith in order to grant it transcendental clarity, and by this means it seeks to triumph over the obscurity of this faith: the reduction is not a transcendental "rejection" of the realistic thesis as to the existence of the world, but is rather its transcendental "redemption" in the sense of restoring this faith to its ultimate foundation. Husserl clearly states his aim as follows:

> The world exists from the beginning, continually pregiven and given without doubt within the certainty of its being and in its self-verification. Even if I have not "presupposed" the world as a basis it is still there for me, the ego within the *cogito,* and is accepted by me in terms of its constant self-verification together with every meaning that it has for me, sometimes objectively correct with regard to particulars, and sometimes not. It is given to me along with all the sciences, arts, personal and social forms, and institutions insofar as it is just that world which for me is the real world. There can be no stronger realism, if this word is taken to mean at least: "I am certain that I am a man who lives in this world, etc., and I do not doubt this in the least." But the great problem is precisely to understand this "self-evidence." Our method requires that, beginning with its concrete world-phenomenon, the ego systematically question itself, thereby coming to know itself, the transcendental ego, in all of its concretion, its systematic constitutive levels, and its undeniably complex foundational acceptances. . . . The ego must be explicated: it must be brought to speech by means of a systematic intentional "analysis" which is to begin with the world-phenomenon.[11]

Yet we shall see that the explicit implementation of this aim leads Husserl into various difficulties.

Introduction

II

The *Ideas* gives us the most well-known formulation of the phenomenological reduction. The formulation was called the "Cartesian way" to transcendental phenomenology by Husserl, and is discussed in detail several times in the following essays. Here we need mention only one essential feature of this "way": its primary aim is to obtain an absolutely indubitable domain of immanent experience by suspending all reference to the actually existent transcendent objects of experience (i.e., by "bracketing" the world of transcendent objects and suspending our convictions as to their actual existence), a domain which shall then function as our proper point of departure for the intentional analysis of the life of consciousness and which shall also serve to realize the Cartesian quest to base our knowledge of things upon absolute and indubitable evidence. We intend to direct our attention here toward Husserl's later observations about the adequacy of this formulation of the reduction, observations which cast valuable light upon its proper goal.

For Husserl himself, the most problematic feature of the Cartesian way is its characterization of the phenomenological reduction as a "disconnection" of the realm of transcendent objects from the realm of pure immanent experience that remains left as a residuum after the reductive bracketing of the world. Given this characterization, we are apparently encouraged conclude that phenomenology is not to concern itself at all with the "real world of things," or the realm of transcendent objects: phenomenological inquiry appears to be limited to the region of pure immanence alone. This interpretation, in Husserl's view, is a seriously misleading "introduction" to phenomenology. "First of all, we should avoid speaking of a phenomenological 'residuum' and should also avoid all talk of the 'disconnection the world.' This easily leads to the opinion that the world is now to dropped from the phenomenological thematic, and that instead of the world this thematic is to concern itself solely with 'subjective' acts, modes of appearance, etc., which are related to the world."[12] This view, in effect is simply to obscure phenomenology's true theme, for, as we have seen above, our true task is systematically to comprehend the world, not deny it. In this sense, the point of departure assumed by the Cartesian way is abstract, for the precise nature of what is to be investigated by phenomenology is left in question. "The shorter path to the transcendental *epoché* . . . which I term the 'Cartesian way' . . . has the one disadvantage that, though it leads directly, as in one great leap, to the transcendental ego, every prefatory explication must of necessity be omitted, and this result in an apparent lack of content in which one can become lost as to what is to be gained by such a leap. Indeed, one is

Introduction

not certain how this is to achieve a completely new kind of fundamental science which is to be decisive for philosophy."[13] The "new kind of fundamental science" referred to here is the science of transcendental clarification. Since Husserl repeatedly defines this science as the systematic investigation of the essential correlation of "world" and "consciousness of the world," the apparent exclusion of the world would render phenomenology's transcendental task senseless. "The *epoché* regarding all natural human lifeinterests appears to disregard them entirely (for the most part, this is a very common misunderstanding of the transcendental *epoché*). Yet if it were meant in this way, there would then be no transcendental inquiry."[14] The formulation of the phenomenological reduction must make it clear that, although it is in one sense correct to say that the phenomenological thematic concerns itself with subjective acts, nevertheless, ". . . when universal subjectivity is properly posited in its full universality, indeed, when it is posited as transcendental subjectivity, then the world itself in every respect and as what it truly is lies within this subjectivity on the side of its correlates as something which exists with justification. Hence a transcendental investigation also includes the world itself in all of its true being within its thematic. . . ."[15] If we still speak of a "disconnection of the world," this must be taken to mean the rejection of the world-acceptance, which constitutes the naive "prejudice" of everyday consciousness, and not a setting aside of the question concerning the *being* of the world.[16]

According to Husserl, then, the Cartesian way fails to give an adequate account of phenomenology by inviting serious misunderstandings of its true goal. More specifically, it does not succeed in directly elucidating the full meaning of the terms "transcendence" and "immanence."

The Cartesian way attempts to erect a basis of absolute evidence as the point of departure of phenomenological inquiry. It does so by establishing a contrast between the type of evidence related to our experience of transcendent objects and the type of evidence related to our reflective apprehension of experience itself. The transcendent object cannot be given absolutely, for it is not present "within" consciousness and can only be given incompletely within the series of appearances that manifest it. On the other hand, there is no such "presumptive horizon" or incompleteness associated with the reflective "experience" of experience itself, for such experience is immanent to consciousness and can be given in a totally apodictic manner. This opposition appears to be established in a straightforward manner. Yet its apparent clarity is, in fact, ambiguous, for it touches only upon one sense of the immanence-transcendence relation, and thus threatens to obscure a very important distinction between "real transcendence" and "transcendence in an intentional sense."

Introduction

Although we can say that the real object of experience is not actually included as a physical part of the sphere of immanence, and that in this sense it is "distinct" from the act of consciousness that apprehends it, nevertheless, from the standpoint offered by the intentional analysis of consciousness, the object of experience can also be said to be immanent. In this intentional sense of immanence, the transcendent object is included within experience as the correlate of an intentional act of consciousness, and its givenness to consciousness can be brought to absolute self-givenness when this experience is subjected to the phenomenological reduction. "In intuiting the pure phenomenon, the object is not external to knowledge nor is it external to 'consciousness,' but is given in the sense of the absolute self-givenness of something purely intuited. . . ."[17] We might say that in this manner the sphere of "immanence" includes the entire realm of intentional objects (and hence also the world) as pure phenomena, and is not simply limited to "real" parts of the psychical life. Moreover, it is this intentional sense of immanence that permits us to understand one of Husserl's central claims: "transcendence is a characteristic of being which is constituted immanently within the ego." If the reduction were meant to display only a totally pure realm of actual immanence, it would be, in principle, impossible for any category of "transcendence" to arise.

If the terms "immanence" and "transcendence" are not clarified through their proper intentional meaning, the realm of "pure immanence" won by the phenomenological reduction can quite easily lead to that impression of the loss of the world-thematic that Husserl considered a misunderstanding. The ambiguity present in the notion of immanence can easily obscure the immanence of the transcendent by suggesting that it is solely an actual immanence that is referred to.[18] It is vital to the entire phenomenological inquiry that the transcendent objects of experience be retained in order to serve as transcendental clues for the elucidation of the ultimate origins of our experience of the world. To be sure, there are later portions of the *Ideas* that make explicit reference to the fact that the world does persist as the "intentional correlate" of the *cogito*, but the question remains as to how this contention can be justified solely upon the basis of the Cartesian way and its elaboration of the immanence-transcendence opposition.[19] Moreover, if this world-thematic, which is definitive for Husserl's transcendental reflection and which essentially relies upon the proper elucidation of the intentional sense of immanence, is not given in and through the very enactment of the reduction itself, we shall have no criterion for determining that the initial stages of our phenomenological inquiry (which are to grant us from the very beginning access to transcendental subjectivity) are in fact uniquely situated within a

11

Introduction

genuinely phenomenological attitude. And if they are not, how does a truly phenomenological reflection emerge from them?

Given this perplexity of the Cartesian way, we can now readily understand Husserl's later dissatisfaction with its general outlines. "The clarification of the theme of 'transcendental subjectivity' and the new perceptions that emerge here which, once posited in their systematic acceptance, provide our new foundation of being, caused greater difficulties than I had originally imagined. . . ." The introduction of the phenomenological reduction given by Husserl in his lectures of 1907 (i.e., *The Idea of Phenomenology*) as well as the later *Ideas* contains a "principal mistake, although it was one which was very difficult to clarify."[20] As we have seen, this "mistake" amounts to an obscurity with respect to what is to be won by the reduction. "It could at first appear with total self-evidence that the subjectivity won as the 'residuum' by the reduction is my own, the phenomenologizing ego's 'pure' subjectivity: my own private ego, so to speak. . . . Thus in this reduction I have overemphasized the stream of consciousness, as if this were the concern of the reduction."[21] But this issue carries with it another aspect as well. We know that the reduction does not simply disclose the sphere of actual psychical immanence. Its aim is to reveal the full intentional life of transcendental subjectivity, and to do so in such a manner that we are granted apodictic evidence concerning this realm over which the phenomenological reduction reigns. We are doubtlessly forced to raise the question about the extent to which the claim to present apodictic knowledge of this subjectivity is dependent upon the "obscure" transcendence-immanence dichotomy, and to what extent this obscurity calls into question the success of the attempt to gain such knowledge through the Cartesian way.

Husserl's later observations again cast light upon this situation. We are now told that the appeal to the immediate apodicticity of the *cogito* is "naive" insofar as the sphere of immanence and the appropriate reflective apprehension of this sphere do not adequately take into account the intentional horizons of temporality that properly belong to transcendental subjectivity.

> At this point we must keep in mind that the apodictic evidence of the *ego cogito* . . . is only a beginning and not an end: namely, it is indeed apodictic, but it also quickly evokes an entire series of puzzling questions within me concerning its true meaning, its extent and its limits. To refer to only one such question: the "I experience," "I think," etc., appear to be actual and apodictically certain within the momentary now, and my transcendental past is certain for me as well. But does not memory deceive me often enough . . . ? Is it not finally possible that my entire transcendental past and future is only a tran-

scendental appearance or illusion? Hence we still face the enormous task of the *apodictic critique of transcendental experience.*[22]

To what extent is transcendental subjectivity given in an apodictic manner? This question will be asked by the "critique of transcendental experience." The Cartesian way affirms that, in principle, there is direct and apodictic access to the subjectivity uncovered by the reductive method, for the sphere of pure immanence dispenses with all transcendent evidence, thus leaving us with only "apodictically" certain knowledge. Husserl now suggests that this sphere of "immanence" does not automatically guarantee apodicticity. In Husserl's later works, we can find at least two major reasons that can be offered in support of such a contention. First, if "immanence" is meant in a factual sense (i.e., in the sense of a particular and actual stream of consciousness), in principle this meaning *excludes* the possibility of apodictic knowledge.

> Knowledge, and scientific knowledge in particular, would be entirely satisfied when and to the extent that it could achieve an absolute and apodictic finality and at the same time *adequation to an apodictic content.* However, no factual knowledge—be this either *mundane* or *phenomenological-subjective* knowledge—*is of this sort.* No temporal being is apodictically knowable: not only for us, but because it is itself apodictically knowable that such knowledge is impossible.[23]

Second, the temporality of transcendental subjectivity is such as effectively to question the Cartesian way with respect to its claim to have immediate knowledge of this subjectivity. Does the reflective apprehension of the immanent life of transcendental subjectivity offered by this way amount to anything more than a naive reliance upon the testimony of the "momentary now" of reflective experience? In claiming to dispense with all evidential transcendence, the Cartesian way focuses upon that which is most *immediate* as the criterion for apodictic knowledge, an immediacy which is apparently guaranteed by direct selfreflection. But there is a sense in which the "immediacy" of this reflective "now" is not truly immediate at all, for it is mediated by the intentional horizons of the past and the future, which themselves belong essentially to the "living, streaming present."[24] Furthermore, how can the fleeting experiential stream of consciousness sustain a knowledge characterized by an *apodictic persistence* that transcends any given "now"? Does not transcendental-phenomenological experience itself, the experience I gain of myself through phenomenological self-reflection, fall prey to this same temporal passage characteristic of experience as such?[25] If transcendental inquiry is

Introduction

to lay bare the ultimate foundation of all experience of the world, and if such a foundation necessarily transcends individual "experiences," can apodictic certainty extend to such foundations, that is, is there an apodictic knowledge that reaches further than the momentary recollection of individual experiences, which can be held before the glance of self-reflection?

Husserl acknowledges that phenomenology must face such questions if it is to continue speaking of transcendental phenomenology as laying bare a new dimension of *experience*. To surmount such difficulties pertaining to the *nature* and *extent* of an apodictic phenomenological self-knowledge and to prevent an initially "naive" point of departure from leaving phenomenological inquiry with an essentially inadequate point of departure, we must raise anew the question "how self-knowledge—knowledge of this transcendentally pure ego in its totality—is possible . . . ,"[26] but it must now be raised upon a reflectively higher level in terms of a theory and critique of phenomenological evidence.[27] We must clarify, through additional and highly complex analyses, how it is possible to attain apodictic access to what Husserl terms the "primordial originality of the immanent in general," and we must also be able to show how this primordial originality of the immanent stands in relation to the temporal modalities of the transcendental ego. Depending upon the success of such analyses, we shall be able to speak of a truly original and "immediate" (i.e., "presuppositionless") apodictic evidence, which will guarantee the absolute nature of phenomenological inquiry. In as much as the Cartesian way lacks such "higher level" reflections upon the nature and extent of phenomenological evidence, it must remain a naive beginning and not a final achievement.

III

Husserl's later reflections upon the Cartesian way disclose several fundamental inadequacies of this way. With these reflections in hand, we are now able to understand why Husserl sought alternate ways of introducing the proper theme of phenomenology that could perhaps avoid the difficulties of the Cartesian way. Our task now will not be to provide an exhaustive catalog of these alternate ways, but rather to attain a more modest goal of mentioning some general features of the most important of these alternate ways.

We shall first consider the way to transcendental phenomenology introduced by Husserl in terms of a phenomenological psychology.[28] What was given by the Cartesian way as

Introduction

. . . pure subjectivity was still not exposed as apodictically indubitable. The disconnection of the world on the basis of its not being apodictically given directed our glance toward the universe of a pure subjectivity which is given in a new type of experience, that of transcendental observation. But the critique of apodicticity must be realized, and this was a task we had postponed. The Cartesian way, therefore, was our first way to the transcendental ego and to its not yet realized apodictic critique.

The next requirement, that of coming to know transcendental subjectivity in terms of the individual forms or types of forms belonging to its transcendental life in order that the *ego cogito* does not simply remain an empty word, was satisfied in another manner which was employed at the same time in order to construct, step by step, *a new way to the ego cogito.*[29]

This way counsels us to refrain from taking up any interest in the kind of being possessed by the world and the kind of evidence associated with it (i.e., the evidential transcendence of the world which leaves open the possibility of its nonexistence). Our reflection is now guided by a new kind of "theoretical interest," an interest simply in pure subjectivity as such. Similar to the theoretical interest motivating the natural scientist in his examination of the "objective" world which requires that he abstract from all "subjective" features of experience, our new inquiry will attempt an explicit abstraction from all interest in the strictly "objective" features of the experience of the world. "Is it not sufficient," Husserl asks, "without having to begin with that lengthy critique of the experience of the world, and without having to bring into evidence the possibility of the world's nonexistence, to directly set the *epoché* of the disinterested self-observer into play upon his individual acts?" He then goes on to state:

In any case, we attempted to carry out this new manner of thinking. Accordingly, our procedure was as follows: we told ourselves to entirely set aside the earlier train of thought. Instead, we proceed from the natural and naive ego which has performed some act or other, thereby relating itself in an entirely natural manner to its respective intentional object. Without thinking first of some sort of transcendental subjectivity, or without already possessing some sort of representation of it, we may then perform a similar *epoché* upon every single act in a manner which is quite easily understood, an *epoché* which is similar to the one which, related to the world and our experience of the world, has been performed in the Cartesian way.[30]

Introduction

Here, in place of the distinction between transcendental and "natural subjectivity, we now distinguish between the ego performing its acts in a naive and straightforward manner and the ego reflecting upon these acts and not taking part in the positional theses or interests (such as "practical intentions"), which are features of the ego reflected upon. The knowledge gained by such reflection is knowledge of the phenomenologically pure act of consciousness. But the "purity" of this knowledge is still incomplete, for we have not yet reached the *transcendentally* pure ego. Similar to what we had noted above concerning the "correct" understanding of the phenomenological reduction, phenomenology, if it is to achieve its transcendental dimension, cannot remain with the isolated analysis of intentional acts and their correlates, nor can it prolong indefinitely the characterization of its thematic as the clarification of pure "psychical" immanence. Both features can be taken as elements belonging to the "first" stage of the reflection operative in a phenomenological psychology, a stage which is therefore transcendentally naive.[31] The phenomenological psychologist must advance to the descriptive analysis of the world-horizon, which attends every experience of individual things, thereby drawing close to the transcendental dimension of inquiry. He must also advance to the explication of that transcendental intersubjectivity which is an *a priori* feature of the world-horizon and which discloses a transcendental horizon of the intentional (and empathetic) interrelatedness of egos that passes beyond a transcendentally naive concern with "my own subjectivity."

The crucial question here, however, is this: does a phenomenological psychology insure a transcendental perspective as its final result? *Is* it a way which leads of necessity to a transcendental phenomenology? A more detailed analysis of Husserl's later texts than we are able to offer here is required to answer this question with certainty. We can, however, at least suggest the following. Husserl does state that a "strict working out of the idea of a descriptive psychology, which is to bring the truly essential nature of the psychical into view, necessarily enacts the transformation of the phenomenological psychological *epoché* into a transcendental one."[32] The possibility for this "transformation" of the psychological *epoché* into a transcendental one rests upon the fact that the phenomenological psychologist has indeed uncovered a "universally pure subjectivity" together with those "anonymous" constitutive activities of consciousness which can in turn be revealed as the ultimate point of origin for the positing of that world which exists for all actual and possible egos (and hence not merely my own). But what necessity is there for the psychologist to make this transcendental turn? In fact, Husserl also states that this turn toward subjectivity as *transcendental,* as world-constituting

Introduction

(and hence its *priority* for all experience of the world), "lies close at hand" and "almost" present, but that the psychologist can nevertheless remain "naively dogmatic: he need not see the transcendental turn of the psychological reduction, which indeed lies close at hand."[33] If this is so, it would then appear that an inherent necessity for transforming the psychologically universal *epoché* into a transcendental one is lacking. A "break" appears at this point which still needs to be completed.

Transcendental phenomenology lies close at hand, but its attainment is not thereby automatically secured. The reason for this is found in the fact that the transcendental and psychological *epochés* remain essentially distinct from each other. The phenomenological-psychological *epoché* not an absolute *epoché*. Although it does accomplish a descriptive-intentional analysis of subjectivity and discovers the intentional horizon of the world-thesis that is co-implicated in individual intentional acts, its scope nevertheless limited. The phenomenological psychologist is guided in his inquiry by a specific interest in the purely psychical as such. This interest requires a theoretical posture that inhibits or "disconnects" that positing of the world which is a feature of naive consciousness and hence signifies a reflection upon experience that has successfully suspended the "nature attitude." But such reflection is still not identical with transcendental reflection. For the phenomenological psychologist, the psychological *epoché* is only a "means of purification"[34] employed in order to "obtain the pure psychical within the world."[35] Hence the concern of the psychological "bracketing" of the world is invested with a concern for a specific mundane region, and as such bears only a superficial resemblance to the methodology of transcendental phenomenology.

The transcendental (or "absolute") *epoché* dispenses with this abstracting of the psychical. Its concern is not the scientific interest in a regional thematic. On the contrary, it is guided by the ideal of an absolute science that will encompass all other sciences and lay bare their ultimate foundations. It is the pursuit of the philosophical task of taking up a stance within that dimension of a universal knowledge-complex which, as the transcendental basis of all knowledge, cannot be adequately brought to light by any particular scientific inquiry The transcendental *epoché* is concerned with ultimate origins and, in accordance with this principle, grasps "subjectivity" not as an abstract domain of psychical immanence but as world-constituting subjectivity. Apart from this transcendental interest subjectivity will remain construed abstractly and the world will remain invested with a "positive" or "one-sided" meaning. Both must receive their "transcendental determinations": subjectivity must be viewed as meaning-bestowing" and the world must be taken back into this source of its meaning.[36] Such determinations cannot be given with full evidence

17

when subjectivity is simply listed as a "part" of the world, for then such relationships become unintelligible.[37]

If the way leading to a transcendental phenomenology through a phenomenological psychology must face its own difficulty, it nevertheless presents several important features that distinguish it from the earlier "Cartesian" introduction of phenomenology's thematic. The central question involved in any attempt to "introduce" transcendental phenomenology is this: how can one motivate the reflective apprehension of experience carried out within the "natural attitude" to assume the thoroughly "unnatural" stance of the transcendental reduction? How can we provide a comprehensible transition from the one attitude to the other? Whereas the Cartesian way had suggested a rather violent break between the two attitudes (the assumption of the transcendental attitude being made in "one single leap"), we now find Husserl suggesting that phenomenological inquiry can take its point of departure from a reflection upon experience (i.e., that of a phenomenological psychology) that can be introduced without obscurity to the nonphenomenologist. Furthermore, it is a way that avoids the specifically Cartesian considerations concerning the evidence for the existence of the world, considerations which, as we have seen above can be dangerously misleading. In this way we discover a broad area of investigation that stands between the naiveté of the natural attitude and the unnatural attitude of the transcendental reduction, an area which we hope can successfully function in a mediatory role between these two opposed stances.

This approach promises two additional gains as well. First, such reflection initially grants us a descriptive contentual analysis of the intentional structures of consciousness (including the intentional consciousness of horizons), thereby preparing the way for the all-important inquiry into the transcendental nature of subjectivity by assuring us insight into the concrete nature of intentional consciousness and preventing that "apparent lack of content" which was a troubling feature of the Cartesian way for Husserl. Second, by displaying the proper role of a reflective interest in the pure subjectivity of the "psychical *per se*," the way of phenomenological psychology actually takes up a misconception encouraged by the Cartesian way and turns it into account. The tendency to interpret the Cartesian way in terms of psychical immanence is now employed for the sake of instituting a more readily comprehensible transition to transcendental phenomenology. By the detailed analysis of this kind of interest in the psychical, and by specifying its difference from transcendental phenomenology, Husserl is now in a position directly to face and "control" the misunderstanding to which the Cartesian way fell victim by

Introduction

making such considerations an integral part of the introduction of the transcendental thematic.

Other ways leading to transcendental phenomenology found in Husserl's later work can be grouped together under the title of "ontological ways. In general, these ways compose a group which Husserl at one point characterizes as "one" of two correlative ways. We may either take the empty *ego cogito* and its "static" essence-typology for our point of departure (where we still face the "difficulty" of distinguishing psychological-subjective knowledge as objective knowledge of the subjective from the purely transcendental knowledge of subjectivity), or we may begin with the *given world* and the universal ontology of the world, a point of departure eventually leading us to world-constituting subjectivity and to the knowledge that all being is the correlate of transcendental subjectivity.[38] The possibility of possessing two correlative points of departure leading to transcendental phenomenology is structurally assured by defining this phenomenology as the inquiry into the fundamental correlation of "world and "consciousness of the world." Hence in principle the adoption of either "correlate" as a point of departure should permit us access to that transcendental dimension wherein the essential relationship between "world" and "consciousness of the world" can be displayed. The point of departure offered by the ontology of the world, however, has two distinct advantages over other points of departure. First, and as we shall see in greater detail later, by assuming the character of a "regressive analysis" and search for the *foundations* of the world as it is experienced, this way effectively introduces what shall turn out to be the "transcendental" character of our inquiry in a more readily understood manner than does the way of phenomenological psychology, for example, since, as we have seen above, there remains the question whether insight into the *constitutive* character of subjectivity can be directly achieved by this way. The explicit search for experiential foundations, which is an essential feature of the "ontological" ways, promises to pass beyond this difficulty by ultimately disclosing transcendental subjectivity as the *answer* to our foundational quest. Along the same lines, our inquiry now will also take on a strong "genetic" character, which shall prove to be better suited for disclosing the constitutive role of consciousness than the *"static* essence-typology" of the Cartesian and psychological ways. Second, by taking the world as it is given for its point of departure, this "way" is in a better position to emphasize the important presence of the world-thematic for phenomenological inquiry and to avoid the impression of a lack of interest in or an implied rejection of the "world." Together, these two features grant the ontological way a preeminent suitability for introducing

19

Introduction

transcendental phenomenology. Let us now consider this approach in somewhat greater detail.

We may, following Kern's recent analysis,[39] distinguish three types of the ontological way: (1) the way leading through the clarification and critique of the positive sciences; (2) the way leading through the foundations of formal logic; and (3) the way through the *Lebenswelt*.

The critique of the positive sciences has a twofold thrust. On the one hand, the positive sciences themselves operate upon the assumption of clarifying "the" world, either in the sense of the totality of the world or of a specific region within the world (i.e., the region of "physical nature"). Hence one direction that the phenomenological critique of the positive sciences can take is that of clarifying the foundation for this belief in the world, a belief which in fact precedes a specifically scientific inquiry and its trust in the achievements of logical reason and whose roots can be found in the "prelogical reason of experience."[40] Scientific inquiry presupposes a persevering "structural style" of experience, a "harmony" which our experience must evidence if there is to be a truly existing world. By raising the question about the ground for this structured experiential whole we move to the consideration of phenomenology's transcendental thematic.

We need not, however, only "critique" the positive sciences by calling for a clarification of the basis upon which all scientific inquiry rests. We may also advance a critique by exposing the abstractness of science by appealing to this same "prelogical reason." By taking mathematical calculability as the true index to reality, the natural sciences have substituted an abstract schema to replace our direct experience of things. This substitution results in the transformation of the world of immediate experience into a machinelike complex of "facts," thereby leaving subjectivity out of account and giving the authentically human life of theoretical reason a vicious turn by reducing nature and freedom into an unintelligible antinomy.[41] Transcendental phenomenology now emerges as the theoretically responsible attempt to set aside the abstractness of science by returning to ultimate origins. Rather than directing its attention to one "part" of reality (i.e., pure subjectivity as such), phenomenological inquiry here returns to a fuller and more concrete apprehension of the world. It is a move to restore the completeness of experience by reinstituting the transcendental correlation of world-ontology and subjectivity. Its procedure here no longer appears "abstractive," but now takes on the role of a critique of abstractions by leading reflection back to that concrete world-apprehension which the various scientific disciplines presuppose but nevertheless continually overlook.

Introduction

Husserl's concern in *Formal and Transcendental Logic* is to show how this quest for origins can be made to emerge within the context of reflections upon the formal dimension of theoretical reason as well. This constitutes the way leading to transcendental phenomenology through the questioning of the ontological foundations of formal logic.

Husserl challenges us to rethink the scientific and logical disciplines that we have inherited from the "cultural tradition." If we are not to be satisfied merely with the invention of "theoretical techniques," we must then accept the radical challenge of taking upon ourselves full responsibility and justification for all areas of authentically human endeavor and reflect upon "the ultimate possibilities and necessities in terms of which we are to take up a position with respect to reality in judging, evaluating, acting."[42] This responsibility must also include the task of providing an account of the effective foundations of "scientific reason."

One of the highest achievements of theoretical reason is reached in the formal theory of deductive systems.[43] The "content" of this level is the systematic connectedness of purely formal propositions. Our concern is with determinate procedural methods whereby such formal theories and structures can be constructed and their lawful interrelationships viewed. By such means, theoretical reason attempts to gain clarity concerning those ultimate laws of formal thought operative in all rational inquiry. The element of "formalism" here, however, carries with it two distinguishable aspects. On the one hand, such an interest in formally determinate structures leaves the possible "objects" to which such structures could be applied completely "uninterpreted," that is, such objects are left materially indeterminate and are designated by the mathematician, for example, as "objects of thought" in order to signify this complete indeterminacy. On the other hand, this theoretical concern need not only focus upon a "pure theory of meaning-forms," or a pure "logic of noncontradiction," but can, and in Husserl's view must, advance toward a "formal logic of truth." At this point the relationship of formal theory to "possible objects must soon become a problem."[44]

The transition to a logic of truth is made within the context of Husserl's view of the proper "orientation" of logic and theoretical reason. Logic must not lose sight of its "epistemological vocation." Just as the sciences view the interest in the analysis of the formal properties of "judgments" *per se* as serving a more primary interest "attached to the things themselves such as they are in truth,"[45] so also must logic remain clear about its "orientation toward the object." "*According to its ultimate meaning . . .* it is not a pure formal apophantic logic, but an ontological-formal logic."[46] Formal logic, construed as the formal theory of science, has an ontological direction. To be sure, an interest in propositional forms as "pure" meanings can be consistently maintained, and such an interest is displayed in the historical development of logic. But the most profound *meaning* of formal analysis is evidenced when logic is viewed as "*the science of possible categorial forms in terms of which objective substrata must be able to exist in order to exist in truth.*"[47] In this sense, the *a priori* truths of formal logic "set forth what holds with formal universality *for all objects as such:* they announce *under what forms objects in general exist,* or the way in which they solely *can exist.*"[48]

The recognition of logic's formal-ontological dimension, however, carries with it a further task. If our formal conception of an "object as such" is not to remain in naive acceptance, we must proceed to the clarification of the "world" as a horizon of meaning that is indispensable to the conception of an object as such. "There is a universal basis of experience which exists *before* all acts of judgment and which is constantly presupposed *as a harmonious unity of possible experience.*"[49] Inquiry into this unity of experience must also advance to the elucidation of a "material syntax," constituting a part of the universal world *a priori,* and complementing the a *priori* syntactical forms of formal logic. This material *a priori* "syntax" assigns "the *a priori* form of a possible universe of existing things"[50] to the content of our world-apprehension, thereby uniting all particular material domains or regions of the world into a synthetic totality of experience. At this level, the terms entering into our "formal" judgments concerning the objective world are no longer abstractly "free" or unbound but are now synthetically "bound" by horizons of intentional implications.

We are hereby brought to the threshold of transcendental phenomenology. If the foundations of logic are to be complete and firmly grounded, and if logic is to fulfill its proper role in seeking out those "ultimate possibilities and necessities" ingredient in our taking a stand with respect to reality, we must systematically return from the ideal formations of logic to that consciousness which constitutes them in order to grant these formations intelligibility and clarity.[51] We must above all investigate that *teleological* nature of intentionality which synthesizes all "particular pulsations" of the life of consciousness, directed in a "unitary manner toward objects,"[52] into that conception of the being of the world which is indispensable to the fundamental concepts of logic.

Perhaps the most well-known of Husserl's later "ways" to transcendental phenomenology is that of the phenomenological inquiry into the *Lebenswelt*. What had been presented in the two ways discussed above as the presupposed basis for all scientific and logical activities, the universal world-apprehension given to consciousness prior to all such activities, is here no longer treated as a "partial theme" oriented within the totality of

Introduction

the objective sciences. Now it is taken up as a "universal philosophical problem" in its own right, encompassing all of consciousness' activities.[53] The "objective-logical" sciences are not the primary ones. What is truly primary is "the 'merely subjective-relative' intuition of the prescientific world-apprehending life of consciousness."[54] A unique kind of "science" is now called for in order to investigate this life, a life which Kant among others had failed to appreciate in its foundational primacy.

Contrasting with the abstractness of the Cartesian way, the phenomenological *epoché* here appears with the full world-thematic at its disposal. The *epoché* is no longer spoken of as the disconnection of one realm of being from another, but as the resolve to dispense with an inadequate set of investigational criteria and to adopt a new set in its place. Instead of the nonintuitive schemata of the objective-scientific attitude, we are to return to the investigation of the world's intuitive self-givenness. In place of the misleading immanence-transcendence dichotomy and its understandable distortion of the phenomenological thematic, the reduction is now introduced in terms of a new polarity: that between the objective-scientific attitude and the subjective-relative attitude. The latter is to be adopted by the resolve to move away from the scientist's interest in the "objectivity" of things toward the manner of the world's givenness to consciousness. Our new attitude does not suggest a rejection of the reality of the objects encountered by consciousness, but discovers the *a priori* correlation of "thing" and "world-horizon," which is the foundation for all further objective determinations. The transcendent object is not disengaged from our inquiry: it is there as a "transcendental clue" or index to the synthetic manifold of appearances that remains anonymous to the natural life of consciousness. Within this new attitude we shall be able to comprehend what had never before been thematically grasped:

> . . . syntheses in an inseparable synthetic totality which are continually produced through intentionally encompassing horizon-acceptances, mutually influencing each other in the form of verificational existence-confirmations or disconfirming cancellations and other possible modalizations. This is the unique character of the synthetic totality in which something previously quite unknown, and never grasped or viewed as a task for knowledge, can come into our possession: namely, the universal achieving life of consciousness wherein the world originates as continually pregiven and as existing for us in its streaming actuality, or in which we now discover for the first time both "that" and "how" the world as the correlate of an investigatable universality of synthetically connected achievements receives the meaning and acceptance of its being in the totality of its ontic structures.[55]

Introduction

IV

Our survey of Husserl's various attempts to introduce transcendental phenomenology, a "survey" which Husserl himself undertook in his later writings under the title of a "phenomenology of the phenomenological reduction," must conclude with three questions: What consequences do the various non-Cartesian ways to transcendental phenomenology hold for the overall character of this philosophy? What further insight do they offer us about possible "motivations" or "grounds" for the adoption of the transcendental-phenomenological attitude? And can we, on the basis of Husserl's later writings, speak of a final "form" or structure of the phenomenological reduction?

The answer to the first question can be given as follows. If we assume that Husserl's search for alternative ways to transcendental phenomenology entails denying any radical priority of the Cartesian way over and against other possible non-Cartesian introductions of the phenomenological problematic, Husserl can also be said to surrender the claim to present phenomenological inquiry with an absolute point of departure.[56] The Cartesian way maintains that an absolute point of departure can be had by bringing to light the evidential autonomy of the self-reflecting ego. The autonomy of phenomenological self-reflection, which is essentially opposed to the dubitability of the world's existence, casts into light a self-enclosed and self-sufficient realm of absolute evidence that cannot be called into question. In opposition to this claim, however, stands a later statement of Husserl: "It is manifestly impossible to proceed otherwise than by first obtaining naive evidence and systematic descriptions which follow (this evidence) in a straightforward manner. . . ."[57] If phenomenological inquiry is now to be served by a "naive" point of departure, the initial evidence at its disposal must be open to further questioning and cannot be directly accepted as conclusive or "absolute."

At least part of the reason for this revaluation of the character of phenomenology's starting point can be found in the inadequacies of the Cartesian way noted above. The "naiveté" in question here clearly has reference to Husserl's later call for an "apodictic critique" of the point of departure offered by the Cartesian *cogito*. We may once again mention the problem of the temporal character of the transcendental ego and the question of its apodicticity and the limits of its apodictic knowability as one which cuts deeply into the "absoluteness" aimed at by the Cartesian way.[58]

Let us be certain that we understand at least the general features of what is entailed by this revaluation. It does not mean that there is *no* "absolute" evidence associated with the self-reflections of the transcen-

Introduction

dental ego, for Husserl still upholds the possibility of an absolute "science" of transcendental origins, a science which is to be based upon absolute evidence. It does mean, however, that such evidence and the goals of such a science are not *immediately* given to phenomenological reflection in the sense of constituting its point of departure. In this way, perhaps, we can suspect a more profound source of Husserl's dissatisfaction with the Cartesian way. Its claim to offer a realm of indubitable evidence as the criterion for distinguishing the *transcendental*-phenomenological standpoint from the naiveté of the natural attitude is in a certain sense misleading. The evidence offered by the radical self-reflection manifested by the adoption of the phenomenological reduction suggests only that the type of evidence phenomenology seeks is simply immediate and directly given, and nothing else. But, in fact, the anonymous constituting life of transcendental subjectivity (which conceals within itself the realm of transcendental origins) is not "immediately" apprehended by phenomenological reflection, but must be disclosed by self-critical reflection rather than by apprehension of the proper domain of transcendental phenomenology in "one great leap."

The issue here is made more complex by the fact that the ultimate locus of transcendental phenomenology is still found within the realm of evidence capable of being disclosed by transcendental self-reflection, therefore allowing phenomenology to be characterized as a science which has its foundations within the scope of autonomous and radical self-reflection. But the domain of transcendental origins, the discovery of which is the mark of phenomenology as transcendental philosophy, is now viewed by Husserl as being attainable only when such reflection has also become *self-critical.* This distinction means that we must constantly guard against any simple identification of the initial realm of self-reflective evidence with the absolute science of transcendental origins. We begin with the availability of naive evidence for the initial stages of self-reflection, and we must repeatedly test such evidence to discover the extent to which it conceals undisclosed presuppositions and to discover new assessments of our subjective-descriptive procedure for the purposes of clarifying and delimiting the scope and weight of such evidence. A universal science of essential descriptions

> . . . which transcendental subjectivity itself enacts as self-knowing and self-thematizing, must carry within itself its own system whereby, systematically advancing from its beginning with naive descriptions, it must necessarily come to descriptions wherein all naiveté is canceled, so that such descriptions lead equally to a critique of its own procedure, to its own justification in practice by the delimitation of its range or scope, and finally, to a universal description

Introduction

in systematic stages whose naiveté is completely set aside and which reaches its completion solely through those higher descriptions which offer the delimitation of its scope.[59]

This dimension of phenomenology's self-critical task plays an increasingly important role in Husserl's thought and separates this thought from the apparently straightforward introduction of absolute evidence that is a hallmark of the "Cartesianism" of the *Ideas*. The more Husserl sees the necessity for greater clarity concerning the transcendental thematic of phenomenological inquiry, the less adequate does he view the contribution of the Cartesian way to this end. It is a lesson we have already learned from Husserl's reflections upon the theory of the phenomenological reduction. In their attempt to clarify phenomenology's transcendental orientation, the "ontological" ways dispense with the immanence-transcendence dichotomy and its attendant claims of apodicticity entirely, and take on the character of a cautious step-by-step advance to transcendental subjectivity through intermediate stages of inquiry calling for self-critical evaluation. Hence Landgrebe, in the last essay of this volume, can justifiably speak of Husserl's "departure from Cartesianism."

At the same time, however, we are also compelled to recognize a continuing significance of the "Cartesian" point of departure for Husserl's thought, a significance which can perhaps best be clarified through our second question: what further insight do the various non-Cartesian ways offer us concerning possible motivations or grounds for the adoption of the transcendental-phenomenological attitude?

Attending the sharp division of the natural and transcendental attitudes is the question about the manner in which the initial reflections of (in Husserl's phrase) the "beginning philosopher" can be intelligibly introduced to those "beginners" who have not yet taken upon themselves the full requirements of the phenomenological attitude. It has often been noted[60] that the first sections of the *Ideas* frequently alternate between the natural and phenomenological attitudes in their attempt to secure an initial foundation for genuinely phenomenological reflection, thereby leaving the actual introduction of the phenomenological reduction in something of an "enigmatic" situation. Eugen Fink also takes clear notice of this problem in the concluding pages of his essay in speaking of a final "paradox" associated with all attempts to introduce the transcendental-phenomenological attitude to someone who does not already share it, thereby confirming his contention that all attempts to introduce the phenomenological reduction and transcendental attitude are necessarily false.[61] Must we therefore conclude that the very attempt to offer a coherent introduction of such an attitude is necessarily doomed to fail? If so, are not all such attempts, including the Cartesian and various non-Cartesian

Introduction

"ways," equally problematic regardless of their specific inadequacies and motifs?

Do Husserl's later reflections offer any clarification of this problem? In one sense, we can affirm that they do. Husserl begins the systematic part of his lectures on "first philosophy" with preparatory meditations upon "The Motivation of the Beginning Philosopher in the Absolute Situation." The concern of these meditations is clear: what can serve as the motivation for the "philosopher" to break with the preoccupations and naiveté of the natural attitude and take up a line of inquiry that necessitates the adoption of a transcendental stance? Husserl's answer to this question is clear and succinct. Such motivation must be sought in two correlative grounds. First, in the idea of philosophy itself as that science which provides an absolute foundation for all knowledge, a foundation whose source resides in transcendental self-knowledge (and hence the idea of philosophy as transmitted to us through the Platonic and Cartesian traditions). And, second, as the *will* of the philosopher to create for himself clarity concerning this foundation. Thus a unique resolve of the will and the aim of such willing emerge as the indispensable conditions definitive for the "beginning philosopher."

> In this way philosophy in principle cannot originate out of acts of knowing that are naive, but only out of free self-reflection, the free self-reflections of the knower himself. It can originate only out of radical reflective clarity concerning himself and concerning the true goal of the philosophical subject, as well as clarity concerning the way and method which this subject must follow in the realization of this aim.[62]

Two correlative and constant motifs of Husserl's thought, that of self-reflection and that of absolute science, are employed here as the only possible index to the point of departure required by truly radical reflection. The irreducible "first step" in the reflective pursuit of transcendental philosophy is now taken to be this "philosophical will" whose sole aim is that of ultimate and absolute knowledge, whose *telos* is properly defined as the "ideal of universal philosophy," and whose sole ground is to be found in the rational and reflective autonomy of the philosophical pursuit itself. The proximity of this stance to the "spirit of Descartes" should be directly visible.

Husserl explicitly emphasizes the freedom and autonomy of this will, characteristics which in principle signify that in the last analysis there can be no necessitating or "coercive" introductions to this will other than its own self-apprehension and initial grasp of its proper aim. It thus appears that transcendental thought can have no other "beginning." The ultimate

Introduction

"way" to transcendental phenomenology is that offered by human reason itself.

Two questions arise from this characterization of the "first step" of phenomenological reflection. Does it offer any resolution of the difficulties mentioned above concerning the problematic character of any "introduction" to transcendental reflection? Is there a presuppositional status to this first step that threatens to darken phenomenology's claim to be free from all presuppositions?

Regarding the first question, we may say that, if the radical autonomy of such reflection is maintained with total consistency, it can be "awakened" only from within. In this sense, the notion of an introductory way leading to transcendental reflection is indeed problematic if we mean by this a way whose beginnings are, as a matter of principle, rooted within a nontranscendental attitude and which can only approach the domain of transcendental thought from "without." A recent author states this issue in the following terms: "But all the richness of transcendental philosophy, especially with regard to its critical implications, cannot do away with the difficulty of how to ever enter it by way of introductory argument. What seems to be the difficulty of taking the transcendental turn, or of introductory argument, is the autonomy of transcendental explanation. The scandal is that it can be explained only from within, not from without."[63]

That Husserl is aware of this issue in terms very similar to these can be adduced from several additional considerations. At one point Husserl explicitly maintains that the "universal science" of which he is speaking (i.e., transcendental phenomenology) must include as a part of its own proper domain treatment of the question about its own point of departure.[64] The latter issue does not stand outside of the scope of transcendental reflection, but must be said properly to belong to it. Clarification of this issue must, therefore, be achieved from within. In addition, and as our previous remarks have already indicated, the implications of this issue were directly confronted by Husserl in his attempt to employ a nontranscendental phenomenological psychology as a potential stepping-stone leading to properly transcendental reflection, not to mention his obvious concern to work out problems of this order through systematic deliberations upon the entire question of the phenomenological reduction. Finally, if we accept Husserl's preface to Fink's essay and its implied agreement with the major contentions of the essay at their face value, we are then permitted to accept Husserl's silence regarding such statements of Fink's as "all introductions of the phenomenological reduction are false" as his tacit approval of such a position.

If our appraisal of this issue is correct, how then are we to treat those various "introductory ways" which Husserl is so earnestly concerned to de-

Introduction

velop? Can a satisfactory account of their introductory character be given in the light of our preceding remarks? Or are they perhaps successive failures, which simply serve to point out the existence of a difficulty that attends all transcendental philosophy?

One, and perhaps the only, possible answer is forthcoming from the fact that the philosophical will which constitutes the irreducible foundation for the "first step" of phenomenological reflection is not at first given with total "clarity." If we wish, a certain naiveté reigns here as well:

> This, then, is the result of our entire reflections up to this point: the idea of a universal science of primordial and foundational subjectivity. . . . Manifestly this idea can by no means already possess the value of a clear and distinct representation of this intended science. At first we have nothing more than a very vague practical aim, that of a certain still to be achieved knowledgeprocess, hovering in the vagueness of its distance before us.[65]

Husserl continues: "How, starting from this point, are we to reach more determinate representations of this idea so that we can arrive at a point from which we may truly begin?" This is the true focus of Husserl's "introductory" ways to transcendental phenomenology. Beginning with an initial and approximate orientation to transcendental philosophy, we must still seek an adequate way to set the further course of our inquiry in motion so that the attainment of our ultimate goal can be secured. We are conscious of pursuing a unique science, but the procedural stages of this inquiry are not thereby guaranteed in detail; hence the need for a careful examination of various approaches to transcendental subjectivity (i.e., the Cartesian way, the way of phenomenological psychology, and the various ontological ways), an examination which at the same time promises greater clarity with respect to the ultimate requirements of our science itself. Most important, however, it is only with such increased clarity that we can be said to be in authentic possession of our point of departure. Its full delimitation can only be achieved as a *result* of advancing phenomenological inquiry. Thus within the autonomous domain of transcendental philosophy itself there exists a tension between possible points of departure and the ultimate goal to which these beginnings are addressed, a tension which makes necessary a course of reflections (such as those of Husserl's which we have followed in these pages) whose aim can finally be none other than illuminating the progressive and self-critical character of this unique science of transcendental origins.

Given the autonomy of transcendental philosophy, this constitutes the proper role of Husserl's "introductory ways." If phenomenology's point of departure is not, however, initially given with absolute evidence, does

Introduction

this not mean that the ideal of a universal science and the philosophical will to pursue such a science, both essential ingredients in the philosopher's "beginning situation," are to be properly termed presuppositions? And, if so, does this not vitiate phenomenology's claim to be a presuppositionless science?

We might reply to such questions by simply stating that the autonomy of transcendental philosophy demands that it "presuppose" itself as its own goal, and that this brings the matter to an end. Husserl has no recourse other than to state that the philosophical will is its own presupposition: it can have no other point of departure or aim. A more complete reply, however, and one in accordance with our preceding discussion, would show that the claim of phenomenology to be a presuppositionless science does require further explanation. If lack of all presuppositions is synonymous with total insight and clarity with respect to ultimate concepts and grounds, such a characterization can only belong to a fully realized science of transcendental subjectivity. Since the beginning stages of phenomenological inquiry are not in possession of such total clarity, this would seem to necessitate something like a presuppositional character for those initially vague and "naive" ingredients of phenomenology's "beginning situation" mentioned above. If they possess this kind of naiveté, this could well be manifested in the initial presupposing of the vague ideal of a universal science. A self-questioning note of Husserl's sheds some light on this. Asking for the truly "radical" nature of philosophy's theoretical aims, Husserl answers that it consists of "total presuppositionlessness." "But is that a possible goal? To formulate all concepts anew, to permit no previous judgment: is that possible? Does this not presuppose a fully developed spirit that has already successfully passed through the school of rigorous science?"[66] A presuppositionless science here appears as the result of phenomenological inquiry and not as its point of departure. From this distinction we are perhaps allowed to draw the conclusion that the lack of all presuppositions is no longer a necessary requirement for phenomenology's point of departure. This does not entail, however, that we are free to make any presuppositions we wish. Our goal is still a science free from all presuppositions, that is, a transcendental science that ultimately dispenses with all presuppositions by virtue of its possessing absolute evidence. All acceptances must be reconstituted upon the basis of absolute evidence if they are to be permitted within this science. This holds equally for the "presupposition of a presuppositionless science." Clearly one of the goals of such a science will be to destroy this ''presupposition'' by ultimately displaying full justification for it, and with such justification it will no longer be a naively accepted "presupposition."

Introduction

Thus a more adequate response to the question concerning the presuppositional status of the ideal of a universal science must take into account the clear distinction Husserl makes between the initial stages and final results of one and the same autonomous science. Such a distinction is crucial if room is to be made for phenomenology's response to the demand for the critical evaluation of its own point of departure. By entering the ideal of a universal and presuppositionless science as an initially naive acceptance (thereby indexing it as a "presupposition" which continually calls for a self-critical review of its own status and justification), we are assured in principle that the unique theoretical interest of philosophical reason will be truly "radical" and that it will not hesitate before the questioning of its own initial orientation.

Let us now turn to our last question concerning a possible "final form" of the phenomenological reduction. It is clear that in one sense there can be no such "finality" apart from the full realization of transcendental philosophy itself. Its completion alone constitutes the adequate expression of the full significance and meaning of Husserl's transcendental reduction. We can, however, perhaps speak of a "final form" in another sense. The concluding pages of Husserl's last major work include a lengthy passage that speaks of the "way" to transcendental philosophy as finally structured by the inherent "teleology" of human reason itself. In part, no doubt, as the result of the increasingly apparent stresses facing phenomenology in the quest for greater clarity concerning its own proper thematic and procedural advance, the theme of the autonomy of transcendental science, already a major element of the various possible ways leading to the transcendental attitude, now thrusts itself more urgently upon Husserl in the dynamic form of the life of human reason. On one level, transcendental phenomenology is to be synonymous with the highest of man's vocations: the perpetual striving for rational self-knowledge and true humanity. Sustained in part by his reflections upon the not always explicitly formulated message contained within the history and inner aims of Western philosophy and in the spiritual crisis of modern man is Husserl's contention that the advance to transcendental thought, and hence the effective deployment of the phenomenological reduction, can be sustained and clarified in terms of the self-realization of reason. Scattered throughout Husserl's writings are suggestive sketches for a philosophy of human culture whose purpose is to illuminate the central features of a rational humanity. For this dimension of Husserl's thought, the theory of the phenomenological reduction culminates in a philosophy of man wherein the ultimate basis for the motivation behind the reduction can be found.

31

Introduction

The specific passage in question here begins with a familiar query: given philosophy's aim to be a "universal science of the world" and to hold sway over a universe of truths about the world "in itself," is the philosopher in possession of "immediately evident" truths with which he can begin his unique science? No such truths appear to be forthcoming given the presumptive and relative nature of our experience of the world. Then, has the idea of a "truth in itself" any meaning for consciousness, or is it merely a philosophical "invention"? From this point on Husserl's discussion focuses upon this category of a "truth in itself" and attempts to delineate its proper status with respect to philosophical reason:

> But yet (this idea) is not a fiction or a dispensable and meaningless invention. Rather is it an idea which raises man to a new height, or to which man is called in a new historicity of human life whose entelechy is this new idea and the philosophical or scientific praxis which is coordinated with it, the method of a new kind of scientific thinking.... The meaning of the setting of this task and its presuppositions (and hence those of all methods) has never been seriously considered, much less scientifically investigated in terms of ultimate responsibility ... Human personal life runs its course through stages of self-reflection and self-responsibility, from individual and occasional acts of this form to levels of universal self-reflection and self-responsibility, and further to the conscious apprehension of the idea of autonomy, the idea of a conscious resolve of the will to form its entire personal life into the synthetic unity of a life lived in universal self-responsibility;[67] correlatively, it is a will to form itself into a true ego, a free and autonomous ego, which seeks to actualize its innate rationality and which strives to remain true to and identical with itself as a rational ego....
>
> The universal apodictically grounded and grounding science now emerges as the necessarily highest of human functions: that, namely (and as I have stated), of making possible its development into a personal and all-encompassing human autonomy—the idea which constitutes the life-force of the highest stage of humanity.
>
> Hence philosophy is nothing other than "rationalism" through and through, but one which differentiates itself in terms of different stages of intention and fulfillment, *ratio within the constant movement of self-enlightenment,* beginning with the first breakthrough of philosophy in mankind, whose innate reason had previously remained entirely hidden as in the darkness of night....
>
> The emergence and recession of historical movements, now a strengthening empirical sensualism and skepticism, now a strengthening rationalism of the older scientific ideals, German Idealism and the

Introduction

reactions against it—all this characterizes the first epoch, that of modern times in its entirety. The second epoch is the renewed beginning, once again taking up Descartes' discovery of the basic requirement of apodicticity, together with the motivational forces of this requirement that grow out of the changed historical situation . . . a radical rethinking of the genuine and not to be forgotten meaning of apodicticity (apodicticity as a basic problem). . . . Herewith begins a philosophy of the deepest and most universal self-understanding of the philosophizing ego as the bearer of that absolute reason which now comes to an awareness of itself . . . (and the understanding) that reason signifies precisely what man in his innermost depths as man must ultimately aim at, and which alone can satisfy and "bless" his existence; . . . that being human is a teleological being, something that ought to be (*Sein-sollen*); that this teleology holds sway in each and every act and intent of the ego and that it can, through self-understanding, know the apodictic *telos* in all; and that this knowing which belongs to ultimate self-understanding has no other form than that of self-understanding in accordance with *a priori* principles, self-understanding in the form of philosophy.[68]

Although this alignment of transcendental science and the ultimate *telos* of philosophical reason can serve to strengthen and clarify Husserl's analysis of the motivational context of phenomenological thought, it must be noted that with respect to phenomenology's own requirements it remains abstract. If Husserl is critical of the failure of Kant and German Idealism to surmount their abstractness by returning to the analysis and questioning of "actual subjectivity" and the concrete life of consciousness, this "final form" of philosophical reason itself cannot be held apart from such analysis. Moreover, this particular passage does nothing to resolve the question whether or not transcendental phenomenology can lay claim to a fundamental "uniqueness" with respect to other philosophies. If its uniqueness rests in its concrete manner of approaching transcendental subjectivity, we fail to note here any specifically "phenomenological" point of departure that makes this approach possible. For these reasons, it can appear that Husserl's teleological reading of man's reflective life threatens phenomenology with a certain anonymity. We must ask whether recognition of this teleology is a sufficient criterion for determining whether or not we are within a properly phenomenological attitude. Similarly, although this passage does indicate that the theme and requirement of apodicticity is to be a basic *problem* for our transcendental science, it significantly does not specify the precise way in which the *telos* of human reason can effectively advance the question of apodicticity to the point of illuminating the details of phenomenology's point of departure.

33

Introduction

There are additional difficulties as well. How are we to treat Husserl's historical deliberations? Can historical judgments be admitted to the realm of phenomenological inquiry? Can they perhaps be introduced through the category of "naive evidence" serving to give some initial formulation to our point of departure, or do they have a distinctive status of their own? If so, perhaps we must add a "way through historical reflection" to the other ways leading to transcendental phenomenology. We must, however, also ask whether the elucidation of reason's teleological character requires such deliberations, for is it not possible to discover this teleology within the concrete personal life of consciousness itself? Finally, is this teleology itself entirely compatible with the possibility of a fully achieved science of transcendental origins, or are human reason and self-understanding by their very nature always "on the way" to such a result? Precisely how can these two motifs complement each other?

The further discussion of such questions can be greatly stimulated by the collection of essays that follows. We can hope that the continued study of Husserl's later works as well as the continuing publication of his unpublished manuscripts will permit a more precise determination of these issues. No matter what the final outcome of such studies may reveal, however, the theme of the phenomenological reduction will continue not only to introduce us to Husserl's phenomenology, but will also serve to lead us across the threshold of philosophy and its undying claims as well.

NOTES

1. Adolph Reinach's *Was ist Phänomenologie?* (*Munich:* Kösel-Verlag, 1951), an address originally presented in 1914—one year after the publication of Husserl's *Ideas*—attempts to strengthen the definition of phenomenology as the "descriptive study of essences," asserting thereby that phenomenology is not intrinsically involved with the question of transcendental idealism. This point is explicitly noted by Conrad-Martius' preface to the published text of the address: "Quite the contrary, the conclusive result of phenomenology is the total surmounting of this transcendental idealism. . . ." (p. 5).

For a recent discussion of this question of the relationship of the *Logical Investigations* to Husserl's later phenomenology see René Scheré, *La phénoménologie des 'Recherches Logiques' de Husserl* (Paris: Presses Universitaires de France, 1967).

2. Edmund Husserl, *Phänomenologische Psychologie* (Den Haag: Martinus Nijhoff, 1962), pp. 20-46.

3. See H. L. Van Breda, *"La reduction phénoménologique,"* in *Husserl: Cahiers de Royaumont III* (Paris: 1959), pp. 307-308; and L. Landgrebe, *"Husserls Phänomenologie*

Introduction

und die Motiv zu ihrer Umbildung," in *Der Weg der Phänomenologie* (Gütersloh: Gerd Mohn, 1967), pp. 9-39.

4. *Phänomenologische Psychologie,* pp. 42f.
5. Edmund Husserl, *Die Krisis der europäischen Wissenschaften und die transzendentale Phänomenologie* (Den Haag: Martinus Nijhoff, 1954), pp. 100ff.
6. Cf. Eugen Fink's essay below, pp. 110ff.
7. Edmund Husserl, *Erste Philosophie: Erster Teil* (Den Haag: Martinus Nijhoff, 6), pp. 268ff.
8. *Phänomenologische Psychologie,* p. 518.
9. Edmund Husserl, *Erste Philosophie: Zweiter Teil* (Den Haag: Martinus Nijhoff, 1959), p. 456.
10. *Ibid.,* p. 457.
11. *Ibid.,* pp. 190f.
12. *Ibid.,* p. 432.
13. *Krisis,* pp. 157f.
14. *Ibid.,* pp. 179f.
15. *Erste Philosophie: Zweiter Teil,* p. 432.
16. *Ibid.,* p. 465.
17. Edmund Husserl, *The Idea of Phenomenology,* trans. Alston and Nakhnikian (The Hague: Martinus Nijhoff, 1964), pp. 27f.
18. In an important study, which in many respects serves to complement his analysis of Husserl's notion of the absolute included in this collection, Rudolph Boehm suggests that "the notion of an 'immanent object' tends to confuse the 'intentional contents' of consciousness which are really transcendent to consciousness with the 'real contents' of this same consciousness which alone are really immanent." "*Les ambiguités des concepts husserliens d' 'immanence' et de 'transcendence',*" *Revue Philosophique,* no. 4 (1959), 502. This essay, as well as the work cited in the following footnote, provide us with indispensable analyses of these crucial Husserlian concepts.
19. Cf. Iso Kern, *Husserl und Kant* (Den Haag: Martinus Nijhoff, 1964), p. 203.
20. *Erste Philosophie: Zweiter Teil,* pp. 432f.
21. *Ibid.*
22. *Ibid.,* p. 169.
23. *Ibid.,* p. 398.
24. *Ibid.,* pp. 149f
25. *Ibid.,* p. 475.
26. *Ibid.*
27. *Ibid.,* p. 478.
28. This way is followed in some detail in the *Krisis,* in the second part of the *Erste Philosophie,* and in the volume entitled *Phänomenologische Psychologie.*
29. *Erste Philosophie: Zweiter Teil,* p. 126.
30. *Ibid.,* p. 127.
31. *Krisis,* pp. 247-260
32. *Ibid.,* p. 259
33. *Erste Philosophie: Zweiter Teil,* p. 445.
34. *Ibid.,* p. 445.
35 *Ibid.,* p. 450.
36. ". . . But meaning is still one-sided and incomplete: namely, all objective meaning is meaning drawn from the meaning-bestowing subjectivity, and only when meaning is drawn from and seen in terms of this source does it win the transcendental determinations which inseparably belong to it." *Erste Philosophie: Zweiter Teil* p. 457.

Introduction

37. It is only the transcendental determinations of "subjectivity" and "world" that can resolve the crucial phenomenological "paradox" between man both as a part of the world (as intramundane subjectivity) and as the constitutive source of the world (as transcendental subjectivity). Cf. *Krisis*, pp. 182-190.
38. *Erste Philosophie: Zweiter Teil*, pp. 255ff.
39. Iso Kern, *Husserl und Kant*, p. 218.
40. *Erste Philosophie: Zweiter Teil*, p. 262.
41. *Ibid.*, pp. 230f.
42. Edmund Husserl, *Formale und transzendentale Logik*, in *Jahrbuch für Philosophie and Phänomenologische Forschung*, vol. X (Halle: 1929), p. 5.
43. Also termed the "theory of possible forms of theory," or the "doctrine of manifolds." For the occurrence of this topic in the *Logical Investigations* see Becker's essay, p. 48.
44. *Erste Philosophie: Zweiter Teil*, p. 255.
45. *Formale und transzendentale Logik*, p. 129.
46. *Ibid*
47. *Ibid.*
48. *Ibid.*, pp. 107f.
49. *Ibid.*, p. 194.
50. *Ibid.*, p. 134
51. *Ibid.*, p. 233.
52. *Ibid.*, p. 232.
53. Cf. *Krisis* section 34, pp. 135-138.
54. *Ibid.*, p. 127.
55. *Ibid.*, p. 148.
56. Cf. Rudolf Boehm, *Editor's Introduction* to *Erste Philosophie: Zweiter Teil*, pp. xxx-xliii.
57. *Erste Philosophie: Zweiter Teil*, p. 477.
58. A very detailed analysis and critique of this question of the temporality of the transcendental ego in Husserl employing many of Husserl's unpublished manuscripts can be found in Klaus Held, *Lebendige Gegenwart* (Den Haag: Martinus Nijhoff, 1966). A valuable discussion of the question of the "point of departure" in Husserl is given in Pierre Thevenaz, "The Question of the Radical Point of Departure in Descartes and Husserl," in *What Is Phenomenology?*, ed. by James M. Edie (Chicago: Quadrangle Books, 1962), pp. 93-112.
59. *Erste Philosophie: Zweiter Teil*, pp. 477-478.
60. See Paul Ricoeur's "Introduction to *Ideas I*," in Ricoeur, *Husserl: An Analysis of His Phenomenology*, trans. E. G. Ballard and L. E. Embree (Evanston: Northwestern University Press, 1967), pp. 16ff.
61. In a later essay, Fink no longer treats this as a *paradox* but as a *problem*. "The fact that this tension between the natural meaning of the *epoché* up to this point and the 'new transcendental meaning' of a neutralization of the belief in the world [Fink is here referring to the *epoché* as a neutralization of the belief in the world which treats this neutralization as an "individual thesis" occurring within this belief, which is then transformed into the suspension of the "universal thesis" of the belief in the world accomplished by the transcendental reduction.—Ed.] is not sufficiently recognized by Husserl as a problem, the fact that, in commenting upon abstaining from this belief when it is reflected upon transcendentally, he expresses himself in a variety of ways all starting from the comprehension-horizon that belongs to the neutralized phenomenon in the natural attitude [which is defined as the meaning of an object when its thetic character has been methodically suspended or bracketed—Ed.]; all this is a symptom of an operative obscurity

Introduction

at the very heart of his philosophy." Eugen Fink, "Les *Concepts Opératoires dans la Phénoménologie de Husserl*," in *Husserl: Cahiers de Royaumont III*, p. 227. However, it is part of Fink's thesis here that such "operative obscurities," present perhaps in the fundamental thoughts of all great philosophies, can never be granted full "thematic" clarity as a result of the finite character of thought itself.

62. *Erste Philosophie: Zweiter Teil*, p. 7.

63. Klaus Hartmann, "On Taking the Transcendental Turn," *The Review of Metaphysics* XX (December, 1966), 248.

64. *Erste Philosophie: Zweiter Teil*, p. 210. Also see *Beilage* VI, esp. p. 358.

65. *Ibid.*, p. 357.

66. *Erste Philosophie: Erster Teil*, p. 313.

67. This notion of self-responsibility can perhaps be best defined as man's ultimate understanding of himself "as being responsible for his own human being," and hence the responsibility involved in being called to live a life of philosophical clarity. *Krisis*, p. 275.

68. *Ibid.*, pp. 270-271, 272-273, 274-276.

The Philosophy of Edmund Husserl

Oskar Becker

Kant was fond of saying that no one could learn philosophy, but only to philosophize. What is that but an admission of philosophy's unscientific character?

1.

IN THANKING those who were present April 8, 1929 for the celebration of his seventieth birthday, Edmund Husserl made specific mention of two of his former teachers: Franz Brentano, of course, and, with particular emphasis, Karl Weierstrass, the mathematician credited with placing the infinitesimal calculus upon a rigorous basis. Just as Weierstrass did away with an unclear way of speaking about the infinitely small and replaced it with precise concepts and methods based on clear and evident insight, so did Husserl's own philosophical goal become that of replacing many splendid but unclear formulations of his contemporaries (and frequently of preceding systems) with straightforward and, for the unbiased, extremely judicious observations which no longer offered room for unclarity. This is the simple but far-reaching meaning of the often misunderstood striving after "philosophy as rigorous science." The fact that Husserl started from mathematics, and that he was schooled in the idea of mathematical exactitude, is of decisive importance for his scientific personality, although this in no way requires that phenomenology must actually begin with the mathematical problematic.

This is clearly shown in Husserl's first philosophical work, the *Philosophy of Arithmetic* (1891, its source being his inaugural dissertation of 1887). The work is subtitled "Logical and Psychological Investigations," and precisely what is new and forward-looking in this work is contained in the word "psychological." Actually it is a question of inquiries, which today we would term "constitutive-phenomenological," even though in the early work the question of method is nowhere subjected to

The Philosophy of Edmund Husserl

basic philosophical discussion. In order to evaluate this terminology, one must recall that in the first edition of the second book of the *Logical Investigations* the manner of observation is still referred to as "descriptive-phenomenological"—and this *after* the appearance of the first, "anti-psychological" book. We know today how and why the characterization of phenomenology as a descriptive-psychological procedure is not unjustified. Current understanding of Husserl's philosophy recognizes that "phenomenological psychology" also plays a decisive and principal methodological role. Everything established phenomenologically in a pure and concrete fashion also possesses a psychological meaning. Conversely, one of the basic systematic approaches to phenomenology leads through a descriptive psychology (which attempts to "understand" experience). In fact, one finds in the *Philosophy of Arithmetic* concepts basic to the "theory of groups" (*Mengenlehre*) and the "theory of numbers"—and primarily the concept of a "collective connecting" itself—discussed by returning to the spontaneous activities of collecting and connecting in which the original and genuine meaning of these concepts are rooted. Here the attempt is made to render "categorial objectivities" (groups and numbers) intelligible within the context of those intentional activities which "constitute" them. These objectivities emerge as the original achievements of such acts. Here it is already clear that it is the *form* of these spontaneous acts which is alone decisive, a form which remains invariant throughout the free variation of their contents (i.e., the elements which are collected). The formal character of arithmetic, together with the formal character of the mathematical analyses constructed upon it, therefore lies in its exclusive relation to "something in general" (objectivity in general). Basic arithmetical-analytical concepts prove themselves to be syntactical derivational forms of an "empty something." It is clear that everything "psychological" in the sense of a description bound up with alleged natural laws of the thought-processes belonging to a determinate and contingent organism *Homo sapiens* living upon the planet Earth is entirely foreign to the inner meaning of this manner of observation. Here, therefore, it is not a question of an actual psychologism such as that attacked by the *Logical Investigations*. This point is of some interest insofar as it is occasionally maintained that Husserl had evolved from an extreme representative of psychologism (in the *Philosophy of Arithmetic*) to a strict anti-psychologist (in the first book of the *Logical Investigations*) and had then once again more or less fallen into psychologism (as early as the second book of the *Logical Investigations*, and subsequently in the later writings). This view does not conform to the historical facts. In general, Husserl's development has proceeded (though not always directly) in a much more continuous

39

fashion, and the seeds of the later thoughts that laid the foundation for his major work are in evidence much earlier than had been commonly believed. In this respect, two points taken from the *Philosophy of Arithmetic* may be alluded to: the basic distinction between "genuine" and "symbolic" number-concepts, and the stress upon the essentiality of symbolic concepts for the meaning of arithmetic in general. "If we had genuine presentations of all numbers, as we do of those which are first in the number-series, there would be no arithmetic because it would be totally superfluous. The most complicated number-relations, now only discovered with difficulty through extensive calculations, would be present to us with the same intuitive evidence as the number-presentations of such propositions as 2 + 3 = 5. . . . In fact, however, our presentational capability is highly restricted. That here certain limits are imposed upon us lies in the *finitude of human nature.* We can attribute a genuine presentation of all numbers only to an understanding which is infinite. . . ."[1] "However, arithmetic in its entirety. . . is nothing other than the sum of technical means designed to overcome the *essential* incompleteness of our intellect already mentioned."[2] "In this respect, Gauss' well-known saying 'ὁ θεὸς ἀριθμντίδει' does not correspond with the notion of an infinitely perfect being. . . . I would simply say 'ὁ ἄνθρωπος ἀριθμντίδει.'" The distinction between "genuine" and "nongenuine" (symbolic) presentations had already been stressed by Franz Brentano (as Husserl explicitly notes, p. 215). Husserl defined symbolic presentation as one which does not directly give its content "as what it is," but gives it indirectly "by means of signs which characterize its content unequivocally."[3] Clearly, the fundamental distinction between the "self-giving" and the "merely signitive" intending of the *Logical Investigations* and the later writings is already present here, a distinction which contains one of phenomenology's most essential and basic methodological ideas: the thought that the merely signitive and empty presentation is to be filled with a self-giving intuition and, where possible, with an intuition which gives the thing "as it is" (*leibhaft*). Of perhaps greater importance, however, is the following more specific condition: the fulfilling (also the "original") intuition has diverse modes, above all the modes of sensibility and categoriality. (Later it is stated that "one cannot play elliptical functions on the violin.") A determinate objectivity has (lying within its essence and therefore quite intransgressible) an entirely determinate mode of givenness. That it is given in this manner and not in any other—no matter what the circumstances—and that it can be given in this manner alone, is neither an accidental nor a necessary imperfection of the intellect which apperceives it, but rather lies in the object itself. With this we come back to the question already touched upon in the quotation cited from the *Philosophy of Arithmetic* concerning the manner in which the "infinite" is given (the simplest case being the infinite number-series). According to the passage cited, it could still appear as if it were the limited character of the finite human intellect which allowed the number-series to be given only symbolically in terms of the "and so forth" of the limitless repetition of adding one (as ἄπειρον δυνάμει ὄν). But further discussion (pp. 246 ff.) indicates that this is not so. The symbolic presentation of an infinite plurality ". . . extends the original concept (of a collection) in such a manner that it *not merely* passes over *certain accidental bounds, but also the bounds necessary to the essence of all knowledge. . . .* The thought that any conceivable extension of our capacity for knowledge can render this capacity capable of either an actual presentation or a successive exhaustion of such (infinite) collections is incomprehensible. *Here our power of idealization itself has a boundary.*" If one compares this later expression with the earlier, one can here find *in nuce* the thought of *transcendental idealism* already expressed in its specifically phenomenological interpretation. Finitude, at first a characteristic feature of the human intellect, appears—at least if one understands it to be an *open* finitude, as the *potential* infinite of the "and so forth" (of an open "horizon")—as a necessary feature of all knowledge which, in general, is capable of being grasped philosophically. "The intention to construct an (actual) infinite plurality" (analogous to an infinite collection) is "absurd." Not only for man but also, in and of itself, for every knowing intellect. It, of course, follows from this that God in Gauss' sense (and therewith in the sense of the traditional ontology) "is to a certain extent an imaginary concept." One can see here how close Husserl, without at that time knowing it, comes to the thought of Kant.[4] Here the thought which plays a decisive role in the *Ideas* is already present: for the ideal intellect also (the divine intellect insofar as God, as is always the case with the later Husserl, is interpreted as a limiting concept, and thus here as an "epistemological limiting concept" in particular) a material thing is always given partially, within a particular orientation and perspective, in a determinate "manner of appearing." The "transcendent" thing is "constituted" in and for itself within a determinate and infinite (i.e., containing an open horizon) manifold of ways of appearing, persisting in this "flow" as something identical. "It is therefore a mistake to think that in principle there belongs to every being the possibility of simply intuiting it as what it is, particularly to grasp it in an adequate perception which would give it 'as it is' (*leibhaft*) apart from all mediation through 'appearances.' God, the subject of absolutely perfect knowledge and therefore of all possible adequate perceptions, naturally possesses (one says) the

41

perception of things in themselves which is denied to finite beings."[5] Here the traditional concept of God, used by Husserl as a basis for criticizing Gauss' arithmetizing deity, is methodologically surpassed. On the basis of the passage quoted from the *Philosophy of Arithmetic*, the second and more precise interpretation of the character proper to an infinite series—that it simply indicates a potentially possible "collection" and that, interpreted as an actual "collection," it is "to a certain extent an imaginary concept"—has taken the place of the first and less precise intuition that arithmetic has meaning only for an "imperfect" human intellect. Strictly understood, the mathematizing intellect is, at least as a finite intellect confronted with any higher-order magnitude whatsoever, not at all imperfect; perfection in the sense of the traditional postulation of an *intellectus infinitus* is nonsensical. This manner of considering the concept of infinity (*implicitly* in the *Philosophy of Arithmetic*; *explicitly* in many passages of the *Ideas* which shed light on these concepts from many different sides) is thoroughly determined by the principle of transcendental idealism: the universal accessibility in principle of all objects which can be meaningfully considered by philosophy. It is surprising that one entire direction of the phenomenological movement which takes Husserl as its point of departure denies this principle, and it is even more surprising that recently one representative of this direction has, as if astonished, questioned its origin. In truth, the principle of transcendental ("constitutive") idealism, if understood correctly and not misconstrued as a "subjective" or metaphysical idealism, is an essential part of phenomenology as such. Correspondingly and as we shall see, the presence of various forms of this principle in every phase of Husserl's philosophy can be demonstrated anew.

We can, looking back, say that a considerable number of principles basic to Husserl's logic and phenomenology (if one can here separate them for external reasons) are already present in the *Philosophy of Arithmetic*: the fundamental distinction between genuine and symbolic presentations (i.e., the intuitively fulfilled "self-giving" presentations and the signitive, emptily intending presentations), the actual carrying out of intentional analyses, consciousness of their form-character and the removal of accidental facticity (concept of essence!), the idea of the "and so forth . . . ," the idea of horizons, and finally the principle of transcendental idealism, which, nevertheless, is not yet expressed without hesitation.

The theory of the phenomenological reduction is still missing; that is, the working out explicitly and in principle of the "transcendental" and the new type of reflection directed toward essences (*eidos*), which will bear the name "phenomenology."

The Philosophy of Edmund Husserl

2.

The first book of the *Logical Investigations,* including the "Prolegomena to Pure Logic" (published in 1900 but already completed in 1899), contains in its first ten chapters a critical discussion of the "psychologism" current at that time, a discussion which resulted in its almost complete and final destruction. Only the eleventh chapter is positive: it outlines the idea of a pure logic. Husserl was not the only one at the turn of the century to oppose the psychologism current in logic at this time. Various Neo-Kantian schools, the Marburg school in particular, did the same, as did Gottlob Frege (whose attack, in the extensive preface to the first book of his *Grundgesetze der Arithmetik,*[6] was mounted with admirable acuteness, but apparently without any telling effect). What gave the Husserlian exposition its incomparable impact was the attentive presentation of the opposing arguments and the thoroughness with which the psychological prejudices were pursued into their last refuge, casting light upon and refuting their ultimate bases. That here a truly radical skepticism (relativism) raised itself had already been seen and forcefully pointed out by Plato. But it was left to Husserl to show and to establish in particular cases and with irrefutable force that, in terms of their ultimate consequences and inner meaning, the many less direct and apparently not so radically relativistic observations in modern logic lead us back to that absurdly radical skepticism. To reproduce the individual and, in accordance with the nature of this discussion, apparently disparate considerations is as impossible here as it is unnecessary. The scientific situation today has changed to such an extent (essentially as the result of the effective consequences of Husserl's work) that these conditions are no longer of such pressing importance as they were thirty years ago. Who today knows of the empiricism, anthropologism, relativism, and psychologism of that period? Today's "theory of knowledge" still certainly evidences an empirical orientation, but it has become "critical," that is, it has become essentially more cautious with respect to questions of logic. Current "critical empiricism" (above all under the influence of Bertrand Russell) is bound up with a logical formalism in the shape of the logical calculus. In the area of logic there is therefore no longer any talk of empiricism.

Even though the particular details of Husserl's "Prolegomena" can be passed over in this brief sketch, it is nevertheless of great importance, particularly with reference to the further development of Husserl's philosophy, to characterize the basic philosophical position which comes into view through these details.

43

Oskar Becker

As already mentioned, there are those who have repeatedly felt (and this has already been voiced by contemporary critics) that the transition from the first to the second book of the *Logical Investigations* constitutes a break. Consequently, some have spoken of a "return to psychologism" in the second book subsequent to the sharp attack upon psychologism in the first. Although this interpretation, seen in terms of the entirety of Husserl's philosophy, is misleading, it is nonetheless quite understandable. The development of the "phenomenology" which is coming into being (the breakthrough to which occurs in the *Logical Investigations*) does not at this time follow a direct path, and this without detriment to the consistency with which philosophy's basic tendency to become a "rigorous science" is subsequently pursued. In opposition to the "subjective" (i.e., toward acts) orientation of the *Philosophy of Arithmetic,* the "Prolegomena to Pure Logic" bears a thoroughly "objective" orientation in focusing upon the purely objective (*gegenständlich*). In the summarizing discussion of "psychological prejudices"[7] which culminates in the presentation of the decisive differences between psychologism and its opponents, "ideal species," "individual facts" (*Tatsachen*), and "intentional unities" are, in repeated application, opposed to the individual and real (*realen*) psychical acts. It is not a question of logical principles constituting "a law for acts of judgment, but rather a law for contents of judgment . . . in other words, for ideal meanings." "We are not considering judgments as real (*reale*) acts," but only "judgments in an ideal sense." "Ideal" indicates here the antithesis to various real (*real*) "subjective-anthropological" phenomena or psychical acts which are, in addition, characterized by their temporality. "In the psychological parts of logical theory one speaks of judgments as being a holding-something-as-true, thus of (determinately) ordered experiences of consciousness. This is no longer the topic in the purely logical parts. Judgment here means the same as *proposition* . . . understood as an ideal unity of meaning." "Whoever, with logical-analytical intent, states: the categorical judgment 'God is just' has the subject-representation 'God,' is surely not speaking of the judgment as a psychical experience . . . and similarly not of a psychical act, but rather of the proposition 'God is just' which is *one*, the diversity of possible subjective experiences notwithstanding. . . ." If, in the *Philosophy of Arithmetic,* the acts of counting, collecting, and so forth, were analyzed with respect to what is necessarily contained within them *as such* (under, to be sure, the misleading title of a psychological analysis), the psychological is now sharply separated from the ideal and the latter is in general related to objects, never to acts. But it will be admitted that the "apodictic *a priori* evidences" which manifest themselves in ideal objects and affair-complexes (*Sachverhalten*) can be made "psychologically useful." "From them we can at any time gather *a priori* possibilities and impossibilities which relate to certain kinds of psychical acts, to acts of counting, additive and multiplicative connecting, etc." Finally, a view, although hardly noticeable at first, is here in the process of being prepared which permits us to interpret the acts themselves as "idealizing" even though they themselves are not yet *ideal*. For it is stated later on: "Therefore these laws are not themselves psychological principles. The subject-matter of psychology as the natural science of psychical experiences is the investigation of the *natural conditions* for these experiences. Thus the natural (causal) relationships for mathematical and logical activities in particular belong to this realm. Their *ideal* relationships and laws constitute a realm of their own. This realm is ultimately constituted by purely general principles, constructed out of 'concepts' which are not class-concepts of psychical acts but ideas which have their concrete foundation in such acts. "The number 'three' . . . is not an empirical particular or class of particulars, but is an ideal object which we apprehend ideally in the act of counting, of judging with evidence, etc." The *evidence* for logical judgments has certain natural "conditions" such as "concentration of interest, a certain mental liveliness, exercise, etc." Psychology's task is to investigate these conditions and here it can only encounter "vague empirical generalities" and not "knowledge of an exact content." But in addition to these "psychological," "external," and "empirical" conditions, judgmental evidence also stands under "ideal conditions." "Every truth represents an ideal unity of a possibly infinite and unlimited multiplicity of correct assertions of the same form and matter. . . . Now the laws of pure logic are truths which are based . . . purely upon the concept of truth. When applied to possible acts of judgment, they express, on the basis of the pure form of judgment, ideal conditions for the possibility or impossibility of evidence. Of these two kinds of conditions for evidence (the psychological and the ideal), one refers to the particular constitution of that type of psychical being which falls within the framework of current psychology; the other, however, as the ideal laws of evidence, is universally valid for every possible consciousness."[8] These words contain the first clear intimation of the phenomenological reduction, for the thought of ideal laws holding for every possible consciousness—and not only for ideal objects—is here clearly expressed. It must be admitted, however, that, within the framework of the "Prolegomena," these words constitute no more than a passing and isolated reference; the positive concluding chapter concerning the "Idea of Pure Logic" refers solely to the "objective or ideal connection" which constitutes "science *qua* science." Science as "anthropological unity, as the unity, namely, of acts of thought, of thought-dispositions, together with certain related external arrangements," "is not our interest here." Nor is the act of evident judging as such to be considered. "If we reflect upon this act, then instead of that objectivity, the truth itself becomes the object and now *it* is *given* in an objective manner. Hereby we seize—in ideational abstraction—truth as the ideal correlation of the fleeting subjective act of knowing, as the *one* in opposition to the unlimited manifold of possible acts of knowing and knowing individuals."[9]

From then on pure logic is sketched out as the "theory of possible theory-forms or the pure theory of manifolds,"[10] as the fulfillment of the Leibnizian dream of the *mathesis universalis* which first becomes possible after the pure categories of meaning and object and the laws based upon them have been fixed. Hence there can be no doubt as to the general and sharply objective orientation of the "Prolegomena."

3.

Contrasting with this orientation, the second book of the *Logical Investigations*, of far greater importance than the "Prolegomena," contains in its most decisive sections "intentional analyses" of acts and act-complexes. The justification for this revised attitude, which repeatedly stands in a much closer relation to the *Philosophy of Arithmetic,* is the task of the significant § 2 of the introduction to the second book entitled, "Clarification of the Goal of Such (i.e., "phenomenological") Investigations." The standpoint of the "Prolegomena" is not thereby surrendered, but only is an accommodation sought for the new task. The first section had already stated that it is a question "of discussions of a most general kind which belong to the wider sphere of an objective *theory of knowledge* and, closely connected with this, to a pure *descriptive phenomenology* of the experiences of thought and knowledge." "Pure phenomenology presents a field of neutral inquiry in which the different sciences are rooted. On the one hand, it serves to prepare the way for *psychology as an empirical science . . .* on the other hand, it discloses the 'sources' out from which the basic concepts and ideal laws of *pure logic* originate." In § 2 it is stated that "the objects which pure logic has neglected to investigate are given at first in grammatical dress: more precisely, as embedded within concrete psychical experiences which, in the functions of meaning and meaning-fulfillment, belong to certain linguistic expressions and which form a *phenomenological unity* with them." It certainly does not follow self-evidently from the fact that "the theoretical realizes itself in certain psychical experiences and is given in them in the manner of a single instance" that those psychical experiences, the logical character of acts, "must be held to be the primary objects of logical inquiry." For it is not the "psychological" but rather the "logical" judgment which interests the logician, the "identical *meaning* of an assertion which is one over and against the diverse, descriptively distinguishable subjective judgment-experiences." Nor is it decisive that the ideal meaning-unity corresponds to "a certain generally common trait in the particular experiences in which the essence of judgment as such is realized." Yet, although "the ideal and not the phenomenological analysis [one should note this opposition here, for it is quite impossible for the later Husserl] belongs to the primordial domain of pure logic," this second type of analysis cannot be dispensed with because all logic "insofar as it becomes our own object of inquiry and insofar as it makes possible the evidence for the *a priori* laws grounded within it" must be given in "subjective realizations." The ideal logical law is given at first in nothing other than the *meaning of words*. The evidence with which we apprehend it is dependent upon this. Unnoticed equivocations can later substitute other concepts and pervert the sense of purely logical principles. Logical ideas must be brought to "epistemological clarity and distinctness" through phenomenological analysis. For "logical concepts, as valid unities of thought, must have their origin in intuition (*Anschauung*); they must originate through abstraction upon the basis of certain *experiences* and are to be continually preserved by the *reenactment of this abstraction* and are to be seized in their ideality with themselves." "We shall certainly not rest content with 'mere words'. . . . We shall return to the 'affairs themselves' (*den Sachen selbst*)."

We see how these later determinations of the task and function of "phenomenological" investigation find themselves in accord with the aspirations of the *Philosophy of Arithmetic*. And this to such an extent that the new direction of inquiry is unhesitatingly called upon to provide "a descriptive (not genetic-psychological) understanding of these psychical experiences to the extent required in order to give stable meaning to all basic concepts of logic. . . ." This is stated more clearly in the third appendix to § 6: "Phenomenology is Descriptive Psychology," a characterization which naturally leads to the objection: "If the critique of knowledge is thus essentially psychology . . . (and if) pure logic thus also rests upon psychology—to what purpose was the entire quarrel with psychologism?" Yet this objection can be answered with reference to the fact that "pure phenomenology" was characterized earlier (see above, p. 46) as "a field of neutral inquiry" from which psychology and logic both originated. "Pure description is simply a stage prior to theory. . . . Thus one and the same sphere of pure description can serve as preparation for very diverse theoretical sciences. It is not psychology as a complete science which is a foundation for pure logic, but only certain classes of descriptions which form the first stage for the theoretical investigations of psychology . . . and which, at the same time, form the support for those fundamental abstractions in which the logician comprehends with evidence . . . the essence of his ideal objects." Therefore, "we would do well to speak of *phenomenology* rather than of descriptive *psychology.*" Here, and already in an appendix to the first edition of the *Logical Investigations* (II, 18), the improper designation "descriptive psychology" is retracted after its initial employment. In the foreword to the second edition of the *Logical Investigations* (1913, I, xiii), Husserl mentions this designation in a highly self-critical way: ". . . The uncertain *Introduction* (to the second book), doing so little justice to the essential meaning and method of the investigation carried out, was radically revised. I felt its defects immediately after its appearance and soon found occasion[11] to raise objections to my misleading designation of phenomenology as descriptive psychology." It is stated that "phenomenological descriptions do not concern subjective experiences or classes of subjective experiences belonging to empirical persons, for it knows nothing of persons . . . of my subjective experiences and the experiences of others, and it assumes nothing concerning them; it raises no question with respect to them, attempts no determinations, makes no hypotheses. . . ." In this critical review Husserl already (1903) found himself on the path leading directly to the complete *phenomenological reduction.* That this principle had, however, already found its first, but certainly not adequate, expression in the first edition of the *Logical Investigations* is indicated by § 7 of the *Introduction* to the second book entitled, "The Principle of the Presuppositionless Character of Epistemological Investigations." Nevertheless, this title itself says very little, for such a principle had already been repeatedly called for from the side of "epistemology." The concrete formulation of this basic principle, however, is new. "In our opinion, the principle can only mean the exclusion of all suppositions which cannot be entirely and fully realized phenomenologically. Every epistemological investigation must be carried out upon purely phenomenological bases." The "clarifying (*aufklärende*) theory of knowledge" will simply "clarify the idea of knowledge in accordance with its constitutive elements or laws . . . will *understand* the ideal sense of the specific connections within which the objectivity of knowledge is documented, will raise the pure forms and laws of knowledge . . . to clarity and distinctness by returning to adequately fulfilled intuition." The characteristic which distinguishes this procedure from other current directions is this: what is of decisive importance in the theory of knowledge is seen in the phenomenon, in the

The Philosophy of Edmund Husserl

clarification (*Aufklärung*)—not explanation (*Erklärung*)—and understanding of the phenomenon, and in the "adequately fulfilled intuition." At the start, this view, later substantiated in the course of the *Logical Investigations* (particularly in the sixth investigation), appears as the principle of the phenomenological method in general. One can view this as a systematic deficiency: the method's basic principle first shows itself to be confirmed in the method's application. But the principal self-referential character of logic shows such a "zig-zag" movement (II, 18) to be unavoidable.

What we have said so far should have at least indicated in outline the nature of the philosophical problems with which Husserl started at the time of the *Logical Investigations*. It remains to refer briefly to the content of the six investigations. In this connection, naturally only what is of principal importance can be taken into account.

Since the theme of the preparatory first investigation finds its proper treatment in the sixth investigation, we shall begin with the important second investigation concerning "The Ideal Unity of Species." The so-called "essential insight," here still entitled "ideation," is demonstrated upon typical examples for the first time and is defended by detailed analyses against the "newer theory of abstraction" of the empiricists (Mill, Spencer, Locke, Berkeley, and Hume) which constitutes its denial. More precisely, it is a question of "defending the kind of justification proper to specific (or, ideal) objects as compared with individual (or, real) objects" and "the different manners of presentation in which the one and the other become clearly given to us." The "act in which we mean something specific (*Spezifisches*)" is "in fact different from the act in which we mean something individual," despite a certain "phenomenal similarity." For in both cases "the same concrete (object) appears, and in both cases, insofar as it appears, the same sensible content is given in the same manner of apprehension." But "in the one case the appearance is the presentational basis for an act of *individual* meaning," and in the other case it is the presentational basis "for an act of *specific* meaning; that is, while the thing appears, or better, while a certain feature appears in the thing, we do not mean this objective feature which is given here and now, but rather do we mean its *content*, its 'idea': we do not mean this moment of red in the house, but we mean *redness* (*das Rot*)." In every concrete instance, the individual red is something else, but the same *species* is realized "in" every instance: this red is the same as that red—viewed *specifically*, it is the same color, but, viewed *individually*, it is an individual trait of different objects. It is a question here of a *categorial* epistemological difference belonging to the "form of consciousness": its "origin" lies in the mode of consciousness, and not in the fluctuating "matter of

49

knowledge." "Talk of universal objects" proves to be unavoidable since there are ineradicable differences between specific and individual judgments (both of which may be either singular or universal): hence judgments such as "Socrates is a man" and "All men are mortal," on the one hand, and judgments such as "2 is an even number" and "All analytical functions are differentiatable," on the other. Here "the strict ideality of the specific in the sense held by the tradition" is supported. We do not only speak figuratively when we genuinely mean a *similar* red coloration which, perhaps, is found in different places. For each likeness refers back to an ideality by virtue of which likeness holds; otherwise one would encounter a *regressus in infinitum*. To these arguments, carried out by way of examples, against opponents of "ideal species," are attached brilliant polemical and critical discussions concerning the empirical theory of abstraction which can be compared with the penetration and telling force of the first parts of the "Prolegomena." From among the several positive descriptions which follow the conclusion of this investigation the important distinction between two fundamentally different conceptions of abstraction might be mentioned: "abstraction in the sense of a lifting out" of "abstract contents," that is, dependent parts ("moments," not "portions"[12]) of an object, in contrast to concept-formation, or the grasping of a species.

The third investigation, "Concerning the Theory of Wholes and Parts," deepens the difference between independent and dependent parts ("portions" and "moments") and explores their *a priori* laws. The concept of object employed in this investigation is extraordinarily broad and encompasses examples of both acts and objects. This occasions the working out of a precise concept of "analytic," which is actually the most far-reaching achievement of the investigation. "Analytic propositions are propositions whose validity . . . is entirely independent of the material uniqueness of their objects; they are therefore propositions which permit complete formalization and which can be grasped as special instances or mere applications of the *formal or analytic laws* which thereby emerge. Here formalization consists of replacing all material-determinations of the given analytic proposition by indeterminate elements which are then interpreted as unbounded (*unbeschränkte*) variables" (II, 247). By contrast, *all* material propositions, also those which are necessary (*a priori*), are "synthetic," such as, for example, the proposition "a color cannot exist apart from something colored." For "color is not a relative expression whose meaning includes the representation of a relation to something else." Although color is not "thinkable," apart from something colored, the existence of any colored something, or, more precisely, an extended something, is not "analytically" grounded in the concept color. By contrast, the following is an analytically necessary proposition: "Correlates reciprocally require each other." The employment of the expression "analytic" is connected primarily with Aristotle (*'Αναλυτικά*) rather than Kant, although relations to the latter are not lacking. Essential is the fact that "generalization" (be this to the highest genus) can never replace "formalization"; the empty-formal "something" is not the *γενιώτατοιν* as is the *τί* of the Stoics (compare the later statement of this theory with § 13 of the *Ideas*). The theory of wholes and parts finally culminates in the proposal of a formal-analytic theory of part relations whose more precise statement would belong to mathematical logic. The fourth investigation turns away from the "formal-ontological" considerations of the third investigation and returns to questions concerning the theory of meaning ("apophantic") as these had been previously defined in the first investigation. The idea of a "pure grammar" is developed as a pure form-theory of meanings. The grammatical laws of individual languages are different, but every language must have certain principles of grammatical structure which refer back to a necessary structural lawfulness of meaning-connections (this also holds for an artificial conceptual "language," such as the logical calculus). One could at first examine the purely combinatorial possibilities of connecting elementary logico-grammatical structures to form complexes of progressively higher intricacy (Husserl has explicitly called for such a theory for the forms of judgment in the widest sense in his latest work).[13] But a theory of meaning-combinations of this type is not identical with pure grammar. Here only those meaning-assemblages (which, if they are "clear," need be meaningful only in an "empty" and "unfulfilled" way) are of interest which *themselves once again possess the character of a meaning.* Thus a propositional meaning is "assembled" from the meanings of the words it contains, but not always in such a way that all partial meanings form *independent* parts of the proposition as a whole. The "dependency" of meaning here does not simply lie in the dependent character of its object, but is of a unique nature. The decisive distinction is that between "syncategorematic" meaning (which does not signify expressions which are incomplete or anomalously abridged) and "categorematic" meaning. They are responsible for the fact (which we cannot here expound in greater detail) that definite laws underlie the combining of meanings to form a whole meaning, laws which exclude the possibility of so-called purely grammatical "*nonsense.*" It is to be distinguished not only from material *absurdity,* but also from purely formal ("analytic" in the sense of the third investigation) absurdity. This difference is pointed out by contrasting "a man is a" (nonsense) with the purely grammatically "sensible" but *ana-*

lytically absurd expression "an A which is not an A." ("A colored something without extension" is *materially* absurd.)

We can consider only the last of the two concluding investigations ("Concerning Intentional Experiences and Their Contents," and "Elements of a Phenomenological Clarification of Knowledge"), which is basic to so much of Husserl's thought. Although the fifth investigation is very important historically, it simply presents the first example of carrying out an "intentional analysis" of greater scope and more encompassing content in which the *essence* of acts is for the first time revealed for what it is. A presentation of its subtle act-analytical content is, however, quite impossible within the present context.

By contrast, the sixth investigation's two basic trains of thought allow brief characterization. Corresponding to the two "sections" of this investigation, the first concerns the idea of "knowledge as fulfilled synthesis," and the second concerns "*categorial intuition.*"

The distinction between "empty intention" and "fulfilled intuition" had already been alluded to in the first investigation. In particular, it was pointed out that an intuition belonging to a determinate but empty representation by way of "fulfilling" it could not be taken to mean that incidental and inadequate kind of imagelike "illustration" with which—particularly from the side of associational psychology—it was predominantly confused. Something "illustrating" the proposition "every algebraic equation to an odd power has at least one real root," can occur to me: "an open book (I recognize it as Serret's *Algebra*) and the physical type of an algebraic function in Teubner print, and, with the word 'root,' the well-known symbol $\sqrt{}$" (II 63). But all this does not give me the least assistance in *understanding* the proposition, not to mention insight into its truth. The intuition which leads to this insight manifestly possesses a character quite different from the sensibly illustrative "accompanying phantasy image." First, it is not at all *sensible* but *categorial*, and, second, it relates to the *same* meaning meant by the proposition as an intentional meaning (not something merely "accompanying" what is intended) solely in the manner of being an appropriate (adequate) intuition of this meaning. This means: a "synthesis of identification" obtains between both, and this alone (and not something else) leads to *insight* (evidence) into the true affair-complex. Indeed, in principle the "truth" of this affair-complex consists of nothing other than this identity of what is meant with what is intuited.

The unity of "expressing thoughts and expressed intuitions" can be either "static" or "dynamic." In the static unity-relationship the "meaning-bestowing thought" is grounded in an intuition and is related to its object in this way. I speak, for example, of "my inkwell" and at the same time the inkwell itself stands before me and I see it. The name names the object "through the ... signifying act." The relationship between name and object in this state of unity evidences a certain *descriptive character:* the name "my inkwell," "is deposited," as it were, "upon" the perceived object (II, 469). By contrast, in the "dynamic" coincidence of meaning-intention and fulfilling intuition "we experience a descriptively unique *consciousness of fulfillment.*" "We can experience *the same* objectivity now intuitively rendered present in an intuition which, previously, was 'merely thought of' in symbolic acts: the objectivity, defined precisely as this so-and-so, now is intuited as what it, at first, was merely thought of (signified) as being" (II, 504). The "intentional essence of the act of intuition is appropriate to the signitive essence of the act of expression." In this connection, a meaning-intention is not always fulfilled: it can also be "disappointed." This expression, just as the expression "nonfulfillment," "does not signify a simple privation of fulfillment," but rather a new "descriptive fact, a form of synthesis which, like fulfillment, has its own unique character" (II, 513). "Conflict" is a "possibility correlative" to harmonious fulfillment. The intuition *conflicts* with the meaning-intention. "Conflict separates," but the experience of conflict is situated within relation and unity; it is a form of "synthesis"—no longer a synthesis of "identification," but now one of "distinction." For, in general, it is true that "an intention is disappointed by way of conflict only by virtue of the fact that it is one part of a more encompassing intention whose complementary part is fulfilled" (II 515).

The fulfillment of an intention can be enhanced. Not only in the sense that real intuitability can be achieved, but also in the sense that the clarity and fullness of this intuition is itself capable of varying degrees. This "points toward a *final goal of the enhancement of intuition* wherein the full and entire intention would have reached fulfillment; not an intermediate and partial one, but a definitive and final one. . . . Where a representational intention has secured a final fulfillment for itself through this ideally complete perception, the genuine *adaequatio rei et intellectus* has been realized: the objectivity is precisely what it was intended as; it is *actually* 'present' or 'given'" (II, 589-590). In this exceptional case, "*evidence* provides us with the ideal of adequation"; indeed, "the epistemologically critical and pregnant sense of evidence is exclusively concerned with this final and unsurpassable goal, the *act of this most complete synthesis of fulfillment* which gives absolute fullness of content, the object itself, to the intention. . . . Since every identification is evidence for an objectivating act, its objective correlate is *being in the sense of truth*, or simply *truth*" (II, 593-594). Specifically, there are four conceptions of truth which must be distinguished:

1. "Truth as the correlate of an identifying act, i.e., an affair-complex"; "truth as the correlate of a coinciding identification of an identity: the *complete agreement between what is meant and what is given* as such." Evidence as the "experience of truth" certainly does not directly mean that this is an adequate *perception of truth*, for one must grant that "the carrying out of the identifying coincidence is not yet an actual perception of the objective agreement, but that it first becomes such through a specific act of objectivating apprehension, through a specific viewing of the existent truth (*die vorhandene Wahrheit*).

2. Truth as "the ideal relation between the cognitive essence of the coinciding acts." Thus not the "objectivity which corresponds to the evidence-act," but "the idea belonging to the act-form," "the cognitive essence apprehended as the idea of the empirically accidental acts of evidence; or the idea of adequation as such."

3. Essence (being, truth) is "the object given in evidence in the manner of the meant object; it is fullness itself" insofar as it "is attentively experienced."

4. Truth as the correctness of intention, especially correctness of judgment; its adequacy with respect to the true object.

How shall the concepts of "truth" and "being" now be distinguished? If one takes into account the fact that the investigation is extended to include both "relating acts" (acts of judgment)[14] and "nonrelating acts" (acts which simply posit), thus encompassing the entire sphere of objectivating acts, it then appears most appropriate to ascribe the concept of truth to acts and "their ideally graspable moments," and the concept of being (true being) to their objective correlates, even though "some room for equivocation remains unavoidable." *Truth* (according to 2 and 4) would be defined as the idea of adequation, or as the correctness of the objectivating positing; being (true being) would be defined (according to 1 and 3) as the *identity of the object meant and the object given in the adequation.* The concepts of *absurdity* (experience of absolute conflict), *falsity*, and *nonbeing* can be treated analogously.

From the definitions given in §§ 38-39 of the sixth investigation, the *principle of phenomenological accessibility*, together with the truly-existing objects first constituted through this accessibility, emerges as clearly as possible. No object "truly is" which is not, at least *ideally*, given "adequately in evidence as the object meant," which could not be experienced as an object "making" an intention "true." And any object which cannot thus "truly be" is not at all.

It remains to glance briefly at the second part of the sixth investigation which introduced "categorial intuitions" (to which the "essential insight" of species in the second investigation also belongs) into phenomenology.

The Philosophy of Edmund Husserl

If all truths, even those relating to grammatical, mathematical, and similar objects, are to be given in evidence through adequately fulfilling intuitions, the concept of intuition must be extended beyond the sphere of sensibility. "How shall we designate the correlate of a nonsensible . . . subject-presentation if the word 'object' (*Gegenstand*) is denied us; how shall we name its actual 'givenness' if the word 'perception' (*Wahrnehmung*) is denied us?" Thus totalities, indeterminate pluralities, numbers, disjunctions, predicates, and affair-complexes become "objects," and the acts through which they appear as given become "perceptions" (II, 615).

There are, of course, phenomenological differences between sensible and categorial intuitions. Every perception indeed apprehends its object directly, but "this direct apprehension has a different sense and character depending upon whether the object is sensible or categorial, real or ideal." In fact, the sensible object is "constituted" in perceptual acts in a "simple (*schlicht*) manner," which implies that it is "not constituted in acts which are based upon other acts which bring objects into view from some other quarter. . . . Sensible objects are given in perception *within a single act-level (in einer Aktstufe.)*" By contrast, categorial intuitions are founded acts. Let us limit ourselves to what is perhaps the simplest example: that of a collection. It is clear that "what corresponds intuitively to the words *and* and *or*, *both* and *one of each*" is not "something tangible . . . indeed, it cannot be depicted pictorially. . . . I can paint A and I can paint B, and I can paint both within the same pictorial space, but I cannot paint the *both*, *A and B.* "Here we can only perform the new act of conjunction upon the basis of both individual intuitive acts, and thereby *mean* the conjunction of objects A and B. One must not confuse the simple perceptions of sensibly unified aggregates, series, clusters, and so forth, with "conjunctive perceptions" in which "the consciousness of plurality alone is truly constituted."

4.

Outside of the essay *Philosophy as Rigorous Science*,[15] Husserl published nothing essential during the years 1902-1912.[16] Nevertheless, this essay suffices to cast light on the state of his inquiries at that time.

The sharpness, indeed, abruptness, with which the ideal of "exact" philosophy is formulated at the very beginning of this essay is noteworthy. " . . . Philosophy, according to its historical purpose the loftiest and most rigorous of all sciences . . . is incapable of assuming the form of rigorous science. Philosophy, whose vocation is to teach us how to carry on the eternal work of humanity, is utterly incapable of teaching in an objectively valid manner. Kant was fond of saying that no one could learn philosophy, but only to philosophize. What is that but an admission of philosophy's unscientific character? . . . I do not say that philosophy is an imperfect science; I say simply that it is not yet a science at all, that as science it has not yet begun. As a criterion for this, take any portion—however small—of theoretical content that has been objectively grounded."[17] Even the "much admired exact sciences" have defects, but present in them is a "doctrinal content continually growing and branching out." "No reasonable person will doubt the objective worth or the objectively grounded probability of the wonderful theories of mathematics and the natural sciences."[18] Such objectivity cannot be obtained for philosophy by a "mere negative criticism of consequences," but only through a "positive criticism of foundations and methods." It appears that such a criticism has not yet grown out of what today is passed off as the exact and basic philosophical science: experimental psychology. Thus the first part of the essay takes a stand against the "naturalization of consciousness" and the "naturalization of ideas." The truly basic philosophical science is not "natural science," but the "phenomenology of consciousness." In the course of these discussions, which we cannot here pursue in detail, the thought of the *phenomenological reduction* (and the thought of phenomenology's peculiar presuppositionless and yet concrete character) becomes unfolded ever more clearly, a thought which is subsequently presented in a rigorously systematic manner in the *Ideas* of 1913.

Still to be mentioned is the brief polemic against *Weltanschauung* philosophy and "historicism" at the conclusion of the essay which occasioned Dilthey's (who had greeted the second book of the *Logical Investigations* so enthusiastically) opposition. Once again Husserl's own ideal of exactitude is displayed. The sciences of man (*Geisteswissenschaften*) are empirical sciences, not sciences of essences. They describe "morphological structure," the *type* of historical forms of art, religion, morality, science, philosophy, "*Weltanschauung.*" The plurality and diversity of the types which thereby emerge easily lead to skeptical relativism. In addition, the sciences of man, qua empirical, are in a position neither to demonstrate the justification for this skepticism nor to refute it. The question of *validity* is an ideal one; it can be decided only by an investigation into essences and never by inquiry into the factual-historical. The "historicist" fails to recognize this; this is his principal mistake. With respect to the concept of truth, Husserl here characteristically fully equates philosophy with the positive sciences. "We can esteem as a great accomplishment the successful solution of a scientific problem that today would belong to a class of problems easily mastered by a high-school student. And the same holds true in all fields."[19] Also that of philosophy. "Profundity is an affair of wisdom; conceptual distinctness and clarity is an affair of rigorous theory. . . . The exact sciences, too, had their long periods of profundity, and just as they did in the struggles of the Renaissance, so too, in the present-day struggles, I dare to hope, will philosophy fight through from the level of profundity to that of scientific clarity."[20] "Of course, we need history too. Not, it is true, as the historian does. . . . But it is not through philosophies that we become philosophers, . . . The impulse to research must proceed . . . from things and the problems connected with them."[21] "To one truly without prejudice it is immaterial whether a certainty comes to us from Kant or St. Thomas, from Darwin or Aristotle, from Helmholtz or Paracelsus."[22]

This statement reveals a fundamental lack of interest in all purely historical development. Only later will Husserl attempt to grasp genesis as such phenomenologically; corresponding to a "static" constitution there will be an "*a priori*-genetic" constitution whose "sedimented history" is to be found in layers of intentional implications.[23]

5.

The *Ideas*[24] remains Husserl's most comprehensive philosophical work to date; not in the external aspect of its relatively modest range, but in the comprehensiveness of its problem-formulation and the depth of its philosophical foundation. It contains the systematic presentation of phenomenology's basic method, the *phenomenological reduction* mentioned above. Husserl proceeds from two basic and interrelated distinctions; namely, those between "fact" (*Factum*) and "essence" (*Eidos*), and "real" (*Reales*) and "irreal" (*Irreales*). Pure or transcendental phenomenology is concerned neither with facts nor with real things (*Reales*). In other words, it "reduces" the real facts which confront us in the "natural attitude" in two respects: first, "eidetically" and second, "transcendentally." That is, it first transforms them into "essences" and then into "transcendental phenomena" in "pure consciousness."

From the very beginning it should be clear that these two directions or "aspects" of the phenomenological reduction comport themselves as two autonomous components which, when set in any relation to each other that you like, produce the same results in two different ways (depending upon their different combinations) and with significantly different midpoints. One can best clarify this relation with the help of an illustration. Beginning with the *natural attitude N,* one can pass over into the *eidetic attitude E* in a "vertical" direction (or, correlatively, from the "natural object," that is, from the "real fact" *N* to the "eidos" *E*) and then move from *E* in a "horizontal" direction to the *full or pure phenomenological attitude P* (or, to the pure, transcendental phenomenon *P*). Or one can first advance in a "horizontal" direction from *N* to *T*, the *transcendental-factual* ("metaphysical") attitude, or to the "transcendental phenomenon as a unique *factum,"* and from there move "vertically" to *P*. The vertical directions signify the "eidetic" components of the reduction, and the horizontal directions signify its "transcendental" components. The midpoints *E* and *T*, traversed by each "way" (*NEP* and *NTP*), the pure, "transcendent" eidos *E* and the "transcendental" factum *T*, are important. ("Transcendent" here means "not yet transcendentally reduced.") The transcendent eidos forms the object of "ontology,"[25] which can be further divided into *formal* and *material* parts, the latter in addition encompassing a group of individual "regions" which are determined by "highest genera."[26] In contrast, the philosophical science of the transcendental factum culminates in *metaphysics*, and is to be sharply distinguished from "ontology."[27]

We need not treat ontology in detail. The first section of the *Ideas* gives us nothing essentially new in relation to the *Logical investigations,* although much is presented in a clearer and more systematic form.

Of particular importance in the *Ideas* are the discussions beginning with the "Fundamental Phenomenological Outlook" in the second section that focus upon the "transcendental reduction." First the "world in the natural attitude" is described, a world which surrounds us with its horizons of distance and indeterminacy. The spontaneity of the *cogito* attaches itself to this world and sets aside its other ideal worlds (the world of arithmetic, for example). This natural world is also an intersubjective world wherein others as well as myself are to be found. The quintessence of this "description prior to all theories" is the "general thesis of the natural attitude": "'The' world is always there as something real. At the most, here and there it is 'other' than I have supposed it to be, this or that is to be struck *out of* it under such titles as 'illusion,' 'hallucination,' etc. I exclude them from this world which—in the sense of the general thesis— is always there."[28] The transcendental reduction simply consists of a "radical alteration" of the natural attitude. The "general thesis" characterized above certainly does not consist of "individual acts of judgment, of an articulated judgment concerning *existence."* But this "potential and unexpressed" existence-thesis can also be "disconnected" or "bracketed," that is, it can be "set out of action" in a unique manner *without its content thereby being disturbed in the least.* What this *epoché* or suspension of judgment means can be illustrated by comparison with the well-known

The Philosophy of Edmund Husserl

Cartesian "attempt to doubt." The very "attempt to doubt something which is present to consciousness . . . necessarily occasions a certain suspension of the (existence) thesis." For such an attempt does not itself belong within the realm of our arbitrary will. "We do not abandon the thesis which we have enacted, we make no change in our conviction . . . and yet the thesis undergoes a modification: while the thesis in itself remains what it is, we, as it were, set it 'out of action,' we 'disconnect it,' 'bracket it.' It is still there, just as what has been enclosed by parentheses is still there. . . . The thesis is experienced, but we make 'no use' of it. . . . In the *attempt to doubt* . . . the 'disconnection' is brought about in and through a modification of the antithesis, namely, with the 'supposition' of *nonbeing*. . . . Here we disregard this possibility for we are not interested in every analytic component of the attempt to doubt. . . . We extract only the phenomenon of 'bracketing' or 'disconnecting'. . . . We can, with respect to *every* thesis, exercise this unique *epoché* with entire freedom, a certain suspension of judgment which is compatible with the unshaken and unshakable (because it is evident) conviction of truth."[29] "If I do so . . . then I do not 'negate' this world as though I were a skeptic, but I employ the 'phenomenological' *epoché* which prohibits entirely *any judgment concerning spatio-temporal existence*."[30] In this way all sciences which are concerned with reality (and also those sciences which are concerned with "transcendentally" pure possibilities) are "disconnected." But in no way are their results to be doubted, for as we have seen it is not within my power to doubt them. The phenomenological *epoché* is not meant "positivistically." It does not turn against "metaphysics," and so forth. According to an often repeated remark of Husserl, it is to be compared to that free suspension of judgment assumed by participants in a scientific discussion that is the very precondition of the possibility of such discussion. At the start both opponents must allow the discussion to remain undecided and are not permitted the use of their convictions no matter how securely these are established, even though they may not be able to give them up for very long: everything must be left to the course of the argumentation.

Now what possibly is achieved by *this epoché*? "What can remain when the entire world, including ourselves and all 'cogitare,' is disconnected?"[31] The so-called "residuum" left by the reduction encompasses a *new region of being,* that of the *essence of "pure" consciousness as such.* Here we find "the insight that consciousness in itself has a being of its own which, in its own absolute mode of being, is not affected by the phenomenological disconnection."[32] It is the *epoché* which first makes this region accessible.

59

Oskar Becker

The most important structure of pure consciousness is *intentionality:* disregarding certain exceptions, consciousness is "consciousness of something." It is not a question here of some connection between a psychological occurrence and a real object, of a "fact of experience in the world," but of "the pure essence" of consciousness "grasped in ideation as a pure idea." To be sure, "not every real (*reelle*) moment in the concrete unity of an intentional experience possesses the basic character of intentionality." The data of sensations, for example, are not intentional. But in the last analysis this is conditioned by the restriction of the analysis to a particular "constitutive level." That is, primordial time-consciousness is only touched upon and not analyzed in the *Ideas* (§§ 81-83). Within this time-consciousness itself every real (*reel*) element is primordially intentional. The data of the senses, which for psychology and also for the phenomenological analyses at the level of the *Ideas* appear to be ultimate elements, prove themselves to be constituted in the primordial time-consciousness by means of the so-called "passive" syntheses of the identification of a manifold of still more original *intentional* primordial-phenomena (*Ur-Phänomen*), the "primordial impressions," "retentions," and "protentions."[33]

The question is now raised whether the "pure ego" is disconnected by the reduction. After an initial hesitation,[34] Husserl had denied that this was the case (*Ideas*, § 57). Of course man as a natural being and "person" in the world falls under the reduction. Subsequent to the reduction, nothing remains other than the "stream" of "pure" experiences which we know are predominantly—and in the last analysis are so without exception—intentional in character. Does the pure ego belong to this stream of pure experience? Never as a particular experience within the stream of consciousness. For as a part of experience it originated within and fell with the experience itself. Actually, however, "it belongs to every experience which comes before us and streams past. Its 'glance' passes 'through' every actual *cogito* toward the object. This ray of intentional glancing changes with every *cogito* . . . but the ego remains identical."[35] No experience *endures of neces*sity; the ego, however, is in *principle necessary.* According to Kant, it must be able to accompany all representations. Hence the pure ego presents "a unique—nonconstituted—transcendence, a transcendence in immanence (the immanent stream of experience)"[36] which cannot be subject to the *epoché.* Correctly understood, this concerns only the *pure* ego: every concrete and personal *habitus*, all so-called "habitualities," are subject to bracketing.[37]

"The transcendence of God," expressed in the teleological character of the stream of consciousness, a teleology which leads along constitutive paths to the natural and cultural worlds, is also disconnected. This teleology is a *factum:* the "rationality of nature" is already an essentially non-necessary *factum.* Perhaps the world of nature is "rational": in any case, however, it is transcendent to absolute consciousness and therefore this "rationality of nature" must be disconnected.[38]

Finally, pure logic itself must be disconnected! This appears to be impossible, since formal logic governs all scientific activity, and hence also phenomenological inquiry. But under the assumption that "phenomenology's inquiry into pure consciousness sets itself and need set itself no other task than that of descriptive analysis," logic can be dispensed with. For "where the formation of concepts and judgments does not proceed constructively, where no systems of *mediate* deductions are built up, the formal theory of deductive systems in general . . . cannot function as an instrument for material research."[39]

Setting aside further details, the "thesis of my pure ego and its personal life which is 'necessary' and absolutely indubitable" stands opposed to "the thesis of the world which is 'contingent'." "Everything corporeally given as a *thing* can also not be, but no experience given as it actually is can also not be."[40] "The being of consciousness would indeed be necessarily modified by the annihilation of the world of things, but it would not be affected in its own existence."[41] "No real being . . . is necessary for the being of consciousness. Immanent being is doubtlessly absolute in this sense: that in principle *nulla 're' indiget ad existendum.*"[42]

"In contrast, the world of transcendent *'res'* is to be referred without qualification to consciousness, and to an actual consciousness, not to one which is merely logically conceived."[43] It is indeed "logically possible" that there can be some world outside of this one, but at the same time this possibility is materially absurd. The mere "assumption of something real outside of this world" is indeed free from formal contradiction, and is therefore "logically possible." But the "essential condition required for the validity" of such an assumption, the kind of "demonstration required by its meaning" (one thinks here of the sixth investigation's concept of truth) demands that the transcendent being which is posited by this assumption "be of necessity capable of being experienced, and not merely by an empty logically conceived ego, but by any *actual* ego, as the demonstrable unity of its connected experience."[44] Furthermore, "what is capable of being known by one ego must be in principle knowable by all." And even if this may not be true in fact, there exist in principle "essential possibilities for establishing an agreement" which would include "spirits dwelling in the remotest stellar worlds."

Husserl's *idealistic* "standpoint" is fixed in this way. It is not achieved as an epistemological thesis, but by analyzing the meaning of all positing of the transcendent as such. Thus Husserl carries on the great "idealistic" tradition of Leibniz, Kant, and—despite his personal aversion to romantic philosophy[45]—German Idealism, and not the "psychologistic" philosophy of Berkeley.

It is very characteristic of Husserl not to have remained content with the general characterization of his position as an "idealism" of the constitution of objects "in pure consciousness" (a thesis which is closely associated with his position), but to have continually attempted to display concretely the structures and movement of this constitution through an inclusive series of careful researches. The greater part of this work remains unpublished today. The *Ideas* itself contains very condensed (and in this condensed state often not easily understood) surveys of important but incomplete areas of inquiry. They must be left untouched by our presentation. Here we can only offer a few general comments on the topic of constitution.

The relationship of the "transcendent" thing to the "real" immanent "parts" of the stream of consciousness ["real" (*reel*) in this sense of immanently real is to be sharply distinguished from "real" (*real*) in the sense of transcendentally real] is defined as a relationship of a unity to a manifold. "For an empirical consciousness of one and the same thing, experienced from all sides and in itself continually confirming itself as being unified, it is essentially necessary that a multiple system of manifolds of continuous appearances and perspectival configurations belong to it, in which all objective moments falling within the perception and possessing the character of corporeal self-givenness are given perspectivally in determinate continuities."[46] This is paradigmatic for every "synthesis of identification" in which a transcendent object is constituted. Furthermore, corresponding to every "truly existing" object is "the idea of a possible consciousness in which the object itself is capable of being grasped in an *original* and hence perfectly *adequate* fashion." This also contains the idea of a reason which "rationally posits" the truly existing object in terms of such an adequate comprehension. This comprehension is not a simple act: every object-category prescribes a "transparent general rule" which lets us know "how, with respect to its meaning and mode of givenness, an object standing under it could be brought to adequate, original givenness."[47] It is a question here of the *constitution* of the object, of "ideal possibilities of harmonious intuitions which can be continued without limit" which express the object's transcendence. In this way a determinate region of objects, the region of "things" perhaps, can serve as a "transcendental clue." The regional idea of things prescribes "series of appearances which are quite determinate, fully ordered, advancing *ad infinitum*, and which, taken as an ideal totality, are strictly limited and closed; their development, which is open to inquiry, presents a determinate internal organization which is essentially bound together with those partial ideas which are generally designated as components belonging to the regional idea of 'a thing'."[48] (Just as *res extensa* is a partial idea of *res materialis*.) Thus much of what appears to the phenomenologically naive as simple fact proves to be an essential necessity; for example, the problem of the "origin of spatial representation" (*Raumvorstellung*), which is decidedly not an empirical-psychological problem. This, however, is only one particular example. The problem of constitution is actually an absolutely universal one. Every kind of object, every kind of actuality, "brings with it *its own constitutive phenomenology and therewith a new and concrete theory of reason.*"[49] In addition to the regions of concrete objects, formal regions have their own constitution, and the same problem of a universal constitution appears outside of all spheres of pure representation in the realms of feeling and willing. The concluding paragraphs of the *Ideas* offer a broad characterization of this problematic and illustrate its various levels and structures with examples. To be sure, all this remains a suggestion, a slender, if not vague, outline of enormous tasks.

It must be kept in mind in this connection that the *Ideas* is incomplete. Only the first book has been published. The second book (a handwritten copy of which was made available to a limited circle of students) contains the draft of an analysis of "intersubjectivity" and "empathy," and advances from these issues to the problem of persons, sociality, and other topics.[50] The predominant concern of the published portion of the *Ideas* with the "material thing" and the strata underlying the constitution of inanimate nature is, therefore, to a large extent determined by the chance selections represented by what has been published so far.

6.

Our presentation has now reached the point of access to Husserl's current philosophy. Here we shall offer a few concluding remarks concerning this philosophy:[51] its basic position is not different from that of the *Ideas*, but it does carry out the various intimations of the *Ideas* in a more radical and comprehensive fashion. Husserl now sees principal modes of access to phenomenology from three different sides.

I.   The establishment of phenomenology from the side of *constitutive-transcendental logic*.

The positive sciences admittedly no longer possess the "naiveté" of the ordinary man, but they do nevertheless possess a "higher form of naiveté" insofar as they forego a justification of their methods "in terms of pure principles and by recourse to pure ideas established in accordance with ultimate *a priori* possibilities and necessities." "If we are not satisfied with the joy of creating a theoretical technique . . . if we cannot separate true humanity from a life lived in radical self-responsibility, and consequently, if we cannot separate scientific responsibility from the totality of responsibilities of human life in general—then we must . . . seek those ultimate possibilities and necessities in terms of which we are able to take a stand with respect to reality in judging, valuing, action."[52] What is required, therefore, is the reflection of science and logic (as the most universal scientific theories) upon themselves, "reflection" here "signifying nothing other than the attempt to establish truly the meaning of what science and logic 'themselves' are . . . understood in a radical manner as an *explication of meaning*." Thus it is a question of "the intentional explication of formal logic's true meaning." The theoretical formulations which the classical tradition in both logic and mathematics (as *mathesis universalis*) has handed down to us must "once again be placed within the living intention of the logician." "The intentionality brought once again to life in every genuine recomprehension is to be questioned as to where it truly aims."[53] This must not be interpreted as an impermissible subjectivization of logic: the "ghost of psychologism" must be completely exorcised. It is not a question of "problems concerning natural subjectivity," but of problems concerning "transcendental subjectivity in the sense of transcendental phenomenology." Thus "the insight that a *truly philosophical logic* . . . can be formulated exclusively in terms of a transcendental phenomenology" is made apparent. "In its naive positivity . . . historical logic proves to be *a kind of philosophical childishness (Kinderei)*"[54]—a remark which should be taken to heart by those who today are still of the opinion that the truly philosophical problems of logic and mathematics can be formulated, or even solved, by means of a dogmatically "realistic theory of objects or relations."

How the idea of a pure transcendental logic is developed from this position cannot be briefly summarized.[55] We can only say that it is primarily a question of once again taking up the issue of psychologism in logic, but upon an incomparably higher level than that presented in the first book of the *Logical Investigations*. It is shown that the questions which arise with the rejection of all naive psychologism, indeed, with every detailed examination of entirely concrete and fundamental problems and principles of formal logic (such as the principles of contradiction and excluded middle, *modus ponens* and *modus tollens,* etc.) can be resolved only by returning to the *constitution* of the relevant logical objectivities. The basic concept of *logical experience* is introduced, whose essential structures parallel the ordinary concepts of "empirical" experience, primarily with respect to the latter's "openness," its unlimited perspective of determinability, its "horizon." The customary formulations of logical principles thus prove to be bound up with "idealizing presuppositions": for example, with reference to the *decidability of all judgments.* (The principle of the excluded middle: the close connection here with the latest mathematical inquiries!) Finally, the older rigid and far too narrow concept of evidence undergoes a thorough purification of its inflexibility and is broken up into an unlimited number of kinds and levels, each with its own essential laws. (Of the major forms, only the newly expounded "evidence of distinction" is named in contrast to "evidence of clarity.")

Conceived in this manner, transcendental logic ultimately joins a universal "phenomenology of reason," an "'ultimate' logic which regulates its own transcendental clarification" and which culminates in the "self-elucidation of transcendental subjectivity."

II. This same goal can also be reached by the way presented in the *Cartesian Meditations.* Indeed, one must interpret this way as constituting the truly central access to phenomenology as such. In essence this train of thought had already been introduced in the *Ideas* as the "Fundamental Phenomenological Outlook." Meanwhile, an extensive problematic has arisen today out of these themes, particularly as the result of taking into account the *intersubjective* problems of the reduction.

Although the experience of the world is always a communal one, the "I am" is nevertheless the "primordial intentional basis for my world," whereby the "world which is there for us all" and which is accepted by me in this sense is also "my" world. "Whether this is agreeable to me or not, whether (by reason of whatever prejudice) this sounds monstrous to me or not, it is a *primordial fact—which I must face up to,* and which I, as a philosopher, dare not for one moment disregard"—irrespective of the "ghosts of solipsism," "psychologism," or "relativism." Intersubjectivity is now to be understood in terms of this "primordial fact." It is a "frankly embarrassing and puzzling question as to how another psychophysical ego with another psyche can be constituted in the ego, since to its meaning as other belongs the impossibility of my experiencing the psychic contents essentially constitutive of the other in any truly original manner comparable to my experience of my own."[56] In addition, it must be made comprehensible how it is possible for me necessarily to ascribe *the same* world of experience to the other ego, and not one which is simply analogous to my own. Beyond this it is also true that precisely insofar as my psyche refers back to my transcendental subjectivity, so also does the psyche of the other point toward a transcendental ego foreign to my own. The complexity of this problem is quite clear, even though here it is simply a question of its first beginnings. It is subsequently shown that one must distinguish between two basic kinds of nature and world: first, the world which is "in itself" "first," the objectivity which is "not yet intersubjective" and which "is constituted in my ego as belonging in a strict sense to me alone insofar as it contains no trace of the alter ego, that is, contains nothing which, by the constitutive inclusion of alter egos, passes beyond the sphere of truly direct and original experience."[57] The second sense of "world" is that of the authentic intersubjectively constituted world which is common to us all. "What might be termed the *transcendental appearance*" of a "transcendental solipsism" can be overcome solely by thinking through this intricate problematic: its resolution must pass through the concrete elucidation of the *meaning of* each emerging possibility for experience given "with the primary character of originally emerging from experience itself."

III. Finally, and this is the third mode of access to transcendental phenomenology, this most radical "Cartesian" problematic admits of a *psychological* turn. All reductions belonging to the "Cartesian" way can also be simply interpreted "psychologically." All possible levels and kinds of ego-logical and intersubjective experience can (if one abstracts from all philosophical or, so to speak, epistemologically "critical" points of view) be observed in a purely descriptive way as possibly occurring psychologically. Subjects (be they singular or collective) remain within the naively accepted world. This in no way hinders casting their subjective representations of the world into relief—a procedure which is more or less consciously exercised in all historical and psychological disciplines (including—if one abstracts from extremely behavioristic methods—the experimental disciplines where the course of the experimental subject's experience must be describable, even though in an incomplete way). One can now take this procedure, so widely applied in life, poetry, and the above-mentioned sciences, as one's point of departure, as something already known and naively exercised, and (as viewed from the course of *our* observation) reach the transcendental method by working back from this point through a "reversal" which brings to light the principal philosophical value of the naive description. This approach, sketched out by Husserl in an article for the *Encyclopaedia Britannica* and worked out in greater detail in a series of lectures given in Amsterdam (1927),[58] would constitute a final surmounting of psychologism as well as refuting the alleged antagonism of phenomenology to psychology.

Our presentation has reached its admittedly modest goal. It has purposely avoided two topics which would have doubtless made it more "interesting": the discussion and comparison of phenomenology with other directions in contemporary philosophy (including those which are to be counted within the so-called "phenomenological movement"), and, irrespective of any particular point of view, the subjective "illumination" of Husserl's work. On the contrary, we have endeavored to unfold the philosophy of phenomenology's founder on the basis of selected texts with the conviction that here alone can it be a matter of *den Sachen Selbst.* It is not Husserl's *opinion*, no matter how "ingenious" or "profound," that is in question, but rather a lasting *accomplishment—non opinio sed opus.*

NOTES

1. Edmund Husserl, *Philosophie der Arithmetik* (Halle-Saale C. E. M. Pfeffer, 1891), p. 213.
2. *Ibid.*, p. 214.
3. *Ibid.*, p. 215.
4. *Critique of Pure Reason* (B 624, note). According to Kant's terminology here the concept of God would be a possible but empty one one cannot conclude from a concept's "logical" possibility a "real" possibility of such things.
5. Edmund Husserl, *Ideas: General Introduction to Pure Phenomenology.* trans. W. Boyce Gibson (New York, Macmillan, 1952), pp. 135-136.
6. Jena, 1893.
7. Chapter 8.
8. *Logical Investigations*, I, 187.
9. *Ibid.*, p. 230.
10. "The objective correlate of the concept of a possible theory, determined only in its form, is the concept of a possible domain of knowledge in general. Such a domain is called a 'manifold' by the mathematician. It is a domain that is determined alone by the fact that it *is* subject to a theory of such a form. . . . The objects are completely undetermined materially. . . ." Marvin Farber, *The Foundation of Phenomenology* (New York Paine-Whitman, 1962), p. 144.—ED.
11. In a review in the *Archive fur Systematische Philosophie* XI (1903), 397 ff.
12. Husserl defines "abstract contents" or "dependent parts" as elements which can exist only as belonging to a more comprehensive whole. By contrast, "portions" are *in–dependent parts*, that is, parts of wholes that are or can be divided and whose essence is independent of all other contents.—ED.
13. Edmund Husserl, "Formale und transzendentale Logik," *Jahrbuch für Philosophie und phänomenologische Forschung* (1929), p. 13, and Appendix I.
14. "Predicating acts."—ED.
15. "Philosophy as Rigorous Science," trans. Quentin Lauer, in *Phenomenology and the Crisis of Philosophy* (New York: Harper and Row, 1965).—ED.
16. Although not published during his lifetime, an important document stemming from this previously little-known period of Husserl's development (a series of lectures delivered

Oskar Becker

by Husserl at Göttingen in 1907) has been published in the collected works: *Die Idee der Phänomenologie* (Den Haag: Martinus Nijhoff, 1958). An English translation has appeared under the title, *The Idea of Phenomenology*, trans. W. D Alston and G. Nakhnikian (The Hague: Martinus Nijhoff, 1964).—ED.

17. "Philosophy as Rigorous Science," pp. 72-73.
18. *Ibid.*, p. 74.
19. *Ibid.*, pp. 128 f.
20. *Ibid.*, p. 144.
21. *Ibid.*, p. 146.
22. *Ibid.*, p. 147.
23. See *Formale und transzendentale Logik* (1929), p. 221.
24. Published in 1913 as the first work in the newly founded *Jahrbuch für Philosophie und phänomenologische Forschung* (vol. I, no. 1).
25. Husserl's use of this word corresponds neither with the tradition of the seventeenth and eighteenth centuries (although points of contact are in evidence) nor with the terminology of Heidegger.
26. Cf. the first section of the *Ideas:* "Essence and Knowledge of Essence."
27. There are only a few references in the *Ideas* to this metaphysics (pp. 5, 96 f., 110 f., 119 note). We cannot pursue them here in any further detail.
28. *Ideen I*, p. 63. (Gibson, *Ideas*, p. 106. Our translations here do not always follow those of Gibson.—ED.)
29. *Ideen I*, pp. 64-66 (Gibson, pp. 108-109).
30. *Ibid.*, pp. 67-68 (Gibson, pp. 110-111).
31. *Ibid.*, p. 69 (Gibson, p. 112).
32. *Ibid.*, p. 72 (Gibson, p. 113).
33. On this topic see the "Vorlesungen zur Phänomenologie des inneren Zeitbewusstseins," reprinted in *Husserliana*, vol. 10: *Zur Phänomenologie des inneren Zeitbemusstseins* (Den Haag: Martinus Nijhoff, 1966).
34. In the first edition of the *Logical Investigations* (II, 1, 340 f.).
35. *Ideen I*, p. 137 (Gibson, p. 172).
36. *Ibid.*, p. 138 (Gibson, p. 173).
37. Compare Husserl's discussion of "habitualities" in the *Cartesian Meditations*, trans. Dorion Cairns (The Hague: Martinus Nijhoff, 1962) § 32.—ED.
38. *Ideen I*, § 58.
39. *Ibid.*, p. 141 (Gibson, p. 176)
40. *Ibid.*, pp. 108 f. (Gibson, p. 145).
41. *Ibid.*, p. 115 (Gibson, p. 151).
42. *Ibid.*, p. 115 (Gibson, p. 152).
43. *Ibid.*, pp. 115 f. (Gibson, p. 152).
44. *Ibid.*, p. 113 (Gibson, pp. 149 f.).
45. "Philosophy as Rigorous Science," pp. 76-77.
46. *Ideen I*, p. 93 (Gibson, p. 131) .
47. *Ibid.*, p. 350 (Gibson, p. 396).
48. *Ibid.*, p. 370 (Gibson, p. 417).
49. *Ibid.*, p. 375 (Gibson, p. 422).
50 . See the essay by Hans Wagner included in this collection.—ED.
51. Husserl's only publication to date is *Formale und transzendentale Logik, Jahrbuch für Philosophie und phänomenologische Forschung* (Halle), X (1929), v-xiii; 1-298. The *Cartesianische Meditationen* will appear next (at first in French translation).
52. *Formale und transzendentale Logik*, pp. 4 f.
53. *Ibid.*, p. 9.

54. *Ibid.*, p. 12.
55. We must also omit a presentation of the very remarkable interpretation of mathematical analysis contained in the first section of Husserl's new logic as a logic of pure consistency in which the concept of truth plays no role.
56. *Formale und transzendentale Logik*, pp. 209-211.
57. *Ibid.*, p. 213.
58. Both have been recently published in Volume IX of the collected works: *Phänomenologische Psychologie* (Den Haag: Martinus Nijhoff 1962).—ED.

The Phenomenological Philosophy of Edmund Husserl and Contemporary Criticism[1]

Eugen Fink

Preface by Edmund Husserl

MANY HAVE occasionally been troubled by the fact that in the past years I have refrained from entering into a discussion with critics of the "transcendental" or "constitutive" phenomenology which has its basis in my writings and which develops with an internal consistency in them. I have from time to time stated my reason for this silence. All of the critiques with which I have become acquainted miss the basic meaning of my phenomenology to such an extent that it is not in the least affected by them, despite their direct quotation of my own words. I held that it is more important to deal with the demands made by problems relating to this new science that emerge upon ever new levels in comprehensive and concrete work, and to bring them, partly through methodical development and partly through a self-reflective clarification of their principally new philosophical meaning, to a level of concrete development where they will in the future be capable of representing their unassailable claim to truth on their own as completed work.

Next to the overabundance of superficial critiques originating for the most part from beginners in philosophy whose work generally lacks the ripeness belonging to those critical achievements which are to be taken seriously, there are well-founded and responsible critiques which are gradually appearing from the side of different philosophical schools. It is quite necessary to come to terms with these critiques—all the more so insofar as the undeniable imperfections in my own presentations, which are scarcely to be avoided with the first breakthrough of new thoughts, are as responsible for misunderstandings as the presuppositions embodied in those viewpoints by which the critics of phenomenology consciously or unconsciously allow themselves to be led. At my request, the author of the following essay has undertaken to outline a discussion with my critics which is necessary in order to clarify the principal misunderstandings of phenomenology. This is a task for which he is well qualified. I have guided his philosophical studies from the very start of his career, and since their conclusion he as been my assistant for the past five years and has had almost daily contact with me. In this way, he has not only become thoroughly familiar with my philosophical intentions, but also with the principal contents of concrete unpublished investigations. I have carefully read through this essay at the request of the able editors of the *Kant-Studien,* and I am happy to be able to state that it contains no sentence which I could not completely accept as my own or openly acknowledge as my own conviction.

Freiburg I. Br., June 1933.

EDMUND HUSSERL

THERE IS A widespread and often repeated opinion that the development of Husserl's philosophy in no way presents a progression continuous with its original motives as portrayed in the *Logical Investigations* (1900-1901), but that under the influence of Neo-Kantianism it undergoes a radical transformation first manifested in the *Ideas.* It is not to be denied that Husserl, in the period subsequent to the *Logical Investigations*, brought about a profound reorganization of his philosophical thought. The *direction* of this "revolution of thought," however, has for the most part remained misunderstood. This internal reorganization occurs as part of the struggle to attain a philosophical self-understanding and self-mastery over the inner aims which constitute the driving force of his thinking. Only within the context provided by these aims can the true "meaning" of the preceding stages of his philosophy be understood. The still rigorously correlational method of inquiry in the *Logical Investigations*—the "objective" stand with respect to structures of logic, and the "subjective" return to experiences (in which the thematic objects of pure logic are given)— this "correlativism" contained, in the unclarity of its methodological foun-

Eugen Fink

dations, a disquieting and urgent topic which finally led to the conception of the "phenomenological reduction" with which Husserl's philosophical aim finally came into its own.[2] The breakthrough to a more profound statement of the problem, accomplished by establishing a *new idea of philosophy* upon the basic thought of the phenomenological reduction, became, with its first published presentation in parts of the *Ideas* (1913), the object of diverse interpretations. On the one hand, it was misconceived as the surrender of the "turning toward the object" and as a collapse into "subjectivism" and a deviation away from problems of ontology. On the other hand, it was construed as a drawing nearer to "Criticism." This latter interpretation is the undiscussed presupposition of that criticism of phenomenology to which we shall now turn. We shall, first of all, attempt to present this criticism through its basic interpretation of and general objections to phenomenology, in order subsequently to question the validity of this criticism by referring to the principal difference between the phenomenological and the critical ideas of a transcendental philosophy. We shall then proceed to point out, on the basis of the different objections, the divergency of these two philosophical conceptions. Our presentation will conclude by indicating the general problematic of phenomenology's "transcendental appearance" (*transzendentalen Schein*) in which all serious misconceptions are grounded.

Even though no actual philosophy can be disputed the right to judge other and opposing philosophies solely in accordance with the idea of philosophy which serves as its guide, there yet remains this indispensable presupposition for all real criticism: that the philosophy to be criticized must be understood on its own terms and from its own perspective beforehand. "Criticism's" critique does not fulfill this requirement.[3] It begins with a critical discussion of phenomenology's epistemological position, and does so because it views all of the phenomenological doctrines with which it takes issue as being based upon these methodological convictions. Criticism's overall judgment of phenomenology: that phenomenology, being solely a prephilosophical science of what is immediately given, possesses only a relative and limited justification (and only as such can it, in apprehending the immediate by means of its own analytical descriptions, possess an estimable methodological dignity); that phenomenology, as "philosophy," is "*dogmatic*" and "*unscientific*"—this judgment also rests in the last analysis upon Criticism's rejection of the "phenomenological method." Granting that a decisive judgment concerning a philosophical doctrine can be made from the point of view offered by a criticism of method, we are still permitted to take as a philosophy's genuine method only what is expressly indicated by this philosophy within the framework of its own methodological self-understanding. The

Husserl's Philosophy and Contemporary Critisicism

"phenomenological reduction" alone is the basic method of Husserl's phenomenological philosophy. It is the epistemological "way" (*Erkenntnisweg*) which leads beginning philosophical reflection to the "thematic" domain of philosophy; it grants us "access" to transcendental subjectivity and it includes within it all of phenomenology's problems and the particular methods associated with them. Criticism's critique of the phenomenological method does not, however, concern itself with this totality of basic knowledge (the "reduction"), but rather presupposes a concept of method which aims at uncovering that capacity for knowledge which is activated by philosophical reflection. In appraising the importance of this criticism it is important to note that phenomenology's critics determine its methodological character on the basis of Husserl's researches *prior* to the discovery of the phenomenological reduction, researches which were published in the *Logical Investigations.* This means that the methodological characterization of phenomenology rests upon a phenomenology which, as yet, is neither explicit nor clear about its basic philosophical intent and whose relevance first generally becomes apparent in the following period. The critique of Zocher and Kreis is convinced that the principal methodological beliefs which serve to guide the entire development of phenomenology can be read off the beginning period of Husserl's philosophy. This is to reverse the situation. The character phenomenology thereby assumes does not advance beyond the current and vague notion whereby phenomenology is designated as a descriptive science that reports on what is simply found.

With respect to method, Criticism raises the reproach of intuitionism against phenomenology, a reproach which takes on its true edge *sub specie* Criticism's own methodological convictions. According to its own testimony, Criticism naturally does not question the legitimacy of intuition and intuitive knowledge, but it does limit its significance. Instead of erasing and smoothing over the principal differences between man's capacities for knowledge, Criticism articulates their duality and grants them their basic distinctiveness by mutually contrasting them. It sees two aspects of phenomenology's intuitionism (i.e., the unjustified extension of the concept of "intuition"): it is first of all an intuitionistic interpretation of knowledge in general (and thus it is related to the customary epistemological concept of experience as directed toward *objects*), and, second, it is an intuitionistic interpretation of *philosophical* knowledge. The first states that phenomenology defines the general concept of knowledge by means of the concept of a self-giving intuition (an original givenness). Here the prototype, so to speak, is perceptual self-givenness (in the paradigmatic sense of an adequate perception). With this the essence of knowledge is transposed from the very start into the

73

Eugen Fink

sphere of the prelogical and the prepredicative. The complete orientation of the concept of knowledge along the lines of the simple intuitive apprehension of what is immediately given (with an "evident self-givenness") now leads—according to the thesis of the critical critique—to an empirical interpretation of knowledge. Not only is the essence of knowledge defined by means of an inadmissible formalization of evident perception (primarily of sensory experience), but the unique nature of discursive and *a priori* thought is also positively misconceived, such as in the doctrines of "categorial *intuition"* and essential *insight.* If phenomenology's intuitionism in its interpretation of objective knowledge results in misconceiving the principal difference between sensory experience and genuine thought by erasing the opposition between sensibility and understanding, intuitionism with respect to *philosophical* knowledge signifies a much more serious danger. From the critical point of view, this danger consists of the sanctioning of naiveté by rejecting all constructive thought with the requirement that the basic methodological principle within the field of philosophical knowledge is also to be given solely by the notion of evident self-givenness. In this way, original and intuitive evidence is raised to the highest court of appeal and the idea of offering a proof or foundation (*Begründung*) is degraded to the idea of "showing" or of self-manifestation. In other words, the notion of philosophical truth becomes defined in terms of a naive theory of correspondence. Criticism not only views one of its basic achievements as consisting in the ability to preserve the naive notions of truth and knowledge belonging to "empirical realism" (the realism of everyday action and the positive sciences) and even methodologically substantiating and justifying them, but also in being able to surpass them by means of a philosophical knowledge which has as its method the construction of a "theoretical object" by means of the synthesis of a transcendental-logical form with a "given content." In this way criticism lets it be known that the characterization of the phenomenological method as a form of intuitionism carries with it the reproach of dogmatism. That is, it remains fixed to the "self-givenness" of the objects of experience and contents itself with "evidence," without raising the question as to the legitimacy of this self-givenness which it simply accepts without making the possibility of experience, together with its objectivity, an explicit problem. In brief: phenomenology's intuitionistic character, which as a theory of objective knowledge already receives its principal orientation from sensory experience, leads to an empiricist misapprehension of the unique character of thought and above all of the unique character of *a priori* knowledge. Phenomenology thereby reveals a hopeless dogmatism with respect to the theory of philosophical knowledge, not only insofar as it transposes a naive (and, in addition, empirically misinterpreted) concept of knowledge to the plane of philosophical problems, but also insofar as, through this transposition, it derives the right to deny all "construction" and, therewith, all questions bearing upon the legitimacy of experience and objective knowledge in general.

Closely related to the reproach of intuitionism is another objection made by Criticism against Husserl's phenomenology: phenomenology is "ontological." Considered more closely, this charge represents only another aspect of the first objection: a characterization of phenomenology in terms of its thematic. "Ontologism" here refers to the unjustified restriction of the thematic of knowledge to "beings" (*Seiendes*). Corresponding to phenomenology's methodological empiricism is a positivism with respect to its theme. Similar to the reproach of intuitionism, the objection that phenomenology is ontological is raised in two respects. First—so it is objected— the concept of the object of knowledge is basically determined with reference to the object of perception, that is, it is determined with reference to what is physically and psychically real, so that, despite the unquestionable service performed by the *Logical Investigations* in defending and guaranteeing the ideality of logical objectivity against a positivism appearing in the crude disguise of psychologism, a remainder of a positivistic interpretation persists uneffaced insofar as the "ideal" becomes posed as an existing objectivity. This is expressed above all in the phenomenological doctrine of the *eidos*. While Criticism held strongly to the division between real existence (which is accessible to the appropriate ontological attitude) and its valid meaning (which is accepted as being valid, but which does not "exist"), phenomenology ontologized the *a priori* and had construed it as an existing objectivity, as the "essence" of a clear and self-giving intuition. Therein lies a momentous misconception of validity (*das Geltenden*): a transformation of the phenomenon of *meaning* into something possessing the character of an entity; a substantialization of value.[4] Its blindness toward the value-character of validity hindered phenomenology from seeing the profound and basic difference between being and meaning, reality and validity, and accordingly prevented it from determining the nature of the knowledge-thematic in an appropriate manner. Consequently, the mistaken intuitionistic starting point which serves to determine the nature of the method used in obtaining knowledge leads to the ontological misinterpretation of the object of knowledge. Even when the "ideal" is expressly opposed to real existence and even though a difference is postulated between perception and "categorial intuition," there nevertheless remains an all too homogeneous equating of ideality and reality: valid meaning-contents become substantialized into "objects belonging to a higher order."

The reproach of ontologism, however, is more decisively directed against the phenomenological determination of specifically *philosophical* themes. Just as the objection of intuitionism with respect to phenomenology's general theory of knowledge had initially meant a defect which could have been repaired by means of a more penetrating reflection on the part of phenomenology itself, and had then later assumed its true destructive bent with reference to phenomenology's theory of philosophical knowledge, a theory which presented itself as an inadmissible transference of a naive conception of knowledge—naive, that is, in Criticism's view— so the emphasis here similarly falls upon the transference of this thematic concept (posited in an ontologistic manner) to the foundational-sphere which is to be known philosophically. Phenomenology's blindness with respect to values, its ontologizing of validity in general, excludes it from passing beyond the "affairs" to the sphere of the *theoretically* valid, a sphere which for Criticism can be exposed through construction and which serves to establish the actuality of all affairs (*die Sachheit aller Sachen*). Phenomenology thus contents itself with what is in principle not final and presents the "affair" as constituting the true theme of philosophy. Since as a result of its intuitionistic and ontologistic beginning phenomenology must remain affixed to the immediate givenness of objects (affairs) without searching for the conditions which determine the possibility of such things being given, thus rendering them ultimately (i.e., philosophically) capable of being understood, phenomenology makes a virtue of necessity and raises this programmatic slogan: "To the affairs themselves!" Viewed "critically," this signifies a renunciation of philosophical understanding, a surrendering of the question of legitimacy which must be asked of what is given (*quid juris*)[5] in favor of an analytical description which simply receives what is given.

The interrelated objections of intuitionism and ontologism receive their radically critical orientation from the contours of the "critical" philosophy: phenomenology's inability to raise the philosophical question concerning the possibility of the theoretical object, a question which transcends all evident self-givenness, and its inability to answer this question, proves it to be a dogmatic philosophy. It is not, however, dogmatic only in the sense of not extricating itself from its naive entrenchment in beings (the "affairs") which constitutes the theoretical *habitus* of both everyday and positive-scientific experience of the world, nor in the sense of being incapable of overcoming the methodological fixity of its concern with the self-testifying and self-exhibiting quality of beings—but its dogmatism is shown in a very elementary fashion by its direct postulation of beings as

Husserl's Philosophy and Contemporary Critisicism

independent of the subject, in its view of things as "things in themselves." Hence, at least for the critics, the period of the *Logical Investigations* appears to be defined by the attempt to restore the naive idea of a pre-Kantian ontology. In this connection (in the view of critical idealism), the fact that Husserl passes over to the correlative consideration of subjective experiences after the thematically objective attitude toward logical objects counts for nothing, for the "subjective-relatedness" is here itself still dogmatic: it is oriented along the lines of the actual knowledge-relation between the empirical content of the subject (its experiences) and the "given" objectivity. Indeed, it seems that this relationship is still interpreted realistically insofar as the phenomenology of logical experience is classified as a "descriptive psychology." As an ontic science, however, psychology (even when it proceeds "eidetically") is dogmatic (in the critical sense) since within the reflexive attitude it naively posits the given being (or the actual essence) as a thing in itself, be this either in the mode of the warranted positivity of a prephilosophical science (which still possesses only limited justification) or in the doctrinaire form of a dogmatic ontology. In any case, the return to the physical givenness of some being within the experience which corresponds to it in no way touches that "subject relatedness," the knowledge of which annuls all dogmatism and forms the essential content of the critical philosophy. According to Criticism, the relationship of an existent being to an empirical subject realized in actual experience is not the fundamental problem of philosophy; philosophy's fundamental problem is the relationship of the *a priori* structures of being (which hold theoretically) to the nonempirical "epistemological ego" (the "transcendental apperception"), which is there *prior* to all experience and which makes experience possible. The orientation toward and mastery of this problem determine the "scientific" character of a philosophy. Now insofar as phenomenology, in Criticism's view, proves to be a form of dogmatism because of its mistaken methodological beginnings (intuitionism and ontologism), its "scientific" character must be denied. This represents a very sharp criticism of the intellectual endeavor which is to lead Husserl toward the realization of "philosophy as rigorous science."

Up to this point we have presented the critique of Husserl's phenomenology as it is based upon the first phase of this philosophy and as essentially represented by the *Logical Investigations*. The major thrust of this critique is not, however, directed against this first phase, but is chiefly aimed at the second phase, which makes its appearance in the *Ideas*. As we have already mentioned, we must note in this connection that this critique of the decisive period in Husserl's philosophy is constructed upon arguments gained from the analysis of the *Logical Investi-*

gations and is based upon their validity. The criticism of the methods thereby cited as "phenomenological" is sustained throughout by the conviction that this criticism touches upon the principal and general character of phenomenology. The guiding thought of the critique of critical philosophy is therefore the following: after phenomenology's initial phase (the *Logical Investigations),* which is shaped by the concern to formulate certain basic methodological beliefs which, from Criticism's standpoint, are dogmatic and (philosophically) unscientific, Husserl's phenomenology surprisingly approaches thoughts central to the critical philosophy in the *Ideas.* By leaving it undecided whether or not this took place under the direct or indirect influence of Neo-Kantianism, Husserl enters upon the path of an idealistic transcendental philosophy and effects a break with the objectivism and ontologism of the *Logical Investigations.* But—the goal to which this path leads is not reached. The methodological theories conceived originally (and which, judged critically, are merely dogmatic prejudices) are not altogether surpassed. They force—in sublimated form—Husserl away from the fruitful and genuine beginnings of a critical philosophy into an intuitionistic and ontologistic reinterpretation of this philosophy. Husserl succumbs to the subterranean force of the urgent and compelling motives of his precritical phase.

Now, despite the fact that Criticism's attacks are predominantly directed against the presentation of phenomenology as given in the *Ideas,* its basic eristic notions are shaped by its judgment of the *Logical Investigations.* Hence it would appear that the refutation of this criticism necessarily begins with a defense of this work. But here we are confronted with a basic difficulty of interpretation: a truly penetrating and exhaustive understanding of the *Logical Investigations* presupposes some insight into the central meaning of the *phenomenological* transcendental philosophy. As we have already mentioned, it is only in terms of the *Ideas* that the vital intention and direction of the *Logical Investigations'* philosophical goal can be grasped. And, since only an interpretation which explicitly has at its disposal those philosophical theories which the *Logical Investigations is approaching* can actually clarify them with respect to their decisive significance, the critical critique's undertaking must necessarily fail. This critique not only fails to see that the treatment of problems in the *Logical Investigations* can be understood only from the viewpoint of the *Ideas,* but also posits the *Ideas* as being methodologically dependent upon these investigations (while not interpreting the latter correctly). Criticism's critique is therefore burdened with two presuppositions: (1) the thesis as to the dogmatic character of the method of the *Logical Investigations* (which, as an "intuitionistic ontologism," also determines the further development of phenomenology); and (2) the thesis that the *Ideas* represents a turning toward the critical philosophy itself. Both presuppositions, however, fail to apply. The theoretical-methodological character of the first phase (the *Logical Investigations*) is not that of a realistic-dogmatic ontology nor is the second phase (the *Ideas*) "idealistic" in a manner reminiscent of the critical philosophy. Precisely because the attempt has been made to define phenomenology in terms of traditional systems, the possibility (in spite of certain affinities and conflicts) of taking cognizance of phenomenology in terms of the principally new idea of philosophy which defines it has been taken away.[6] Nevertheless, there is no doubt that this version of phenomenology's development is to some extent justified insofar as the transition from the problematic belonging to the *Logical Investigations* to that of the *Ideas* is formally similar to the transition from a naive and empirical knowledge of things to the "critical" knowledge of the possibility of experience. For the phenomenologist, the way leading from the *Logical Investigations* to the *Ideas* can also be characterized as the surmounting of dogmatism and as the attainment of a truly philosophical attitude. But the formal similarity and the correspondence of terminology here constitute a dangerous facade which conceals the great distance between Criticism and phenomenology. Only when such concepts as "dogmatism," and so on, are left within the haze of formal indefiniteness can one succumb to the attempt to postulate a similar direction for these two different philosophies.

The refutation of the critique cannot concern itself *in extenso* with the objections raised against the *Logical Investigations,* for their invalidation not only assumes the exposition of the true meaning of the *Ideas* in opposition to the Neo-Kantian critique, but must also assume an intensive inquiry into the hidden history of the motivations at work in Husserl's development. We shall only make a few basic comments to this end and shall then investigate the criticism made of the *Ideas* and phenomenology's decisive phase.

First, the objection of intuitionism raised against phenomenology's method does not hold with respect to the *Logical Investigations.* There the concern is not with the primacy of intuition as a capacity for knowledge, but rather with the primacy of the intuitable nature of all knowledge as opposed to the merely *signitive* act of knowledge. The concept of knowledge is in no way oriented along the lines of perception (primarily sensory perception) to the end that its character of intuitability, of immediate and simple self-apprehension (the pure self-givenness of the object), is proclaimed to be the basic character of all knowledge whatsoever, thereby committing violence to logical knowledge. Rather knowledge is (in the pregnant sense of actual evidence) at all times and for all types of evidence the self-givenness of those affairs which are given with evidence in the act of knowing (affair-complexes, values and value-complexes, etc.); that is, their comprehension and possession as "they themselves are." A direct self-givenness (characteristic of sensory knowledge) which presents itself in one stroke is a special instance of this principle. Categorial knowledge and knowledge of essences stand opposed to this instance, for their self-givenness is essentially possible only by means of a synthesis constructed upon the basis of eventually highly diverse founding-acts. The critique is thoroughly blind to what is basically new in Husserl's theory, which counts as the first clarification of the intentional essence of evidence, that is, evidence as a basic mode of intentionality in general (of all kinds of acts) which everywhere has its opposite mode in "signitive" and "empty" intentions. Furthermore, these two basic modes of intentionality are bound together by possible transitional forms of fulfillment and disappointment, forms which are constantly functioning in the life of consciousness' activities and which can clarify the evident consciousness of correctness. Again, with respect to what is consciously known in the consciousness of evidence, objects given in the evident intention are differentiated according to whether the evidence is simple or established upon the basis of other acts (*fundiert*), thus differentiated into purely sensible objects and categorial objects (pluralities, affair-complexes, totalities, etc.), to which it essentially belongs that the one is given only in simple acts, whereas the other can be known with insight only through determinate and categorially founded acts. We shall not pursue the further analytical identification of these characteristics (whose further development is found chiefly in Husserl's last work on logic, the *Formal and Transcendental Logic*). In any case, one must see that the theory of evidence, which has been widely discussed ever since Descartes' *clara et distincta perceptio* (but which has been conceived of with empty words and concepts), a theory without which every theory of knowledge remains so many empty words, becomes, as a basic component of the general theory of intentionality which here begins to emerge, a theme of analysis for the first time in the *Logical Investigations*. Nor is there any trace of "empirical intuitionism" in the phenomenological theory of the *eidos*. The often misunderstood "essential insight" is in no way defined as some sort of mystical act, as a receptive intuition or a pure "seeing," as it were, of the nonsensible. Rather, the *eidos* is the correlate of an operation of thought, or of a spontaneous intellectual act. The *eidos* is known as the invariable element of something held fast in terms of its self-identity throughout its variation and the reflective running through of its possible modifications. Since mention of essential insight was to have indicated the manner in which a thought-intention was fulfilled (and whose meaning, therefore, was only *analogous* to sensory perception), the phenomenological definition of essence itself as an actual objectivity does not signify its hypostatized substantiality, but simply indicates the *eidos*' "categorial" existence, that is, its being engendered through spontaneous acts of thought. If it were a question in the first book of the *Logical Investigations* of raising the independence of idealities to the first line of defense against psychologism, it is also true that an occasional over-emphasis of the ontological independence of the "ideal" does occur. If the entire position of the *Logical investigations* with respect to this question is taken into account, all "realism" with respect to the ideal disappears. For after the naive thematic attitude toward the forms of pure logic in the first book, the second book already proceeds to establish the objectivity of logical forms as a problem. Here the "correlative" attitude toward subjective experience already claims the dignity of being a philosophical foundation of pure logic. The problem of ideal being (taken in its widest sense) here appears as the intentional analysis of its givenness.[7] The critical objection that in the phenomenological theory of the *eidos* what is accepted as valid falls victim to "ontologization" results from a distinction made between what *is* and what is accepted as being *valid.* As a matter of fact the phenomenology of the *Logical Investigations* does not employ this distinction. Instead of narrowly limiting the concept of beings (*Seienden*) to real things, it employs it rather freely,[8] and we find here a point open to a criticism that does not presuppose an interpretation alien to phenomenology. A positive establishing of the phenomenological position and its defense against the critical theory belongs to a dialogue between phenomenology and Criticism which, where it is only a matter of rejecting a false interpretation of phenomenology, we cannot here attempt to carry out.

To some extent, however, the anti-formalistic state of phenomenology at its beginning (documented by the often repeated phrase "to the affairs themselves") does provide an occasion for the critical reproach of ontologism (i.e., the fixed concern with things, affairs, contents, the given). The charge, however, must be decisively rejected. "To the affairs themselves": this is not a prior decision as to what themes are possible for phenomenology and what themes are to be specifically appropriated for it. Nor does it fix a particular region of objects which could be characterized as "affairs." Only if one interprets the concept "affair" with respect to "content," and, furthermore, only if one brings it within the context suggested by the critical thought of the constituted nature of "affairs" (as objects of experience) through transcendental-logical forms and a given material, can one succeed in interpreting the demand for a return "to the affairs themselves" as proclaiming a prephilosophical naiveté to be constitutive of philosophy's epistemological method. From the standpoint of this misinterpretation, phenomenology has the appearance of being a science which simply describes what is directly found and lays hold of it eidetically, thereby betraying a basic and thoroughly positivistic methodological character.

The concept "affair" must first of all be understood *formally* if we are to grasp the true meaning of the slogan "to the affairs themselves." Everything which can be brought to the point of manifesting itself as it is, be this real or ideal, a horizon, a meaning, the refusal of meaning, nothingness, and so forth, can be an "affair" in the sense maintained by this phenomenological *maxim of inquiry*, a maxim which intends to cut through all concealments brought about by historical and traditional interpretations and which opposes all argumentative attempts to invent solutions by attacking the actual content (*Sachgehalt*) of the problem itself. "Affairness" in this sense can and must also be a "construction" if it is to carry true philosophical knowledge with it. Second, this imperative does not simply signify the self-imposed obligation of phenomenological investigation to concern itself with the nature of affairs: it also has the meaning of alluding to that apprehension of the nature of affairs which is first made possible by the phenomenological method, that is, their nature as intentional-analytic concretions. The completely new methodological feature of the intentional analysis introduced by Husserl brings it into the strictest opposition to a naive thematic-attitude of knowledge toward the given. Although the natural positivity of experience consists of a directedness toward the object presented to it, the intentional explication of the knowledge-relation not only leads to what is present (present subjective experiences, etc.) but also leads beyond the sphere of what is present to consciousness in order to enter into the meaning-horizons which belong to intentionality, into the entire operative system of presentational and appresentational intentions, anticipations, and habitual acquisitions. Except for the fact it remains undisclosed and "anonymous," the system of intentional achievements on the basis of which an object comes to actual givenness is at work in any simple act of knowledge. The analysis of such knowledge first permits us to encounter the bewildering fullness of those intentional bestowals of meaning which make up the "presupposition" for the direct givenness of the being which is known. In other words, intentional analysis (in a broad sense) is an exhibiting of the "conditions for the possibility" of the givenness of an object in experience. It is clear that this exhibiting does not possess "critical" significance. When—from the standpoint of Criticism—it is called "dogmatic" insofar as it constitutes an analytical interpretation of actual experience-relationships which, as such and in general, are grounded by the relationship of theoretical acceptances to the judgmental functions of the "transcendental apperception," and when it begins within the sphere of "founded" experiences (and not the "foundational" sphere itself), it is not to be confused with the naive, thematically positive attitude toward knowledge and should not be framed within the methodological character which might be appropriate to the latter. The critique of method exercised by Criticism upon the *Logical Investigations*, which supposedly lays bare the methodological principles which continue to influence phenomenology, passes over the decisive theoretical *habitus* of this philosophy: the development of the method of intentional inquiry. Because the critique believes that the phenomenological method can be explicated in terms of the guiding thought of a descriptive eidetic science instead of that of a descriptive intentional analytic, it must fail to appreciate the as yet quite opaque and veiled methodological structure of the phenomenology beginning in the second book of the *Logical Investigations.* If the suitability of the charges of "intuitionism" and "ontologism"—quite apart from the fact that the phenomenological method can be successfully defined only with reference to the period of its mature and developed self-understanding inaugurated by the *Ideas* (a period still not concluded)— remains questionable because they are misled in conceiving of phenomenology as a descriptive science which is embedded in the natural positivity of experience, the critics may still retreat to their strongest objection, that of "dogmatism." Admittedly, the basic "transcendental" question concerning the possibility of objective knowledge (in the critical sense) is neither posed nor answered in the *Logical Investigations.* Nor is it contained within its methodological horizon. Yet it is equally absent in the *Ideas,* the second phase of Husserl's phenomenological philosophy, a phase which Criticism interprets as a turning toward its own problematic.

Through the method of *intentional* inquiry and exposition, the *Logical Investigations* had already set in motion a problematic which subsequently led to the "phenomenological reduction." The *Logical Investigations* thereby moves beyond the "dogmatism" within which both the naive "empirical realism" of the everyday and positive-scientific attitude toward knowledge and the "transcendental knowledge" (in the critical sense) of the possibility of the "theoretical object" principally remain. The significance of Husserl's starting with the analysis of the actual knowledge-relation, or with the intentional investigation of ontic experience, and therefore of his starting with (as it might well appear to Criticism) a "dogmatic" situation, could have been pointed out only if the basic relationship between intentional and "constitutive" analyses had been clarified. This clarification would have been nothing other than the demonstration of the internal coherence of the first and second phases of Husserl's philosophy. The transformation which took place between these phases could then have been grasped as an immanent necessity within the development of the central transcendental-phenomenological motive, the seeds of which are already effectively at work in the *Logical Investigations.* If the *Logical Investigations* is interpreted with a disregard for this inner finality (which is first disclosed in the *Ideas),* the turn taken by the *Ideas* simply becomes unintelligible. It then becomes easy to explain it as the result of some external "influence" and to see the projected outline of a transcendental philosophy made in the *Ideas* as a form of "Criticism" distorted by the methodological prejudices of the first phase.

Now if the thesis, expressed in the charges of "intuitionism" and "ontologism," as to the *Logical Investigations'* dogmatic method forms the presupposition supporting the agreement of phenomenology's critics (insofar as the motive for and the direction of the alleged distortions of basic critical ideas are thereby indicated), the prejudicial identification of the critical and phenomenological ideas of a transcendental philosophy is a fundamental presupposition of this criticism to an even greater measure. Although this "identity" is located only in the similarity of goals and problems, it nevertheless proves itself to be the *cardinal insinuation* hindering a true coming to terms between Criticism and phenomenology: through this prejudical assumption the critique has concealed from itself the uniquely *different* nature of its opponent. The deep-seated misconception of the essential nature of Husserl's phenomenological philosophy, accomplished by equating it with the tendency of the critical philosophy, does not, however, rest upon an external misunderstanding or upon an inattentive exposition, but has—and this is to be admitted frankly—what appears to be a legitimate cause in the first published objectification (in the *Ideas*) of phenomenology's basic ideas. There are three major reasons which make this mistaken interpretation seem intelligible. In the first place there is an extensive terminological correspondence between basic concepts and definitions which masks and conceals widely different meanings. ("Transcendental," "transcendental ego," "constitution," and "transcendental idealism" have a radically different sense with respect to the critical and phenomenological philosophies.) Second, in addition to this similarity, it is possible to detect a certain similarity of *form* in the elements composing the critical and phenomenological systems, a similarity which all too easily permits itself to be used as evidence for their internal identity (for example, the relationship of philosophy to the sciences, transcendental idealism as constituting the justification of empirical realism, etc.). The third reason is to be found in this peculiar feature of the *Ideas:* since at the time of the *Ideas* Husserl was primarily concerned with providing evidence for making the transcendental subjectivity exposed by the "reduction" a region of thematic inquiry, the breakthrough

Husserl's Philosophy and Contemporary Critisicism

to a new idea of philosophy is expressed in a very cautious and reserved manner. Although the actual accomplishments of the *Ideas* are to be retained even today, there are still many statements in the *Ideas* (i.e., in the first part, which, because of unfavorable circumstances, is the only part to have appeared) which require comment since they permit the conception of "philosophy" (which lies included within their own understanding of their philosophical significance) to remain in the background and postpone its consideration to the projected third part. The inadequate formulation of the genuinely phenomenological idea of philosophy, the externally formal relatedness of system-composition, and the terminological similarity between Criticism and phenomenology all might have contributed to the fact that Criticism's critique of phenomenology is built upon an absolutely false presupposition.

What are the basic elements of this critique? Let us, condensing it to its most essential train of thought, briefly repeat the critique first with respect to its presentation of the (presupposed) "similarity" between Criticism and phenomenology. The similar directions of the critical and phenomenological philosophies are shown in the sameness of their problem-formulation, a similarity which remains no matter how different their theoretical answers might appear with reference to specific details. Common to both philosophies is the fact that they do not remain within the dogmatism of the naive view of the world, but overcome it insofar as they make it an explicit *problem*. Although the *Logical Investigations* is epistemologically naive in that a being's self-givenness here serves as an instance of a foundation (*Begrundungsinstanz*), Husserl does break through in the *Ideas* to the basic problem of the critical philosophy: that of raising the question concerning the possibility of knowledge. Such a question, however, cannot be answered through the analysis of the factual knowledge-relation between subject and object. An answer can be given only insofar as the knowledge-relation is itself traced back to the presuppositions which make it possible and only insofar as the question as to how the character of objective validity can belong to knowledge is discussed. If the naiveté of the everyday knowledge-practice and positive-scientific inquiry consists in living nonproblematically within the enactment of experience and knowledge and in holding the self-givenness and self-manifestation of beings in knowing apprehension (intuition, thought, experiment) as the unquestioned source of their judgments, and, if the objectivity of beings in general, the in-itselfness evidenced in experience (the "empirical reality" of beings), does not indicate a problem but rather a primary state of affairs (*Urverhalt*), then the problem of philosophy is directly defined as the question of the justification for this positivity of ontic knowledge. It must be kept in mind, however, that the philosophy which, as a "theory of knowledge," overcomes "dogmatism" is not simply a theoretical interpretation of ontic knowledge, but is also the theory of the *possibility* of ontic knowledge. The understanding of ontic knowledge in terms of its possibility means casting light upon a sphere of "presuppositions" which serves to characterize philosophy's thematic field and problem-dimension. Criticism, in a modified relation to Kant, now defines the judgmental functions of the "transcendental apperception" (i.e., the *a priori* relatedness of the pure ego—that is, the ego as a pure form, as the ego-principle—to that which is theoretically valid, a relatedness which is prior to all experience) as constituting the "foundational sphere."[9] Phenomenology (the phenomenology of the *Ideas*) similarly effects a transition from the natural-dogmatic attitude, within which the possibility of knowledge is not itself made a problem, to the "posing of the question transcendentally." If Criticism further defines the ego of the "transcendental apperception" as a nonempirical, pure ego, Husserl similarly quite sharply separates the "transcendental ego" from the psychical and empirical ego. Indeed, Husserl, just as Criticism, defines the transcendental ego as *irreal.* In this way the "critical" tendency inherent within the basic origins of Husserl's theory of knowledge receives unmistakable documentation. Husserl's concept of the transcendental ego is identical with Criticism's basic concept of "transcendental apperception." But this not only shows an identity in their formulations of the problem, but also an identity in the principal direction of the theoretical solution of this problem. Criticism and phenomenology coincide (at least insofar as their intentions are concerned) by sharing the concept of a "transcendental philosophy." Just as the characterization of Criticism as a "theory of knowledge" indicates only one aspect of its problematic, we shall find phenomenology being related to it in terms of other perspectives as well, for example, in the principal definition of philosophy's relationship to the positive sciences. All positive sciences begin within a dogmatic situation, that is, they are based upon presuppositions which they are no longer capable of acknowledging. Now in so far as philosophy expressly relates these sciences to the sphere of their presuppositions, it renders the ground upon which the positive sciences rest transparent and establishes them in a sense which they, in their own attempts to lay a foundation, cannot realize. Thus philosophy takes on the aspect of a transcendental theory of science. Furthermore, for Criticism as well as for phenomenology, the transcendental-philosophical problem of knowledge can be converted into a corresponding theory of beings, into a fundamental ontological thesis: viewed philosophically, beings (i.e., the theoretical objects of knowledge) are principally the result of a "constitution." Both Criticism and Husserl expressly and emphatically define the "idealism" expressed in this thesis as "transcendental idealism," thereby distinguishing it from all "subjective idealisms." Here, as before, the characterization "transcendental idealism" reveals traits common to both philosophies. First, in both positions the "transcendental ideality" of beings is not only compatible with their "empirical reality" but also the latter is directly grounded in the former and is only comprehensible with reference to it. Second, the "idealistic" thought of the constituted nature of beings includes within it a primacy of meaning (*Sinn*) over being (*Sein*). According to Criticism, meaning, or theoretical validity, whose recognition in the pure judgment-forms of "transcendental apperception" first makes possible the objective givenness of the real, is prior to reality and prior to the real object of knowledge. (Hence Zocher, for example, terms critical idealism an "idealism of meaning.") Phenomenology directly formulates the problem of constitution as the problem of "the bestowal of *meaning*."

In all these correspondences the inner accord of phenomenology with the spirit of "critical idealism" shows itself in an apparently irrefutable way. But, according to Criticism, phenomenology presents a remarkable alter ego, an internal division and disunity which once again forces it into crude opposition with Criticism. Although Husserl's conception of the idea of philosophy presses forward to authentically "critical beginnings" (whether these are literally determined by Criticism or not) which could have proved fruitful, he surrenders them in carrying out his "point of departure." The shadow of his dogmatic past falls upon his present venture. Methodological ideas conceived in the epoch of the *Logical Investigations* obscure the clear picture of the basic critical determinations which now undergo an intuitionistic-ontologistic reinterpretation. This deviation from critical beginnings not only occurs by way of a marked relapse into the dogmatic position of the *Logical Investigations*, but also as a remarkable *sublimation* of its methodological position. The resulting opposition between critical and dogmatic motives produces an internal imbalance in the structure of phenomenological philosophy whose basic view, because of its fluctuation and vacillation, can be grasped and fixed only with great difficulty. Only the direction of its fall away from the pure idea of Criticism, conditioned by its concealed dogmatism, remains unambiguous. The most important reinterpretations of critical positions can be briefly summarized. The phenomenological definition of "transcendental apperception," the central concept of all "transcendental philosophy," is (although in an indirect way) completely intuitionistic and ontologistic. Its aversion to "construction," an aversion which rests upon its methodological biases, makes it impossible for phenomenology to free the epistemological ego from all empiricism and to recognize it as a *pure form*. For this reason, Husserl posits the "transcendental ego" as an individual, *existing* ego. Even if he holds fast to this ego's nonempirical character, he does not attain to a transcendental concept of this ego as belonging to a "nonontological subject" (Zocher), but simply draws a questionable "metaphysical" distinction between an ego existing within the worldly "apperception," where it is the object of inner experience and empirical psychology, and an existing ego which is detached from this apperception. The content of the empirical and the pseudo-"transcendental" ego is, for Husserl, the same. This indicates that the transcendental ego is *ontic*.

In addition to its general methodological dogmatism, a further and particularly significant motive for phenomenology's misconceiving the "foundational sphere" as ontic is present in the naive transference of the *eidetic* method, which is developed with reference to beings found within the prephilosophical experience of the world, to the level of philosophical problems. If an unacceptable (intuitionistic) ontologization of validity is already present in the naive-theoretical attitude of the phenomenological theory of the *eidos*, a more fateful "ontologism" is revealed in the transference of this same method to the thematic area of transcendental knowledge. The application of the eidetic method to the "transcendental ego" constitutes an ontologization of the latter.

The ontic interpretation of the "foundational sphere" attacks Criticism's innermost meaning: the universal priority of the forms of validity which, as theoretically valid within the correlative relationship to a preobjective "content," are the transcendental conditions for the possibility of the objects of knowledge (i.e., are constitutive of beings), is surrendered for the sake of the priority of *a single being*. The "foundational sphere" is misconceived as the region of being (*Seinsbereich*) of inner experience. The "critical idea of immanence" is thereby transformed into a naive conception. As a consequence of phenomenology's intuitionistic bias, everything from the "immanence" of beings in general (the objects of inner and outer experience) to the transcendental world-forms (the pure form of the ego, the *a priori* functions of judgment, theoretical acceptances, and all these taken together within the context of their reciprocal meaning-relationships) is replaced by the relationship of transcendent beings to "consciousness." Even though Husserl will not acknowledge it, his conception of "transcendental idealism" displays certain traits which place him in close proximity to a "subjective idealism." Despite repeated emphasis that the "empirical reality" of beings can persist without detriment to their "transcendental ideality," one must distrust this thesis if one investigates Husserl's concept of "constitution." Here also, Criticism argues, we are able to witness the degeneration of an original and genuinely critical point of departure. Critical idealism is an idealism of "constitution." It surmounts naive dogmatism (which holds fast to given reality) through a tracing of reality back to a "theoretical consciousness." But this "consciousness" is not at all a being, but is the pure form of consciousness in general and, as such, is the "presupposition" of all beings. Now, since phenomenology, entrapped by its bias, misconceives this consciousness as an existing one (*ein Seiendes*), it strikes upon a thoroughly *ontic* idea of "constitution." This is shown by the fact that phenomenology mistakenly transfers the idea of "constitution" into the relationship between objects of "inner perception" and those of "outer perception" and determines it as a relation of "immanent" acts (of subjective experience) to the "transcendent" object as intentional forms of meaning.

In summary: phenomenology's decisive deviation from Criticism, with which it shares certain *problems* and the *direction* of their solution, is to be seen in the fact that phenomenology, as a sublimated working out of the intuitionistic and ontologistic character of its method, does not, as does Criticism, "clarify" beings with respect to their transcendental "presuppositions," but *clarifies beings by means of other beings* (*Seiendes durch Seiendes eklärt*).

How can this critique of phenomenology, repeated here only in its principal features, be answered? Is it justified? The critique itself places its negative evaluation in the presentation of phenomenology's deviation from thoughts basic to Criticism and in exhibiting the "intuitionistic-ontologistic deviation from a critically initiated thought of immanence" (Zocher). The answer to this critique cannot consist of protesting against these unfavorable charges and showing that in fact phenomenology does not distance itself from Criticism's problematic, but it must necessarily be an overthrowing of the presupposition upon which this critique is constructed. Phenomenology cannot distance itself from Criticism because it was never close to it. If one grasps it in terms of the critical aspect of a "deviation" from a Kantian or Neo-Kantian starting point, one has from the very beginning discarded proper access to phenomenology, and phenomenology itself has become concealed as a result of an insinuation. As a direct consequence, one fails to see phenomenology's inner character of unity and one must interpret it as a contradictory totality of opposing ("critical" and "dogmatic") tendencies. The overthrow of the critique's fundamental presupposition entails demonstrating phenomenology's own individual character by singling out the difference between it and Criticism. Such an undertaking encounters serious difficulties.[10] Here we can make only a limited attempt to indicate, within the context of one *single* perspective, the *original essence* of Husserl's phenomenological philosophy. This will be no more than a suggestion or an intimation of the direction in which any authentic re-creation of Husserl's thought must advance. Although phenomenology has developed a series of methodological "introductions" to the essential content of its philosophizing by taking different points of departure from traditional problems (the theory of knowledge, the universal theory of science, radical self-reflection, laying the foundations for logic, etc.), we must here renounce accompanying these introductory paths. The interpretation of the alteration of problems from their traditional form into their phenomenological setting cannot be briefly accomplished. We must, so to speak, use "force" in order to create for ourselves a view into the innermost meaning of phenomenology. The unrefined and oversimplifying concepts we shall come to employ in this process are to serve as provisional signs and are to be continually understood in terms of their reference to the analytic work.

If it is true that every philosophy reveals its innermost essence less in its theoretical accomplishments—which always remain human piecework—than in the basic question which is its motivating force, the difference between phenomenology and Criticism is principally defined as a difference in their basic problems. No matter with what diversity Criticism formulates its basic problem, whether as the question concerning the possibility of objectively valid knowledge or as the question "How are synthetic judgments *a priori* possible?" and so forth, there remains in all such variations the question concerning that realm of meaning which forms the presupposition of all beings. This "foundational sphere" is the thematic region of the philosophical problematic. How can it be characterized more precisely? The raising of this philosophical question signifies surmounting naive stupefaction in the face of beings, surmounting the attitude which focuses upon the ontic, and elevating oneself to the meaningful *a priori* form of the world which first makes the experience of beings in their givenness as "theoretical objects" possible. The *a priori* world-form is not, so to speak, a perceivable universe of essences given in direct immediacy (a type of knowledge related to objects); rather it is the relationship of theoretical validities, which are prior to all experience, to the pure form of consciousness, to the "transcendental apperception," a relationship which first makes the knowledge-relation to objects possible and which is accessible only through "construction." We intend, by designating the area of the critical problematic with the concept of an "*a priori* world-form" (in the sense discussed above), to indicate the *mundane character* of the critical philosophy. A concept thereby emerges which is of decisive importance for distinguishing phenomenology from Criticism. Even though Criticism raises itself above the positivity of experience and works out a philosophical questioning which, in opposition to all dogmatic metaphysics, "clarifies" beings by returning to a *meaning* which is prior to all beings and makes beings what they are, its formulation of the problem fundamentally rests upon the basis of the world. Its interpretation of the problem of the world remains *world-immanent* (precisely because it returns to an "*a priori* world-form"). (Indeed, Criticism's "critical" pathos is essentially determined by the world-immanent character of its clarification of the world: the denial of any knowledge of "things-in-themselves," etc.)

The basic question phenomenology is in the process of raising by introducing it in conjunction with traditional problems and the question which reveals its radical opposition to Criticism can be formulated as that concerning the *origin of the world.* The fullness of meaning sounding within the indeterminacy and openness we shall initially grant to the formulation of this question indicates its elemental character. It is man's eternal question concerning the origin of things which myth, religion, theology, and philosophical speculation each answer in their own way. The questionable and puzzling character of the being of the world is grasped with recourse to a "world-transcendent" cause, a world-ground, God, and so on. Basic "metaphysical" notions which express the relationship of world-ground and world along the lines of the intramundane relations of one being to another (for example: ground and consequent, creation and product, the emerging into light of something concealed, etc.) offer skepticism the weapons for the "critical" critique in which metaphysical systems are indeed destroyed, but not the problems which run through them. To the extent that the critique destroys naive forms of answers to this problem of origins it serves to reveal all the more the problem-character of this question. The destruction of dogmatic metaphysics is the first task in laying the foundations for philosophy. The critique can also go so far as to dispute the possibility of having knowledge of the world with respect to a "transcendent" world-ground in general and remove the problem of philosophy to the level of a world-immanent knowledge of beings, be this either in the form of a naive positivistic fixation upon beings or in the form of having recourse to the *a priori* presuppositions of beings.

In the basic question of Edmund Husserl's phenomenology, motives which have worked against each other in the history of philosophy have entered into an inner accord. The problem which until now has appeared in speculative form is retained in its central meaning, but is at the same time modified by a radicalization of the critique. The question concerning the origin of the world cannot be posed with the naiveté which sees the world as made up of the totality of things existing in themselves, for this must necessarily lead to a dogmatic metaphysics, that is, to a metaphysics which clarifies beings by means of beings. The superiority of the critical tendency in philosophy over every dogmatic metaphysics not only consists in the fact that it does away with the naive point of departure for such metaphysics by indicating the inapplicability of ontic concepts and relationships of being to a "world-transcendent" dimension (the "immanent employment of the categories"!), but also in the fact that it exposes a prior problem. Before beings can become a problem with respect to their factual being or facticity, it must first be understood *what* beings are in general. Criticism, which gives its answer to this problem by the constructive disclosure of the "transcendental" presuppositions of meaning or the "foundational sphere of meaning," does not proceed to pose the question of origins as a *theoretical* problem. Therefore, whereas Criticism's problematic comes to rest with the interpretation of the *meaning* of beings, phenomenology sees its decisive problem in the question concerning the origin of the world, a problem which it in principle keeps free from all naive (precritical) interpretations of being. If the basic motivating question of dogmatic metaphysics concerned the origin of *beings,* by contrast phenomenology explicitly raises the question concerning the origin of the *world.* This means that phenomenology places the unity of beings and world-form in question, that is, it questions the bond (in Zocher's terminology) between the "founded" and the "foundational sphere." If Criticism justifiably charges dogmatic metaphysics with using beings to clarify beings without having at all posed the nature of beings as a problem (i.e., without having sought the conditions for the possibility of their givenness), from the perspective of phenomenology the "critical" philosophy (insofar as both it and dogmatic metaphysics repudiate their guiding *problems)* can be characterized as a clarification of that which is within the world (beings) by means of the world-form and therefore as a basically *mundane* philosophy.

Defined with reference to its central problem, phenomenology raises the claim to realize a philosophical understanding of the world which transcends all worldly forms of clarifying, making intelligible, grounding, and so forth. It intends to make the world comprehensible in all of its real and ideal determinateness in terms of the ultimate ground of its being. It aspires to an absolute knowledge of the world. The *hybris* of this claim appears to place phenomenology within the ranks of the speculative systems of traditional philosophy which, in spite of the magnitude of their systematic project, have failed in justifying their speculative theses. However the essence of philosophical speculation is to be defined by phenomenology, phenomenology's theoretical *habitus* is not itself "speculative." It desires to be an absolute knowledge of the world in the form of

Husserl's Philosophy and Contemporary Critisicism

"rigorous science." This signifies neither a reduction of speculative metaphysics to science or a treatment of problems with "scientific methods" (whereby the concept of science remains oriented along the lines of the mundane sciences), nor a "speculative" definition of the scientific character of philosophical knowledge as the setting into play of a particular knowledge-capacity. It means simply this: phenomenology makes the "world-ground," be this posed either in the doctrinaire form of belief or in the form of speculative presentment, the *object of theoretical experience and knowledge,* and renders it accessible, exhibits it, and allows it to be seen and brought to evidence as it is in itself by means of a genuine method. In other words, phenomenology lives exclusively within the pathos of inquiry. What "object of knowledge," "exhibit," "demonstrate," and so on, mean in this connection can be understood only by gaining access to the dimension of the origin of the world. It is by no means a question of simply transposing methods of knowledge and demonstration aimed at worldly beings into the sphere of phenomenology's problems, so that the (in the critical sense) "transcendental" theory of the possibility of knowledge would assume a foundational role in establishing the specifically phenomenological experience. If phenomenology intends to be a "science," this indeed retains the formal sense of a concern with the theoretical unity of its "knowing," but at the same time it primarily denotes a transformation of the *idea of science.* Since phenomenology, through knowledge of the *world in terms of its origin,* realizes a knowing which in principle transcends all forms of mundane knowledge (including knowledge of the sphere of meaning which lies prior to all experience as well), it develops a *new* concept of science. While the traditional "universal" concept of science is basically related to "world-immanent" knowledge, phenomenology, so to speak, "extends" the concept of science by developing a knowing which is "world-transcendent." Phenomenological knowledge of origins does not take its place next to the mundane sciences, thereby falling under a common "higher concept" of a "science in general" with them, but is in a definite sense *prior to* all worldly knowledge. To the extent that everything known by the world-immanent sciences by means of experience (the positive sciences) and "construction" (for example, the critical-transcendental philosophy) is to constitute the thematic field of a demonstrative and explicative experience belonging to the world-transcendent knowledge of the absolute "ground," the rigorous science of phenomenology "grounds" all worldly sciences in a radical sense which cannot be viewed in terms of the mundane relationships of establishing one science by means of another. Phenomenology appears to share with Criticism the thesis that all of the positive sciences can only be established in an ultimate sense through philosophy. Nevertheless there is a fundamental difference. For Criticism it is a question of a world-immanent establishing of the positive sciences (whose concern with beings is naive) by philosophy viewed as the constructive exposition of the sphere of meaning which is the foundation of reality (beings). Phenomenology presents the establishing of all mundane knowing in general by a philosophy which knows *the origin of the world.* Thus phenomenology raises the claim of establishing all mundane knowing in a manner which is opposed to all knowledge of that problem-sphere to which Criticism is related in its own way

But how can phenomenology justify this claim? How can its questioning meaningfully transcend the world, and how can it give an answer to the concern for a nongiven origin, this traditional theme of theology and speculation, in terms of a theoretical knowledge? In radical opposition to all metaphysics of faith and speculation, phenomenology develops a *method of knowing* which leads to the origin of the world itself and makes it the thematic object of a possible knowledge. This method and way of knowing, which is the most essential feature of phenomenology's unique character, is the "phenomenological reduction."[11] It is the systematic totality of basic knowledge by means of which we "transcend" the world as the encompassing horizon of every knowledge-problematic, and by means of which we are led back to the world-transcendent origin.

Phenomenology's opposition to dogmatic metaphysics, however, not only consists in the *theoretical* form of its transcending of the world, but also consists in its different *direction.* Whether as belief or speculation, dogmatic metaphysics agrees in principle with the critical philosophy (only that the one maintains what the other denies) in positing the relationship of world and world-ground (or the origin-relation) as a "*transcendent*" relation between the world on the one hand and the world-ground on the other. Phenomenology surmounts the "transcendent" starting point (which is oriented along the lines of ontic relations) by laying hold of the *problem* theoretically and by determining the relationship of world to world-origin as one which is "transcendental" in character. The transcending of the world which takes place in performing the phenomenological reduction does not lead outside of or away from the world to an origin which is separate from the world (and to which the world is connected only by some relation) as if leading us to some *other* world; the phenomenological transcending of the world, as the disclosure of transcendental subjectivity, is at the same time the *retention of the world* within the universe of absolute "being" that has been exposed. The world remains *immanent* to the absolute and is discovered as lying within it. In this way, the phenomenological reduction does not purely transcend the world, but only transcends the *limitedness* of the "natural attitude"

Husserl's Philosophy and Contemporary Critisicism

(which simply views the world as the universe of beings) from which mundane philosophies originate and to which they remain related when they speculatively postulate a "transcendent" world-origin. To be sure, the movement of knowledge occurring within the reduction is a transcending passage from the world to "transcendental subjectivity," but it remains in principle within the unity of the absolute (which we come to recognize in working through phenomenological philosophy) as the world's "constitutive becoming" which emerges from origins within "transcendental" life. Just as the world is what it is only in terms of its "origin," so is this origin itself what it is only with reference to the world. To know the world by returning to a "transcendence" which once again *contains* the world within it signifies the realization of a *transcendental* knowledge of the world. This is the sole sense in which phenomenology is to be considered as a "transcendental philosophy." The difference in meaning of this concept reveals the radical difference between Criticism and phenomenology. Criticism's knowledge-problematic is essentially determined by transcending beings (or, ontic knowledge) to their *meaning,* to the *a priori* relationships between "transcendental apperception" and the theoretical ("transcendent") acceptances which render the givenness of beings possible, and hence is determined by the passage from innerworldly beings to the *a priori* form of the world. The meaning of critical "transcendental philosophy" is therefore determined throughout by a world-immanent character. By contrast, phenomenology's basic problem involves a transcendence with a completely different orientation. It is a transcendence beyond the *world* and not only beyond inner-worldly beings; nevertheless it is not, as with dogmatic-speculative metaphysics, a transcendence to some other-worldly "absolute." Phenomenology explicitly and knowingly wins back the world from within the depths of the absolute in which—*before* the phenomenological reduction—the world itself lies concealed.

Up to this point we have purposely employed broad concepts in order to expose the decisive difference between Criticism and phenomenology with respect to their *basic problems.* Precisely because this basic difference is concealed by their common definition as "transcendental" philosophies, it is necessary for us first to set this concealment aside by employing unrefined and forceful concepts. These formal explanations should not, therefore, be taken as definitions of phenomenology's meaning, but should only be taken as signs pointing to the direction in which true definitions can be won. These cannot be obtained by considering phenomenology within the context of its literary "objectification," but only through a true penetration into the basic problem motivating all of its particular analyses. Even though positing a general characteristic before the initiation of analytical work strongly contradicts the spirit of phenomenology, nevertheless the foregoing indications of phenomenology's basic meaning cannot be avoided in guarding against unwarranted insinuations

Even though our glance at phenomenology's inner essence has been indeterminate and emptily formal, it nevertheless does permit us to recognize that the difference between Criticism and phenomenology is one which concerns their *basic problems* and, therewith, their *ideas of philosophy*. In giving this difference the highest degree of sharpness and depth, and in bringing these two philosophies into extreme opposition, we have succeeded in destroying the presupposition which forms the basis of that entire criticism which is our concern to reject here. The root of this misunderstanding of phenomenology shows itself to be the impermissible identification of the critical and the phenomenological problematics. This questionable identification is not so much the result of explicitly establishing the similarity of basic problems as it is the result of an unexpressed assumption documented by the thematic interpretations of phenomenology's central and basic thoughts. The theory of the "phenomenological reduction" as well as the theory of "transcendental constitution" are both interpreted by relating them to critical methods and theories, and this is a principal mistake. Indeed, these theories are misconceived in two ways: first, to the extent that Criticism evaluates them positively as "genuine critical beginnings" and, second, to the extent that they are negatively judged as "deviations." If we look for the reason for this misunderstanding we are seeking for the reason why Criticism's critique, despite an intensive study of phenomenological texts, could relate both the phenomenological reduction and the theory of transcendental construction to its own basic (critical) problematic. We now discover one reason for this in the concealment of the basic problem which motivates phenomenology. If a philosophical theory is to be understood with reference to that particular problem which it attempts to master so that the *motive* for the formation of its theory can be manifested, from the very start phenomenology carries with it a certain "unintelligibility" precisely because it cannot, in principle, be grasped with reference to mundane problems; with reference, that is, to questions which stand within the horizon of the "natural attitude." Its basic problem is concealed in this way: it is at first not an unsettling problem which is somehow present *before* phenomenological theory, so that by virtue of its threatening character it can serve to provoke philosophical reflection. It first originates *as a problem* in and through the phenomenological reduction itself, which is already the first step to be taken in mastering it. Outlining the "transcendental" problem of the world can first occur only in

Husserl's Philosophy and Contemporary Critisicism

transcending the world. The phenomenological philosophy therefore cannot be coordinated with any worldly problem which might serve to provide its motivating occasion. There is the constant danger that, instead of giving oneself to the movement of knowledge contained within the reduction (even though this movement at first appears unmotivated), the reduction is reduced from the very start to a mundane problematic in order to understand first what might conceivably serve as motivation for it. If one has referred it to a question situated within the horizon of the "natural attitude" (the question, for example, concerning the possibility of knowledge as a question of theoretically valid presuppositions), not only phenomenology's general and principal character is of necessity missed, but also the sense of its unique epistemological methods. The concealment of its basic problem is, however, not the sole contributor toward its being misunderstood. There is also the particular way in which the problem from which the phenomenological philosophy can take its point of departure is posed. It can be conjoined with mundane problems in many ways (as a theory of knowledge, a theory of science, an ontology, the theory of universal self-reflection, etc.) with the final end of essentially *altering* these mundane problems by allowing them to branch out into the phenomenological reduction. In principle, however, phenomenology does not concede the character of *philosophical* reflection to its own departures from within a worldly problem-formulation. Phenomenological philosophy first begins with the "reduction." The concealment of its basic problem, together with the worldly givenness of its initial problems, permits the emergence of the belief that phenomenology can be defined in terms of its more or less accidental beginning with mundane problems. The critique of phenomenology exercised from the side of Criticism misses its "object" and is in the truest sense "objectless" because, in addition to reducing phenomenology to a mundane philosophy, it cannot endure phenomenology's "unmotivated" character and must posit its own problematic as the motive antecedent to the phenomenological reduction. Here we can only indicate how this critique can be rejected. We must make the attempt to free phenomenology's two central and basic systematic ideas, the theory of the reduction and the theory of constitution, from the mistaken interpretations to which both have been subjected (both their positive evaluations as "critical beginnings" and their rejection as "deviations") at the hands of the critical critique. Since we are here not able to present the phenomenological theories themselves within the context of their direct performance, but are compelled of necessity to speak *about* them, our previous look at phenomenology's *basic problem* (as the question concerning the origin of the world) gives a certain, although dim, light in terms of which the unclear phenomenological concepts of "reduc-

Eugen Fink

tion" and "constitution" gain some form. Do we not contradict ourselves at this point? Are we in fact able to cite a *motive* for the reduction in advance: the problem, namely, of the "origin of the world"? There is no problem already given within the world which can serve to occasion our setting phenomenology into practice, that is, our actual advancing along its way to knowledge. The form which the problem of the origin of the world assumes in theology and speculative philosophy does not serve as the motivation for phenomenology's basic question. Phenomenology rejects both as being mundane forms of the authentic problem of origin, forms which it recognizes as being only "symbolic anticipations" of its own basic question. If, therefore, phenomenology's basic problem does not exist *before* the performance of the reduction, since this problem itself takes shape in and through the reduction, its basic motivating problem can nevertheless be indicated (even though in a provisional and quite vague manner) by way of anticipation in speaking about phenomenology, for speaking *about* phenomenology presupposes having actually passed along its way. Though it may seem strange and surprising to characterize as "knowledge of the origin of the world" a philosophy whose pathos is determined by the rejection of all overly bold systematic constructions and the uncompromising demand that philosophy be a rigorous science, this does not signify the later attempt, as it were, to claim a "metaphysical" character for phenomenology, but is only a summarizing expression for the totality of knowledge, made possible by the reduction, belonging to the phenomenological "transcendental philosophy."

The interpretation which the "phenomenological reduction" finds within Criticism's critique is false in two respects. First, the reduction is fixed as the method for obtaining the "foundational sphere" and thus as possessing an orientation similar to the abstractive steps which lead Criticism to the conception of the "epistemological ego." Although a difference in method is admitted, at least the thematic to which the different methods lead is determined as being the same: "transcendental apperception" (the epistemological ego) is identified with the "transcendental ego." This implies further identifications: the "natural attitude" is interpreted as the positivistic comportment of knowledge (the attitude concerned with beings) and the transition from it to the "transcendental attitude" is misconceived (by overlooking the essential difference in the notion of "transcendental") as the transition to what in the *critical* sense are the "transcendental" presuppositions of the possibility of positive knowledge (to the "transcendental-logical" model of the object of knowledge). On the other hand, the "irreality" (*Irrealität*) of Husserl's transcendental ego is given a new meaning in connection with the critical notion of the "irreal" and is identified with *pure form*. The phenomenological *epoché* is, as the disconnection of the real, a method for exposing the irreal presuppositions of the real. For the critical philosopher, Husserl's genuinely critical beginnings take shape in terms of such "explanations." In reality, however, such a beginning is not at all considered by Husserl. Equally mistaken is the asserted "deterioration of the critical beginning." In the opinion of the critical philosopher, Husserl debases the transcendental thought concerning the relatedness of beings in general to the theoretical form of consciousness in general to a dependency of the objects of "outer experience" upon the sphere of immanence.[12] In the final analysis, Husserl turns "transcendental idealism" back into a subjective idealism. The phenomenological *epoché*, which, in itself, is well suited for disconnecting beings in general (and hence both immanent and transcendent beings) for the purpose of exposing the sphere of meaning (the "foundational sphere") which first makes beings in general possible, becomes in Husserl's hands a method for disconnecting transcendent beings and obtaining the "region of consciousness." Let us briefly discuss the reduction and attempt to show that this is neither a method for exposing the (in the critical sense) "transcendental" validity-*a priori,* nor a method for obtaining and purifying human (and this is the same as worldly) "immanence"; that the transcendental ego which is accessible through the reduction is neither the pure form of the ego, the ego-principle, nor is it identical with the worldly existing ego (the empirical object of both self-experience and psychology); that the reduction establishes the basis for neither a critical "transcendental philosophy," nor a dogmatic and subjectivistic philosophy of immanence. The primary concern of this discussion will also be to understand motives for these misconceptions, which could have their source in the *Ideas*' all too condensed presentation of the reduction.

Every discussion of the phenomenological reduction, no matter how incomplete, finds itself faced with the unavoidable difficulty of being compelled to speak about it as if it were an activity of knowledge which it is always possible to perform, and which from the very start lies within the horizon of our human possibilities. In truth, however, it does not at all present a possibility for our *human* existence. The unfamiliarity of the reduction is therefore not only an unfamiliarity with it as a fact, but is also an unfamiliarity with its possibility. Although we also say that all talk about a particularly difficult kind of knowledge quite remote from our everyday knowing (for example, the knowledge of physics) presupposes *actually having been involved with it* (precisely for the reason that it does not belong to the everyday familiarity we have with our knowing and experiencing), a discussion of the reduction not only signifies an appeal to its actual performance, but also imperatively requires the performance of an act which places us beyond the horizon of our own possibilities, which "transcends" our *human* possibilities. The unmotivated character of the phenomenological reduction (the absence of any worldly problem which could serve as its real motive) expresses the reduction's unfamiliar nature in a similar way. Because it is the suspension of the "natural attitude" it cannot appear within this attitude and it therefore must be unfamiliar. The reduction becomes knowable in its "*transcendental* motivation" only with the transcending of the world. This means that the reduction is its own presupposition insofar as it alone opens up that dimension of problems with reference to which it establishes the possibility of theoretical knowledge. This strange paradox of the beginning of philosophical reflection finds expression within the fundamental perplexity into which all attempts to explicate the phenomenological reduction fall. Unmotivated and unfamiliar with respect to its possibility, every exposition of the phenomenological reduction is in a unique way *false.* This falsity is caused by the exposition's *worldly point of departure,* that is, its starting upon the basis of the "natural attitude" which the performance of the reduction is to suspend. Hence the phenomenological reduction first appears to be one theory among many which in its own way answers to the philosophical problematic within which we already stand as men philosophizing in the face of the questionable nature of the world. In truth, however, we do not stand within the problematic of philosophy (as this must be understood by phenomenology) from the very start, but are in a radical sense *outside of this problematic.* As long as we exist within the natural attitude the problem of philosophy, insofar as it is not factually given, is not only "unfamiliar," but also is indeed inaccessible. *Being shut off* from the dimension of the "transcendental" belongs to the essence of the imprisonment within the world which defines the natural attitude. Phenomenology's problem is not one which can be explained within the compass of the natural attitude. The introduction to philosophy presents itself as the *exemplum crucis* of the *leading out* of the natural attitude which begins within the natural attitude. In other words, the "falsity" of the initiating exposition cancels itself when it is carried out: in principle, all initial determinations of the reduction must be surmounted. This also means that from the very first the true theory of the reduction cannot be restricted to its beginnings: the first provisional and necessarily "false" determinations of the beginning stage of the reduction must not be taken as constituting the definitive theory of the reductive method. This point is the occasion for widespread misconceptions of the reduction. Instead of truly submitting oneself to the movement of knowledge which belongs to this basic phenomenological method and instead of leaving behind those determinations which are bound up with its point of departure from within the natural attitude by *actually performing* the reduction, one remains attached to the explications given by the provisional exposition and finally reaches interpretations which make the reduction a return to the conditions for the possibility of experience, or a return to the sphere of psychical immanence. The presentation of the phenomenological reduction in the *Ideas,* the presentation upon which Criticism entirely rests its critique, is, as the first published formulation of the reduction, still very much bound up with its point of departure. The straightforward introduction of the reduction makes it difficult to recognize the radically new meaning of the problem which is here raised for the first time. In a very real sense, the presentation of the reduction here (in the *Ideas)* is an appeal for its actual performance. There is also the specific purpose which guided Husserl in writing the *Ideas:* although he very strongly emphasized that it was a question here of a fundamentally new kind of science, nevertheless the major emphasis falls upon presenting a wealth of concrete intentional analyses. His primary interest was to disclose a new theme for investigation and to show that a totally new kind of knowledge and insight could be in fact obtained. He could be satisfied with this first and provisional account of the reduction in trusting that the actual carrying out of the given analyses (and not simply their being read) would create the disposition to set authentically the phenomenological reduction in motion. We must stress that even today this account is not false in the sense of being "incorrect," but only that it possesses that unavoidable "falsity" which is the property of every first exposition of the reduction, that is, it appeals to an act the performance of which is to transcend it.

We shall now, with constant reference to the account given in the *Ideas*, bring several essential moments of the reduction into relief for the purpose of indicating at what point Criticism's interpretation deviates from a true understanding of the reduction. In the *Ideas,* phenomenology's basic thought is first introduced as the universal alteration of the general thesis of the natural attitude. The full and most profound meaning of the concept of the natural attitude is, however, not thereby developed, but is, so to speak, explicated only with respect to its most readily understood features. The limited character of the analysis of the natural attitude gives further cause for misunderstanding the reduction. Yet in spite of this limitation the concept of the "natural attitude" cannot be fully developed and unfolded from the start because this concept is not at all a worldly one which is in some way already given. Rather is it a "transcendental" concept. We are, in the natural attitude, imprisoned and engrossed within it, so that we are not at all able to dismiss it without breaking out of it completely. The phenomenological reduction is just this breakthrough. Hence a true explication of the imprisonment within the natural attitude which is essentially constitutive of human experience presupposes the reductive escape from this imprisonment. A description of the natural attitude which is carried out *prior to* the reduction is itself accomplished at the level of the natural attitude and only has the significance of preparing for the introduction of the phenomenological formulation of problems. The provisional and inauthentic delineation of the natural attitude in terms of a moment which is grounded within this attitude, the moment of the thoroughly thetic character of our worldly relation (either theoretical or practical) to beings, allows this attitude to appear as a *thematic attitude.* One could attempt to equate this with the straightforward attitude of our living within the world, or with the positive attitude toward beings in general (the objects of both inner and outer experience), so that a modification of this attitude could signify either a thoroughly reflective thematic or a turning toward the *a priori* presuppositions of beings. Both interpretations of the phenomenological transcendental attitude advanced by Criticism's critique are thus perhaps occasioned by a misinterpretation of that "attitude" against which this transcendental attitude directs itself and which it discards. In truth, however, the natural attitude is not an attitude for which the psychological thematization of immanence or the philosophical position of Criticism with respect to knowledge can be substituted. All human attitudes remain in principle *within* the natural attitude. At its onset, Husserl's description, which first starts within the natural attitude, casts into relief the belief-character of our human experience of the world. Thus his initial point of departure is apparently psychological. The world which we know and within which we know ourselves is given to us as a *universe of acceptances*, is given to us in terms of a universal belief in the world in which all particular positings of being in experience come together as the "general thesis of the natural attitude": the belieflike positing of the world's reality. To be sure, this human belief in the world is not expressly made use of, nor is it unfolded in accordance with its belief-components as the concrete flowing world-apperception (already an unavoidable task of performing the reduction), but is simply determined as constituting the essence of the natural attitude. The understanding of what actually occurs by defining the natural attitude in this way is of decisive importance for appropriating the true meaning of the reduction. The discussion of the natural attitude which starts from within this attitude characterizes its essence as the standing-within-the-belief-in-the-world. It now becomes a question as to what is really contained within this determination. We have already stated that the problem of the phenomenological introduction to philosophy consisted in the paradox of beginning within the natural attitude in order to lead out of it. Does this indication of the essence of the natural attitude conceal a possible point of departure for leading us out of it? Standing-within-the-belief-in-the-world first of all signifies the position of *man* within the belief in the world, that is, man is the subject who accepts the world (and, included within this, himself as man) in his life of meaning, and he does this in a variety of ways. Comprehensive intentional analyses are necessary in order to be able to understand the inner structure of the world's being-for-us, this immensely complicated complex of acceptances which is in constant metamorphosis. Not only must we analyze the actual and potential positings of being which belong to our own experience together with the acquisitions of acceptances and the components of habitual opinions which originate with these positings, but also we must above all consider the multiple modes of our taking over acceptances from the experience of others, and so forth. Our life of meaning not only relates to transcendent beings, but is also directed to our psychical being itself, to immanent being, and furthermore not only to beings (objects) but also to horizons of beings, and ultimately to that universal horizon which encompasses all horizons. The general thesis is not one positing of being running alongside of other individual experiences and which is just added to them, but is the universal, constant, self-modifying consciousness of the world whose contents are in constant flux: the constant world-apperception. It is the belief in the world which persists throughout the alteration of single apperceptions and the breakdown of its particular beliefs (the modification of being into appearance) and which endures throughout these various corrections. Now is this belief in the world, viewed in the context of such an all-encompassing scope, the belief which makes up the essence of the natural attitude? Is this standing-within-the-belief-in-the-world the thetic act of *man's* universal believing in the world? The definition of the natural attitude which is given within the confines of this same attitude starts with the *intramundane* world-belief in the being of the world: belief in the world is the unique way in which one being, namely man, exists within the world. We repeat our question: is the ontic (intramundane) belief in the world the essence of the natural attitude? Or is starting with the intramundane belief in the world an attempt at definition which is still fastened to its point of departure (and hence "false") and whose truth is first revealed when it is adopted? That man's believing in the world is itself within the world is just a fact which still belongs to the content of this belief. To call myself or someone else "man" already implies being certain of myself as one man among others and hence a knowing of myself as existing within the world as a being related to the world in a conscious manner. Existing-within-the belief-in-the-world and believing oneself to be a man are one and the same. And in such a way that just as every belief in a particular worldly thing is within

Eugen Fink

the world as a psychical occurrence, so is the universal belief, the universal apperception of the world, also within the world as a psychical occurrence. Clearly the belief in the world does not permit itself to be explained by the clue offered by the intentional nature of single human acts. Here we find, in an "objective" direction, that which is noematically intended, and, in a "subjective" direction, the noetic intending. In the belief in the world, however, the world is not objective in this sense, as if the world stood over and against man as a universal unity of acceptances, but rather is man, within the context of his intending of the world, included within this belief itself and encompassed by it. After the first and necessarily provisional determination of the essence of the natural attitude as a believing in the world, as the universal flowing apperception of the world which is carried out on its own terms (i.e., upon the *basis* of this belief itself), what is of decisive importance is the awakening of an immeasurable astonishment over the mysteriousness of this state of affairs (*Sachlage*). To accept it as a self-evident fact is to remain blind to the greatest mystery of all, the mystery of the being of the world itself, the world which first receives meaning and the acceptance of its being from the flowing world-apperception, and this in terms of every content with which the world could conceivably be given to us at any moment. This naturally also holds for ourselves and for our human nature, the latter itself implying the being of the world just as the being of the world implies the being of man. For we have hereby reached that fundamental view which the transition from the provisional to the authentic determination of the natural attitude shall only *transform* more deeply.

This transformation, however, occurs in performing the phenomenological *epoché*. As the disconnecting of the belief in the world, the *epoché* is not a refusal to hold a belief which is already known to be a belief, but is in truth the first authentic *discovery of the belief in the world:* the discovery of the world as a *transcendental dogma*. In other words, the *epoché* first makes the primordial depths of the belief in the world accessible: this belief must be bracketed by the *epoché* so that it can become a "phenomenon" and thereby a theme for phenomenology. Insight into this basic correlation of *epoché* and belief in the world is of the utmost importance for understanding the reduction. The *epoché* is not a mundane inhibiting of the ontic and intramundane belief in the being of the world. As the persistent and radical deactivation of the belief in the world, the *epoché* is the disconnecting of the belief in the human performer of beliefs, that is, the bracketing of the world-belief's self-interpretation by which it apperceives itself as being in the world. But the belief in the world does not disappear when "man" himself, as a unity of beliefs (*Glaubenseinheit*), as a self-apperceived acceptance, falls within the scope of the reduction; rather can the true "subject" of belief now be uncovered for the first time: the transcendental ego, for whom the world (the intramundane subject and the totality of its objects) is a universe of transcendental acceptances. To perform the phenomenological reduction is to disconnect the belief in the world in the depths of its transcendental primordiality. It is important here to guard against a possible misinterpretation. One does not perform the transcendental *epoché* in two steps, first disconnecting the belief in the being of the external world, and then, by means of a supplementary disconnecting, the self-apperception of the subject of beliefs as man. The reverse order is equally incorrect. Such a procedure would imply that one could adequately carry out the act of bracketing the world, the universe of spatio-temporal objects, by means of an all-encompassing gathering together of those single acts of bracketing which are thought of as continuing *ad infinitum*. In this case, the philosophizing ego would run through an ideal process composed of single acts of a possible human world-consciousness and follow it with a universal resolution that, for a "phenomenology," the results of such acts are not, so to speak, to be permitted as premises. From this the following arrangement closely follows: first the universal bracketing of all acts concerned with the external world (all objects of the external world) and then the bracketing of one's own existence with regard to all actual and possible acts related to one's being *qua* man. But what is overlooked here is that for every act and its acceptance-relation to and attainment of its object, the universal space-time world is already presupposed as something which is constantly and in advance there for me, the subject of such acts, as the space-time horizon of the world which is known along with the acceptance of being and out from which the respective individual object—in accordance with the nature of consciousness—is taken, brought to the acceptance of its being, and made the theme of either a theoretical or some other pursuit. In the widest sense, every act is an act of thematization and presupposes a "pregiven" world as its nonthematic background. This holds for all wakeful consciousness as a continuing life of activity. This implies that the truly concrete life of consciousness is a universal, flowing, and continuing apperception which flows through all modifications as a constant motivational background of continually new acts which draw their motive from it and which alone, therefore, are concrete and also motivated in their (modalizable) acceptances.

A radically reflective reflection brings this flowing and concrete life into the view of experience. Despite its constant change, it is the unity of a world-apperception which restores and preserves its belief in the world through a continuing self-correction accomplished by the "crossing out" of empty "appearances" and the revaluation of individual experiences as being other than what they seem to be. The foundations and motivations for the life of act-performances enter into view, foundations and motivations which are given as rooted in the horizons of this constant pre-givenness. All stimuli, without which no turning toward, comprehending, earnest pursual, or achievement can take place, stem from the current mode of the pregiven apperception. They are already meaningfully present (although in modes of determinateness and indeterminateness, familiar and unfamiliar) within the acceptance-horizon "world." In opposition to the universal *epoché* of the natural attitude (the bracketing of all objects which can be grasped individually, an *epoché* which, in its "abstractness," is not free from presuppositions), the possibility of a truly concrete and fully universal *epoché* becomes intelligible in connection with this universal world-apperception, this absolute and concrete life which carries the meaning of the world's being totally and concretely within itself, an *epoché* which has reference to the constantly pregiven world and which thereby relates to all acts and act-achievements which have taken and which are to take their motivation from it. In one act, which cannot be made more radical, and with one stroke, the absolute and concrete apperception of the world, or the belief in the world located within it, is bracketed. Included within this bracketing is the constant self-apperception of the "human ego" with respect to its being and its possession of a particular nature. All single and natural human acts, together with the pregiven world which is their constant acceptance-background, are *eo ipso* subject to the reduction. Through this *transcendental reduction,* and only in this way, we can also win the transcendental world-phenomenon, or the transcendental world-apperception, as a phenomenon in a correlative sense. This is the absolute and concrete life within which the world and I myself as a human subject are ontic phenomena. Only now is that dimension disclosed which permits us to inquire into the nature of absolute life, construed as the ultimate intentionally constituting life, and which in particular permits us to investigate the life of act-achievements, the "results" of which pass over from the mode of actuality to that of inactuality, thereby entering into the flowing reservoir of the pregiven world as "tradition." All tradition lies preserved within the world's current changing givenness. Yet in opposition to the natural concept of tradition, this concept of tradition receives a new character and requires new modes of formulation (for example, "apperceptive transmission" as the mode of this living tradition).

What the true transcendental reduction has caused to enter into view as the absolute and concrete stream of experience is something which, by virtue of an essential necessity, has remained inaccessible to all experience and thought belonging to man's life in the world, his life within the "natural attitude." It is accessible solely through the transcendental reduction. With the reduction, the transcendental, absolute, concrete, and constantly flowing world-apperception comes to *experience*—a new, transcendental, experience. Now an experiencing explication of the infinity of constitutive and synthetically merging apperceptive achievements must be disclosed, and upon this foundation a new and primarily eidetic thinking (a theorizing and transcendental thinking) must come into play. Everything revealed in this experience transcends the universe of all natural familiarities and unfamiliarities, transcends the universe of what, in the natural-psychical sense, is known and unknown. For all this itself is essentially accessible to the phenomenological method as the intentional origin of its meaning for worldly being, and therefore belongs to the universe of phenomenology's problems.

After all this has been said, it would be incorrect to treat the reduction in question as an easily summarized mental technique, the various forms of which could be easily given, a technique which traverses natural-psychical paths and which, given the appropriate instructions, could be performed by every scientifically educated person, as if it were simply a matter of bracketing the "natural concept of the world" in order to place acts of both theoretical and practical consciousness of the world out of play. The *epoché* structures the basic problem of phenomenology, the transcendental problem of the world, by discovering the true "subject" and subjective life out from which the belief in the world emerges (inquiring beyond man as a unity of acceptances lying within the belief in the world), thereby recognizing and breaking with this imprisonment of man as such. In disclosing the world as a universe of transcendental acceptances, the *epoché* makes possible for the first time a problematic which does not itself stand *upon the basis of the world* (i.e., which does not stand within the natural attitude's imprisonment within the world, but which is "opposed" to the world). Phenomenology's inquiry into the *being of the world* passes beyond all questions raised by a philosophy with a "natural orientation." This inquiry is not preoccupied with the being of the world itself, but investigates this being by recognizing that the being of the world is "transcendental acceptance" and by tracing it back to the "transcendental subjectivity" in whose life the world is accepted and "held to be valid." If the guiding question of every philosophy can be defined as knowledge of the world, then this definition holds for phenomenology also, but with the sole reservation that phenomenology exposes the world as a problem and that it places the world in question through a questioning which surpasses the world itself. Breaking free from all naive and mundane concepts in its advance toward knowledge and maintaining that the meaning of mundane being is, in its otherwise

Eugen Fink

constantly concealed depths, "*acceptation*" ("*Geltung*"), phenomenology's formulation of its problem transcends the world since the world becomes questioned with reference to the dimension of transcendental life which, in principle, stands "outside of" the world. Phenomenology transforms the question concerning the being of the world into the question concerning the essence of transcendental subjectivity, that subjectivity which ultimately accepts the "world" and within whose life the belief in the world, together with the meaning of the world's being belonging to it, is constantly being enacted and shaped into the unity of a universal apperception.

But is phenomenology's formulation truly a modification of philosophy's basic cosmological question? Do we, through the *epoché*, actually provide ourselves with a hitherto unknown possibility for giving an answer to the problem of the being of the world? Do we not simply exclude this being? Here we discover an important clue to the essence of the phenomenological *epoché*, which it is all the more necessary to point out since not only the mistaken interpretation of the reduction advanced by Criticism but also more generally widespread misunderstandings rest upon a *misconception of the reducing ego*. It must nevertheless be admitted that the inadequate presentation of the *epoché* in the *Ideas* had not sufficiently developed and differentiated the structure of this ego. Wherein lies this misunderstanding? Even if one does not, as Zocher and Kreis, view the *epoché* as an attempt to exclude beings, "reality" (thus interpreting it as not being a "genuine critical beginning"), or as the disconnecting of the positings of transcendent being (the distorting of the critical beginning to a "philosophy of immanence")—even if one comprehends it as being universal (as the disconnection of the world)—the *epoché* still remains thoroughly misconceived when it is explicated as a *mere abstinence-modification* of the universal world-thematic, of all acts belonging to natural life in the world. It then acquires the character of being a casting off and a distancing from the thematic which exists *before* the *epoché*. It then means: instead of living in the belief in the world we bracket it; we no longer posit being, rather do we offer no opinion concerning it. But such a description is still misleading, for the *epoché* appears to be a method for setting aside and disconnecting a previously existing thematic, and thus a method of *turning away* and withdrawal. This is strongly expressed in Criticism's mistaken interpretation of the *epoché,* where the *epoché* is misconstrued as the bracketing of "reality" in order to get away from the real to the *a priori* presuppositions for the givenness of the real, or as the bracketing of the "transcendent" in order to preserve a pure sphere of psychical immanence. The reduction is not understood in its transcendental-phenomenological meaning as long as one directly identifies the ego living within the belief in the world with the ego exercising the *epoché*, so that the same ego is posited as first actively involved with the belief in the world and then as inhibiting this belief by "bracketing." Phenomenology does not disconnect the world in order to withdraw from it and occupy itself with some other philosophical thematic, but rather, as philosophy, does it stand within the question as to what the world is: phenomenology disconnects the belief (as the universal world-apperception) in the world in order ultimately to know the world. Yet how, when the world is recognized by the *epoché* as a being-meaning (*Seinssinn*), as a correlate of the belief in the world which has already given and which continues to give the world, can we prevent robbing ourselves, by disconnecting that belief within which the world is and continually "holds" for us, of the possibility of knowing what it is? This apparent *aporia* disappears when we make the "identity" of the ego which believes in the world and the ego which disconnects the belief in the world itself a problem. This identity is not the self-sameness of the simply active ego, which "until now" lived within the naive performance of its positings and which "from now on" will suspend such performances and hold them in abeyance, but is rather the unique *identity* of the phenomenological reduction's *three egos.* In truth, the *epoché* is not a "direct" refraining from belief paralleling the believing life of the thematic experience of the world which directly enacts its beliefs, but—and this cannot be overemphasized—is a structural moment of *transcendental reflection.* The *epoché* is a reflexive *epoché,* that is, it is a refraining from belief on the part of the reflecting "observer" who looks on the belief in the world in the actuality of its live performance *without taking part in it.* Transcendental reflection, however, is essentially different from every natural reflective attitude. Every reflection *prior to* transcendental reflection is a reflection of man upon himself and maintains itself within the boundaries of the human self-apperception and moves within the bias of the natural attitude. The transcendental bracketing of the world, and here this implicitly means the disconnection of self-acceptances (the "human ego"), renders possible for the first time the establishing of a reflecting-self which does not from the start stand within the human self-apperception, but which is rather "*outside*" of it. This ego knowingly directs itself toward the universal world-apperception as its *theme.* The disconnection of the world, however, not only makes possible the formation of a nonworldly reflecting-self, but, as we have already mentioned, also makes possible the discovery of the true "subject" of the belief in the world: the "transcendental subjectivity" which accepts the world. Thus the three egos belonging to the performance-structure of the phenomenological reduction are: 1. the ego which is preoccupied with the

Eugen Fink

world (I, the human being as a unity of acceptances, together with my intramundane life of experience); 2. the transcendental ego for whom the world is pregiven in the flow of the universal apperception and who accepts it; 3. the "onlooker" who performs the *epoché*. Therefore, while the transcendental ego who accepts the world does not suspend this belief in the world, but rather enacts it with greater intensity, thus leaving the ego which is preoccupied with the world, the self-apperception "man," in acceptance, the transcendental theoretical "onlooker" renounces all sharing in the belief in the world, renounces all taking part and concurrence; he makes no use of individual mundane positing, be this theoretical or a-theoretical. He abstains from any world-thematic, but not from all thematic entirely. His thematic field is the transcendental intending of the world, and this not as set out of action or neutralized, but in all the liveliness of its positive functioning. Because he observes this belief without taking part in or becoming involved with it, he does not accept the world as such, but only accepts the world as "phenomenon," as the correlate of that transcendental belief which has first been thematized by this ego. These indications of the reduction's formal performance-structure, no matter how vague and indeterminate they might be, point to a tension existing between the "egos" which can be distinguished within the framework of an all-encompassing unity, a tension which essentially belongs to the carrying out of the phenomenological reduction and which defines phenomenology's *pathos*. Entire disciplines of the phenomenological philosophy and the most basic insights into the architectonic of the phenomenological system are concealed within the problem of the "identity of the three egos," and we are not in a position here to indicate these even in a very general way. Our glance at the triadic structure of the ego which emerges with the performance of the reduction serves above all as a basis for rejecting the interpretation of the *epoché* which sees it as a "straightforward *epoché*" and permits us to define it as a structural moment of a unique kind of reflection, thereby eliminating one of the presuppositions for Criticism's mistaken interpretation. In addition, our glance reveals the entirely universal structure of the transcendental problem of the world (in the phenomenological sense): the world in itself becomes a problem (its disconnection does not signify its loss as a theme, but signifies that, as such, it has first truly become subject to questioning). Neither the "foundational sphere" of the meaningful *a priori* world-form nor the intramundane region of consciousness constitutes the object of phenomenology, for these stand from the start within philosophy's guiding cosmological question, a question which can never set them aside but which can only transform them so that the philosophical question concerning the world takes on the style of experientially and *knowingly* exhibiting the world's origin. Our glance finally reveals that the phenomenological reduction is at bottom a transformation of the "self"; it transcends the pure and "indissoluble" unity of the human ego, divides it, and brings it together within a higher unity.[13]

This brief sketch of the phenomenological *epoché's* true nature as the leading out of the natural attitude and the formation of the transcendental problem of the world is burdened by a striking ambiguity, an ambiguity to which we shall now briefly call attention. This ambiguity concerns the almost unavoidable expressions: "belief in the world," "acceptance," and so forth, which originally possess a psychological meaning but which nevertheless enter into the theory of the reduction as transcendental concepts. These terms must therefore not be taken in their usual sense, but first take on their integral philosophical meaning from the performance of the reduction itself. This ambiguity, which encumbers every one of the phenomenological *epoché's* self-interpretations, is caused by the unavoidable "falsity" of its point of departure from within the natural attitude. The countless misunderstandings which Husserl's philosophy had to suffer are caused by the fact that one retains and works with primarily "psychological" concepts within the familiar ease of their worldly meaning, thus failing to participate in their decisive modification by performing the reduction. Hence one fails to discover that the being of the world is that of a "transcendental unity of acceptances." Thus misunderstood, phenomenology assumes the character of being an exclusive thematization of psychical immanence which, however, in its working out of an initially "critical" formulation of problems, can be charged with overstepping the legitimate boundaries of psychology in wishing to be "more" than simply psychology, thereby finally arriving at a confused conception of the ego in which "the pure transcendental consciousness and the individual empirical subject remain merged in a peculiar fashion" (Kreis). Criticism errs with this objection because it overlooks the positive difference between phenomenology and psychology. Phenomenology is not to be distinguished from psychology because it aims (even though only at the start) at a critical, "transcendental" concept of the subject. To show how the difference might be suitably determined would require extensive phenomenological investigations. Here we can only give one indication of this difference.

Psychology is a science which rests upon the basis of the natural attitude and which is thematically directed toward the "psychical," that is, the level of psychical animal life, and primarily that of human life. Whether its procedure is inductive or *a priori*, its theoretical interest is exclusively concerned with that being which exists "consciously," that is, the object of psychology is *regional.* In order to secure the purity of its

Eugen Fink

own particular area, psychology must perform a certain kind of *"epoché,"* namely, the consistent disconnecting of all beings *transcendent* to the psyche, even though these beings are known within this psyche.[14] The domain of psychological investigation left over is the sphere of my own immanence, as well as the spheres of immanence belonging to other psyches which come to be identified through empathy. This *epoché* clearly has the character of holding in abeyance those objects not belonging to the thematic. But the transcendent being which is "disconnected" in this way is, in a certain manner, nevertheless present within psychological objectivity in that the transcendent is experienced, known, valued, meant, and, in the widest sense, believed in, within the sphere of immanence. The nonpsychical appears within psychology's thematic as the "intentional object," intended meaning, noematic content. Of fundamental importance, however, is the sense in which the emergence of the nonpsychical within the psychical is to be determined, that is, what character is possessed by the knowledge-relation as such. What does the transcendent's givenness within the immanent mean? Knowing (in the widest sense) is a one-sided relationship of one being (existing in the manner of consciousness) to another being. Being-known is of no concern to the being which is itself known. It is what it is whether it is known, meant, valued, believed, or not. In other words, the being-given of a being within the consciousness of another being does not touch its reality; it is ontically independent of the knowing being. So certain is it that we can only encounter beings in our experiencing and intending (in one word: in our believing in the world), nevertheless this being does not originate *out of* this belief. This means that the experience of the world, the having-the-world-in-acceptance thematized by psychology, is in itself impotent. To the essence of the natural attitude belongs the differentiation of beings in themselves from beings for us, or, as we say with less precision, the differentiation of the world from our "representation of the world." (A "thing-in-itself" is not thereby posited in any philosophical sense, just as the givenness of beings in consciousness is not defined by the "picture theory.") Developed as a positive science, psychology moves from the start within the self-explication of human experience as being only receptive and impotent. Psychology can now also degenerate into "psychologism" if it should attempt to reduce beings to their being-given, if it should discount the evidence of outer experience and proclaim the transcendent to be a mere acceptance-image, a mere correlate of a subjective meaning, or if it should orient the concept of all nonimmanent being along the lines of a "merely intentional object," thereby making the reality of the world an illusion in order ultimately to end with the absolutization of immanence. (One motive for this can be found in the always possible reflection that, as the concept contrasting with that of the representation of the world, the "world in itself" is also just *meant* by us as "being-in-itself.") We can, in distinguishing phenomenology from both psychology and psychologism, characterize phenomenology in the following way: 1. Phenomenology *is not a regional science;* it is not related to an area of the world (which could be regionally delimited by a method which holds in abeyance those beings which do not enter into consideration) but, as *philosophy*, has the world in its totality for its object, and this in a way unknown to all philosophies situated within the natural attitude insofar as phenomenology, through the reduction's transcending of the world, questions beyond the world and expressly situates itself within the universe of the absolute. In contrast to the psychological "*epoché*," the phenomenological *epoché* is not a method for delimiting (*Einschränkung*) an area within the world, but is rather a method for going beyond the world by *removing limits* (*Entschränkung über die Welt hinaus*): the totality of beings signified by the title "world" is made a problem by viewing the world as a unity of acceptances lying within the life of the reductively disclosed transcendental subjectivity. 2. Within the context of the belief in the world which has become its theme, phenomenology cannot in principle distinguish between the simple givenness of that which is accepted and a "something" which might be independent of it. In other words, the *transcendental* acceptance-relation is not identical with the intramundane acceptance-relation which is alone relevant to psychology. Transcendental "acceptance" (expressed concretely: the streaming life of transcendental subjectivity shaping itself into the unity of an apperception) does not possess the inner character of impotence and receptivity. 3. Phenomenology is in principle also different from every form of psychologism. It does not pass over the difference, essential to the natural attitude, between the thing in itself and the thing as it is for us: it does not dissolve the world into mere being-for-us, but by suspending the natural attitude it primarily inquires into the transcendental belief from which this difference (and accordingly the antithesis of world and our representation of the world) itself springs. Phenomenology's interpretation of everything which in one sense or another exists in the world as being an "acceptance" is not the thesis that the being of the world is "subjective" in the sense of *psychical* subjectivity, nor is it the denial of the existence of things independent of *human* knowledge. It signifies the discovery of an otherwise continually concealed meaning of being and the beginning of a transcendental interpretation of the intramundane relation of "independence."

The theses which serve to indicate the difference between phenomenology and psychology are to give us only those concepts needed for rejecting Criticism's interpretation of phenomenology as a philosophy of immanence. The ambiguity of such concepts as "belief in the world," "acceptance," and so on, which dominate the introduction of the reduction, necessarily expose phenomenology to the danger of being understood as a psychology or even as a psychologism. The true significance of the phenomenological reduction's beginning with the general thesis remains opaque as long as one does not himself participate in it and as long as one judges it in terms of the customary understanding of the mundane concepts of belief, and so on, thus failing to grasp the new meaning of these mundane words emerging with the reduction's performance. Phenomenology greatly looks forward to taking leave, at some time, of *all* knowing accepted by us and to give itself entirely to the uncertainty of the movement of knowledge initiated with the bracketing of the world (i.e., without retaining knowledge belonging to any acceptance tradition in the widest sense of the term). Criticism's interpretation remains attached to the situation within which the *epoché* is initially placed. It will not be contested that there is some reason for this. It is to be found in the inappropriate abstractness peculiar to the *Ideas'* characterization of the transcendental subjectivity disclosed by the *epoché* as a "region of pure consciousness," as the "residuum" left after the nullification of the world. The inappropriate character of these expressions is not only caused by the unavoidable ambiguity of all concepts expounding the *epoché*, but is also primarily the result of defining transcendental subjectivity in terms appropriate to psychical immanence alone. Yet this all too easily misleading characterization does not concern a self-interpretation of phenomenology which is simply erroneous; rather must these questionable terms be understood within the context of the very unique train of thought in the *Ideas*. They are a source of misunderstanding only when one does not grasp them within the context of the specific and not strictly necessary position of the *Ideas*. What procedure is peculiar to the *Ideas*? The radical difficulty of expounding phenomenology's basic thought, which is present as the paradox of leading out of the natural attitude by starting within it, consists of transforming the intramundane departure from the intramundane belief in the world into the discovery of the *transcendental* belief in the world, and is therefore the transition from the being-for-us of beings to the world's being-for-transcendental-subjectivity. Carrying out the *epoché* moves the phenomenological problematic out of the range of the apparent problem concerning the relation of psychical immanence and transcendence into the dimension of the acceptance-relation between the world in its totality (and hence both immanence *and* transcendence) and transcendental subjectivity. Such a movement, however, presupposes a prior methodological securing of the mundane correlation of subjective immanence and objective transcendence as a point of departure. In the *Ideas* Husserl saw before him the task of first of all anticipating this methodological assurance by characterizing the difference between immanence and transcendence as a difference of *intentionality*. In the *Ideas* these definitions are in no way meant to be phenomenologically definitive conceptual determinations. The intentional analysis of the givenness of the immanent over and against the givenness of the transcendent is in no way a formulation of the "criterion" for their definitive concepts, but only presents the transformation of their traditional difference (meant primarily as a difference of regions) into an *intentional* one. Thus, after the first presentation of the phenomenological *epoché*, Husserl must again return to the natural attitude in order to carry out an intentional characterization of the worldly consciousness on its own terms, that is, a characterization of the relation between immanence and transcendence. This does not occur as a result of a predominantly mundane interest in knowledge. Here it is neither a question of a traditional epistemological problem nor of a foundation for psychology, but rather of an interpretation of the essence of consciousness preparatory to the performance of the *epoché*. In other words, all these analyses are already aimed at the *epoché* which is to be carried out. This being "aimed at . . ." is the decisive peculiarity which we are not permitted to overlook. In § 34 Husserl once again provisionally returns to the basis of the natural attitude, yet in a manner determined by the "intimation of pure or transcendental consciousness. . . ." In this peculiar and, so to speak, indecisive posture between the natural and transcendental attitudes, Husserl brings consciousness, seized purely with respect to its ownmost essence, into relief as a *region* and, through the interpretation of the epistemological dignity of inner and outer experience, comes up against the priority and indubitability of immanent experience. The construction of a radical disharmony in all transcendent experience—a hypothesis whose methodological presuppositions remain unclarified—then serves to point out that the "negation of the world" (*Weltvernichtung*) leaves the region of consciousness "untouched," thereby indicating its separability from the world.

In all of these explications the difference between the mundane and the transcendental consciousness is not brought into sharp relief, for these interpretations are carried out precisely within the unstable transitional stage. Husserl himself terms them "preparatory transcendental observations" (§ 51). Only when one places the analyses concerning the priority and separability of the region of consciousness given under this title within the back and forth transitional movement from the reduction's intramundane starting point to the developed and clear transcendental

Eugen Fink

statement of the problem can one understand why Husserl pointed to the a-regional transcendental subjectivity as constituting a "region" or "residuum." All concepts occurring in this connection are in a state of striking fluidity.[15] The equivocal terminology of the *Ideas* is not, however, the result of literary negligence, but is rather a specific expression of the basic perplexity which overshadows the beginning of phenomenological philosophy, the presence of which had to be very much in evidence with the first introduction to this philosophy.

Criticism's misconceiving of phenomenology as an epistemological attitude stemming from an originally "critical" beginning and directed toward the sphere of inner experience, and its resulting interpretation of the reduction as a disconnecting of the transcendent and a restriction to what is psychically immanent, does not follow solely from the generally raised objection that phenomenology, as a result of its hidden but operative ontologistic-intuitionistic methodological concepts, denaturalizes the intended "transcendental apperception" into an ontic one, and ends up with an empirical conception of the subject (even if this be sublimated in a psychological or "metaphysical" way). That this is so is clearly shown by the objection viewed as decisive by Zocher: phenomenology invalidates itself with a "dialectic of the concept of experience" which cannot be accounted for in terms of its dogmatic method. We do not have space here to develop the details of this carefully worked out objection and answer each point individually. We shall only clarify the basis upon which it rests. The objection gains its weight from the question concerning the nature of the noema. Is the noema itself "immanent" or "transcendent"? Does it constitute a legitimate theme for phenomenology, or is a noematic phenomenology a contradiction? In this connection Zocher expressly proceeds from the assumption that phenomenology is the thematization of the immanent, the sphere of subjective experiences, and that this immanent sphere is further defined by the "criterion" of not presenting itself through perspectival configurations (*Sich-nicht-Abschatten*). If the noema is given through such configurations, then it cannot be immanent and therefore cannot belong to phenomenology's thematic. If, however, it does not present itself perspectivally, then the criterion is false and phenomenology is extended to a sphere which has not been methodologically legitimized. Zocher sees the true cause for this *aporia* in the ontologistic context of the noema-concept, a context which he views as requiring to be surmounted for the sake of a critical (i.e., developed in terms of a theory of meaning) concept of the noema. Thus, here also "critical" motives are suspected in Husserl, motives which have been distorted by his method's harmful dogmatism. Essential for us is the fact that this objection clearly shows the equation of phenomenology with an epistemological position related to the sphere of "subjective experiences." The basis for this objection can only, however, be destroyed by referring to the performance of the reduction. We must carry out the principal division between the psychological and the transcendental concepts of the noema. In an intentional psychology (a psychology which remains upon the basis of the natural attitude) the object of investigation (be this inductive or eidetic) is the actual and potential conscious life of a being existing in the manner of a "subject": thus its acts of experiencing, valuing, willing, and so on, its habitual convictions, views, and so on. Acts, however, have their essential intentional meaning. They are what they are only as an act of *meaning (meinende)*. This, however, signifies that they cannot be thematized without taking into account the moment of meaning (*Sinn*) lying within them. The real, factual being of the immanent is always a "having-a meaning." To ask here where this "meaning" is located, whether inside or outside, is in principle senseless. (But we certainly do not wish here to contest the legitimacy of raising the ontological question concerning the being of the noema.) Understood psychologically, the noema is not in itself transcendent and does not present itself through perspectival configurations; only the object of a transcendent perception is presented in this way within a manifold of noematic meaning-constituents. Defining the psychological noema as the *meaning* of an experience has nothing to do with the critical concept of "meaning" (as a transcendental-logical acceptance, perhaps) but must be grasped with reference to the essence of intentionality. The transcendental, that is, the truly phenomenological, concept of the noema can, however, be characterized solely within the horizon of the phenomenological reduction. Just as the *epoché* does not disconnect the intramundane belief and is not a reduction to the inner sphere of the psychical (together with the "representation of the world" lying within it) but discovers, by bracketing the world, that belief in the world which is to be bracketed (more precisely: the true world-apperception which gives the world in advance and which places this new thematic into play, and the belief in the world which is continually functioning within this apperception), so also does the *epoché* present the possibility of determining the correlate of this belief, which, formally expressed, is its "noema." In other words, the transcendental noema is the world itself viewed as the unity of acceptances contained within the belief which belongs to transcendental subjectivity's flowing world-apperception. If the psychological noema is the *meaning* of an actual intentionality which is to be distinguished from the being itself to which it is related, then by contrast the transcendental noema is this being itself. That it would be quite incorrect to discuss this with reference to some "criterion" of immanence is as clear as the absurdity of the question whether or not there is a being which "corresponds" to the transcendental noema; whether, that is, the transcendental noema is related to an object. Do we not here openly contradict the *Ideas*? To be sure, the *Ideas* treats the question of the noema's relation to the object, but it does so by distinguishing between the noema considered as an object within the context of how it is given and the object considered as that which is noematically identical within the continually changing noemas. The *Ideas* does not give a thorough discussion of the difference between the psychological and the transcendental noemas. But, as continually carried out within the attitude of the phenomenological reduction, the correct distinction of noema and object is *eo ipso* meant transcendentally. The extensive and important analyses of noesis and noema are nevertheless invested with a peculiar ambiguity, for with respect to content they are equally valid in the psychological attitude; they are, so to speak, indifferent to the distinction between phenomenology and psychology. The noema's proper relation to the object must then be commented upon differently according to whether the psychological or transcendental concept of the noema is involved. Insofar as it is related to a thing which transcends the psyche, the psychological noema is not a mirror image of the thing which exists somewhere "out there," but is rather that meaning of experience through which the object which exists in itself is made accessible in itself through a certain infinite relativity in the course of the fulfilling identification of this object. The psychological noema refers to an object which is independent of it and which announces and exhibits itself within this noema. The transcendental noema cannot refer to a being beyond and independent of the infinity involved in such endless identification; the transcendental noema is the being itself, and is so in the hitherto unknown depths of its hidden meaning of being as transcendental acceptance. Here "relation to the object" only has the sense of referring an actual noema (i.e., the correlate of an isolated transcendental act) to the manifold of act-correlates which, through the synthetic cohesion of constant fulfillment, first forms the unity of the object as an ideal pole.

What does this disturbing indifference displayed by the *Ideas* to the differentiation of phenomenology from psychology mean? The difference as such is adequately known. Nevertheless, the primary interest in the first book of the *Ideas* (the only one, unfortunately, which has been published) must have focused upon demonstrating the real possibilities of working along the lines of *intentional* inquiry and therefore, after the basic introduction of the phenomenological reduction, the principal interest in working out the new idea of phenomenology remains in the background. Although philosophically initiated by the reduction, the phenomenological analysis of subjectivity occasionally moves ambiguously between phenomenology and psychology and analyzes, so to speak, the most elementary and basic forms of intentionality within the context of a twofold relevance. The ambiguity in terms of which the thematic analyses of the *Ideas* are to be understood (in having both phenomenological and psychological relevance) is not a dangerous one so long as one genuinely moves along with these analyses—purposely neutral with respect to this differentiation—and keeps the overall sense of the transcendental-phenomenological aim firmly in view. It becomes fateful for understanding the *Ideas*, however, if these intentional expositions of the active life of transcendental subjectivity are viewed as being so complete that the idea of the phenomenological transcendental philosophy could be adequately defined, judged, and criticized with reference to them. Only by entering thoroughly into what is gained by each person carrying out the outline of the reduction given in the *Ideas* can this text provide full insight into the essence of phenomenology. Since Criticism's critique has deferred access to the original meaning of the phenomenological reduction by assuming a similarity in the basic problems of phenomenology and Criticism, it must necessarily mistake the *Ideas'* methodological character and interpret the increasingly evident deviation of the phenomenological concept of transcendental subjectivity from the critical concept as phenomenology's becoming lost in an empirical ontologization of the "epistemological ego," an ego which, although "spiritualized" by phenomenology as a consequence of its "critical" ambition, coincides in content with the sphere of physical immanence.

However, if the phenomenological reduction cannot be understood from either the critical position or from the ("subjectivistic") position of philosophical immanence, how can its character be formulated in a positive manner? It can be formulated in certain theses. The phenomenological reduction is not primarily a method of simply "disconnecting," but one of *leading back*. It leads, through the most extreme radicalism of self-reflection, the philosophizing subject *back through itself* to the transcendental life of belief (a life which is concealed by the subject's human self-apperception) whose acceptance-correlate, the world, "is." In other words, it is the method for discovering and exposing a knowledge-thematic which is in principle *nonworldly:* the dimension of the origin of the world. This means that the thematic is neither a realm of beings in the world nor the *a priori* form of the world itself. Does not phenomenology thereby fall into an abstruse "metaphysics," whose *Organon* would be some sort of "mystical" intuition? Does it not posit some sort of "speculative world of the beyond"? Not at all. The *epoché* is not a "royal path," but the most extreme striving for a theoretical self-surmounting of man, a *way of knowledge* to the "absolute" which traverses transcendental experience and

Eugen Fink

thought. This knowledge is intuitive (*intuitive*) if we understand by this *true self-givenness* and not "intuition" (*Anschauung*) as a human capacity for knowledge opposed to discursive thought. (The "epistemology" of phenomenological knowledge is a particular problem within the transcendental theory of method.) But where does this knowledge lead, and what does it prove? To the transcendental consciousness in which the world is accepted? Every characterization of this consciousness as a "field," realm, dimension, and so on, is *false,* even when we designate it as a domain lying outside of the world. No matter how important it is to determine the *irreality* of the transcendental subject (in opposition to the critical critique) as something nonworldly, we have thereby only indicated a task: the keeping of all mundane representations belonging to any sort of knowledge-thematic at a distance. Every being in the world is situated within horizons of familiarity and is manifested within the essential regional character of the worldly domain which belongs to it. The reduction, however, does not lead to a being already familiar in its general structure, for transcendental subjectivity is not disclosed by the pregivenness of its "*a priori*" forms of being. The reduction leads us into the darkness of something unknown, something with which we have not been previously familiarized in terms of its formal style of being. The reduction is not a technical installation of a knowledge-attitude which, once established, is finished and complete once and for all, and which one must simply accept in order to wander subsequently through a domain which lies upon one and the same level, but is rather an unceasing and constant theme of phenomenological philosophy. The first stage of the reduction leads to the transcendental ego, the "point of breakthrough" to the absolute. A *life-stream of acts* thereby comes to phenomenological self-givenness. The intentional explication of this first and provisional theme of phenomenology is exposed to the constant danger of stepping beyond this self-givenness in being misled by the mundane meaning of concepts required by this explication. The "presence" of this actual flowing life is not to be grasped in terms of the mundane understanding of the totality of time, thus immediately assigning a past and a future to this present, nor can the "egoness" of the transcendental ego be sketched out beforehand in terms of our understanding of the human ego (its individuation). The transcendental ego has no "limits," that is, it cannot be known from the start in the full extent of its being. Here the opposition to the psychological thematization of subjectivity is particularly striking. The subjective time of the psychical life of acts is ordered in terms of world-time and is viewed as being in the world. In the psychological interpretation we move beforehand within an understanding of the totality-structures of the human subject. The object of inquiry is always the psychical, which is identically valid for all, not a factual and solitary psychical life. By contrast, transcendental knowledge of egological subjectivity is not carried out within the medium of universality, that is, of validity for every transcendental subjectivity, but is limited to the *one* factual streaming life of acts. But the concepts "one" and "factual life of acts" are *worldly concepts* in origin. They contain everything superfluous in the sense of requiring an explicit reduction. To this extent phenomenology is in a state of permanent perplexity as to how to express what it makes visible in evident self-givenness. But the streaming life of acts alone does not constitute the object of the first phenomenological knowledge. There is also the world as the transcendental "noema" which belongs to the life of acts. The theorizing "observer" posits as existing transcendentally both the "life of acts," which does not stand within any horizon of structural prefamiliarity, and the *world as phenomenon.* Phenomenology's methodological advance, which we can only briefly indicate, is determined by elucidating the "ego" in making use of the "world-phenomenon" as a clue. From the acceptances which, in their totality, come together to form the acceptance-totality "world," the phenomenologizing observer inquires into the life from which they originate, and thereby acquires the motivation (which abides in the "transcendental" itself) to push the reduction further in the direction of a complete unfolding of transcendental being.

Transcendental egology becomes transcendental "monadology." The questioning of intentionality, in which the other is first accepted as another human being who stands within the "world-phenomenon," leads to the transcendental exhibiting of a coherence of being among a uniquely structured plurality of transcendental egos, a coherence which the "metaphysical" title "monad" only serves to point out and not exhaustively characterize. Just as the transcendental ego cannot be thought of in terms of the idea of worldly singularity, this "monadology" in no way signifies that a massive plurality has been transposed into the transcendental sphere. The mutual *implication* of monads is the important title of a problem concerning the nonextensive being of the monadic plurality: the nonindividuated relation of one monad to another, a relation which is possible only transcendentally. (In the *Cartesian Meditations* Husserl has presented the first stages of an explication of the transcendental monad-totality. The analysis of the "experience of another ego" in the fifth meditation is only a *development* of the reduction, and not a thematic interpretation of "empathy.") Yet the transcendental monad-totality is not the final and adequate concept for transcendental subjectivity, for it designates only the *first stage* of the phenomenological conquest of absolute subjectivity. Reference to this fact is important here because Criticism's critique of phenomenology presupposes that phenomenology's meaning can be fully determined on the basis of the published fragments of the *Ideas*. (Wherever Husserl's later writings are taken into account their principal meaning remains subject to the critical interpretation of the *Ideas*.) Since the "critique" thus does not break into the idea of the phenomenological philosophy by actually performing the reduction, but on the contrary determines its meaning with reference to the thematic analysis of subjective acts, by construing it as a method for acquiring the sphere of immanence, or by construing phenomenology's provisional self-explication (as the return to an irreal, nonempirical subject) as a method for constructing an "epistemological ego," it basically remains affixed to misinterpretations of the most provisional preparatory concepts. It not only misconstrues its "object," but also fails even to come close.

Can this, however, be raised as an objection against it? In Husserl's published writings the idea of phenomenology is not fully developed in terms of a complete formulation of the phenomenological concept of philosophy. The reason for this is a conscious repressing of all empty anticipations of the system. If the reduction can be presumed, thereby granting the possibility of each one grasping the meaning of phenomenology for himself, the phenomenological inquiry can humbly begin with the elucidation of "consciousness." With the method of intentional analysis, phenomenology realizes a manner of knowing which, upon the basis of the natural attitude, not only possesses significance for the radical reform of psychology, but which is also suited for converting the highest surmises of speculative philosophy into a genuine and accountable inquiry.

As phenomenology's permanent *desideratum,* however, the reduction not only has stages relating to the thematic disclosure of transcendental subjectivity, but also has stages belonging to methodological considerations of the concepts which serve to explicate this subjectivity. We must note this here because the critique with which we are concerned can first be answered with reference to these stages. The issue is that concerning the reduction of the idea of being and the reduction of the idea of eidetics. To what extent is the critical objection that phenomenology clarifies beings by means of beings justified? Even if intramundane beings are not clarified by having recourse to other mundane beings (clarifying transcendence, perhaps, by means of immanence), is not the world as the totality of beings clarified by returning to a being which exists apart from this totality: transcendental subjectivity? By no means! Even though it is impossible to define the transcendental life without making use of the concept of being, the mundane and the transcendental are not simply distinguished as two universal regions of being; rather are they distinguished in the *mode of their being.* The idea of being which is originally given within the horizon of the world (and whose formalization as the predicative concept of the "is" still remains related to the world) must be *reduced.* The transcending of the worldly idea of being must be taken up into the concept of "transcendental being." If, in the eristic judgment of the Neo-Kantian critique, phenomenology is "ontological," then it must first be determined whether or not the critique attributes the *mundane* concept of being to phenomenology. This also holds for Zocher's objection that the eidetic carries ontologizing tendencies into the determination of the transcendental subject. To be sure, the *Ideas* does not distinguish between the mundane and transcendental eidetics. But the very difficult separation of the two cannot be brought into view and explicitly enacted at the provisional stages of the *Ideas.* It is a fundamental mistake to wish to understand the nature of the reduction in terms of the opaque eidetic presented, instead of, on the contrary, viewing the question of the nature of the transcendental eidos as a problem emerging out of the performance of the reduction.

Although the determination of transcendental subjectivity in the *Ideas* is thematically and methodologically provisional, an important anticipation of the further course of the phenomenological problematic is yet given by the explicit indications of the transcendental problem of *constitution.* We hereby encounter the central and fundamental concept of phenomenological philosophy. The true theme of phenomenological inquiry can be determined only in relation to this concept. While (to the extent that this is explained in the *Ideas)* the performance of the reduction could, by exposing the nonworldly sphere of transcendental subjectivity, carry with it the impression of establishing a *world-transcendent* thematic for philosophy in contrast to the traditional world-related thematic, insight into the phenomenological theory of constitution does away with this impression and clarifies the *transcendental* (i.e., the retention of the world in transcending the world) character of phenomenology's answer to the world-problem. The true theme of phenomenology is neither the world on the one hand, nor a transcendental subjectivity which is to be set over and against the world on the other, but the *world's becoming in the constitution of transcendental subjectivity.* As the *logos* of the world which is discovered by the reduction as the transcendental acceptance-phenomenon, "phenomenology" is the theoretical exhibiting of the world-forming constitution: it is essentially *"constitutive* phenomenology." Although the sole meaning of the philosophical understanding of the world is that of the constitutive analysis of the world, this cannot be set in motion immediately after the performance of the reduction. As the elucidation of the transcendental monad-totality, the first stage of the reduction moves indeterminately within the explication of the relationship between transcendental subjectivity and the world, its "noematic correlate." It necessarily speaks of the transcendental "belief in the world," "experience of the world," "meaning of the world," of "having-the-world-in-acceptance," and so forth. This means that it still expounds this relationship in concepts which are essentially worldly. Their meaning still retains the moment of *receptivity* which makes up the inner essence of *human* experience. Only by adding the term "transcendental" can the difference be indicated, although in a purely negative and prohibitive manner. Whatever positive meaning such terms as transcendental "experience," "intending," and so forth, have, this meaning cannot yet be determined on the provisional problem-levels. Phenomenology's further advance occurs by clarifying the inner character of the relation between transcendental subjectivity and the world as one of "constitution." (We can only suggest at this point that the constitutive relation cannot be construed along the lines of a *"relation between. . . ."*) Let us now briefly outline the initial formulation of the question of constitution.

The phenomenological reduction first exposes a subjectivity which *already* accepts the world, and which therefore does not first begin to construct its "transcendental" acceptance (a subjectivity which in this case could be known theoretically directly in terms of its construction of these acceptances). The transcendental subject's (or the monad-totality) *possession of the world,* which is disclosed by the reduction, is the *problem* with which the analysis of constitution begins insofar as the true character of this problem remains indeterminate. The initial mastery of this problem is to be found in the thorough analysis of the actual flowing transcendental "experience" of the world. Methodological access to the hidden inner essence of the processes of transcendental achievement is gained by the intensive interrogation of intentionality. Insight into the secret nature of the actual being-"acceptances" which are in the process of being formed in the stream of intentional life (but which nevertheless already rest upon the foundation of a universal possession of acceptances, the possession of a world) now becomes the clue for interrogating the transcendental world-possession: the inquiry into constitution. The awakening of sedimented constitutive processes is held together by the unity-title "world," but is differentiated into a manifold of constitutive disciplines corresponding to the regional structuring of the "world-phenomenon" (e.g., the constitutive theory of nature, animal life, man, etc.). Not only does the world as the universal unity of all regions present its own constitutive problem in terms of which all particular and regionally oriented "disciplines" must undergo principal revisions, but there are other necessities for such revisions as well. The problematic of constitution does not lie upon one methodological level. Thus, for example, the egological (primordial) analysis of constitution is essentially provisional and must be revised by bringing in the constitutive problematic of transcendental intersubjectivity. Nor does this latter designate the ultimate ground of constitution. Reference to the need for revising the initial constitutive analyses only serves to indicate the internal *multiple-leveled* character of phenomenology, thereby calling attention to the difficulty of a definitive determination of the essence of "constitution." In the *Ideas,* as well as in almost all of Husserl's published writings, the uniqueness of the constitutive analysis has not been explicitly presented.[16] The reason for this lies in the fact that setting about the analysis of constitution necessarily requires that the basis for all inquiry into constitution be unfolded to its full extent. This means that, in the *indeterminateness* of its relation to the world, transcendental subjectivity must first undergo a provisional explication of its most elementary structures. Such an explication, which still foregoes the closer determination of the relation between the transcendental ego (or the monad-totality) and world, moves within the context of elucidating the intentional character of "subjective" *acts* in which the "world" (as actual transcendental noema) comes to be accepted and the *habitualities* in terms of which the having-in-acceptance holds as such. Since, however, at one point this elucidation analyzes intentionality chiefly in terms of the totality-forms within which intentionality is already uncovered in intentional psychology (and thus upon the basis of the natural attitude), and since the inner character of transcendental intentionality (over and against the psychical and intramundane intentionality) still remains provisionally indeterminate, the misunderstanding can arise which equates the transcendental and provisional analysis of acts and habitualities with a psychological analysis. A particular motive for such confusion lies in Husserl's occasionally speaking as if the act-intentional explication of transcendental subjectivity is already a constitutive analysis. This, however, can only be understood as an *anticipation* which becomes intelligible in terms of the fundamental relationship between the act-intentional explication of transcendental subjectivity and its analysis in terms of constitution. This relationship can be briefly characterized as the relationship between *constituted* and *constituting* intentionality. The intentionality which is *given* is the psychical intentional life (as the manner in which man is in the world) prior to all philosophical illumination. The course of this life is cast into determinate relief and becomes differentiated into acts, opinions, and so on. Through the reduction, however, the transcendental life which is continually *concealed* by the given worldly life is exposed and first becomes visible in terms of a structure which accords and coincides with the psychical life. Seen in this perspective, the reduction acquires the character of a method which

Eugen Fink

inquires beyond the worldly and objectivized intentional stream of life (as an intramundane psyche). The reduction *deobjectifies* transcendental life and casts off its worldliness by removing the self-apperception which makes it worldly by situating it within the world. The reduction thereby succeeds in penetrating into those depths of the intentional life of belief where the psychical life's self-apperception is first validly constructed. The phenomenological reduction has led out of the imprisoning bias of self-interpretation by returning to the transcendental "life of belief" for which this bias is a correlative acceptance-constituent. But what exactly "acceptance-constituent" can signify at this point remains indeterminate. It is important to sustain this indeterminacy and first to acquire the full breadth of the reductively disclosed apperceiving coherencies of transcendental life in its proper context: the transcendental monad-totality which is implied by the ego and which constitutes phenomenology's first and provisional problem-level. Once this first stage has been unfolded, the assault upon the inner character of the "possession of the world through acceptance" can and must be initiated, thereby disclosing the deeper constituting strata of transcendental life. Not only does the meaning of the "relation" between world and transcendental subjectivity become fully discernible here for the first time, but also now the *act-intentional* analysis of transcendental life can be recognized as a necessary mid-stage which, however, must be surmounted. The transition from the provisional act-intentional explication of subjectivity *after* the reduction to the clarification of the constitutive essence of intentionality is not only carried out by way of differentiating them and revealing their inner implications, but is, above all, also carried out as an exhibiting of transcendental intentionality's *productive* (*produktiven*) character. Here the opposition to the given, intramundane intentionality is stressed. The psychical intention is essentially *receptive;* in terms of its own self-illumination, it is performed as a *means of gaining access* to a being which in itself is independent of this intention. As we have already stated, through the reduction we return to an intentional life for which the intramundane life's self-interpretation as a passive life is an "acceptance-correlate." If we can no longer interpret this transcendental life as being receptive, its true character still remains indeterminate. Its constitutive interpretation identifies it first as a *creation.* No matter how harsh and doctrinaire this definition of the essence of constitution as a productive creation may sound, it at least indicates the opposite to the receptive character (the requirement of something existing in itself) of the ontic and mundane (psychical) life of experience. (Here we cannot give further clarification of the fact that "constitution" signifies neither a receptive nor a productive relation, but one which is unattainable through ontic concepts and which can be indicated solely through the enactment of constitutive investigations.)

Up to this point we have indicated three different concepts of intentionality: 1. psychical (or receptive) intentionality; 2. the transcendental act-intentionality (whose nature is indeterminate); 3. the transcendental-constitutive (productive-creative) intentionality. We do not mean to signify different intentionalities with these different concepts, but only *one* intentional life viewed at different levels. Thus the intramundane psychical "life" is in fact none other than the transcendental world-preceding life, but is such in being *concealed* from itself in a form of "constitutedness." The reduction breaks through this "constituted" layer which is documented by worldly self-apperception and exposes the pure transcendental life. But even the latter life can be viewed as a *constituted* life (and even constituted with the "indeterminacy" peculiar to it) so long as the explication moves upon the first and provisional stage of phenomenology described above. Insofar as the reduction has provided access to the constituting essence of intentionality, however, Husserl can, by way of looking ahead to phenomenology's higher levels, designate the transcendental life explicated within the first stage of the problem (a stage which is essentially defined by act-intentional explication) as a "constituting" life. Only in this limited sense does the *Ideas* speak of constitution. It is important for us to discuss this limitation, since Criticism's objections to the phenomenological idea of constitution are entirely directed against the merely anticipatory passages of the *Ideas*. It must be admitted that the critique could indeed have no other point of departure for its attack, but, by neglecting the prior appropriation of the reduction, it has destroyed the possibility of seeing the provisional indeterminacy in the idea of constitution as presented in the *Ideas* and has pushed it into the "determinateness" of a critically established (and then ontologically divergent) theory of constitution. Here the critical critique also remains true to its interpretational schema: it identifies the "critical" and phenomenological problems of constitution in order to confirm immediately the fact that a deviation has occurred as a result of phenomenology's methodological dogmatism. A formulation of the problem of constitution is now assumed for Husserl in which the two defining moments of intentional "meaning" and hyletic matter correspond to the heterological moments of the critical idea of constitution (*a priori* valid form and given content). But Husserl's critical start already falls short of Criticism's more pregnant formulations in that he has limited the concept of given content to purely sensory contents (*sensualism*) and has posited the concept of "meaning not with reference to a thinking (judging) epistemological ego" but to a contemplative one. This partially correct critical beginning is now modified by phenomenology's basic and unsurmounted "intuitionistic-ontologistic" character into a psychologistic-subjectivistic idea of constitution.

How can we answer this objection? To the extent that this is absolutely required, we shall first attempt to formulate the principal difference between the critical and phenomenological ideas of constitution. Starting from Criticism's basic epistemological position, we can designate its problem as the question of the possibility of objective knowledge. In contrast to the naive interpretation of knowledge which simply accepts the object as something existing in itself, Criticism refers to the *a priori* conditions of objective knowledge which lie at the basis of every real and objectively true act of knowledge. For Criticism this prior basis is the *a priori* constitution of the object of knowledge which we can bring into view by "constructing" a model of the theoretical object in general. However it may stand with respect to the validity of this sort of philosophical theory, it is important for our purposes that phenomenology does not develop its idea of constitution, which possesses an entirely different nature, from the same epistemological problem. For phenomenology, it is not a question of a constitution of the knowledge object by means of a prior ("transcendental"-subjective) projection of the objectivity of objects (in the theoretical judgment-functions of the epistemological ego) but of the *constitution of the world.* In other words, the critical idea of constitution is still *mundane* insofar as it permits beings (as the correlate of objective knowledge) to be constituted through the *a priori* form of the world, whereas the phenomenological concept of constitution is directed toward the structure of the world in its totality, a structure which is first made accessible by the world-transcending method of the reduction which, although in principle "*outside*" of the world, yet *retains the world within itself.* The extent of Criticism's misunderstanding of "transcendental" constitution in the phenomenological sense cannot only be seen in the fact that it equates it (as a "start") with Criticism's world-immanent idea of constitution, but also in the fact that, as a "deviation," it is mistakenly equated with the intramundane relationship of immanence and transcendence. Even if (with respect to the phenomenological reduction) one clearly understands the entirely different directions of the critical and phenomenological ideas of constitution, it is still possible that one could hold the opinion that in one respect there is a certain affinity between these explicitly opposed ideas in that phenomenology, like Criticism, posits a heterological basic principle in the idea of constitution: "sensual *hyle*" and "intentional *morphe*"; subjective form and given content. Is this, however, actually meant as a heterological distinction? Not at all. This distinction is to be understood solely by explicitly observing the clearly provisional character of reference to the idea of constitution in the

Ideas. We have already indicated that this is the *naiveté of phenomenology's first problem-level*, which explicates intentional life in terms of its act-intentional articulation and leaves its internal character within that "indeterminateness" which indicates that intentionality's self-interpretation as essentially passive in nature is to be no longer held, but does not yet indicate the transcendental interpretation of intentionality as constitution. In the anticipatory indications of the constitution-problematic, constituting achievement is identified with an *act's* intentional bestowal of meaning so that, measured by this anticipatory concept of constitution, the deeper-lying constitution affected by transcendental temporalization (*Zeitigung*) cannot be cast into relief, thus permitting the "hyle" to appear as pure matter for this kind of intentional activity. In truth, however, there is no dualism of heterological moments in the phenomenological idea of constitution but only relative strata within the unified constitutive disclosure of the world's origin from within the depths of the transcendental subject's life. Both the hyle, which is first exhibited as the act's nonintentional moment, and the totality-form of the act itself are constituted within the depths of the intentional self-constitution of phenomenological time, a constitution which, however, does not proceed by means of acts.

Closely connected in both philosophies with the theory of constitution is their principal self-characterization as "transcendental idealism." Just as the critique which here concerns us generally passes over the difference between the phenomenological and the critical concepts of the "transcendental" and furthermore overlooks the distinctive differences between their ideas of constitution, its evaluation of phenomenology as "transcendental idealism" also rests upon a misunderstanding. Here we can only attempt to substantiate this with brief suggestions. We shall not enter into the extensive problematic of the question of idealism itself.

In addition to its "interpretations" of the basic phenomenological ideas of constitution and the reduction, the critique believes itself capable of showing identical beginnings in the definition of transcendental idealism with respect to the stand taken against subjective idealism common to both Criticism and phenomenology. That phenomenology turns against "subjective idealism" for quite different reasons remains concealed from the critique. This becomes clear to us when we keep in mind the two central conceptual polarities that play a decisive role in the critical and the phenomenological expositions of idealism. Whereas in the critical philosophy the opposition between "empirical" and the "transcendent" is dominant, and whereas, as transcendental idealism, the critical philosophy directly secures an empirical realism, phenomenology stands under the opposition between *"mundane"* and *"transcendental."* If Criticism discards subjective idealism as constituting the absolutizing of an (empirical) being because it clarifies beings by means of beings, thereby moving within a prephilosophical problematic, phenomenology turns against subjective idealism because it constitutes a definite form of that mundane idealism which it in general rejects. Phenomenology is not concerned with either a necessary relationship of transcendent beings to the intramundane sphere of immanence or a necessary relationship of beings in general to the *a priori* world-form. Phenomenological idealism concerns neither an intramundane priority of the existing human subject in contrast to all other beings, nor *a priori*ty of the form of subjectivity (the transcendental *a priori*) with respect to intramundane beings in general (as theoretical objects of knowledge); rather is it a question of the world-priority (*Weltvor-gängigkeit*) of a subjectivity, first discovered by the reduction, which is "transcendental" in a completely new sense. Phenomenological idealism is a *constitutive idealism* which essentially contains the world within itself by returning to constitutive origins. Such an idealism does not in principle signify "subjectivism." It is not a subjectivization of the totality of beings, nor is it their dissolution into the mundane kind of being belonging to the subject (as long as by "subject" we understand some sort of worldly concept, be this the being which we are, or the form of consciousness, or any such concept whatsoever). Phenomenology does not skip over the mundane independence of beings from man, his unimportance and insignificance in the cosmos, or the pure receptivity of our human knowledge; rather does it allow the unreflected realism of the natural attitude to remain. But *phenomenology* does not remain there; it brings the natural attitude to the point of being philosophically comprehended in a radical way by the reductive disclosure of the transcendental origin of the world, a disclosure with reference to which the world acquires an entirely new dimension which is capable of being inquired into and interpreted. What are unquestionably "primordial phenomena" for the natural attitude (and quite justifiably so for this attitude) are now accessible as a constitutive problem for a new kind of philosophical explication. Through the reduction phenomenology also transcends the possibilities of mundane philosophy. The world in its entirety, formerly the universal theme of all philosophy, can, through the reduction, be known as the result of a transcendental constitution: it is expressly taken back into the life of absolute subjectivity. This "reacceptance" has nothing at all to do with an ontic (philosophically immanent) or transcendental-*a priori* ("critical") subjectivization of the world, nor is it a means for relating the world to a mundane subject defined in one way or another: it is a transcendental comprehension of the world as a constituted objectification of absolute subjectivity. Since the natural attitude, the attitude within which all philosophy first begins, is essentially closed to the depths of the "transcendental," and, since as imprisoned within the world it can encounter no subjectivity other than intramundane or human subjectivity, the advance to a "subjectivism" which transcends all mundane forms of subjectivism requires the efforts of the phenomenological reduction. This phenomenological subjectivism is not opposed to the immediate truths of the natural attitude, an opposition which might, for example, take the form of disputing the independency of beings from the intramundane subject, but retains all such truths within itself; only it knows them as truths which belong to a determinate and relative (and, until now, absolutized) situation. It suspends them by raising them into the full transcendental truth which contains the mundane as a moment within it. The world is interpreted idealistically in phenomenology, but this does not signify a subjectivism which is burdened with the natural attitude's concept of the subject, but rather the scientific exhibiting and systematic unfolding of the *world's constitutive ideality.*

How can we further indicate the nature of this idealism? It is important first of all to keep all representations which would relate the world as the "one" back to a transcendental subject as the "other" at a distance. We have already indicated that by means of the phenomenological reduction we have for the time being come upon a provisional concept of transcendental subjectivity which is to be later surpassed by higher levels of phenomenology, and which is to be subsequently exhibited as making up a stratum of the self-constitutedness of the transcendental life which lies within the transcendental itself. We have thereby anticipated the problem of revealing transcendental subjectivity with recourse to strata of self-objectification up through the final, no longer objectified, primordial ground. Accordingly, we are now permitted to view the world itself as a "stratum" within transcendental life, a stratum which functions as the terminating level of all constitutive processes and which allows the world to arise. In the natural attitude we know nothing of the status of the world within the universe of absolute life. The world is accepted by us as a self-sufficient "universe" within which we ourselves are present as beings among other beings. It is the reduction which first knowingly draws the world back to its origin and discloses the world's transcendental ideality (as the terminating objectification of the absolute spirit). No matter how speculative this advance notice of the meaning of phenomenological idealism may sound, it is not a "metaphysical construction" issuing from a conviction in some previously adopted position, but is rather the simple formulation of the basic knowledge won by the phenomenological reduction, which says nothing when taken as an empty formula, but which can

131

say a great deal when taken as the guiding thought for concrete constitutive analyses.

In both this sketch of phenomenological idealism and in the provisional discussion of the basic phenomenological concepts of the reduction and constitution, the differences between phenomenology itself and the image of phenomenology which Criticism has shaped have become quite noticeable. Here we can desire no more than this. But what significance does such a critique have for phenomenology's own self-understanding? With this question we strike out in two directions. First: Is the problematic to which phenomenology is reduced in this critique one which, in one way or another, occurs within the totality of the phenomenological philosophy? If so, how is it to be characterized? Second: Does a critique which is mistaken, even though it is based upon a thorough study of phenomenological texts, have positive value? We shall now, by way of conclusion, attempt to answer these two questions.

The critical critique views phenomenology in terms of the interpretational schema with which we are now familiar and which, we maintain, is both false and inadequate in both directions. In this schema phenomenology (no matter what its philosophical aspirations are) is first treated as a positive science (as the thematization of the sphere of immanence) and then (at least at the start, where it coincides with Criticism) as a "transcendental-*a priori*" theory of the possibility of objective knowledge. The fact that every positive science first of all finds itself at home within the natural attitude from which it emerges and within which it remains, and the fact that the equation of phenomenology with the positive science of psychology signifies a removal of the former to what is in principle a prephilosophical problem-level, is illuminating. But what does the characterization of phenomenology as a "transcendental philosophy" akin to Criticism mean? Does not this problematic, presumably merely affixed to phenomenology by the critique, actually occur within phenomenology itself? We indeed encounter this problematic and we do so upon the basis of the natural attitude. In order to justify this assertion, however, we must investigate the problem to which Criticism gives an answer. This problem is that of the "*a priori.*" Criticism clarifies the puzzling priority of the universal preacquaintedness with beings prior to the experience of determinate beings as the *a priori* form of the world (which is shaped prior to all experience in the judgmental functions which belong to the epistemological ego and which are related to the "transcendental acceptances"). Now in what form does the same problem genuinely appear in phenomenology? Phenomenology already characterizes the problem of the *a priori* upon the basis of the natural attitude (and thus in an essentially prephilosophical attitude) as the problem of the *world's pre-*

Husserl's Philosophy and Contemporary Critisicism

givenness.[17] The givenness of beings in human experience is always situated beforehand within the horizon of prefamiliarity, the regional familiarity with the factually given. We always move *a-thematically* within the boundaries of a unique knowledge of essences, even though this is not a movement within the determinateness of an eidetic fixation of essences. As human beings we are always open to nature, animals, other men, and the realm of beings in general. Just as surely as this standing open of man to the horizon of being which forms the style of the world prior to the determinate experience of individual beings belongs to the very essence of man, thus presenting a purely *a priori* "habituality" which cannot, like various empirical habitualities, be traced back to an original intuition in time, so in principle does every explication of the *a priori* pregivenness of the world remain upon the basis of the natural attitude as long as man remains defined as that subjectivity with reference to which this problem is to be answered. It is still a human subjectivity which is at issue when a definite and abstract method purposely disregards man's empirical and concrete being and returns to the pure unindividuated form of consciousness in general. Man, at least minimally, is still the basis for abstracting to the epistemological ego. Phenomenology does not remain attached to the prephilosophical (i.e., taking place within the horizon of the natural attitude) explication of the world's pregivenness. Through the reduction it acquires not only the possibility of inquiring into the transcendentally reduced experience of individual beings, but also the possibility of a *constitutive* inquiry into the knowledge of essences which essentially belongs to man, thereby making the *a priori* style of the world itself the theme of a constitutive analysis. The constitutive interpretation of the mundane *a priori* made possible by the reduction is alone first capable of transforming the problem-basis to which the critical critique attempts to reduce phenomenology into a philosophical one. We can now see at least this much: for phenomenology, both forms of interpretation (as a critical beginning and as a deviation from this beginning) must, when measured against its own self-understanding, signify its projection upon a prephilosophical problem-basis. That is, both interpretations place phenomenology into a situation which is *dogmatic.* Now what are we to understand by the phenomenological concept of dogmatism, and how is it different from the critical concept with which it is occasionally identified by the critique? If the latter concept formally signifies a biased attitude toward beings (the positive knowledge-attitude) together with the naive positing of objects as things in themselves which are independent of the experiencing subject (a bias, consequently, toward truth as correspondence in terms of which our knowledge is directed toward things), dogmatism, understood phenomenologically, signifies a biased preoccupation with the

Eugen Fink

natural attitude, that is, every philosophy which does not pass through the reduction is, in phenomenology's judgment, necessarily dogmatic. Thus the thematic comportment of our everyday experience as well as the theoretical procedures of the positive sciences, the epistemological attitude toward eidetic affairs (mathematics, for example), and also the philosophical knowledge of the *a priori* form of the world are all dogmatic in the phenomenological sense. They are only internal differentiations within the natural attitude, that is, within dogmatism itself. In terms of this determination of the phenomenological concept of dogmatism (even though it is somewhat vague), we are now able to reject Criticism's critique of phenomenology as the attempt to reduce phenomenology to the level of a dogmatic philosophy.

Is, however, the critique's significance for phenomenology's own self-understanding only that of presenting a mistaken interpretation against which phenomenology must guard itself? Has it no positive value for which phenomenology could be grateful? In rejecting the principles at work in Criticism's critique, we repeatedly found ourselves in the position of defending the meaning of phenomenology against the actual wording of certain texts. Herein lies the true significance which a careful critique, even though it is not successful, has for the phenomenologist himself: it focuses attention upon sources of misunderstanding; not in the external sense of drawing attention to certain textual "inaccuracies," but by calling attention to the unavoidable difficulties with which every phenomenological statement is involved. In other words, it brings the *"transcendental appearance"*[18] which phenomenology undeniably carries with it clearly into view. The major dimensions of this important problem of "transcendental appearance," which in various ways dominate the entire constitutive phenomenology, cannot be developed here. We shall content ourselves with pointing out a three-fold paradox which continually obscures the phenomenological problematic.

First of all, there is the *paradox of the position from which statements are made* (*Paradoxie der Situation der Äusserung*). Phenomenology is established by the performance of the reduction. The philosophizing ego thereby transforms itself into the phenomenologically theorizing ego, the "transcendental observer." As we have already seen in our consideration of the formal structure of the reduction's performance, the acceptance of the world has been set out of action for this ego and the world has become a pure "phenomenon." As we have stated, this theorizing ego stands in the transcendental attitude. No additional problem presents itself as long as this ego consistently proceeds in an inquiring manner, its self-giving knowledge being organized within the unity of a theoretical context. A unique paradox arises, however, when, philosophically directing itself to others, it first turns to the *communication* of its knowledge. Here the transcendental attitude now appears within the natural attitude as a philosophy which announces itself within the world. The "phenomenologist" addresses himself to the "dogmatist." Is such communication possible? Does not the phenomenologist withdraw from the transcendental attitude when he communicates? The phenomenologist's statements clearly presuppose a basis shared by both him and the dogmatist. Is such a basis given, or can one be produced? While all men, no matter how different their manner of thinking, share the common basis of the natural attitude, the phenomenologist has broken out of this basis in performing the reduction. Considered more closely, however, he must not step out of the transcendental attitude and return to the naiveté of the natural attitude in communicating with the dogmatist. Rather does he place himself within the natural attitude as within a transcendental situation which he has already grasped. His communication with the dogmatist is now burdened by the difficulty that, for the speaker, the position from which statements concerning phenomenological knowledge are made is transparent with respect to its transcendental meaning, whereas it is not so for the listener. Is it therefore possible for them to speak about the same things? In order to understand phenomenology, we must presuppose that one has developed the "transcendental attitude." Communication with the dogmatist thus has the meaning of a provisional transmission of phenomenological knowledge whose purpose is that of leading the other to the performance of the reduction on his own. We can in this way understand beforehand why it is necessary first to insert the reduction within the natural attitude in an "unmotivated" and "false" way, and we can also recognize the pure impossibility of an integral presentation of the reduction from the very start.

The second fundamental paradox is grounded within the first: it is the *paradox of the phenomenological statement.* The primary cause of this is the fact that the phenomenologist who desires to communicate has only worldly concepts at his disposal. He must express himself in the language of the natural attitude. The mundane meaning of the words available to him cannot be entirely removed, for their meaning can be limited only by the use of other mundane words. For this reason no phenomenological analysis, above all the analysis of the deeper constituting levels of transcendental subjectivity, is capable of being presented adequately. The inadequacy of all phenomenological reports, caused by the use of a mundane expression for a nonworldly meaning, also cannot be eliminated by the invention of a technical language. Since phenomenological communication is chiefly a communication addressed to the dogmatist, such a language would be devoid of meaning.

Eugen Fink

Phenomenological statements necessarily contain an internal conflict between a word's mundane meaning and the transcendental meaning which it serves to indicate. There is always the danger that the dogmatist will grasp only the mundane meaning of words and overlook their transcendental significance to such an extent that he will imagine his mistaken explication of phenomenology to be correct and capable of calling upon the text for its justification.

The third and final paradox is closely connected with the first two. It is the *logical paradox of transcendental determinations*. This does not mean that the sphere of transcendental subjectivity is a sphere in which no logic whatsoever would be valid, but indicates solely those logical *aporias* which occasionally occur in the determination of basic transcendental relations, relations which cannot be mastered by logical means (which, even in their formalization, are still related to the world). This can be clarified by an example. How are we to determine the identity of the transcendental and human egos? Are they simply the same ego viewed from two different perspectives, or are they separate egos? One is first tempted to determine this singular identity-in-difference, this sameness in being-other (*die Selbigkeit im Anderssein*), in terms of the clue offered by determinate relations of identity which persist throughout a variation of content (perhaps as identity in becoming, analogous to the identity of an organism, etc.). In principle, however, all *ontic forms of* identity are unable to define "logically" the *constitutive identity* of the transcendental and human egos. The two do not exist in an identical or analogous manner. The "identity" which prevails here is not a form of identity that can be determined within the horizon of the mundane idea of being, but is rather a form of identity which holds between a mundane being (defined in terms of the ontic idea of identity and its forms of content-variation) and a transcendental being (which in principle transcends the mundane idea of being). Is man therefore the absolute? Not at all. But neither is the absolute a "transcendent" reality beyond man and not encompassing him. Separating and distinguishing them is as false as their direct equation. In place of a "transcendent" relation between man and the world-ground we must posit a "transcendental" relation which does not overlook man's worldly finitude, frailty, and impotence, but which comprehends it as a constituted meaning, thereby taking it back into the infinite essence of spirit.

Perhaps our glance at the ineradicable "transcendental appearance" which accompanies all phenomenology provides us with deeper insight into the motive which forces the critical critique away from its object. We have not opposed this critique merely for the sake of polemic, but rather for the sake of formulating the possibility of a true discussion between Criticism and phenomenology. Prior to such discussion, both philosophies must be held separate. In this sense alone, our presentation here constitutes a small step in the direction of preparing this dialogical situation.

NOTES

1. The present article deals with the objections raised against phenomenology by the criticism represented by Rickert and his school. We shall essentially limit ourselves to the statements made by Zocher and Kreis, who have voiced the "critical" evaluation of phenomenology in an extremely penetrating and carefully thought out manner. Cf. Rudolf Zocher, *Husserls Phänomenologie und Schuppes Logik: Ein Beitrag zur Kritik des intuitionistischen Ontologismus in der Immanenzidee*, 1932: Friedrich Kreis, *Phänomenologie und Kritizismus,* in "Heidelberger Abhandlungen zur Philosophie und ihrer Geschichte," 1930.

2. The first manuscript notes concerning the phenomenological reduction appear in 1905. Two years later Husserl had already presented the reduction in his Göttingen lectures.

3. This is not intended as a reproach against those critics, particularly Zocher and Kreis, who investigate Husserl's publications intensively and with care (although, unfortunately, they have not sufficiently concerned themselves with the *Formale und transzendentale Logik*), but refers to the basic question as to whether in general, beginning from a mundane position (i.e., a philosophy which has not performed the phenomenological reduction), the essential content of phenomenology can be apprehended.

4. The Neo-Kantian Rickert defines the object of knowledge as nonexistent. It is a value which is held, an "ought." On this level the object of knowledge betrays a thoroughly normative character, a character the loss of which is threatened in Criticisms view when the object of knowledge is exclusively interpreted in terms of something which "is."—ED.

5. Kant, *Critique of Pure Reason*, A 84.—ED.

6. In this connection Husserl's phenomenology is not only misconceived by opposing directions in contemporary philosophy, but is also misconceived by the "ontological realists" within the so-called "phenomenological movement" itself. Even though their standards of evaluation differ, they are at one with the critical philosophy in their evaluation of Husserl's development. They interpret the period of the *Logical Investigations* as a "turning towards the object," as the discarding of an unfruitful epistemology by means of asking ontological questions, and see in the *Ideas* the influence of "Neo-Kantianism."

7. That the naive ontological question concerning ideal being is, with its very introduction, transformed (although this is still latent) into the phenomenological-*constitutive* problem of ideal objects becomes clear from Husserl's later writings, in which he repeats the problematic of the *Logical Investigations* upon the level of an explicitly transcendental philosophy (cf. *Formal and Transcendental Logic*).

8. The wide range of the concept of "being" (*Seiende*) does not signify the doctrinaire thesis that the real and the ideal are homogeneous just by virtue of their being two different

Eugen Fink

kinds of "being," but precisely leaves open the possibility of initiating an ontological inquiry into the different modes of being characteristic of the real and the ideal. The concept is thereby secured the free space required for the working out of its problematic from the very start.

9. Zocher's phrase.

10. In the first place, a general characterization counts as nothing with respect to understanding a philosophy which believes that it approaches its own thesis only by traversing comprehensive analytical evidences. In the second place, phenomenology's general self-interpretations in Husserl's published writings are *provisional*; i.e., are related to certain problematics taken as points of departure (for example, "ontology," and the "theory of knowledge"), which are subsequently modified in a radical manner and possess dangerous similarities to certain historical philosophers.

11. All phenomenology passes through the "reduction." A "phenomenology" which renounced the reduction would in principle signify a mundane philosophy, that is (understood, of course, phenomenologically), a dogmatic philosophy.

12. Kreis cites as a particular motive for this (next to the general ontologistic-intuitionistic tendencies) Husserl's holding fast to a precritical concept of knowledge. While Husserl obviously surrenders this concept with respect to knowledge of the transcendent and advocates a critical-transcendental constitution of the object, he yet attempts to save the precritical concept of knowledge for one sphere of beings, and this leads to the positing of the sphere of "immanence" as a sphere of absolute being.

13. It is precisely at this point that phenomenology's opposition to all forms of Kantianism becomes particularly evident. Kant's "transcendental apperception" is not at all opposed to the empirical ego as a higher self-dividing unity, but is simply the principle of the ego's indissoluble unity. In other words, it is the form of unity belonging to the world-imprisoned ego, the mundane ego.

14. We find an extensive characterization of this "psychological *epoché*" in Husserl's *Phänomenologische Psychologie* (Den Haag: Martinus Nijhoff, 1962). Just as the natural sciences "disconnect" all subjective elements of experience in order to arrive at a purely objective theme of inquiry, we can reverse this procedure in order to make the theme of inquiry the purely "subjective." Husserl's primary interest in this work, however; is to identify the "psychological *epoché*" as a preparation for and a way leading to the full transcendental reduction.—ED.

15. Thus, for example the concept "pure," which we mention only because Criticism's critique occasionally falls prey to the equivocation of the concept "pure ego." The pure ego does not signify the transcendental ego, but primarily signifies the ego-pole in contrast to the concrete ego of the stream of experience. Only with the reduction does the pure ego *qua* abstract ego-pole also become transformed into the "pure" ego in the sense of the transcendental ego.

16. By contrast, Husserl's unpublished manuscripts already constitute an extensive carrying out of the constitutive interpretation of the world.

17. And this indeed in a more rigorous form as the pregivenness of the surrounding world (*Umwelt*) which gives itself harmoniously in the flowing advance of perceiving modes of givenness—a world-unity which persists throughout the constant and endlessly open change from one surrounding world to another.

18. *Transzendentalen Schein*, a phrase referring to the feet that, seen from the point of view of the natural attitude, phenomenology's transcendental dimension gives rise to a distinctively enigmatic, paradoxical, and "misleading," appearance. The phrase itself is taken from Husserl. In the Formale und transzendentale *Logik* Husserl speaks of the "transcendental appearance of solipsism" (p. 213), meaning thereby that a certain "enigmatic" (the word is Husserl's own) quality is bestowed upon transcendental

subjectivity by the reductive procedure—the ego "appearing" to be solely a solipsistic ego—an enigma which, in this particular instance, is to be solved by the "systematic unfolding of the constitutive problematic," and this essentially by way of carrying out the analysis of the intersubjective strata of constitution. (See the article by Wagner below.) Husserl's employment of the word "enigma" is closely connected with another of his expressions which Fink has taken up in the present context. In the *Krisis* Husserl speaks of the "emergence of paradoxical obscurities" (§ 52). Phenomenology appears "opaque" to the natural attitude, an opaqueness which is perhaps best summed up by Husserl's well-known formulation of the "paradox of human subjectivity," a paradox which focuses upon the "contradictory" nature of human subjectivity as both an object within the world and a subject which constitutes the world (§ 53).—ED.

The Decisive Phases in the Development of Husserl's Philosophy[1]

Walter Biemel

SINCE its inception, phenomenology has grown so rich (I might almost say, has so richly proliferated) that today almost anyone can search out something from phenomenology's virgin forest without being unfaithful to or literally betraying phenomenology. It is just this rich development, however, which makes it advisable for a genetic reflection to consider carefully what Husserl's original intentions were and how they developed. For it is far from correct to say that phenomenology sprang with one leap from Husserl's mind fully armed and equipped; rather Husserl himself reached it through a step-by-step struggle.

If we should desire to search out phenomenology's point of origin, we must apparently go back quite a distance, back, namely, to Husserl's *Philosophy of Arithmetic* of 1891, or to the still earlier working out of the first chapter of this work, which appeared in 1887 under the title: *Concerning the Concept of Number.*

As justification for the author's aim in working with the concept of number, the preface to this work states: ". . . since by contrast with the older logic, the newer logic has understood its true task to be that of developing a practical discipline (the technique of making correct judgments) and has striven for a universal theory of the methods of science as one of its most important goals, it has found many urgent occasions to direct particular attention to the question of the nature of mathematical methods and the logical character of its basic concepts and principles" (p. 4). Husserl then immediately points out that the newer *psychology* has also directed its attention to this area, particularly with reference to the "psychological origin of the representations of space, time, number, continuum . . ." and it is assumed as self-evident that "the results of this same (psychology) must also have importance for metaphysics and logic" (p. 5). It would not be extraneous to consider this point of departure for a moment. It serves to indicate that at the start Husserl did not wish to modify, overthrow, or reestablish logic and psychology upon a new foundation, but rather that he borrowed the justification for his own investigations from the existing logic and psychology. This is not so astonishing in this case since it is a question of an inaugural dissertation.[2]

Both sciences upon which Husserl rests his investigation (logic and psychology) do not yet, however, provide the occasion for Husserl's kind of investigation. For Husserl, after a period of great discoveries in mathematics and their utilization, it is now time to inquire into the nature of its basic concepts.[3] The real impulse for Husserl's philosophizing, that which sets it in motion, is the inquiry into these basic concepts: more precisely, into "number," the basic concept of arithmetic.

It might first appear surprising that Husserl should attempt to clarify the concept of number by means of psychological investigations. One would assume that mathematical or logical discussions would have been much more appropriate. The concept of number and the activity of counting are viewed as one of the simplest psychical thought-processes which must be clarified if we are to advance to more complex activities (p. 9). The investigation of the concept of number is thus already directed to the analysis of an original phenomenon of thought in order to come to know something like the "essence" of consciousness.

How does Husserl proceed? He first cites the Euclidean definition of number. "Number is a plurality of unities." But Husserl sees at once that this definition is meaningless so long as the concept of plurality is not also thought out and analyzed. We do not reach the concept of plurality simply by abstracting from given contents. We reach this concept only by paying attention to *how* individual elements are *connected* to form a whole. It is this *connecting* which is decisive. We reach the important phenomenon of plurality by means of similarly formed connectings. Husserl clarifies this with another concept, that of the continuum. A continuum involves a continual connecting, for example, a continual connecting of line-points, moments of a duration, and so forth. In a concrete instance, for example, we can make note of the elements, points, and the extended parts which are composed of these moments, and then we can note "how they are actually connected." When we speak of a continuum we are not concerned with the kind of elements which are involved (for these can vary) but with the manner of composition which is common to all continua. But this manner of connecting is not exhibited in the immediate grasping of what is presented, but only in *reflecting* upon what is presupposed by the parts being related to each other in this way, for it is this which is decisive for a continuum.

Since the manner of connecting the parts is decisive, to reach the concept of a class of wholes it is, according to Husserl's theory, always

141

necessary that the manner in which the parts of this class are united to form a whole be brought into view through *reflection.*

What is the manner of connecting which defines an aggregate (plurality)? According to Husserl it is a *collective connecting.* In contrast to other ways of connecting, collective connecting is very loose, but it is nevertheless a connecting whose result is the concept of plurality. To reach the concept of plurality a spontaneous activity is required on the part of consciousness. We never reach something like plurality in a passive manner.[4]

Concerning the mode of being belonging to numbers, Husserl states: "Numbers are mental creations insofar as they form the results of activities exercised upon concrete contents; what these activities create, however, are not new and absolute contents which we could find again in space or in the 'external world'; rather are they unique relation-concepts which can only be produced again and again and which are in no way capable of being found somewhere ready-made" (*Concept of Number*, p. 37). This accords with this phase of his thought: numbers are relation-concepts and they *are* only insofar as a determinate kind of relation is produced. There *are* numbers only insofar as they are produced.

One could object that when we come across a plurality of objects in space we do have something like a numerical quantity. Husserl would be correct in rejecting this. Even when several spatial objects are set in some relation to each other, this connection is not yet the collective unifying performed within consciousness "through the act of taking interest and notice, an act which casts these elements into relief in a unified manner" (p. 37).

If the particular manner in which the parts stand related to each other is decisive for the concept of plurality, this must be discussed further. Husserl, by way of anticipation, points to two classes of relations: physical and psychical relations. He also terms physical relations "content-relations": for example, the relation of similarity, sameness, and so forth. This relation is established within the particular beings in question (be they physical or psychical). With respect to psychical relations, these are not founded in the affair itself but in our way of considering this affair (or affairs); it is also for this reason that the relations cannot be pointed at but can only be performed in thought. It is of decisive importance that the collective connecting is of the latter sort. Thus Husserl can state: "While . . . in all content-relations the degree of variation permissible in its foundation in order to preserve this specific kind of relation is limited, this foundation can, in the case of the collective connecting, be varied arbitrarily and without limit while the relation remains the same. . . . Not every content can be thought of as being similar to, continuously

The Development of Husserl's Philosophy

connected with, etc. (=content-relation), but they can always be thought of as being different and as collectively unified. In the two latter instances the relation is not immediately present within the phenomena themselves but is to a certain extent external to them" (p. 57). This externality means that it depends upon certain psychic acts whether the given contents are to be collectively connected or not, whereas it is not exclusively dependent upon consciousness if two objects are viewed as being similar or dissimilar. Husserl summarizes: "An aggregate arises when a unified interest, and within and along with it at the same time a unified taking notice, brings into relief and includes certain contents for itself" (p 58).[5]

In order to grasp the connecting-character of this collective connecting, a *reflection upon* the psychical act which causes this connecting is required.

How are these considerations related to the concept of number? "The concept of plurality . . . is a representation which concerns contents simply insofar as they are collectively connected" (pp. 59 f.). Something and something else, or this, this, and that, and so on, are brought together. "Something" here signifies any kind of representational content whatsoever; "something" expresses indifference to content, it being solely a matter of there being a content. The "and" indicates the manner in which the relate are connected, namely, that it is nothing beyond simply placing things together. If the indeterminacy associated with the concept of plurality is removed, if it is determined how many pieces ("something"), how many unities or individuals are placed together to make up the plurality, then we reach the concept of number. The plurality is thereby specified. When Husserl states that interest in and taking notice of such placing together are requisite for thinking of an aggregate, this means that an apprehension of unities qua unities and a placing together of unities which are noticed as such are needed. "We can imagine no collective unifying without unified contents, and if we should represent these *in abstracto* then the contents must be thought of as some kind of thing" (p. 63).

This somewhat detailed presentation of Husserl's thoughts was necessary not only because this early work is little known, but also because it is our opinion that the origin of his later phenomenology can be shown to be already present here, even though Husserl himself (primarily as a result of Frege's criticism[6]) abandoned this point of view as psychologistic. It is therefore not a question of showing that Husserl's interpretation of number is the only exhaustively correct interpretation, but only of pointing out the extent to which the first beginnings of the phenomenological procedure are detectable within it.

Which elements are truly fundamental? The concept of production (*Erzeugen*), the concept of *reflection,* the *method of exhibiting* the essence

143

of an affair by returning to the origin of its meaning in consciousness, and the description of this origin. We believe that within these elements we can discover the origin of the concepts of *constitution, reduction,* the exhibiting of the *origin of the bestowal of meaning,* phenomenological *description,* and phenomenological *essential insight.* Indeed, here is the origin of the fact that throughout his life Husserl considered psychology to be a thoroughly crucial science; not the traditional psychologism, be this either experimental or "external" psychology, but introspective psychology in Brentano's sense, a psychology whose structure and meaning Husserl delineated with increasing clarity up to the *Crisis.* Phenomenology's basic insight is that something essential is understood when psychical acts are grasped through reflection as being intentional. One may question the justification for this insight and one may discuss and criticize the metaphysical presupposition which posits the subjectivity which is its basis. These are moments of an interpretation which clearly cannot be attempted here.

One additional illustration of the significance of reflection. Husserl states: "The collective connecting can only be grasped by reflecting upon the psychical act through which the aggregate comes into being" (*Concept of Number*, p. 58; *Philosophy of Arithmetic*, p. 79). This statement remains unchanged in both versions, the first from 1887, the second from 1891. In the first version this statement was italicized. This is not accidental, for Husserl knew that it was a question here of a very crucial assertion, an assertion which would be decisive for his entire later thought. The psychical act through which a significance, a meaning, comes into being is to be grasped through reflection. Certainly in time the acts grasped in this way become differentiated and increase in number, but this does not change the fact that Husserl, presumably under the influence of Brentano's lectures on psychology, discovers and takes over this position at this point. (The extent to which Meinong's influence also plays a role cannot be discussed here. The edition of 1891 contains a marginal note alluding to Meinong: *Ps. Anal.* 27.)

One further reference to the thesis that the idea of constitution originates here. After commenting upon the origin of the concept of plurality from the unifying interest and the act of taking notice, through which the contents come to be presented together at one and the same time, Husserl refuses to designate numbers as "purely mental creations of an internal intuition" because "creation" for him signifies the production of a being which, as the being which is produced, possesses an existence independent from the act of production, as, for example, a work of art. On the other hand, he concedes that they can be viewed as mental creations insofar as they are the result of a mental activity. "Numbers are mental creations insofar as they are the results of activities we exercise upon concrete contents; however, what these activities create are not new and absolute contents which we could find again in space or in the 'external world'; rather are they unique concepts of relations which can only be produced again and again and which are in no way capable of being found ready-made" (p. 37). That there are structures which must be produced in thought in order to exist, and which therefore exist only insofar as they are produced in this way, that is, insofar as determinate thought-processes are set in motion, is *in nuce* the *idea of constitution* which occurs to Husserl in his attempt to grasp the essence of number. Formulated in this way, this idea is naturally exposed to the danger of psychologism, and is here even understood psychologistically. Consequently, the removal of this danger, the gaining of distance from himself insofar as he himself has fallen into psychologism, is the next decisive step in Husserl's philosophy. In this connection Husserl will also grasp in purer form what psychologism contains by way of justification.

The transition from Husserl's work on the *Philosophy of Arithmetic* to the *Logical Investigations* in which the well-known stand with respect to psychologism is taken is at first unclear. For the most part it appears to be an arbitrary jump which is nevertheless justified insofar as logical structures doubtlessly possess a certain kinship with mathematical objects when seen from a purely formal point of view. But this way of speaking, instead of actually exhibiting a new stage of development, remains too general. A recently discovered letter of Husserl's dating from 1890 sheds light on this development which was definitive for Husserl at that time (Husserl's letter to Carl Stumpf, February 13, 1890). Here we can see how the sudden shift, that is, the extension into the area of logic, was brought about. Husserl questions his view that the concept of number forms the basis for the universal arithmetic. "The opinion, which still guided me in working out the inaugural dissertation, that the concept of number formed the basis of universal arithmetic soon proved to be false. (The analysis of the ordinal numbers already led me to this conclusion.) No technique, no 'imaginary representations' can lead one to deduce the negative, rational, irrational, and the various complex numbers from the concept of number. The same holds for the concepts of ordinal numbers, concepts of magnitude, etc. And these concepts themselves are not logical specifications of the concept of number. The fact is that 'universal arithmetic' (including analysis, theory of functions, etc.) finds *application* to numbers ('theory of numbers') and *similarly* finds application to ordinal numbers . . ." (p. 2). Husserl then asks the question: "Now since these different applications of arithmetic have no common concept at their basis from which this science can be deduced, what makes up its content? To what conceptual objects are its principles directed?" They are directed to a system of signs. Indeed: "The system of signs belonging to the *arithmetica universalis* is articulated within a definite series of levels comparable to that of a system of concentric circles. The deepest level (the innermost circle) is filled by the signs 1, 2 = 1 + 1, 3 = 2 + 1, etc.; the next level is filled by the signs for fractions, etc. The signs belonging to the lowest level, and these alone, are independent; the higher signs are formally dependent upon the lower and, ultimately, upon the lowest. To every circle belong rules for calculation ('formal laws'), and those of the higher are dependent upon those of the lower: they are formally included within them" (p. 5). The conclusion drawn by Husserl from this is that ". . . the *arithmetica universalis* is not a science but a piece of *formal* logic; I would define the latter as a 'technique for manipulating signs' (*Kunst der Zeichen*) . . . and I would designate the former, as a particular, and one of the most important, chapters of logic, as the 'technique of knowledge' (*Kunstlehre der Erkenntnis*)" (p. 6). It is instructive to point out that Husserl's idea of levels actually originated from considerations made in the area of arithmetic. At the same time we can see how the difficulties encountered by Husserl in defining arithmetic as a theory of signs brought him to the study of logic. In the nineties he made a thorough study of the contemporary literature in logic, and, in 1897, in the *Archiv für systematische Philosophie* (Vol. 3), he published a *Survey of German Writings on Logic in 1894.* The *Survey of German Writings on Logic: 1895-1899* appeared in the same journal (Vol. 9) in 1903.[7]

The interest in and transition to logic is therefore not at all arbitrary but the result of a coherent development. In this development Husserl distinguishes between logic as a *technique* and logic as a *theory of science.* In Husserl's lectures on logic in 1906-7 (*Signatur F I 25*) this distinction is treated in detail. The idea that logic is a *theory of science* is taken up once again in *Formal and Transcendental Logic.* In the *Logical Investigations* Husserl discusses how logic places basic logical concepts in question and attempts to clarify their origin and meaning.[8] We can also say that it is therefore a question of a phenomenology of logical experience. "The goal of the phenomenology of logical experience is to provide us with as rich a descriptive understanding of these psychical experiences and those meanings contained within them as is required in order to give all the basic concepts of logic fixed meanings . . . in short, meanings such as are required by the interest in pure logic itself and above all by the interest in critical-epistemological insight into the essence of this discipline."[9]

By an entirely consistent development of the idea of reflection which had already appeared in the *Concept of Number,* phenomenological

The Development of Husserl's Philosophy

inquiry is defined by "reflection" and an "unnatural" direction of thought insofar as it is not the objects we are to pay attention to but the acts through which these objects are given.[10] In contrast to the *Philosophy of Arithmetic,* however, reflection, or the investigations carried out within the reflective attitude, is more clearly distinguished from "internal" or introspective psychology. To be sure, this inquiry can be compared with psychological introspection, but in contradistinction to this introspection it is not an immediate description but is rather an abstracting and ideational description, a description which is concerned with exposing essences or an *eidos.*

In the lectures given in the summer semester of 1925 (F I 36) Husserl gives us his own interpretation of what he wanted to achieve in the *Logical Investigations.* "The individual investigations of the second volume concern the turning of intuition back upon those logical experiences which occur within us when we think but which we do not notice at the time, which we do not have attentively in view when we perform these activities of thought in a natural and original way. We are to grasp this hidden course of the life of thought by means of a subsequent reflection and fix it by means of truly descriptive concepts; in addition, we are to solve this new problem: namely, that of making comprehensible how the formation of all these mental structures takes place within the achievements of this inner logical experience, structures which appear in explicitly judgmental thought as diversely formed concepts, judgments, conclusions, etc., and which find their general expression, their universally objective mental character, in the basic concepts and principles of logic" (Bl. 16a).[11]

Here is not the place to attempt an interpretation of the *Logical Investigations;* we shall simply determine what decisive step is taken by Husserl in this work, the step which inaugurated phenomenology and made it effective. Husserl's attack upon psychologism is sufficiently known. We must, however, add a word concerning the sudden change which Husserl brought about in his own thinking, since it easily could have been claimed that his investigations in the *Philosophy of Arithmetic* were thoroughly psychological. It had already troubled Husserl that, as we have seen, the act of collecting (in the analysis of the concept of number) was indeed exhibited in reflecting upon the act which corresponded to the presentation of an aggregate, but that the act of collecting was finally not identical with the concept of number. The attempt to escape from this difficulty becomes clear in the *Outline of a Preface to the Logical Investigations* edited by Eugen Fink (*Tijdschrift voor Philosophie,* 1939). Here Husserl explains how the discarding of psychologism was first prepared for by his studies of Leibniz and how it had then been carried out

147

by his study of Lotze's *Logik* and Bolzano's *Wissenschaftslehre.* "Even though Lotze himself was unable to escape from inconsistencies and psychologism, nevertheless his ingenious interpretation of the Platonic theory of ideas evoked a great and dawning light within me and qualified all my further studies. Lotze already spoke of truths in themselves, and so the thought that all of mathematics and a greater part of traditional logic were to be transposed into the realm of ideality was close by" (pp. 128 f.). Concerning Bolzano, Husserl states: "Now it came to me at once, at first from the sphere of traditional logic, that the first two volumes of Bolzano's *Wissenschaftslehre,* under the titles of a theory of ideas-in-themselves and a theory of propositions-in-themselves,[12] were to be viewed as a first attempt at a self-enclosed presentation of the realm of purely ideal doctrines, and that here, therefore, a complete outline of a 'pure' logic was already at hand" (p. 129).

Thus Husserl was now prepared to expose a realm of ideal objects (the realm of numbers and logical universals), a realm whose validity was independent of the psychical performances through which the ideal objects were understood. With this, however, came the following question which had to be resolved: How did the ideal objects come to be given? In other words, it is the question concerning the correlation of subject and object. "When it is made evident that ideal objects, despite the fact that they are formed in consciousness, have their own being in themselves, there still remains an enormous task which has never been seriously viewed or taken up, namely, the task of making this unique *correlation* between the *ideal objects* which belong to the sphere of pure logic and the *subjective psychical experience conceived as a formative activity* a theme for investigation. When a psychical subject such as I, this thinking being, performs certain (and surely not arbitrary but quite specifically structured) psychical activities in my own psychical life, then a successive formation and production of meaning is enacted according to which the number-form in question, the truth in question, or the conclusion and proof in question . . . emerges as the successively developing product" (F I 36, Bl. 19a f.).

This quotation expresses Husserl's real concern and the real theme of his phenomenology. Is this not, however, a falling back into psychologism? In the same manuscript Husserl, taking a sentence from the *Philosophy of Arithmetic* almost word for word, states: "We accordingly find ourselves compelled to say that numbers are produced in counting, and that propositional judgments are produced in the act of judging" (F I 36, 18b). Is this not precisely the thesis of psychologism? Taken out of context this assertion does in fact have a doubtful appearance. The decisive passage is the parenthetical statement concerning psychical activities: "(and surely not arbitrary but quite specifically structured)." The subject cannot arbitrarily constitute (and surely the issue here is that of constitution) any meaning whatsoever; rather are the constitutive acts dependent upon the essence of the objects in question. To cite a simple example, the essence of the number three is not dependent upon what psychical activities are required in order to form the number; the essence of the number three is determined by its being a number, and that means that it is determined by its place in the number-system. In order to understand the meaning of the number three, however, we must perform determinate acts of collective connecting, otherwise the meaning of 3 in general will remain entirely closed to us. There is something like the number three for us when we can perform the collecting-unifying activity in which three becomes capable of being presented. This does not mean that the essence of the number three would be arbitrarily determined by this activity so that the number would in each case change according to the manner in which I constitute it. Either I perform the acts which disclose the essence of the number three, with the result that for me there is something like three, or I do not perform them and then there is no 3 except for those who have performed this activity.

The problem of constitution is the source of many misunderstandings. The ordinary use of "constitution" equates it with any kind of production, but "constitution" in the strong sense is more of a "restitution" than a constitution insofar as the subject "restores" what is already there, but this, however, requires the performance of certain activities. There is a highly instructive passage concerning this question in a letter which Husserl wrote to Hocking (January 25, 1903). Regarding the meaning of the concept of constitution employed in the *Logical Investigations* Husserl states: "The recurring expression that 'objects are constituted' in an act always signifies the property of an act which *makes the object present* (*vorstellig*): not 'constitution' in the usual sense!" This is indeed the best way to discuss the concept of constitution: *the-becoming-present-of-an-object.* The acts which make this becoming-present possible, which set it in motion, are the constituting acts. Twenty-five years later Husserl will formulate this in the *Formal and Transcendental Logic* in the following way: ideal objects "are what they are only 'through' an original producing. This does not mean, however, that they are what they are only *in* and *during* the original producing. They are *in* the original producing: this means that they are known in it as a certain intentionality of the form: *spontaneous activity,* and this in the mode of being *originally what they themselves are.* This *manner of being given by such original activity* is nothing else than *the way of their being 'perceived' which uniquely belongs to them.* Or, what amounts to the same, this original activity which acquires something is the *'evidence'* for these idealities" (p. 150). This is essentially the same interpretation as is given by the letter; it is simply formulated in a more explicit way.

The equating, in the *Lecture on the Thing* from 1907, of the term referring to what is "constituted" with what is "self-manifesting" also throws light on this matter. Constitution means solely an advancing toward a being in such a way that this being is capable of announcing itself within this advancing-toward. We certainly need not say that all difficulties associated with this question are thereby resolved; in particular, the presuppositions connected with this matter have not been illuminated. But now at least the ambiguous term "idealism," which Husserl himself employed for the purpose of designating this question, can be fixed within certain limits.

The problem of constitution first appears in the *Logical Investigations* and from then on remains one of phenomenology's basic problems. According to the interpretation which Husserl himself advanced in the twenties, the guiding motif of the *Logical Investigations* is: "What do the hidden psychical experiences appear to be which are correlated with specific idealities and which must terminate in the determinate kind of producing which belongs to them so that the subject can, and with evidence, be conscious of these idealities as objects?" (F I 36, Bl. 19b). Here once again the "must" expresses the fact that lawfulness belongs to this termination which the subject is compelled to follow.[13]

In the *Logical Investigations* Husserl was concerned with the constitution of ideal objects.[14] The next decisive step which is to be taken will consist of extending the idea of constitution to areas of other kinds of objects, a step which is by no means self-evident. The first move in this direction is found in the *Lectures on the Phenomenology of Inner Time-Consciousness,* given in 1904-05 and edited by Heidegger in 1928.[15] These belong to a series of lectures given at Göttingen under the title of *Principal Elements of a Phenomenology and Theory of Knowledge.* Husserl's concern is the phenomenological investigation of those simple acts, primarily *acts of perception,* which lie at the basis of all higher knowledge. They are investigated here with reference to their temporality. Husserl shows how the present, past, and future are *constituted* by perception, retention, and protention. Perception as "primordial impression" (*Ur-impression*) permits the constant now to originate. Without perception there would be no "now," no present, and consequently no past or future.

If perception were not apprehended by the glance of the reflective attitude, it would be impossible to grant it the role assigned to it by Husserl in the constitution of time, for normally the perception of the perceived object is focused upon what is given and not upon the mode of

The Development of Husserl's Philosophy

givenness itself, a mode which can be equated with a "continual originating," and which indeed can itself be apprehended as originating.

The central insights given by the lectures on time seem to me to be expressed in §§ 35 and 36 where Husserl effects the return from the constituted objectivities or, as he states, the constituted unities, to the constituting flux which is now disclosed as the being of consciousness. Scarcely has Husserl disclosed the full extent of the problem of constitution by making the step from the constitution of ideal objects to the constitution of other kinds of objects, when he advances to the astonishing point where consciousness is now disclosed to him as lying prior to all constitution and as making possible the constitution of all objects through its own self-constitution. Therefore it should not surprise us when he confesses in several important passages that we lack words for grasping the process which serves as the basis for and which precedes all other processes; but he at least exposes the dimension to which we must reflectively turn. The lectures on time are therefore a decisive step in the development of the problem of constitution. They constitute the first decisive step after the *Logical Investigations* in which Husserl undertakes the task of identifying the self-constitution of that unity which provides the foundation for all other given unities.

The next step is taken in the *Lectures on the Thing* from 1907. These lectures are important in several respects. In the introduction Husserl thematically develops the thought of the phenomenological reduction for the first time. (This introduction is published as vol. 2 of *Husserliana* under the title: *The Idea of Phenomenology.*)[16] In essence, the thought of the phenomenological reduction is only the consistent development of the reflective attitude whose importance Husserl had already singled out in the *Philosophy of Arithmetic.* If the direction of our attention is to be turned away and removed from the naive "straightforward" attitude, so that consciousness becomes its own observer and gains the opportunity of seeing its own constitutive achievement, then the reduction is the appropriate instrument for accomplishing this change in orientation. More specifically, this is the *phenomenological* reduction, that is, the reduction which apprehends beings as they are manifested in their being present to consciousness and hence as phenomena.[17] From this point on the phenomenological reduction becomes a guiding motif of Husserl's thought, a motif which shall occur again and again until the end of his life and which shall find a particularly significant development in the twenties. The reduction is not the goal of Husserl's philosophizing but is a basic methodological concept by means of which the hidden and anonymous life of consciousness is to come into view.

151

Walter Biemel

It is also important that, after the constitution of time, Husserl here for the first time extends the thought of constitution to the constitution of the thing. In a lecture from 1925, Husserl, looking back, states:

"What had to make itself urgently felt in requiring a universal extension of the *Logical Investigations* (a requirement already awakened by the formal universality of the *mathesis universalis*) was the extension of *a priori* and formal logic and mathematics to the idea of an entire system of *a priori* sciences for every conceivable category of objective objects, and therefore a primary need for a universal *a priori* of possible worlds in general in addition to those of formal mathematics. As a correlate, there was the need for extending the purely *a priori* observation of the knowing consciousness, which had previously taken only formal universalities into account, to the knowing consciousness of more determinate contents, a consciousness which is related to all categories of objectivities in general. From this must develop, in complete universality, a pure *a priori* theory of consciousness encompassing every kind of valuing, striving, willing, and, in general, consciousness of every type, thus apprehending the entire concrete life in all forms of its intentional nature and opening up the problem of the constitution of the world in its totality and the problem of the unity of conscious subjectivity, the individual-personal subjectivity and the subjectivity in community with others" (F I 36, 28a).

As long as it remained a question of the constitution of ideal objects, it could always be rejoined that such objects were there merely by virtue of the subject insofar as they were produced as a result of its activities and had no existence independent of thought; but things, spatially extended objects, are a quite different affair. Can we here in a general way still speak of constitution? We can indeed if we understand this concept in terms of the unique meaning which it had for Husserl and to which we have already referred, namely, as the "self-manifestation of the object." When the concept of constitution is interpreted in this way, it is quite meaningful to ask what achievements on the part of the subject are necessary in order for a spatial body to become present to a subject. Directly following Descartes, his favorite philosopher, Husserl announces the procedural principle of advancing from the simple to the complex, from the surface to the depths. The lowest form of experience is to be clarified so that, using this as our point of departure, we can subsequently advance to higher forms. It is therefore presupposed that the lower form is not only the more simple form, but that it is also the form which serves as the foundation for other forms (just as Husserl had stated within the context of the *Philosophy of Arithmetic*). It is thoroughly to the point for Husserl to view perception, the immediate apprehension of the object, as the lower form, since for Husserl perception presents the form of pri-

The Development of Husserl's Philosophy

mordial givenness. Here it is impossible for us to give a precise analysis of the important *Lectures on the Thing* which, in their entirety, amount to 750 pages of transcript. Only a few elements can be emphasized. The essential insights are taken up later in the second volume of the *Ideas* (*Ideen II*). Husserl points out what act-performances are necessary even in the lower sphere in order to gain something like a unified thing, and also points out what at any given time corresponds in the sphere of subjectivity to the respective characters of the thing: the quality of its properties, extension, duration, unity, and whatever else there may be of a similar order. Here he constantly employs phenomenological descriptions in the sense of focusing upon processes within the subject; descriptions, however, which are not concerned with portraying the individual givenness in its immediacy, but only those essential correlations which are constitutive for perception in general.

But the *Lectures on the Thing* are not only important for their extending the investigation of constitution, but also because Husserl here discusses his real aims. "It is a question of the foundational elements of a future phenomenology of experience, one which takes its departure from the nearest and first beginnings, advancing from there as deeply and as far as possible in clarifying the essence of the givenness of experience, at least in its *lower* forms and levels" (F I 13, p. 162). Here for the first time Husserl offers an analysis of the world of experience—another decisive moment which will be maintained to the end[18] and which will enter the foreground in the *Crisis* as the "life-world." Husserl already refers to the fact that the scientific world presupposes the world of experience and that it could not develop apart from the prior givenness of the latter.[19] In contrast to his later position, however, the beginnings of which are in evidence at the close of the twenties, Husserl is *not* concerned with tracing the sciences back to their foundation in the life-world, thereby disclosing the concealed questionability of science, but is rather concerned with preparing "for the most important problem of the constitution of scientific reality in scientific knowledge" (F I 13, p. 170) through the analysis of the world of experience. In this phase of Husserl's thought the knowledge which belongs to the natural sciences represents a fund of truth whose true appropriation will be first accomplished by constitutive investigations. Here we find preparation for what Husserl stated several years later (in the *Logos* essay) concerning philosophy as rigorous science.[20]

In order to understand the tension experienced by Husserl at this time as a result of his recognizing that the constitution-problematic must be extended to include every kind of conscious object, a recognition which required the analysis of often extremely complex problems which could be unraveled only with great difficulty, we may once again refer to a passage

153

from a letter written to his friend Albrecht (January 7, 1908): "I see golden fruit which has been seen by no one else, and I see it within reach before my eyes. But I am Sisyphus for whom the golden fruit disappears when he reaches out for it. And this reaching out is difficult work, the most difficult. I am constantly making advances, even great advances. But the range of investigations which must be completed and the resolution of problems that must be taken up, none of which admit of being settled or delimited, is without precedent. I find myself in much the same situation as in previous years, and age has not made me more accommodating. . . . And naturally it is once again a question of important publications with the ultimate goal of a completely new critique of reason, the fundamentals of which are already contained in my *Logical Investigations.*"

That this struggle with difficulties is not simply empty talk is also shown by the *Lectures on the Thing.* Here the simplest investigations relating to the givenness of spatially extended things in perception are to be presented, and already, and hence still at quite a distance from the truly scientific apprehension of the world (which Husserl at this time viewed as the true apprehension because it is intersubjectively valid in contrast to the merely subjective-relative and changing apprehension of immediate experience), difficulties mount up so that the carrying out of the next step is once again postponed.

The thematic formulation of the phenomenology which develops during the ten years after the *Logical Investigations* is found in the *Logos* essay ("Philosophy as Rigorous Science"). Here let us only recall the principal thesis requiring that philosophy, in order to fulfill its true meaning, must become a rigorous science. This does not at all mean that philosophy must be subordinated to science or even "mathematized" along the lines of the mathematical natural sciences by being raised to the level of mathematical formulae. Quite the opposite. Husserl refers to the fact that the natural sciences are not in a position to explain "the reality in which we live, move and are," and that this is not only a factual incapacity which could eventually be overcome but one which is *essential.*[21] Of what, then, does the scientific character of philosophy consist? Of what sort is that unshakable rigor which is itself to excel mathematically exact calculations and inquiry?

Its rigor is to be found primarily in the requirement that nothing which is given to us in advance, nothing which has been handed down to us, is to be recognized as valid even if it is connected with the most significant names in history.[22] But this is simply a negative criterion for Husserl's radicalism. The positive criterion consists of the return to origins: ". . . it must not rest until it has attained its own absolutely clear beginnings, i.e., its absolutely clear problems, the methods preindicated in the proper

The Development of Husserl's Philosophy

sense of these problems, and the most basic field of work wherein things are given with absolute clarity."[23] The scientific character of philosophy is also made up of the requirement that perfect clarity must reign in every step which is taken and that the philosopher's procedure is to be perfectly transparent to him. Husserl criticizes the exact sciences in this respect for they rely too heavily upon indirect methods and "misconceive the value of direct apprehensions."[24] We must nevertheless ask whether Husserl's "lack of presuppositions" is not a direct assumption of the Cartesian presupposition that the *clara et distincta perceptio* is the guarantee of truth. This presupposition of Husserl's becomes particularly clear when we look at the following statement: ". . . philosophy (is to) adopt the form and language of genuine science and (is to) recognize as an imperfection one of its much praised and even imitated qualities: profundity. Profundity is a mark of the chaos that genuine science wants to transform into a cosmos, into a simple, completely clear, lucid order. Genuine science, so far as its real doctrine extends, knows no profundity. Every bit of completed science is a whole composed of thought-steps each of which is immediately understood and so not at all profound. Profundity is an affair of wisdom; conceptual distinctness and clarity is an affair of rigorous theory."[25] We need not emphasize that this point later serves to separate Husserl and Heidegger. Nevertheless, the questionability of Husserl's view that profundity corresponds to a period of beginnings in which unclarity still reigns, a period therefore which must be surpassed, must not go unnoticed.

Thus Husserl does not understand *philosophia* from the standpoint of *sophia*, but from the standpoint of science in the sense of the *scientia* of modern philosophy, that is, *mathesis.* But these are empty words if we do not have in view *what* these roots are that concern Husserl and *how* they are to be understood. They are not the Aristotelian *archai* or *aitiai* which seek to grasp the *episteme tis.* What, then, are they? The origin of meanings in terms of which beings are accessible to us. The basis of this origin, however, is consciousness. Consequently, through the phenomenological reduction we must grasp beings as they are given to us, thereby apprehending their *eidos* in immediate intuition.[26] As is well known, the critique of the *Weltanschauung* philosophy (actually Dilthey's) contained in the *Logos* essay led to an exchange of correspondence in which Husserl communicated to Dilthey that he did not mean to criticize him. Of interest to us in this correspondence is Husserl's more precise clarification of the "return to origins" as the return to the meaning-formative consciousness.

Husserl here names his philosophy "metaphysics": "That a metaphysics in this sense is in principle required over and against the natural sciences and the sciences of man which have grown out of the great work of the

155

modern period originates out of the fact that a stratification, and consequently a twofold attitude toward knowledge, is grounded in the very essence of knowledge: the one is purely directed toward the being which is consciously meant, thought of in such and such a manner, and given through appearances; the other, however, is directed toward the puzzling essential relation between being and consciousness. All natural existential knowledge, all knowledge gained within the first attitude, leaves open a range of problems whose solution depends upon the ultimate and final determination of the meaning of being (*Sinnesbestimmung des Seins*) and the ultimate evaluation of the alleged truth reached in the 'natural' (first) attitude. I believe that I have insight into the fact that there can be nothing meaningful beyond the entire complex of problems relating to being (including the 'constitution' of being in consciousness), and that therefore there can be no science beyond the phenomenologically extended and established (universal) science of being [*Daseinswissenschaft*] whose work encompasses *all* the natural sciences of beings); i.e., that to speak of a being (*einem Sein*) beyond this science and which is *in principle* incapable of being known is absurd" (Letter of July 5th and 6th, 1911).[27]

By exhibiting the formation of meaning as this comes to be carried out in every science (and carried out without achieving insight into this formation), the sciences are also to be brought to self-understanding through phenomenology.

The *Logos* essay is the foundation of Husserl's thought. The development of his philosophy up to the point at which this foundation is established has been treated in detail because this is required by our genetic point of view. Its subsequent development, more widely known through his publications, need only be briefly indicated.

The first volume of the *Ideas,* published in 1913,[28] is the first attempt at a systematic presentation of phenomenology, its methods, problems, and specifically the essence of that pure consciousness which is won by phenomenology. To some extent it can be said that Husserl here realizes his earlier plan of a *critique of reason.* The reductive method developed since 1907 receives particular emphasis. The first volume of the *Ideas* is to serve simply as the *introduction* to pure phenomenology and is to lay the ground work for carrying out the real task: the phenomenological analysis of constitution which makes up the content of the second volume and to which Husserl devoted the next ten years of his life (a volume revised and reworked until 1928).[29] The *Ideas* couples the idea of constitution with the idea of strata insofar as the manner in which the *Ideas* is constructed (constitution of animal nature, psychical reality, and the spiritual world) serves at the same time to make visible an essential stratification. Husserl was chiefly occupied with the constitution of the

The Development of Husserl's Philosophy

spiritual world up to the end of the twenties, as is clear from various manuscripts which have as their theme the difference between the natural sciences and the sciences of man.[30]

The third volume of the *Ideas* was to have actually contained the "First Philosophy" (*Erste Philosophie*). Husserl nevertheless postponed this project and in place of the *First Philosophy* presented certain scientific-theoretical investigations. The *First Philosophy* was worked out in the lectures of 1923-24, the text of which is to be soon published by R. Boehm. But in my opinion no real revolution occurs during these years: there is only the extending and deepening of the statement of the problem given by the *Ideas*.[31] It is informative to note in this connection that the second part of the *First Philosophy* is actually a theory of the different reductions which are built upon each other for the purpose of finally exposing the fundamental constituting consciousness. Husserl is particularly concerned with clarifying the nature of the transcendental reduction, the reduction which leads back to the transcendental ego, the ultimate basis for the constitution of meaning. There is a definite connection between the *First Philosophy* of 1923-24 and the *Cartesian Meditations,* whose final reworking falls within the years 1929-32, so that we can justifiably state that the *Cartesian Meditations,* viewed as "*meditationes de prima philosophia,*" presents Husserl's "first philosophy," and hence forms the third volume of the *Ideas* to which Husserl already made reference in 1913. Husserl, after he was inspired by the thought of philosophy as rigorous science, suffered throughout his entire life from the difficulty of attaining that systematic mastery over the fullness of insights and material for which he strove. For this reason we have a series of starts in this direction beginning with the *Five Lectures* (*The Idea of Phenomenology*) from 1907, continuing through the *Ideas, First Philosophy, Formal and Transcendental Logic,* and the *Cartesian Meditations,* and ending with the *Crisis.* Even as late as 1930 Husserl wrote to Roman Ingarden: "On the whole it is a real misfortune that I have come so late to the point of being able systematically to project the shaping of my (I must unfortunately say) transcendental phenomenology."[32]

The last phase of Husserl's thought is defined by his work on the *Crisis.* It is part of Husserl's tragedy that this work also remained a fragment, and the question arises whether "fragmentariness" is not an essential feature of Husserl's thought insofar as it constantly appears with systematic claims, but finds that its true passion is directed toward analysis through phenomenological intuition, so that it is torn away from the former.

157

Walter Biemel

What is the truly new feature in the *Crisis* project that justifies our giving this later work its own phase in the development of Husserl's philosophy. What reason is there for Husserl himself viewing this work as constituting a new beginning, a new "way" which he unfortunately cannot carry through to its conclusion?

It is not at all difficult to discover and enumerate the so-called "guiding motifs" which dominate Husserl's thought since the *Logos* essay in the *Crisis:* the critical opposition to the sciences, the attempt to set philosophy apart from the sciences, the striving for an apodictic truth, the discussion of the *epoché* by way of imitating Descartes. It can indeed be said that two-thirds of the work is really dedicated to the reduction, and has this not been the recurring motive for his philosophizing since 1907? What reason, therefore, is there for attributing such significance to the *Crisis,* a significance which indeed amounts to the desire to view it as the turning point of his thought? Are we not allowing ourselves to be carried away by reading something into Husserl which is not at all there?

In order to understand what is truly new in this work one must not (as Van Breda once stated) only look at what Husserl says but also at what he does. And this is Husserl's attempt to interpret and come to terms with history. It is the insight that it is of the very essence of philosophy to enter into such a dialogue with history. Husserl had not easily come to this insight; we have an entire series of manuscripts from group K III in which Husserl asks himself why philosophy should need history. He was forced to raise this question by the attempt to understand how it was possible for Science to have fallen into the critical situation which, as the *Vienna Lecture* states, finds its immediate expression in the fact that science offers an imposing and useful knowledge of nature but fails to know man.

A coming to terms with history is needed to understand this situation— the history of knowledge as the struggle to attain *universal knowledge.* It must be shown how and why this universal knowledge becomes divided into the two directions of physicalistic objectivism and transcendental subjectivism. Husserl sees the beginning of this division in Descartes, a division which leads on the one hand to the development of the mathematical natural sciences and on the other to the development of transcendental philosophy. We shall not repeat the train of thought presented in the *Crisis*, but shall simply lay bare the motivating force and core of this work.[33]

This, in exaggerated form, is the insight that the essential knowledge of man is not a final possession which is acquired once and for all—as the phenomenological essential insight would teach—nor is it an apodictic truth in the sense of the mathematical natural sciences; rather such knowl-

The Development of Husserl's Philosophy

edge *is* only as the self-attainment of reason. Reason actualizes itself in striving for knowledge, so that the way of knowledge is at the same time the way of reason's self-clarification, a reason which is on the way to self-attainment. Reason is interpreted as being historical in its very essence, as concealing historicity within itself. This was not the case with the transcendental ego even though it was interpreted as temporalizing. This relation of the transcendental ego to reason deserves to be explored. *Reason* is not viewed by Husserl as a structured whole whose articulated moments must be investigated, but is viewed as an *essential becoming,* a constant unfolding, an unfolding which is interpreted as a necessary *coming-to-itself.* This not only means that man has insight into what he is, but also that man (and this, for Husserl, is a self-evident assumption) lives in harmony, in self-responsibility with his insight, so that his will is necessarily in harmony with his knowledge. It is necessary to refer to the fact that a teleological moment is already placed within the concept of evidence developed in the *Formal and Transcendental Logic* (pp. 143 f.), a moment which then becomes quite central in the *Crisis.* Through the concept of evidence the life of consciousness receives a teleological, goal-directed structure. Evidence is not simply given but is won step by step. Evidence is a basic kind of experience whose goal is the self-givenness of the object, that is, the possessing of the object itself (p. 144). The raising of this "possessing" to perfection is fulfilled within the historical dimension of the perfecting of self-understanding, wherein the essence of reason is also fulfilled. This is what is new for Husserl, and this in fact designates a turning point in his thought. Not as though he were to abandon all hitherto decisive concepts,[34] for they now receive a new meaning and a new dimension. Let us take the concept of apodicticity, to mention only one such concept here. Apodicticity no longer signified that absolutely certain knowledge modeled after mathematical knowledge, but rather the completely enlightened knowledge of reason, a knowledge which is of compelling force precisely because reason *qua* reason cannot act irrationally, but must decide in accordance with its insight so that its decision is also its own self-realization. Thus Husserl speaks of a life of "apodictic freedom," an expression which at first appears to be contradictory if one simply sees an element of restraint within the concept of apodicticity. But, when the concept of reason is thought through radically and consistently, and when man is understood as a rational being, then insight into rationality is actually the highest certainty, that certainty which unequivocally defines human activity.

Thus the goal set by Husserl is that of "self-understanding as being called to living within apodicticity."[35]

A final comment concerning the concept of the life-world (*Lebenswelt*) which is of decisive importance for this period. It is constantly maintained that the true significance of the *Crisis* is the tracing of the scientifically "true" world back to the life-world, as if opposing these two worlds were already a goal in itself. This is not at all the case. Rather does this tracing back first gain its significance because the scientific world, as the "in-itself true world," is placed in question. The constitution of the scientific world presupposes the constitution of the life-world which is primary. The scientific world originates through transforming the life-world. The purpose of the central paragraphs concerning Galileo is to show by what process of idealization Galileo achieved a scientific conception of nature, a nature thoroughly determined by causality and capable of being calculated and reduced to formulae. Insofar as Galileo was not aware of this transformation as such, he was at the same time responsible for concealing this primordial world, this life-world which is necessarily presupposed by this transformation. "Galileo . . . the consummate discoverer of physics, i.e., physical nature, is a genius who *discovers* and at the same time *conceals*."[36] Nature as idealized and mathematized, and thereby a nature which has become subject to calculation, is for Husserl no longer the in-itself true nature. The apprehension of the world as the primordial life-world must now emerge on its own terms.

It seems to me that the actual steps which prepare the way for the problematic of the life-world can be exhibited in the *Formal and Transcendental Logic*. We found reference to the need for an analysis and theory of the world of experience as early as 1907, but it is in the *Formal and Transcendental Logic* that the first decisive step is made, namely, that of tracing predicative evidence back to the nonpredicative, the latter being equated with experience (cf. § 86, pp. 186 ff.). In § 86 it is explicitly stated that "the judgment of experience is the judgment of origins" (p. 187). The return to origins in logic requires a theory of experience (p. 188). Landgrebe has edited elements which are essential to this logic of experience in the volume entitled *Experience and Judgment*.[37] It is just this flexibility, the openness to modification, and the being-in-movement of the world of experience, that is a presupposition for the possibility of historicity.

Husserl did not rest with exhibiting the structures belonging to the lifeworld (nor do we find any consistent and systematically exhaustive presentation of these); rather will he inquire into those constitutive achievements which make the life-world itself possible, for only in this way can we come closer to the anonymous achieving of the transcendental ego which, in the *Crisis*, is revealed at the same time as historical reason.

The Development of Husserl's Philosophy

NOTES

1. The present text was delivered in a shorter form at the *International Phenomenological Colloquium* held at Royaumont in April, 1957.

2. A. D. Osborne, in his work *"Edmund Husserl and His Logical Investigations,"* correctly refers to Stumpf's influence, particularly the influence of his *Tonpsychologie* (p. 41). Cf. also Marvin Farber, *The Foundation of Phenomenology* (New York: Paine-Whitman, 1962).

3. "Only later, when the most important or most immediate consequences *of* the new principles are drawn out, when errors resulting from unclarity with respect to the nature of auxiliary means and the limits of the reliability of certain operations become more frequent, does there continually arise a more lively and finally unavoidable need for logical clarification; for sighting and securing what has been won; for precise analysis of the basic and the mediating concepts; for logical insight into the dependency of the loosely organized and inextricably entangled mathematical disciplines . . ." (*Concept of Number*, p. 3) .

4. "We can, according to our arbitrary interests, put discrete contents together and take away or add new ones to them. There is a unifying interest directed toward the total content and with it and within it at the same time . . . an act of taking notice lifts out the contents, the intentional object of this act is precisely the presentation *of* the plurality or aggregate *of* these contents. In this way the contents are present to gather at the same time, they are one, and with reflection upon this union of separate contents through these psychical acts arise the general concepts of plurality and (determinate) number" (p. 36).

5. Husserl is, however, against the view (represented by Jevons in particular) that the representation of difference belongs just as much to the aggregate as that of identity. Certainly the parts of the aggregate are apprehended as being different from each other or else we should not reach a plurality, but they are not apprehended *as* being different, for if they were apprehended in this way we would have a representation of difference and not a plurality. "Where a plurality is given, our apprehension is primarily directed toward purely *absolute* contents (namely, an apprehension which places these contents together); by contrast, where a representation of difference (or a complex of such representations) is given, our apprehension is directed toward *relations* between contents" (p. 44).

6 . Cf. Osborne, "Husserl and His *Logical Investigations*," pp. 43 ff.

7. Cf. Farber, *The Foundation of Phenomenology*, pp. 95-98, 170-195.—ED.

8. "Logical concepts as valid unities of thought must have their origin in intuition; they must emerge through ideational abstraction on the basis of certain experiences," *Logical Investigations* II, 5.

9. *Ibid.*, p. 6.

10. "Instead of becoming involved with the actual *performance* of the manifold of acts constructed upon the basis of each other and, as a result, to naively posit, so to speak, the objects meant by their meaning as existing and to determine what they are . . . we shall rather 'reflect,' i.e. make these acts themselves, along with their immanent meaning-content, into objects," *ibid.*, p. 9

11. "Phenomenology does not speak of conditions which belong to animate beings; it speaks of perceptions, judgments, feelings, etc., *as such.* It speaks of what belongs to them *a priori* and in unconditioned universality precisely as *pure* singularities of *pure* kinds [and Husserl proceeds with what is for us an interesting comparison, a comparison which, as we now understand, is not undertaken casually since it expresses Husserl's own development] quite analogous to the ways in which pure arithmetic speaks of numbers and geometry speaks of spatial figures: on the basis of pure intuitions of ideational universality," *Investigations,* II, sec. 1, 18. Nevertheless, this quotation is an addition which does not

161

appear in the first edition, since at that time Husserl had not gone far enough to see that perceptions and feelings could also be addressed as themes for investigation.

12. According to Kneale, ideas-in-themselves are "ideal contents or ideas in the sense in which many people may be said to have the same idea." Propositions-in-themselves are "true propositional contents, something thinkable or expressible but not necessarily thought or expressed," *The Development of Logic* (Oxford: Clarendon Press, 1962), pp. 363, 360.—ED.

13. "What was partly new was the task, or attempt, starting from the relevant categories of objectivities, to radically and consistently inquire into the determinate modes of consciousness belonging to these categories, into the subjective acts, act-structures, and experiential bases within which the so-and-so structured objectivities became known, and primarily, came to evident givenness" (F I 36, B1. 20b).

14. ". . . Whether we take ourselves to be thinking subjects, or whether we imagine angels, devils, gods, or any kind of being whatsoever who counts, calculates, and does mathematics, the inner activity and life of counting and mathematical thought is, if it is to produce logico-mathematical results, universally the same by virtue of an *a priori* necessity. To the *a priori* of pure logic and pure mathematics itself, this realm of unconditionally necessary and universal truth, there corresponds as a *correlate* an *a priori* of a psychical nature: namely, a realm of unconditionally necessary and universal truths related to mathematical *experience*, mathematical presentation, thought, and entailment as the manifold psychical life of a subject in general. . . ." Manuscript as cited above, Bl.26a.

15. An occasionally voiced opinion that the published text is not to be viewed as authentic because of a reworking by Heidegger must be discarded once and for all. Heidegger strictly held himself to the original and undertook only minor stylistic corrections.

16. English translation by Alston and Nakhnikian (The Hague: Martinus Nijhoff, 1964).—ED

17. Cf. the author's article: "*Husserls Encyclopaedia Britannica-Artikel und Heideggers Anmerkungen dazu*" in *Tijdschrift voor Philosophie*, 1950.

18. Cf. *Formal and Transcendental Logic*, § 86.

19. "No matter how far the scientific interpretation of the world may distance itself from the world of prescientific experience, and even if it should declare that the sensible qualities do not have the immediate significance assigned to them by natural experience, it still remains that direct experience, immediate perception, recollection, etc., give it *those* things which, deviating from the customary modes of thought, it proceeds to determine theoretically. . . . All judgments of reality established by the natural scientist lead back to direct perceptions and recollections, and relate themselves to that world which comes to its first givenness within this direct experience. All mediate founding such as that enacted by the scientist rests upon immediate givenness, and those experiences in terms of which reality is immediately given are perceptions, recollections, anticipations (taken in a certain degree of immediacy), and anticipatorylike acts" (F I 13, pp. 168 ff.).

20. At this time Husserl spoke of the necessity of writing a critique of reason. (Cf. his journal entries published in the *Journal of Philosophy* XVI, no. 3.)

21. "The natural sciences have not in a single instance explained for us actual reality, the reality in which we live, move and are. The general belief that it is their function to accomplish this and that they are merely not yet far enough advanced, the opinion that they can accomplish this—in principle has revealed itself to those with more profound insight as a superstition. The necessary separation between natural science and philosophy—in principle a differently oriented science, though in some fields essentially related to natural science is in process of being established and clarified." Edmund Husserl, *Phenomenology*

The Development of Husserl's Philosophy

and the Crisis of Philosophy, trans. Quentin Lauer (New York: Harper and Row, 1965), p. 140.

22. *Ibid.*, pp. 145 f.—ED.
23. *Ibid.*, p. 146.—ED.
24. *Ibid.*, p. 147.—ED.
25. *Ibid.*, p. 144.—ED.
26. "However, to the extent that philosophy goes back to ultimate origins, it belongs precisely to its very essence that its scientific work move in spheres of direct intuition. Thus the greatest step our age has to make is to recognize that with philosophical intuition in the correct sense, the phenomenological grasp of essences, a limitless field of work opens out, a science which, without all indirectly symbolic and mathematical methods, without the apparatus of premises and conclusions, still attains a plenitude of the most rigorous and, for all further philosophy, decisive cognitions," *ibid.*, p. 147. It is therefore not at all surprising that Husserl (as J. Hering reports: "La phénoménologie il y a trente ans" in *Revue Int. de Phil.* I, no. 2), after a lecture given by Koyré on Bergson to the *Göttinger Philosophischen Gesellschaft,* stated: "Consistent Bergsonians, that is what we are" (p. 368).
27. The Husserl-Dilthey correspondence from this period has been published in the *Revista de Filosofía de la Universidad de Costa Rica,* no. 2, 1957.
28. *Husserliana,* vol. 3, contains the text of *Ideen I* together with Husserl's revisions, additions, and improvements.
29. Cf. the introduction to *Ideen II (Husserliana,* vol. 4) by Marly Biemel.
30. Here we can refer to the lectures on psychology from both 1925 and 1928, *Signatur* F I 36 and F I 33. The text of F I 36 will soon appear under the title *Phänomenologische Psychologie* as vol. 9 of *Husserliana.*
31. Cf. Rudolf Boehm's "Introduction" to this text where a different view is presented: Edmund Husserl, *Erste Philosophie: Zweiter Teil* (Den Haag: Martinus Nijhoff, 1959), pp. xi-xliii. Compare also the essay by L. Landgrebe included in this collection.—ED.
32. Cf. Strasser, "Introduction" to the *Cartesianische Meditationen* (Den Haag: Martinus Nijhoff, 1950), p. xxvii.
33. Cf. the reviews by A. Gurwitsch in the *Journal of Philosophy and Phenomenological Research* XVI, no. 3, and XVII, no. 3. [Reprinted in A. Gurwitsch, *Studies in Phenomenology and Psychology* (Evanston: Northwestern University Press, 1966), pp. 397-447. ED.]
34. We must not forget that with the working out of the *Crisis* Husserl had passed the age of seventy.
35. Edmund Husserl, *Die Krisis der europäischen Wissenschaften und die transzendentale Phänomenologie* (Den Haag: Martinus Nijhoff, 1954), p. 275.
36. *Ibid.*, p. 53.
37. Edmund Husserl, *Erfahrung und Urteil,* ed. Ludwig Landgrebe, 3rd ed. (Hamburg: Claasen Verlag, 1964).

Husserl's Concept of the "Absolute"

Rudolf Boehm

THE SUBJECT of dispute often remains unobserved in the dispute itself. Husserl's most disputed thought doubtlessly was and is the thought of "absolute consciousness," the basic thought of the *Ideas* which permitted this philosophy to be characterized as idealism. The following considerations serve as a clarification of this basic but seldom treated concept of the absolute in Husserl's thought.

1. Absolute Phenomena

The *idea of phenomenology*, which Husserl developed under this title in the *Five Lectures* of 1907,[1] is established or "motivated" by the need for a metaphysics. Husserl's idea of metaphysics is the idea of a *science of beings in an absolute sense.* "What is needed is a science of beings in an absolute sense. This science, which we shall call metaphysics, grows out of a 'critique' of the natural sciences which is based upon the insight into the essence of knowledge and into the distinctive basic *forms* of knowledge-objectivities (in the sense of the different fundamental correlations between knowledge and its objectivity) won by the universal critique of knowledge."[2] Husserl distinguishes the *universal* critique of knowledge (or the *theory* of knowledge) from the critique of knowledge in the narrower sense of a critique of the "natural" knowledge found in all "natural" sciences. Phenomenology is to serve as the basis for a universal critique or theory of knowledge. Established in this way, "the theory of knowledge can become the *critique of the natural knowledge* found in all natural sciences. It will then enable us to interpret the results of the natural sciences with respect to beings in a correct and definitive manner. For the epistemological perplexity into which natural (preepistemological) reflection upon the possibilities of knowledge (upon a possible correctness of knowledge) has cast us is not only the cause of false views concerning the essence of knowledge, but is also the source of basically perverse (because self-contradictory) *interpretations* of the being which comes to be known in the natural sciences. . . . Only epistemological reflection can produce the distinction between natural science and philosophy, and only through this reflection is it clear that the natural sciences of being are not the ultimate sciences of being. We require a science of beings in an absolute sense. . . ."[3]

We require a metaphysics, an ultimate science of being, a science of beings in an absolute sense; for this purpose we require an epistemological critique of the natural sciences; in order to provide a basis for this critique of science we require a theory of knowledge or a universal critique of knowledge, and for this purpose we require phenomenology.

Phenomenology stands in the service of a critique of knowledge whose ultimate goals are of a metaphysical order. As the critique of knowledge, however, phenomenology itself will first establish the need for a metaphysics by showing that this need is established by a critique of the natural knowledge found in the natural sciences. Precisely for this reason the theory of knowledge must establish itself by ignoring its metaphysical goals—and this means: as phenomenology. "If we ignore the metaphysical goals of the critique of knowledge, if we hold ourselves purely to the task of clarifying *the essence of knowledge and of the objectivities which belong to knowledge*, then this is the *phenomenology* of knowledge and of the objectivities which belong to knowledge. . . ."[4] Only a critique of the natural knowledge found in all natural sciences which has this kind of "pure" phenomenology as its basis is capable of bringing to light in a convincing manner the fact that the natural sciences of being are not the ultimate sciences of being and that we *thoroughly require* metaphysics as a science of beings in an absolute sense.

In the interest of establishing the metaphysical needs which lay at its very foundation, the philosophical *discipline* of phenomenology requires that phenomenology hold itself "purely to the task of clarifying the *essence of knowledge and the objectivities belonging to knowledge*" entirely apart from all metaphysical goals, and this means *apart from all questions concerning beings in an absolute sense.*

"Phenomenology designates a science, a connection of scientific disciplines; at the same time, however, phenomenology primarily designates a method and a manner of thinking. . . ."[5] Phenomenology's manner of thinking is defined by the method of an "epistemological" or "phenomenological" *reduction.* This signifies the "exclusion of the transcendent in general as an existence which is not an evident givenness in the genuine sense, the absolute givenness of pure intuiting (*Schauen*)."[6] The "phenomenological sphere" is to be "the sphere of absolute clarity, the sphere of immanence in the genuine sense,"[7] a "sphere of absolute givenness."[8] It

165

Rudolf Boehm

is the reduction to the sphere of absolute givenness that establishes a pure phenomenology, for "only the *pure phenomenon,* that which has been reduced, is truly an absolute givenness."[9] The sphere of absolute givenness is "the field of absolute phenomena."[10] This "is a field of absolute knowledge which offers no opinions concerning the ego, the world, God, the mathematical manifolds or any other scientific objectivity; a knowledge which, therefore, is not dependent upon these objectivities, a knowledge which is to be accepted just as it presents itself whether one is a skeptic with regard to it or not."[11]

If metaphysics is the science of beings in an absolute sense, the critique of knowledge whose purpose is to awaken the need for this metaphysics is established apart from all metaphysical goals as a pure phenomenology by means of a return to what is *absolutely given.* The exclusion of all questions relating to *beings* in an absolute sense and the return to the absolute phenomena as the return to what is absolutely *given* amounts to one and the same procedure—the phenomenological reduction. Accordingly, the absolute of phenomenology is not the absolute of metaphysics. The absolute of metaphysics is that which exists absolutely (*das absolut Seiende*). Phenomenology's absolute is that which is absolutely given. Its basic principle runs: "absolute givenness is something ultimate,"[12] and this is so *because* it divorces itself from the critique of the metaphysical goals of knowledge. This is how the *idea of phenomenology* is defined in Husserl's *Five Lectures.*

2. Absolute Being

Several years after presenting the *idea of phenomenology,* "the *theory of knowledge* and the *metaphysics* which, historically and by way of content, is bound up with it,"[13] and their reciprocal relationships, Husserl published a *General Introduction to Pure Phenomenology* as the first volume of his *Ideas for a Pure Phenomenology and Phenomenological Philosophy.*[14]

This work is incomplete. Not only was Husserl unable to make up his mind with respect to the publication of very extensive and partially completed sketches (which were then edited from Husserl's posthumous works in 1952 and published as the second and third books of the *Ideas,* containing the *Phenomenological Investigations of Constitution* and discussions of *Phenomenology and the Foundations of Science*),[15] but the entire work is also lacking its conclusion. A glance at Husserl's introduction to the first volume indicates that what are now the "second" and "third" volumes correspond simply to what in the original plan was en-

Husserl's Concept of the "Absolute"

visaged as being two parts of the second volume.[16] "A third and concluding volume," according to this plan, "will be dedicated to the idea of philosophy. Here we are to awaken the insight that true philosophy, which has as its idea that of realizing absolute knowledge, is rooted in pure phenomenology, and this in such an earnest manner that the systematically rigorous establishing and completion of this first of all philosophies is the unavoidable precondition for every metaphysics and every other philosophy which would desire to emerge as *science*."[17]

The third volume of the *Ideas*, which was to present the conclusion of the entire work, was never written.[18] Nevertheless, the "insight" of which Husserl speaks and which this volume was to have awakened in the reader must have been fixed clearly in his own mind and must have presented the basis for his conception of the work. This insight contained one (if not *the*) basic concept of his *Ideas*, a concept central not only to a pure phenomenology but also to a phenomenological philosophy. It is in terms of this idea that "pure" phenomenology can and must be understood as a basic element of phenomenological *philosophy* insofar as this pure phenomenology is itself the "first of all philosophies" and proves itself to be "the unavoidable precondition . . . for every metaphysics and every other philosophy."

In fact, the "insight" in question already appears to have been expressed in the *Five Lectures*. The quotations above bear witness to this. One of these quotations must be completed as follows: "phenomenology designates a science . . . at the same time and above all, however, phenomenology designates a method and a manner of thinking: the specifically *philosophical manner of thinking,* the specifically *philosophical method.*"[19] Here "pure" phenomenology is meant in the sense of the *Ideas*. This is a "pure" phenomenology in the sense of the Idea of *Phenomenology* insofar as it holds itself "purely" to the task of returning to the field of absolute phenomena as the sphere of absolute *givenness* by ignoring all metaphysical goals and by ignoring all questions concerning *beings* in an absolute sense. This "method" and "manner of thinking" can and must be termed the "specifically *philosophical manner of thinking,* the specifically *philosophical method"* because "establishing and carrying out" a pure phenomenology in this sense is also "the unavoidable precondition for every metaphysics and every philosophy."

It appears as though it is simply the formulation of this "insight" that is sharpened in the *Ideas*. It is expressed in this formula: the first of all philosophies must be a pure phenomenology: pure phenomenology is the *First Philosophy*.[20]

In truth, however, it is not simply a question here of a mere formula.[21] The name "First Philosophy" is itself the oldest title for "metaphysics."

167

Rudolf Boehm

A phenomenological philosophy in Husserl's sense is a philosophy for which the "First Philosophy" is not metaphysics but pure phenomenology. With the establishing of a phenomenological philosophy, metaphysics not only loses its title of being the "First Philosophy," but also loses its foundation-laying function. It must then cease to be a *metaphysics* in the sense in which it has been thought of ever since the time of Aristotle. Yet does not Husserl's pure phenomenology itself *become* metaphysics precisely insofar as it takes on the title of the "First Philosophy," thereby taking over the foundation-laying function which had at one time been attributed to metaphysics? It can be shown in Husserl's work that this does happen.

In the *Five Lectures* pure phenomenology is contrasted with metaphysics insofar as pure phenomenology does not inquire into *beings* in an absolute sense, but returns solely to what is absolutely *given*. In the first volume of the *Ideas* the "absolutely given" (and it alone) is itself posited and appealed to as absolute being and absolute reality.

In § 44 of the *Ideas* Husserl contrasts the *mode of givenness* of things and of the transcendent in general with the mode of givenness of the immanent or experience. He states that "transcendent being in general, no matter of what sort, understood as being *for* an ego, can be brought to givenness in a manner analogous to that mode in which a thing comes to givenness, and thus only through appearances."[22] By contrast, "experience does not present itself in this way. This implies that the perception of experience is the pure intuiting of something which is *given as being absolute in this perception* (or which can be given in this way) and is not given as something which is identical throughout its modes of appearing, i.e., through perspectival configurations."[23] "We therefore conclude that while it belongs to the essence of givenness through appearances not to give any affair as absolute, but to give it only through partial presentations, it belongs to the very essence of immanent givenness just to give something which is absolute and which cannot present itself perspectively and partially."[24]

This is the sole topic of the paragraph. It discusses the "merely phenomenal" *givenness* of the transcendent and the absolute *givenness* of the immanent. The title of these paragraphs states, however: "The Merely Phenomenal *Being* of the Transcendent and the *Absolute Being* of the Immanent."[25] Insofar as absolute givenness is thus spoken of directly as absolute being, the *Ideas*' "Fundamental Phenomenological Observations," the section in which the passages quoted assume a central role, directly emerges as a metaphysics insofar as a "science of beings in an absolute sense" can be called "metaphysics."

Husserl's Concept of the "Absolute"

3. Absolute Positing

The direct claim that what is absolutely given is absolute being (presented in § 44 of the *Ideas)* permits us to conjecture that Husserl in general (in accordance with basic principles as much as with self-evidence) makes givenness as such the "absolute" measure of being; that he speaks of absolute givenness as being constitutive of absolute being because in principle (although implicitly) he identifies being with givenness. The self-evidence which this equation might have had for Husserl appears questionable in view of the care with which the differentiation of the "objects" of metaphysics from those of a pure phenomenology is carried out in the text from 1907. Taking into account the fact that the *Five Lectures* was unknown to most readers of the *Ideas,* the "self-evidence" of this step must be something Husserl imagined.

But this claim is not simply an "immediate" pronouncement. It is "mediated" by the concept of absolute positing. This occurs in § 46 of the *Ideas.* The "Fundamental Phenomenological Observations"[26] reach their climax in these paragraphs.[27] They are entitled: "Indubitability of Immanent Perception and Dubitability of Transcendent Perception."[28] The first lines state: "Every immanent perception necessarily guarantees the existence of its object. If the reflecting apprehension is directed toward my experience I have apprehended an absolute self whose existence is in principle undeniable, that is, the insight that it does not exist is in principle impossible; it would be absurd to hold it possible that an experience *given in this way* does *not* truly exist."[29] Thus "I am simply compelled to state: I exist, this life is, I live: cogito."[30]

"By contrast, it belongs . . . to the essence of the world of things that no perception, no matter how perfect, gives us anything absolute in its domain, and essentially connected with this is the fact that every encompassing experience leaves open the possibility that what is given does *not* exist, despite the continuing consciousness of its bodily self-givenness. It is an essential law that the *existence of things is never a necessity required by their being given* but is in a certain manner always *contingent.*"[31]

"It is clear then . . . that everything which is present for me in the world of things, in the world of realities in general, is in principle *only a presumptive reality,* and that on the contrary *I myself,* for whom these things or realities are there . . . or the actuality of my experience, is an *absolute* reality given by means of an unconditioned and absolutely retractable positing."[32] "In this absolute sphere there is no place for conflict, illusion, and being-otherwise. It is a sphere of absolute positings."[33]

The objects of immanent perception are given absolutely. But immanent perception guarantees that the being of that which comes to absolute givenness in this perception is an absolutely indubitable being. Absolute givenness thereby *necessarily* requires (and requires *as* a necessity) the *absolute positing* of that which is absolutely given as existing. The sphere of absolute givenness is a "sphere of absolute positings."

Here it could appear as if the formula: "*absolute* reality—given by means of an unconditioned and absolutely unretractable positing"—in the end exhaustively defines Husserl's concept of absolute being or absolute reality. For actually the expression "absolute being" does not designate a being which exists in the absolute sense or the *mode of being* of something which is absolute in the metaphysical sense, but simply designates a *positional-modality*. "Existing absolutely" would then signify nothing other than "being absolutely indubitable." Absolute givenness would then not be *posited* as absolute being, but (at least within the framework of a "pure" phenomenology) by absolute being nothing more would be understood than absolute givenness. *Absolute* being would also mean nothing other than an absolute (namely, an absolutely indubitable) "being *for* an ego."[34] Attesting to this would be the fact that, for Husserl, the concept which here contrasts with "absolute" is that of the simply "presumptive."

These passages, however, "include premises" for more radical "consequences which we shall want to draw out from the possibility of separating in principle the entire natural world from the domain of consciousness, the sphere of the being of experiences."[35] These are drawn out by Husserl in § 49 which presents "Absolute Consciousness as the Residuum of the World-Nullification."[36] Regarding "the results . . . we have obtained at the conclusion of the last chapter" (i.e., the results of § 46), Husserl now maintains "that the being of consciousness, of every stream of experience in general, is to be sure *necessarily modified by nullifying the world of things, but its ownmost existence is not thereby touched.*"[37]

With this statement Husserl clearly infers relationships of *being* from *positional* relationships. If "transcendent being in general . . . understood as being *for* an ego, can only be given in a manner analogous to the givenness of a thing, and therefore only through appearances,"[38] then what holds specifically for "*thinglike existence*" also holds for all being which is not the being of consciousness: "its necessity is never a necessity required by its being given."[39] For it is possible for consciousness to exist without the necessity of positing the existence of any real being. Consciousness can be posited absolutely without necessarily positing a

Husserl's Concept of the "Absolute"

real being along with positing the being of consciousness. Therefore no real being, no being of a kind such that it presents itself and exhibits itself through appearances in accordance with the consciousness that we have of it, is *necessary for the being of consciousness* (consciousness in the widest sense as the stream of experience).

"Immanent being is therefore doubtlessly absolute being in this sense: that in principle *nulla 're' indiget ad existendum.*"[40]

The statement: "Therefore no real being *is necessary for the being of consciousness*" is ambiguous. Indeed, the move asserting the absolute being of consciousness rests upon this ambiguity. Real being, understood as being for an ego, is never to be posited as necessary: it neither can nor must come to be given to consciousness or come to be posited by consciousness as necessary being. From this Husserl concludes: no real being is itself necessary for the *being* of consciousness.

Yet Husserl's meaning is clear. Nothing can be posited absolutely, and hence nothing can come to absolute givenness (which is required by absolute positing), whose very being would not itself be absolute. Whatever is given absolutely and, accordingly, whatever requires that it be posited absolutely, thereby *proves* itself to be absolute being. Absolute being is the necessary foundation for absolute givenness.

The basis for this thought lies in the concept of "absolute being" which Husserl here sets forth. This concept is expressed in the form: immanent being is absolute being insofar as absolute being is the being of something which "in principle *nulla 're' indiget ad existendum.*" The Latin phrase Husserl employs in this definition of absolute being originates in Descartes' definition of *substance:* "By substance, we can understand nothing else than a thing which so exists that it needs no other thing in order to exist."[41] Quite apart from the fact that Husserl is not speaking of "substance," his formula would be translated in the following way: absolute being is being which "in principle requires no other being for its existence."

To the extent that an absolute being is now a being such that it can exist without being "conditioned" in its being by some other being, then clearly only an absolute being in this sense can be "posited unconditionally" on the basis of its coming to "absolute givenness." In principle, the possibility of absolute givenness has its foundation in absolute being: *absolute being establishes the possibility of absolute givenness.*

171

Rudolf Boehm

4. Absolute Consciousness

Of course, Husserl's modified Cartesian formula for "absolute being" can be interpreted this way: by placing the word "*re*" in quotation marks ("*nulla 're' indiget ad existendum*") Husserl signifies that he does not understand this word in Descartes' sense (Husserl does not name the being defined as possessing absolute being a "thing"), but that he understands it in his own and more restricted sense. With this interpretation, however, his *definition* of absolute being not only presupposes his terminological distinction between "consciousness" and "reality," but it also implies the thesis that consciousness *alone* is absolute being. Or, it directly places this distinction in question and for this reason is reduced to introducing another distinction between consciousness, called absolute being, and real being. In any case, Husserl's stated definition of absolute being can be understood as being modeled upon the presupposed proof of the absoluteness of consciousness' being: that consciousness requires no *other* being for its existence means that it requires no *real* being (in Husserl's sense) for its existence. Formulated in this way, the definition implies the further assumption that all being apart from the being of consciousness of real being, or the definition establishes a possibly more limited concept of "absolute being."

In this connection, and with particular reference to the already mentioned possibility that Husserl's "nominal definition" of absolute being already includes his thesis that *only* the being of consciousness is absolute, we must not forget that, after the cited definition of "substance," Descartes immediately continues: "And in fact only one single substance can be understood which clearly needs nothing else, namely, God. We perceive that all other things can exist only by the help of the concourse of God."[42] Descartes' definition of substance essentially includes the thesis that God alone is substance.

One is inclined to accept the implication that, in the end, Husserl's definition of absolute being similarly implies the assertion of the absolute being of consciousness and of consciousness alone. Furthermore, since his concept of absolute being is the same as Descartes' idea of substance, it is implied that Husserl conceives of consciousness as being the sole substance. Since he posits absolute consciousness as the sole substance, this absolute consciousness is analogous to God for Husserl.

Nevertheless, Descartes proceeds further: "That is why the word substance does not pertain *univoce* to God and to other things, as they say in the schools, that is, no common signification for this appellation which will apply equally to God and to them can be distinctly understood."[43]

Husserl's Concept of the "Absolute"

We must note a corresponding ambiguity in Husserl's concept of absolute being, an ambiguity which is attested to by the following: God, in Husserl's view, is "an *'absolute' in an entirely different sense than the absolute of consciousness.*"[44]

If the being of God can be thought of as a possibility, the definition of absolute being we are now discussing directly sets forth a *limited* concept of absolute being; if by *"res"* (in quotation marks) we mean solely real being in the narrow sense of the *Ideas,* "immanent being" would be "absolute being only in the sense that it in principle *nulla 're' indiget ad existendum.*" Consciousness would be absolute being only insofar as it does not require being sustained (*concursus*) by *real* being in order to exist—although it might indeed require being sustained by another being "and have its source in what is ultimately and truly absolute."[45]

Perhaps the ambiguity of the definition of absolute being concentrated in the word *"res"* as set off by quotation marks was intended by Husserl.

The statement that "immanent being is thus doubtlessly absolute being in the sense that it in principle *nulla 're' indiget ad existendum*" does not at all prejudice the possibility that in addition to consciousness *reality is also absolute being.* Neither the definition of absolute being nor the thesis that consciousness is absolute being allows the conclusion that real being is *not* absolute being. To be sure, the following occurs immediately after the statement quoted above.

"On the other hand the world of transcendent *'res'* is referable without qualification to consciousness, and not simply to a logically conceived consciousness, but to an actual consciousness."[46] Here Husserl asserts the nonabsolute, purely relative being of reality. But this assertion is not a consequence of the preceding statement from which it is separated by the opening phrase "on the other hand."

The importance of the relationships encountered in this connection rests upon two considerations: first, the relativization of reality—indeed, making it relative *to* absolute consciousness—radically strengthens the absoluteness of absolute consciousness; and, second, the concept of the absolute being of consciousness does not in itself *require* this relativity of the being of "reality." "In themselves," according to Husserl's concept, immanent consciousness and transcendent real being could exist next to each other as *two modes of absolute* being and could even possibly be subordinate to God as the "ultimately and truly absolute," just as in Descartes *res cogitans* and *res extensa* exist as two substances subordinate to the "infinite" substance of God.

That reality, the being of things, real being, transcendent being in general, is truly not absolute but relative, and indeed relative to consciousness, is maintained by Husserl in certain well-known and very pointed

173

formulations which, quite understandably, caused a sensation among both followers and opponents of "phenomenology" much more than did the statements concerning "absolute consciousness." The most important passages are found in the second part of § 49, in the beginning of § 50, and in the first of the concluding summarizing paragraphs (§ 55) of the third chapter of the "Fundamental Phenomenological Observations."

Throughout it is understood that the titles "reality" and "consciousness" do not serve to distinguish two kinds of absolute being: "Between consciousness and reality there yawns a veritable abyss of meaning. Here a being which manifests itself perspectivally and which is never to be given absolutely, a purely contingent and relative being; there a necessary and absolute being which in principle cannot be given perspectivally through appearances."[47]

"The entire *spatio-temporal* world within which man includes himself and the human ego as subordinate individual realities, is, *according to its very meaning, simply intentional being,* a being which therefore has the merely secondary, relative meaning of a being *for* a consciousness. It is a being which consciousness posits in its own experiences, which in principle is only the identical element which is intuitable and determinable by motivated manifolds of experience, and which, above and beyond this, is nothing at all."[48]

"Thus the common meaning of talk about being is inverted. The being which for us is first is in itself second, i.e., it is what it is only in 'relation' to the being which is first. Not as if a blind order of laws had made things in such a way that the *ordo et connexio rerum* must direct itself in accordance with the *ordo et connexio idearum*. Reality, the reality of individual things as well as the reality of the entire world, essentially lacks (in our strong sense) independence. Reality is not in itself something absolute whose bond with some other being is only secondary; it is, in the sense of being absolute, nothing at all; it has no 'absolute essence,' but the essence of something which in principle is *only* intentional, *only* consciously known, presented, appearing."[49]

And finally: "To identify the totality of realities . . . with the totality of being, thereby making the former absolute, is nonsensical. An *absolute reality is as valid as a round square.*"[50]

The basis for the statement that the being of reality is not absolute but simply relative is not contained in the fact that consciousness has already proven itself to be "the" absolute being, but *in the meaning of real being or in the essence of reality itself:* "Reality . . . essentially lacks (in our strong sense) independence." "To identify the totality of realities . . . with the totality of being" is not only false but is also nonsensical to the extent that such an identification implies making real being absolute. The thought of an *absolute* being of things and realities *runs counter to the meaning* of the being of things and realities. The concept of an "absolute reality" is not a concept at all.

Insofar as the absoluteness of absolute being, that is, absolute consciousness, does not remain untouched by the relationship in which reality stands to absolute consciousness, we must investigate Husserl's interpretation of the meaning of real being over and against which the idea of an absolute reality is nonsensical.

5. *Givenness and Being*

The discussion required to establish the thesis that something real "is in an absolute sense nothing at all" is found in § 43 of the *Ideas;* hence in those paragraphs immediately preceding the ones we have discussed up to this point. This part is entitled: "Clarification of a Basic Mistake."[51] The essential content of these paragraphs is found in the first fifteen lines, which follow.

"It is therefore a basic mistake to think that perception (and, in their own special way, every other kind of intuition of the thing) does not encounter the thing itself; that the thing is not given to us in itself and in terms of its in-itselfness. To every being there belongs in principle the possibility of intuiting it as it really is, and particularly of perceiving it in an adequate perception which gives us the corporeal thing itself *without any mediation through 'appearances.'* God, the subject of absolutely perfect knowledge and therefore also of every possible adequate perception, naturally possesses what is denied to us finite beings: the perception of things in themselves.

"But this view is nonsensical. It implies that there is *no essential difference* between transcendent and immanent; that in the postulated divine intuition a spatial thing is a real constituent (and therefore an experience) belonging with other experiences to the divine stream of consciousness and stream of experience."[52]

If these lines actually seem to contain the entire explanation of Husserl's view that real being is "a being which is posited by consciousness in its experience, and which in principle is only the identical element which can be intuited and determined by motivated manifolds of experience and is nothing at all above and beyond this," this information is at first disappointing. These lines appear to lead us back to the "purely phenomenological" questions of *givenness*, and, more specifically, back to the question concerning the possibility of reality's being given *absolutely* in terms of adequate perceivability. And yet is not the question concerning

175

the absolute *being* of the real contained precisely in the question whether an absolute *being* would be conceivable even where absolute *givenness* is absent? In maintaining the absolute being of consciousness, Husserl, on the contrary, seems simply to presuppose that the absolute being of what is given absolutely is subordinate to absolute givenness.

The text of § 43 does not, however, only speak of the factual absence of reality's absolute givenness in "our" experience, but also speaks of the impossibility *in principle* of an absolute givenness of beings whose mode of being is that of reality. However, and we have already established that this is Husserl's conviction, *absolute* being establishes in principle the possibility of absolute givenness. If it can be now shown that the possibility of absolute givenness is in principle *excluded* for real being as such, real being is not to be thought of as absolute, and the thought of an absolute being of things and realities is, as Husserl maintains, contrary to the very meaning of the being of things.

By relying upon the results of his preceding analyses, Husserl can produce the required proof in a few brief words. Yet the task of conducting this proof is connected with that of "clarifying a basic mistake." What mistake?

Husserl is at the point of establishing the assertion that *by its very essence* real being cannot be absolute being by proving that in principle the mode of being which belongs to reality excludes the possibility of a real thing's ever being given absolutely: he thereby conceives "the possibility in principle of absolute givenness" as the measure of absolute being. The basic mistake, however, to which he simultaneously turns his attention, is, paradoxically enough, the mistaken opinion that "every being has in principle the possibility" of being given absolutely, and this clearly means that the possibility of absolute givenness belongs to *every* being as a *principle* because it belongs to *being as such.* Accordingly, absolute givenness as a "possibility in principle" belongs to "beings in an absolute sense" and yet not at all as a "possibility in principle" to beings as such.

Husserl's thesis that real being is "a being which consciousness posits in its own experiences and which in principle is only the identical element which can be intuited and determined by motivated manifolds of experience and is nothing at all above and beyond this"[53] is based upon the conviction that "the perception of things . . . makes present and apprehends something itself in its corporeal presence."[54] Hence, for Husserl, it is "a basic mistake to think that perception (and, in their own special way, every other kind of intuition of the thing) does not encounter the thing itself; that the thing is not given to us in itself and in terms of its in-itselfness."[55] What is the source of this mistake? On the one hand, it

Husserl's Concept of the "Absolute"

clearly lies in establishing the *fact* (which Husserl does not dispute but rather stresses) that things and realities in general "are not given to us" in absolute givenness; on the other hand, however, it also has its source in a more fundamental mistake *in principle* which is concealed within the above-mentioned "fact": "To every being there belongs in principle the possibility of intuiting it as it really is and particularly of perceiving it in an adequate perception which gives us the corporeal thing itself *without any mediation through 'appear*ances'."[56] From this mistake in principle and from the above-mentioned "fact" the following conclusion results: it is simply "an accidental feature of 'our human constitution'" which, in turn, does not at all concern the being-in-itself of things, "that 'our' perception can only encounter things themselves through their perspectival configurations."[57] The impossibility of our having things given to us absolutely, the impossibility of our adequately perceiving them, lies in the imperfect constitution of our knowledge-capacity as "finite" beings. "God, the subject of absolutely perfect knowledge and therefore also of every possible adequate perception, naturally possesses what is denied to us finite beings, the perception of things in themselves."[58] According to this interpretation, the absence of the real's absolute givenness as this is experienced by us would not reside in the lack of absolute being on the part of things and realities, but merely in the deficient constitution of ourselves as beings who experience things in a "finite" manner.

Husserl clearly reproaches Kant with having made the mistake characterized here even though he does not mention him by name.[59] The criticism of Kant implied by the *Ideas'* § *43* in turn implies a basic interpretation of the *Critique of Pure Reason* which Husserl himself had not carried out, but which agrees with the "exposition of the *Critique of Pure Reason* as laying the foundation for metaphysics" initiated by Heidegger in his book (published in 1929), *Kant and the Problem of Metaphysics.*[60] This connection appears to us to be important for the history of philosophy.

The view that "to every being there belongs in principle the possibility" of its absolute givenness, and that this possibility therefore belongs to beings as such, is clarified by Husserl as a "mistake in principle" on the basis of the presuppositions won in providing the demonstration that this postulate conflicts with the very meaning of the being of beings whose mode of existence is that of reality. The requirement of the possibility in principle of an absolute givenness of the real is the requirement of the possibility in principle of its adequate perceivability. Only *immanent* perception, however, can be an *adequate* perception, for only in "the case of an immanently directed, or, more succinctly, an *immanent perception* (the so-called 'inner' perception) do *perception and perceived essentially*

177

constitute an unmediated unity, the unity of an individual concrete cogitatio. Here perception contains its object within itself in such a way that it can be separated from it only by abstraction and only as a moment which *by its very essence cannot be independent*."[61] The requirement of the possibility in principle of an absolute givenness of the real is thus equivalent to assuming the possibility of converting beings existing in the mode of reality to beings existing in the mode of experiences. This runs counter to the meaning of the being of beings whose mode of existence is that of reality. The assumption of an actual possibility *in principle* of absolute givenness for beings as such is in truth ultimately equivalent (paradoxically enough) to a *principal* misconstrual, if not an actual denial, of the independent mode of existence of the real as a being which is in principle "transcendent" and incapable of being dissolved into "immanence."

6. Transcendent and the Transcendental Absolute

In accordance with the essential meaning of its being, real being in principle excludes the possibility of its absolute givenness. Consequently, real being is *essentially not* absolute being. "Reality is not in itself something absolute whose bond with some other being is only secondary, but is in the sense of being absolute nothing at all. It has no 'absolute essence'; it has the essentiality of something which in principle is *only* intentional, *only* consciously known, presented, appearing."[62] Not only is consciousness absolute being, but also consciousness *alone* is absolute being. By contrast, real being is "a being which merely has the secondary, relative meaning of being *for* a consciousness."[63] "Reality, the reality of the individual thing as well as that of the entire world, essentially lacks (in our strong sense) independence."[64] Real being "in principle" is "being which is relative to consciousness."[65]

The paradox which we have already touched upon several times is this: Husserl *denies* the absolute being of the real *on the basis of affirming* the independent mode of existence of the real as the "being-in-itself" of the transcendent which in principle excludes the possibility of its absolute givenness. The "independent" essence of the real, rooted in the being-in-itself of things, excludes in principle the "independence" of reality. In Husserl's words: "To the thing as such, to every genuine reality . . . belongs in essence and 'in principle' the inability to be perceived immanently and the inability in general to be found within the system of experience. Thus the thing itself, simply as such, is transcendent. Disclosed therein is the difference in principle between modes of being, the

Husserl's Concept of the "Absolute"

most crucial difference there is: that between consciousness and reality."[66] In a footnote to the phrase "in principle," Husserl further emphasizes: "Here, as in this work generally, the phrase 'in principle' is used in a rigorous sense with reference to the *highest*, and therefore the most radical, essential universalities or essential necessities."[67] Accordingly, one of the highest and most radical essential necessities must correspond to the difference in principle between the modes of being of consciousness and reality. And yet, when this difference is maintained as an essential necessity, it appears to dissolve itself through its own consequences.

As we have seen, from these consequences the fact emerges that the "essential difference" between the modes of being of consciousness and reality, of the immanent and the transcendent, is none other than the difference between *absolute being* and a being which is simply relative to absolute being. That is, real being "is what it is only in 'relation' to"[68] the absolute being of consciousness. This "relation" is not a fortuitous occurrence, but is itself an essential necessity for the being of the real. In § 49 Husserl himself states: "Thus we see that consciousness (inner experience) and real being are not coordinate modes of being living peacefully next to each other and occasionally 'relating' to each other or being "connected' with each other."[69] As a result, it becomes a question as to what meaning the assertion of a difference *in principle* between consciousness and reality could have. If real being has "the essentiality of something which" is "in principle *only* intentional, *only* consciously known, presented, appearing,"[70] clearly it is merely a mode of being which is *subordinate* to the absolute being of consciousness. Real being itself is only in a relative sense. In this context, real being would in general not be an independent mode of being, but, in accordance with the purely limited sense of its being, would be ultimately reduced to a relative moment within the one single totality of absolute consciousness, or consciousness and reality would ultimately form one single whole which would be the whole of absolute being itself, and that actually means the whole of absolute consciousness. And yet: "To be connected in the true sense, to form a whole, can apply only to what is essentially related, each part having its own essence and on the same lines as the other."[71] Husserl continues with this sentence after he has established that "consciousness (inner experience) and real being are not coordinate modes of being. . . ." Husserl himself seems to be on the verge of canceling the assertion concerning the "difference in principle between the modes of being of consciousness and reality," for he raises the question: "Can the unity of a whole be unified other than through the essence proper to its parts, and which must accordingly have some *community of essence* instead of essential heterogeneity?"[72]

179

Rudolf Boehm

Yet, surprisingly enough, we must affirm the fact that Husserl *denies* just this formation of a "whole" of absolute being out of consciousness and reality, and that he furthermore denies any "*community of essence*" between consciousness and reality. "Only what is essentially related can form a whole in the true sense, each part having its own essence and on the same lines as the other. Both immanent or absolute being and transcendent being are indeed termed 'being' (*seiend*) or 'object,' and each has its objective determination of content. It is evident, however, that what on either side goes by the name of object and objective determination are similar only in terms of empty logical categories. Between consciousness and reality yawns a veritable abyss of meaning. Here a perspectival, never absolutely given, merely contingent and relative being; there a necessary and absolute being. . . ."[73]

What does Husserl's insistence upon the "heterogeneity in principle" between the essence of the real and the essence of immanent experiences signify? What is the meaning of this steadfast holding to the "difference in principle" between these two modes of being? Finally, what is the significance of this mention of a "veritable abyss" between the meaning of absolute being and the meaning of that being which is simply relative to the former when it appears to be the case that real being, as purely relative, can only establish and draw its ownmost and complete meaning of being from the absolute being which is consciousness?

Certainly there is a difference between absolute and relative being. Descartes agrees with the scholastic doctrine concerning the equivocal nature of the concept of substance in discussions of God's "infinite" substance and "finite" substances. Accordingly, Husserl's theory of the "abyss of meaning" could be taken as an indication of the concept of being's ambiguity in its application to absolute being or consciousness on the one hand, and to purely relative or real being on the other.

Yet Descartes will say that ultimately God alone is truly substance (or "*absolute* being" in Husserl's sense). That is, Descartes' theory of the "abyss of meaning" between God and finite things in the concept of substance corresponds to the Husserlian distinction between the "*absolute of consciousness*" and an "ultimate and true absolute" which would be "*an 'absolute' in a totally different sense.*"[74] If Husserl's theory of an abysslike difference between the meaning of consciousness' being and the being of reality is to be brought into strict analogy with Descartes' emphasis upon the equivocal nature of the concept of substance, and, if accordingly, it is also to be understood in terms of Husserl's own further distinction between absolute consciousness and God, then this would mean that for Husserl an "abyss of meaning" would not only hold between the being of consciousness which, apart from God, is alone truly *absolute*, and the being of reality which is ultimately not truly absolute, but that it would also hold between that which is alone true *being* (which would be *absolute* being), and that which, as the simply relative, is not truly *being*. That is, viewed as an analogy to the Scholastic-Cartesian doctrine, Husserl's thesis signifies that *being as such* would be *absolute being* (and therefore consciousness), and that in truth, therefore, there would be nothing outside of this absolute being. Such a thought, however, would contain the very *opposite* of what Husserl clearly means, for this would constitute the thought of an absolutely unequivocal concept of being—the thought of an absolute being which, to be sure, would be subject to a relative "phenomenal" influence, but one which would be incapable of compromising not simply the one and only absolute, but also the *absolutely unique meaning of being* which is construed as the being of the absolute.

Thus Husserl's most extreme formulation: a thing, real being in general, "is in the absolute sense nothing at all, it has no 'absolute essence'," cannot mean that reality has "absolutely" no true being at all. It can only mean that reality is not to be understood in an absolute sense, but in terms of the meaning of being which uniquely belongs to it. To think of measuring the being of things and of the real, no matter in what fashion, in terms of absolute being is senseless and absurd.

Formerly, it could have been thought that a "*dissolution*" (*Aufhebung*) of reality *into* the absolute would show itself as capable of being carried out in the form of the phenomenological *reduction,* a reduction where the "transcendent" essence of reality would remain directly *preserved* insofar as it would be equally "suspended" *within* the absolute and—thus perishing within the absolute—would preserve the abysslike differentiation of the meaning of its being from being in the absolute sense. Thus the difference in principle between the modes of being of consciousness and reality, and the equally essential relativity of all reality to the absolute being of consciousness as its absolute ground, would be made intelligible in one stroke, for the absolute ". . . is the ground into which (reality) has been swallowed up."[75] At the same time, reality would be understood as having "the absolute for its abyss (*Abgrund*), and as also having the absolute for its ground (*Grund*)."[76] In this case, absolute being itself—as the necessary ground which is the foundation for (*zugrunde liegt*) all givenness of transcendent being as a givenness which is always only relative—would be the necessary ground for the reality of that "abyss of meaning" into which reality would perish through the reduction to what is absolutely given.

Such an Hegelian interpretation of the basic relation between the "transcendental absolute" and transcendent reality as Husserl views it

181

appears to be justified insofar as Husserl himself, directly after the enactment of the phenomenological reduction in § 50 of the *Ideas*, explicitly states that "We have lost literally nothing, but have won the whole of absolute being which, properly understood, contains all worldly transcendences within itself, 'constituting' them within itself."[77] The word "literally" in the phrase, "lost literally nothing," can in this connection mean only that we have lost nothing "in the absolute sense." Only in the absolute sense is real being not lost through the reduction to consciousness, since, "in the absolute sense," it is itself "nothing at all." The view that even in some "postulated divine intuition a spatial thing is a real constituent of experience, and is therefore itself an experience belonging with other experiences to the divine stream of consciousness and experiences" is expressly labeled by Husserl as nonsensical. "This view, however, is nonsensical" insofar as ". . . it implies . . . that there would be no *essential difference* between transcendence and immanence."[78] This essential difference, however, establishes "the separability in principle of the entire natural world from the domain of consciousness, or the realm of the being belonging to experience,"[79] for "*the being of consciousness . . . is not touched in its ownmost existence . . . by nullifying the world of things.*"[80] Accordingly, we can first truly win absolute being by conceiving of a possible "nullification of the world of things." It is only here that the absolutely given first truly comes to absolute givenness, and in the final analysis absolute being is preeminently what it is according to its essential possibility of absolute givenness.

With Husserl, real being, so to speak, is only "imperfectly dissolved (*aufgehoben*)" into the absolute, for "*no real being . . . is necessary for the being of consciousness itself.*"[81] The being of things—of the real in general—is indifferent to the being of consciousness in an absolute sense, just as, conversely, the meaning of absolute being, in possessing the possibility in principle of absolute givenness, is totally foreign to the being of reality: "Between consciousness and reality there yawns a veritable abyss of meaning." Yet: "*On the other hand, the world of transcendent 'res' is referable without qualification to consciousness. . . .*"[82] By modifying Heidegger's statement "that Being indeed comes-to-presence without beings, but a being never is without Being,"[83] Husserl's thought can be reduced to this formula: "absolute being (consciousness) indeed comes-to-presence (namely, is essentially able to be) without things, but a thing never is without absolute being (the being of consciousness)." This (in the strict sense of the word) *foundational-problematic* relation between the absolute being of consciousness and the being of reality as the being of things is what occasions Husserl to state: "Thus we see that consciousness (inner experience) and real being are not coordinate ways of being, living peacefully next to each other. . . ."[84] The opposition between the "absolute" relatedness of reality to absolute consciousness and the "absolute" indifference of the absolute with regard to the meaning of the being of reality—or the entanglement of indissoluble relation (of reality to the absolute) and abysslike difference in meaning—create a fundamental *conflict* within the basic relation of the one mode of being to the other. Corresponding to this situation are Husserl's "contradictory" assertions, which both deny the "independence" of reality in principle and steadfastly affirm its "heterogeneity" in principle over and against the absolute.

The basic relation which holds between consciousness and reality can now be characterized in two words: as one which is both *fundamental* and *transcendental*. The basic relation between absolute being or consciousness and real being (which is simply relative to consciousness) is a *fundamental* one insofar as a *foundation* is a necessary basis or an indispensable and essential "condition for the possibility" of the Being of a being; not, however, that it is thereby a "sufficient reason" or an "efficient cause" of the Being of this being. Here Husserl's observations concerning the basic relation between "Consciousness and Natural Reality"[85] are indeed "Fundamental Observations"[86] in this sense of "foundation." In a fundamental relation where something is posited in relation to, and is to be necessarily referred to, a ground, and the requisite ground is indifferent to that which requires it as a ground and does not itself require what it serves to ground for its own emergence, is rooted the possibility of a relation of conflict.

The "fundamental observation" is characteristic of a transcendental philosophy. The *transcendental* itself is nothing more than something fundamental which everything that is requires simply in order to be, or in order to be capable of being, without the transcendental ground of all being and all givenness thereby constituting more than an "absolutely" necessary "condition for the possibility of," that is, without this condition as such also becoming the sufficient or efficient cause for all being and givenness. A transcendental ground as such is simply a foundation, even though it is a transcendental foundation.

7. The Transcendental Absolute and the "Ultimate" Transcendent Absolute

Consciousness at first appears as an absolute being in a *substantial* sense, in which terms, and by way of exhibiting the possibility in principle of its absolute givenness, it "requires in principle no other being for its existence." This is how we translated the Cartesian formula employed by

Husserl in the sentence "Immanent being is therefore doubtlessly absolute being in this sense: that in principle *nulla 're' indiget ad existendum.*" Considered more closely, this formula leaves open the possibility that immanent being or consciousness would require "no other being for its existence" merely in a limited sense, a sense which could be conditioned by the use of the word "*res*" in place of the word "*being.*"

This absolute and "substantial" being of consciousness was conceived of as being independent of some "second" being. It is in fact this "second" being which is spoken of in the sentence which directly follows: "On the other hand, the world of transcendent '*res*' is referable without qualification to consciousness, and not simply to a logically conceived consciousness, but to an actual consciousness."[87]

The relativity of all real being to the "substantial" absolute being which consciousness already is "in itself" must, we had stated, also serve to confirm more deeply the absoluteness of absolute consciousness. The notion employed here is that consciousness is not only absolute being in a "substantial" sense, but is also a *transcendental* absolute. The meaning of this concept has already been given by our last considerations. Consciousness is the transcendental absolute insofar as *no* being, no real being, can exist or can be given *without* the foundation of this "in itself" substantial absolute being.

In an extreme formulation, this signifies that *nothing* could be if there were no absolute consciousness. This does *not* mean, however, that everything which is exists *by means of* absolute consciousness. Formulated still more extremely (a formulation so extreme that its understanding is totally dependent upon understanding all that has been said above), we could say: *there is nothing without absolute consciousness, although there is also nothing with absolute consciousness alone.* Namely, consciousness is a transcendental absolute insofar as it is the "absolutely" necessary foundation for all other (real) being. But by no means does—or can—all other being exist if there is simply absolute consciousness. I speak of "ability to exist" in this respect with reference to the heterogeneity in principle of real being in *opposition* to the simply fundamental and essential condition of transcendentally absolute consciousness. Transcendental consciousness is not an absolute being such that it is able to create all other (real) being from the being that is its own.

Corresponding with this is the fact that Husserl's concept of absolute consciousness as the *transcendental* "absolute" clearly *deepens* the absolute sense of the "in itself" purely *substantial* absolute being of consciousness, but at the same time also decisively limits it: "The transcendental 'absolute' which we have exposed through the reductions is in truth not ultimate; it is something which constitutes itself in a certain profound and

Husserl's Concept of the "Absolute"

entirely unique sense and which has its original source in what is ultimately and truly absolute."[88] In terms of what is "ultimately absolute," absolute consciousness, as the simply *transcendental* absolute, is itself only an "absolute" in quotation marks. Thus characterized, the fundamental delimiting of the absolute sense of the being of transcendental consciousness serves as motivation for Husserl's *theological* ideas concerning the "ultimate and true absolute" here referred to. The idea of God as the idea of the "ultimate and true absolute" is motivated by the idea of a "sufficient cause" for the being of everything which, in general, factually exists.

From this point on, however, the paths taken by Husserl (or those which he could have taken) in the *Ideas* are lost in obscurity.

How are "both" absolutes, the transcendental absolute and the ultimate and true absolute, absolute consciousness and God, related? The idea of an ultimate and true absolute (correctly termed "God") above and beyond transcendental consciousness seems to me to be established to the extent that *real* being appears to be only inadequately grounded in the transcendental absolute (consciousness) to which it is relative. Yet Husserl repeatedly indicates and explicitly states that the "transcendental 'absolute'" also "constitutes itself in a certain profound and entirely unique sense and . . . . has its original source in what is ultimately and truly absolute." Is it therefore "ultimately" not a "true absolute" in the substantial sense granted it at the beginning? If it is *not* absolute in this sense, how then is it possible for it to be absolutely *given?* In this case, how is a phenomenological reduction to the "absolute" givenness of this transcendental consciousness possible? By explicitly "disconnecting" the being of God as a "transcendent" absolute being? In fact: how does Husserl motivate the disconnection and reduction enacted here? "We naturally extend the phenomenological reduction to include this 'absolute' and this 'transcendent.' It *should* remain disconnected from the new field of investigation which we are to institute insofar as this is to be a field of pure consciousness itself."[89] We italicize: "It *should* . . .": *must* and *can* it be disconnected? Why should it be disconnected? ". . . All this does not concern us further. Our immediate aim concerns not theology but phenomenology. . . ."[90] Is this truly a phenomenological reduction, or is it finally only a "convenient" abstraction?

Husserl now informs us that the return to "the *theological principle,* which could perhaps be rationally assumed," could also be established on the side of consciousness by means of a "*facticity*": "the facticity in the given order of the course of consciousness in its differentiation into individual forms and the *teleology* immanent within them (could) provide the occasion for raising the question concerning the ground of this same

185

order"[91]—an order which moreover is clearly conditioned by the *facticity of real being.* Accordingly, one could perhaps think that transcendental consciousness is *essentially* an absolute being which, in a certain manner, existed *factually*—as if it were entangled in reality—a manner of existing which could only be an "outflow" from an "original source in what is ultimately and truly absolute," but which yet could be said to retain possession of the possibility *in principle* of its absolute givenness. Here again, however, intrudes the "abysslike" ("*abgründige*") thought that in principle the *nullification of the* world would be the *condition* for actualizing this possibility and therewith a condition for displaying the absolute essence of consciousness. Hence we return to our first question concerning the relationship of absolute consciousness to the absolute being of God.

On the other hand, God, the "ultimate and true absolute," is the "'Absolute' and 'Transcendent'"[92] in opposition to the absolute being which, as consciousness, is "immanent being" as such. Hence "after abandoning the natural world we come up against yet another transcendence which is not . . . immediately given in connection with the reduced consciousness, but which comes to be known in a highly mediated form. . . ."[93] Nevertheless, if it is to be a being which is truly absolute, the being of God clearly cannot exclude in principle the possibility of its *absolute givenness:* "thus the *theological principle* which could be rationally assumed . . . *cannot* for essential reasons be accepted *as a transcendence in the sense of the world.* . . . The ordering principle of the absolute must be found in the absolute itself and in pure and absolute reflection. In other words, since a mundane God is evidently impossible, and since on the other hand the immanence of God in absolute consciousness cannot be grasped as the immanence of being as experience . . ., there must be in the absolute stream of consciousness and its infinities other ways of manifesting the transcendent than the constituting of thinglike realities as unities of harmonious appearances. . . ."[94] These suggestions of Husserl's are clearly established in their contexts, but are still purely postulative. Yet the formulation of these postulates bypasses the (in the strict sense) truly *fundamental* question: does absolute consciousness, even though it is not the "ultimate and true absolute," remain "to the end" and without qualification that *transcendental* absolute without which there would also be no God, and, consequently, without which God would not be able to be at all? Does God, in order to be God, *require* a transcendental consciousness different from him?

Once the question is raised, Husserl could in fact appear to think so insofar as he himself views the thought of God as grounded more in the *teleology* immanently given in the facticity of the being of realities than in this *facticity itself:* "for example, the factual evolution of the series of organisms up to man himself, and within the evolution of humanity the growth of culture with its care for the spirit, etc."[95] To be sure, "the transition to pure consciousness by means of the method of the transcendental reduction already necessarily leads to the question concerning the ground for the facticity of the corresponding constituting consciousness which now emerges." Yet Husserl immediately proceeds: "It is not the *factum* in general, but the *factum* as the source of infinitely extending possible and actual values that compels us to seek for the 'ground'" and which furnishes "rational grounds for the existence of a 'divine' being beyond the world."[96]

For Husserl (as well as for *Leibniz*[97] and *Schelling*[98]), the question which Heidegger had formulated and had termed the "basic question of metaphysics":[99] "Why are there beings rather than nothing?"[100] immediately takes on the meaning of the further question: "To what end is everything that is?" This is the question Husserl has in mind when, going beyond the absolute position of transcendental philosophy, he thinks of God. A discussion of how these two questions stand related to each other, to what extent the one implies the other, and to what extent the one cannot find an answer without the other has provided the occasion for our observations here.

NOTES

1. *Husserliana*, II, ed. H. L. Van Breda. [English translation by Alston and Nakhnikian, *The Idea of Phenomenology* (The Hague: Martinus Nijhoff, 1964).—ED.]
2. *Ibid.*, p. 23.
3. *Ibid.*, pp. 22 f.
4. *Ibid.*, p. 23.
5. *Ibid.*
6. *Ibid.*, p. 9.
7. *Ibid.*, p. 10.
8. *Ibid.*, p. 14.
9. *Ibid.*, p. 7.
10. *Ibid.*, p. 8.
11. *Ibid.*, p. 9.
12. *Ibid.*, p. 61.
13. *Ibid.*, p. 22.

Rudolf Boehm

14. This work first appeared in 1913. A "new (4th) edition expanded and prepared on the basis of the author's handwritten supplements" appeared in 1950 as *Husserliana*, III. I shall limit myself in the following pages to the attempt to develop Husserl's concept of the "absolute" in the *Ideas*. Where I do not note otherwise I will quote from the text of 1913: yet for the sake of simplicity I shall refer to the page numbers of the *Husserliana* edition exclusively.
15. *Husserliana*, IV and V.
16. Cf. the editor's *Introduction* to *Husserliana*, IV.
17. *Husserliana*, III, 8.
18. Cf. Husserl's lectures on the *First Philosophy* (1923-24) in *Husserliana*, VII and VIII. Also the editor's *Introduction* to VII.
19. *Husserliana*, II, 23.
20. As regards the passage quoted above from p. 8 of the first volume of the *Ideas*, Husserl later added this explicit marginal note (this, certainly, was written after 1923): "phenomenology as First Philosophy." Cf. *Husserliana*, III, 463.
21. For the earlier history of this formula see my *Introduction* to *Husserliana*, VII, xvi—xx.
22. *Husserliana*, III, 101 (Gibson, p. 138). Prior to 1923, Husserl modified this sentence as follows: "In general we can see that for the ego, transcendent being, or real being in general, no matter of what sort, can only be given in perception through appearances," *ibid.*, p. 472.
23. *Ibid.*
24. *Ibid.*, p. 102 (Gibson, pp. 139-140). After 1923 Husserl added the following phrase to the end of this sentence: ". . . and which thus proves to be absolutely uncancelable," *ibid.*, p. 472.
25. *Ibid.*, p. 100 (Gibson, p. 137). My italics. Between 1913 and 1923 Husserl desired to reformulate the title of these paragraphs as follows: "Merely Phenomenal Givenness of the Transcendent as (? or rather 'and'?) Absolute Givenness of the Immanent." During the same period he added this marginal note: "The entire § 44 is useless!" Cf. p. 472. This fact is important for the considerations which follow. A particular problem, which we here must ignore, is raised by Husserl's speaking of the "merely phenomenal."
26. The title of the *Ideas'* second section.
27. *Husserliana*, III, 109 (Gibson, p. 146).
28. *Ibid.*, p. 106 (Gibson, p. 143).
29. *Ibid.*
30. *Ibid.*
31. *Ibid.*, p. 108 (Gibson, p. 144).
32. *Ibid.* Husserl added the phrase "in the world of realities in general" after. Cf. p. 473.
33. *Ibid.*
34. As already cited; *ibid.*, p. 101. Cf. note 22.
35. *Ibid.*, pp. 109f. (Gibson, p. 146).
36. *Ibid.*, p. 114 (Gibson, p. 150).
37. *Ibid.*, p. 115 (Gibson, p. 151).
38. As cited above; cf. note 22.
39. As cited above; *ibid.*, p. 108 (Gibson, p. 144).
40. *Ibid.*, p. 115 (Gibson, p. 152).
41. *Principia Philosophiae*, pt. I, 51; eds. Adam and Tannery, VIII, 24. [English translation by Haldane and Ross, *The Philosophical Works of Descartes*, I (Cambridge: Cambridge University Press, 1911), 239.—ED.] There is no Latin edition of the *Principia* among the books in Husserl's library (now preserved at the Husserl-Archives at Louvain).

Husserl's Concept of the "Absolute"

In Husserl's copy of *René Descartes' philosophische Werke,* trans. J. H. v. Kirchmann, pt. III, *Die Prinzipien der Philosophie* (Berlin, 1870), the passages here in question and other passages connected with them are underlined or marked out in pencil by Husserl.

42. *Ibid.*
43. *Ibid.*, pp. 239-240.
44. *Husserliana,* III, 140 (Gibson, p. 174). Cf. the concluding section of this essay.
45. *Ibid.*, p. 198 (Gibson, p. 236). Cf. Descartes, *Principia Philosophiae,* § 52: "Created substances, however, whether corporeal or thinking, may be conceived under this common concept; for they are things which need only the concurrence of God in order to exist."
46. *Husserliana,* III, 115f. (Gibson, p. 152).
47. *Ibid.*, p. 117 (Gibson, p. 153). Between 1913 and 1923 Husserl wrote "relative to consciousness" in place of "relative." Cf. p. 474.
48. *Ibid.* Between 1913 and 1923 Husserl added, by way of clarification, to the end of the sentence: "or, more precisely, for which the thought of something-beyond is nonsense." In a new formulation of the entire sentence (written after 1923) the end of the sentence simply states: "... *above and beyond,* however, is nonsensical." Cf. p. 474.
49. *Ibid.*, p. 118 (Gibson, p. 154).
50. *Ibid.*, p. 134 (Gibson, p. 168).
51. *Ibid.*, p. 98 (Gibson, p. 135).
52. *Ibid.*, (Gibson, pp. 135 f.)
53. As quoted several times above; *ibid.*, p. 117 (Gibson, p. 153).
54. *Ibid.*, p. 99 (Gibson, p. 137).
55. As quoted above; *ibid.*, p. 98 (Gibson, p. 135).
56. *Ibid.*
57. *Ibid.*, p. 97 (Gibson, p. 134).
58. As quoted above; *ibid.*, p. 98 (Gibson, pp. 135 f.).
59. Proof of this is not required here. I will discuss the context of Husserl's relationship to Kant in a study of *Husserl's Relations to Classical Idealism* which will appear shortly. [Cf. Boehm's *"Husserl et l'idéalisme classique"* in *Revue Philosophique de Louvain* 57 (August, 1958), 351-396.—ED.]
60. In particular § 4 and § 5 of this work. [*Kant and the Problem of Metaphysics,* trans. James S. Churchill (Bloomington: Indiana University Press, 1962)—ED.] Heidegger explicitly acknowledges "that the concepts 'appearance' and 'thing in itself' which are fundamental to the *Critique* can be made intelligible and the object of further investigation only if they are based *explicitly* on the *problematic of the finitude* of man." (Churchill, p. 39.—ED.) Of course Heidegger does not see a "mistake in principle" in Kant's "characterization of the finitude of human knowledge" which reveals "what is essential to the dimension within which the laying of the foundation for metaphysics takes place." (Ibid.) Nevertheless "The Laying of the Foundation for Metaphysics in a Repetition" (the title of the fourth section of Heidegger's Kant book) leads to a radical transformation and revaluation of the idea of finitude itself: especially § 41 where the following sentence is found: "There is and must be such as Being only where finitude has become existent." (Churchill, p. 236.—ED.) Husserl had thoroughly come to terms with Heidegger's Kant book; his marginal notations in his own copy of the book preserved in the Husserl-Archives at Louvain reminds one in many respects of the discussions in § 43 of the *Ideas.*
61. Husserliana, III, 85 f. (Gibson, p. 124).
62. As quoted above, *ibid.*, p. 118 (Gibson, p. 154).
63. As quoted above, *ibid.*, p. 117 (Gibson, p. 153).
64. As quoted above, *ibid.*, p. 118 (Gibson, p. 154).
65. As quoted above, *ibid.*, p. 118 (Gibson, p. 154).

66. *Ibid.*, p. 96 (Gibson, pp. 133 f.).
67. *Ibid.*
68. As quoted above; *ibid.*, p. 118 (Gibson, p. 154).
69. *Ibid.*, p. 116 (Gibson, p. 152).
70. As quoted above; *ibid.*, p. 118 (Gibson, p. 154).
71. *Ibid.*, p. 116 (Gibson, p. 152).
72. *Ibid.*, p. 88 (Gibson, p. 126).
73. *Ibid.*, pp. 116 f. (Gibson, pp. 152 f.).
74. *Ibid.*, pp. 140 and 198 (Gibson, pp. 174 and 236).
75. Hegel, *Wissenschaft der Logik: Zweiter Teil*, ed. Lasson (Hamburg: Felix Meiner, 1934), p. 158: the chapter entitled "*The Absolute*"—"*A. The* Exposition *of the Absolute*" [English translation by Johnston and Struthers, *Science of Logic, vol. II* (London: George Allen & Unwin Ltd., 1929), p. 162.—ED.]. Here it should be noted that the absolute, which can only be "approached" at this stage of the *Logic*, ". . . *is* only *the Absolute of* an *external reflection* . . . and is not, therefore, the Absolute-Absolute, but only the Absolute given in a determinate form," or, "it is the Absolute as attribute," *ibid.*, p. 160 [Johnston and Struthers, p. 164].
76. *Ibid.*, p. 159 [Johnston and Struthers, p. 163]. [Boehm here alludes to three complementary terms present in this section of Hegel's *Logic: untergehen, zurückgehen,* and *zugrunde-gehen*. The essential movement of the dialectic referred to is that of leading a term of the dialectic back (*zurückgehen*) to its ground (*zugrunde-gehen*), a movement whereby this element can be said to "perish" or be "swallowed up" into its ground in order to shed this term of its abstractness. Boehm here suggests that the phenomenological reduction might be said to parallel this Hegelian process of *Aufhebung* wherein one element of the dialectic, which appears as only a partial and "relative" truth, is "nullified" in terms of its abstractness by the dialectical advance toward the completion of its true meaning within some higher synthesis. The phenomenological reduction suspends or "nullifies" transcendent reality, and leads it back into its true ground, or absolute consciousness, a movement which is at the same time the disclosure and "preservation" of the true meaning of reality's being by revealing its relativity to absolute consciousness. Reality then possesses the "absolute for its abyss (*Abgrund*)" precisely insofar as the disclosure of the former's relativity is at the same time its "perishing" as being in an absolute sense, for it is disclosed as fundamentally lacking its own ground, and therefore as *ab-gründig*.—ED.]
77. *Husserliana*, III, 119 (Gibson, pp. 154 f.).
78. As quoted above; *ibid.*, p. 98 (Gibson, p. 135).
79. As quoted above; *ibid.*, p. 110 (Gibson, p. 146).
80. As quoted above, *ibid.*, p. 115 (Gibson, p. 151).
81. *Ibid.*
82. As quoted above; *ibid.*, pp. 115 f. (Gibson, p. 152).
83. Heidegger's *Nachwort* to *Was ist Metaphysik?*, fourth edition (1923), p. 25. In the fifth edition (1949) this sentence is replaced by another: "Being never comes-to-presence without beings, . . . a being never is without Being"; p. 41 ["What is Metaphysics" in *Existence and Being* (Chicago: Henry Regnery Co., 1949), p. 354.—ED.]
84. As quoted above; *Husserliana*, III, 116 (Gibson, p. 152).
85. The title of the central second chapter of the second part of the *Ideas*.
86. Cf. above, note 26.
87. As quoted above, *Husserliana*, III, 115 (Gibson, p. 152).
88. *Ibid.*, p. 198 (Gibson, p. 236). It should be noted that § 81, from which this passage is taken, nowhere explicitly speaks of God. Husserl's theme is indicated by the title of this section: "Phenomenological Time and Time-Consciousness." Because it is within this context that Husserl speaks of the "ultimate and true absolute" which lies beyond the simple

Husserl's Concept of the "Absolute"

"transcendental absolute," further clarification of this theme can be had only with the investigation of Husserl's still unpublished notes of 1930-35 on the problem of time preserved at the Husserl-Archives at Louvain. This is a task which still remains to be completed, even after the indispensable preparatory work accomplished by G. Brand's *Welt, Ich und Zeit* (1955). [A portion of this work can be found in an English translation in Joseph J. Kockelman's *Phenomenology: The Philosophy of Edmund Husserl and Its Interpretation* (New York: Doubleday, 1967), pp. 197-217.—ED.] Equally indispensable would be Husserl's lectures on the *Phenomenology of Inner Time-Consciousness* from 1905-1910 and edited by Martin Heidegger, where Husserl already refers to "the absolute time-constituting flow of consciousness."

89. *Husserliana*, III, 140 (in § 58: "The Disconnection of the Transcendence of God") (Gibson, p. 175).

90. *Ibid.*, p.122 (Gibson, p. 157).

91. *Ibid.*, p. 121 (Gibson, p. 157).

92. As quoted above; *ibid.*, p. 140 (Gibson, p. 174).

93. *Ibid.*, pp. 138 f. (Gibson, p. 173). Instead of the phrase "highly mediated," between 1913 and 1923 Husserl wrote: "in an entirely different way"; cf. p. 477.

94. *Ibid.*, pp. 121 f. (Gibson, p. 157). In the sentence: "The ordering principle of the absolute must be found in the absolute itself . . ." the phrase "the absolute itself" clearly means absolute consciousness; by contrast, "God" means "the ordering principle of the absolute."

95. *Ibid.*, p. 139 (Gibson, p. 174).

96. *Ibid.*; also the note to § 51, pp. 121 f. (Gibson, pp. 158 f.).

97. *Principes de la Nature et de la Grace fondees en Raison*, § 7; ed. Robinet, p. 45. [*Leibniz: Philosophical Papers and Letters*, ed. Loemker (Chicago: University of Chicago Press, 1956), II, 1038. ". . . The first question which we have a right to ask will be, 'Why is there something rather than nothing?' For nothing is simpler and easier than something. Further, assuming that things must exist, it must be possible to give a reason *why they should exist as they do* and not otherwise."—ED.] The meaning which this question has for Leibniz must be drawn from the answer he finally gives to it.

98. *Philosophie der Offenbarung, Erste Vorlesung, Collected Works*, II-III, 7. The meaning which this question has for Schelling is immediately evident from the context. [The relevant passage in this text is as follows: "One generation passes away and another generation comes in order to once again pass away in its turn. We wait in vain for something new to occur wherein this unrest will finally find its goal, everything that happens takes place only in order for something else to happen and which itself becomes past in opposition to something else. Essentially, therefore, everything happens to no purpose, and all of man's actions, endeavors and labors are themselves sheer vanity: everything is vanity, for vanity is simply that which lacks a true aim. Quite removed from the view that man and his acts make the world comprehensible, man himself is the incomprehensible, and I am unavoidably driven to the view that all being is wretchedness, a view which announces itself both in our times and in the past in grievous words. It is precisely man who compels me to raise this question which is so full of doubt: Why are there beings? Why not nothing?" *Ibid.*—ED.]

99. Martin Heidegger, "What Is Metaphysics," trans. R. F. C. Hull and Alan Crick in *Existence and Being* (Chicago: Henry Regnery Co., 1949), p. 349.—ED.

100. *Ibid.* Cf. also Martin Heidegger, *An Introduction to Metaphysics*, trans. Ralph Mannheim (New Haven: Yale University Press, 1959), pp. 1 ff.—ED.

Critical Observations Concerning Husserl's Posthumous Writings

Hans Wagner

1. The Point of Departure

AN ENTHUSIASTIC preoccupation with Husserl's posthumous writings has been at work since 1939. It is carried on partly by those of Husserl's students who are still living and partly by individuals associated with the Husserl-Archives. The publication of the greater part of these highly voluminous writings (amounting to some 45,000 pages) is planned. So far the first five volumes of the *Collected Works* have appeared.[1]

At the same time a new and intense interest in Husserl and phenomenology has arisen, particularly outside of Germany. Indeed, it is quite possible that this renewed interest may lead to a kind of "Husserl-Renaissance."

As far as Germany is concerned, an intensive and critical coming to terms with the later Husserl has not yet taken place. To me such discussion appears to be highly desirable, indeed, even necessary. I wish to initiate this discussion in a fundamental and earnest way with my following remarks.

Published discussions of Husserl's thought in Germany began in 1933. Rudolph Zocher and Friedrich Kreis, both speaking from the Neo-Kantian Critical standpoint, had eventually taken a stand with respect to Husserl.[2] Zocher's investigation is in this connection by far the most important. After the publication today of Husserl's later works, which Zocher was not able to take into account, one would certainly not wish to place the same systematic concepts at the center of criticism which Zocher had to accept as being of key significance at that time. Apart from this, however, this critical study is still in most respects of great significance, and as yet it is still unsurpassed in the soundness of its distinctions, the clarity of its analyses, and its pointing out inadequate explications of important Husserlian concepts. It must still be studied today.

In 1933 Eugen Fink had responded to Zocher's critique with Husserl's explicit authorization.[3] Some notable features will strike those who study this response today. For example, a position is scarcely taken with respect to the results of Zocher's *individual* analyses and criticisms, that is, to the most important results of his close attention to individual topics which is the strong point of this work and whose value is independent of any particular philosophical orientation. Husserl and Fink were clearly concerned with something else. For both of them it was a question of offering a general resistance to "Criticism." If, however, one looks more closely, one will see that this is not the real point of Fink's article. The actual arguments reveal that it is simply a question of delimiting phenomenology over and against the position of Rickert alone, and furthermore only against the (early) Rickert of the "object of knowledge." What is important in Fink's article cannot, therefore, lie so much in what could have been and must be said against Zocher (and Rickert); rather its importance lies in bringing into view several new (and therefore not criticized by Zocher) moments of phenomenological idealism: the transcendental We, the essentially nonmundane character of subjectivity, and the central thought of the constitution of the world. These three moments serve to distinguish in principle phenomenological idealism from Criticism and, quite naturally, from all nonidealistic philosophy. We too will have to concern ourselves in detail with these three moments.

The published critical discussion of Husserl in Germany comes to an end with the Zocher-Fink debate. It is important to keep in mind that this discussion could never concern itself with the *entire* Husserl. Zocher's book did not deal with the *Formal and Transcendental Logic* (*1929*), not to mention the *Cartesian Meditations*, which first appeared in France in 1931, or the "Crisis-article," first published in 1936.[4]

The phenomenological school itself had produced a series of valuable expositions and discussions of Husserl. Oskar Becker's article appeared in 1930,[5] a clear and intelligent presentation of the direction Husserl had taken up to the *Formal and Transcendental Logic.* Unfortunately, the basic thoughts of this work and the *Cartesian Meditations* are only sketched out on a few pages. In 1938, the year of Husserl's death, Eugen Fink published a first inclusive presentation of the entire Husserl.[6] For the person today who is concerned with the entire, and thereby also the final, Husserl, it is in point of time the first document to which he must refer. Finally, in 1949 Ludwig Landgrebe published a collection of essays on Husserl.[7]

The last German reviews of Husserl's work appeared in 1933: a relatively brief review of the *Formal and Transcendental Logic* by Roman Ingarden[8] and a moderately detailed and admirable review of the *Cartesian Meditations* by Helmut Kuhn.[9]

In the following period Husserl is overshadowed by his most important and independent student, Martin Heidegger. Heidegger increasingly became the leader of the phenomenological school. Consequently, Heidegger himself was for a long period viewed as a phenomenologist, and his work was understood as radicalizing phenomenological concerns and rendering them more concrete.[10] On the other hand, Husserl does not appear simply for what he himself is, but as a point of transition leading to Heidegger. Thus Heidegger is seen from the perspective of Husserl, and Husserl is seen from the perspective of Heidegger, although both resisted each other from the very beginning.

Nicolai Hartmann also helped to effect the waning interest in Husserl. He took up the Husserlian theme of formal and regional ontologies and carried it out in a fruitful manner. To be sure, this was accomplished by suspending Husserl's truly basic aim, that is, by suspending all transcendental reductions, by disregarding all pure subjectivity-problematics, and by expressly reinstating the "natural" attitude in the opinion that only in this way could beings come to be accepted in their character of in-itself-ness.

The situation today is entirely different. Husserl and Heidegger, as well as Husserl and Hartmann, are clearly distinct from one another. Each must be studied on his own terms. For us today it is a question of those problems which each of them has worked with and left behind for further development. Each receives his own importance in terms of these problems, different from each other in nature and extent. Consequently, the following remarks will be concerned solely with clarifying *the meaning of Husserl's accomplishment within the current state of philosophical problems,* a state which Husserl himself has helped to bring about, but for which he is in no way entirely responsible.

Reduced to its central and essential elements, Husserl's accomplishment and its contribution to the current state of problems can be centered around the following four systematic concepts: *reduction* as the method for establishing ultimate foundations; *pure subjectivity,* which can on the one hand be characterized in terms of a primordial temporality, and as the subjectivity of a pure (transcendental) intersubjectivity on the other; the universal theme of the *constitution of the world;* and, finally, the *problem of reason* as the idea of a universal critique of reason.[11]

Husserl's Posthumous Writings

2. *The Principal Themes*

It would be inconvenient to begin our discussion of Husserl's hitherto published posthumous writings by taking each volume individually. This would lead to a troublesome and fruitless repetition and recapitulation of references. There remains only the possibility of arranging this discussion *thematically*. Nevertheless, in order to provide a view of the contents of the individual volumes as well, I shall (first) allow a brief indication and characterization of their contents to proceed this thematic discussion, and (second) I shall insert numerous textual references into the thematic discussion itself.

The *Cartesian Meditations,* which first appeared in a French translation in 1931, now appears in the original German text. It is the most important posthumous work which has appeared so far and quite simply represents the later Husserl. It undertakes to provide all knowledge with an ultimate foundation. This foundation can be given only through the method of the phenomenological reduction. Through this method alone can we reach pure subjectivity, the ultimate source of all knowing. The reduction opens up a nonmundane field of pure experience: that of the constitutive accomplishing of the meaning of all beings. Here the return from the object-noema continually leads back to the specific noeses within which these noema are built up. "Noeses," "the life of acts" in general, is not thereby understood as something mundane, but rather as being as pure as that which is accomplished within them. It is not a question of the facticity of these acts of experience; rather we are concerned with their indestructible essential structure: the reduction is thus equally transcendental and eidetic. If I have returned to my pure ego and its life of acts in this way, I am confronted by *this universal question: how does everything which I designate as the world and as something within the world originate from within me in my pure accomplishment?* How is the world constituted for me (the world with all its regions and the world as a whole) with the character of in-itselfness, of objectivity, of being true for everyone? True for everyone: that means for every (actual and imaginable) Other. I can justifiably interpret the world as objective only when I interpret it as existing for every other consciousness just as it exists for me, that is, only when the world is constituted for me as one which is *eo ipso* similarly constituted for every other consciousness. Correlatively, this means that for me the world has the meaning of being true for everyone when another consciousness, and all ether consciousnesses, has the meaning for myself of beings who possess the one world just as I. What is required is that other consciousnesses be singled out as *objects which, like myself, are subjects,* and indeed subjects which, taken

195

together, and thanks to the constitutive accomplishments of their pure consciousnesses, are related to one and the same world.

The entire sense of my speaking of the world as being in-itself and objective is thus bound up with the constitution of the transcendental *We,* a community of monads, a monadological intersubjectivity. And the pure subjectivity to which the sense of all talk of beings and world refers is just as much the one pure ego as the one pure We. More precisely: it is *the subjectivity of the pure ego which contains within itself the conditions for the pure We.*

Of less significance than the *Meditations,* this most important of the currently published posthumous writings, is the *Paris Lectures.* It is shorter than the *Meditations* and in its entirety treats the same themes, although the problem of intersubjectivity (the high point of the *Meditations*) recedes somewhat into the background.

Also of less importance for us today is the *Five Lectures* concerning "The Idea of Phenomenology," which Husserl gave in Göttingen in 1907. The thematic content of the lectures is repeatedly developed later on: universal *epoché*, analysis of essences, evidence, internal time-consciousness, categorial givennesses, the noesis-noema correlation, and so on. I may surely assume knowledge of the first volume of the *Ideas.*

The second volume of the *Ideas,* while in some places carrying out with more precision certain topics which were merely suggested elsewhere, nevertheless offers us something new and important with its researches into the theme of the constitution of the world in general and into the world of nature and the world of spirit in particular. The constitution of the world advances through clearly distinguishable stages. It begins as the constitution of nature. Nature in this connection signifies at first nothing other than the sphere of simple affairs (*Sachen*). The mark of "objectivity" is in no way an original feature of this sphere, a mark which today, because of the centuries-old work of the natural-scientific attitude, is attributed to this sphere as if it belonged to it self-evidently. Rather this is precisely the central question among the complex of problems related to a constitution of nature: how and by what means does the basic conviction that its manner of being is that of something "in-itself" accrue to our speaking of nature, this basic conviction which is already and constantly dominant, but which is thereby no less needful of an explanation of its justification. How and by what means can we think of nature as something "in-itself"? What is the meaning of this speaking of the in-itselfness of nature and how does it originate?

We must first of all understand how we arrive at the constitution of affairs, things (i.e., parts of nature). What belongs to things originally is the appearance of a spatiality and extension which follow certain schemata, a (temporal-spatial) process-character and mobility, a thorough dependency upon variables and varying circumstances. All these, however, belong to things only to the extent that a first and fundamental condition has been fulfilled: their aesthetic relatedness to the living body. The body and its capacity for sensation is the prior condition for a constitution of natural things; admittedly, the body under "normal" perceptual conditions and with "normal" psychophysical capacities. Ultimately, all natural things and the entirety of nature are constitutively related to me as a psychophysical being. And at first the entirety of nature is there *for me alone* (as such a being), that is, as yet without the sense of objectivity.

Additional stages are required in order that this latter characteristic can attach itself to things. The first of these is the constitution of animate nature, that is, those parts of nature which are not simply material bodies but bodies with a psyche. What does this mean and how is it possible to think of and comprehend certain parts of nature as being such bodies? How is the sense of our speaking of living bodies and, within them, real psyches, constituted? How does "life" or the psyche come to be given to us? How do I arrive at the point of attributing to others a life and a psyche similar to mine? In accordance with the fact that both (as something inner) are accessible to me only within myself, that both cannot be directly given to me insofar as they belong to another, I clearly transfer to the Other what is given to me with an original presence only in myself: life and subjectivity. It is, therefore, the appresentation of something which does not manifest itself to me in its original presence. It is only through the accomplishment of this appresentation (or "empathy") that I no longer think of myself as the sole living subject in the world but as one subject among others who are more or less like myself and who, as psyches, are at hand in the natural world along with myself.

This has a double significance. Not only does this mean that there is now for the first time a complete nature, that is, that in addition to simply material bodies there are now living bodies and the psyches which belong to them, but also and primarily this: I now for the first time no longer think of myself as the sole subject but as one subject along with others. As a correlate to this, the thought can now occur to me for the first time that this world of nature and every part in it is no longer simply what it is "for me," but that it is what it is "for us," that is, that it is for other subjects precisely as it is for me. Hence arises the thought of a complete subjectivity (not only myself, but all of us; everyone like myself) as well as the thought of the intersubjectivity of the natural world (as being one and the same world for us all, for everyone). Intersubjectivity, the constant presupposition for speaking of the objective world, is now for the first time something whose meaning can be established in relation to myself insofar as a plurality of subjects has been constituted within myself through the constitution of other psyches, so that I can now think of my world as a world for *all* of these subjects.

The second half of the work treats the constitution of the *spiritual* world. The two halves, however, are not related simply in an external way, as if both nature and spirit existed and one had simply to review the constitution of the one and the other in turn. Rather (and it is important to note this) does the thought of constitution advance of necessity to the spiritual world for internal reasons; namely, the manner in which the world of nature has been constituted so far proves itself to be inadequate and in need of supplementation. In order to bring *this* constitution to its end it is necessary to advance to the constitution of spirit: the completion of the constitution of nature presupposes the constitution of spirit because it is only upon the basis of and within constituted spirit that the constitution of nature can be brought to its conclusion.

That the manner in which we have hitherto constituted nature has not attained its goal can be seen by the following consideration. Neither the hitherto discovered meaning of the "ego" nor of the "We" is the meaning of true and ultimate subjectivity. I am a body with a psyche; "we" are bodies with psyches. The subjectivity which has been spoken of so far is simply a natural, and thus only a real, mundane, subjectivity, and therefore certainly not the true and ultimate subjectivity. It is one which is itself also constituted because it is the subjectivity of beings who are not simply subjects but who are also existing members of existing nature (as bodies with psyches belonging to and connected with them). If this subjectivity is itself constituted, nature up to this point has not yet been constituted in terms of its *ultimate* ground. To lead the constitution of nature to its ultimate ground thus means to pass beyond the subjectivity which we have been able to reach so far and return to one which is more fundamental. Our discussion thus comes to spirit and to the world of spirit.

As long as the constitution of nature remains affixed to bodies and their psyches it still remains affixed to nature, for the subjectivity taken into account so far belongs to nature. If the constitution of nature now becomes the accomplishment of spirit, spirit extends beyond nature, for the subjectivity of spirit is no longer a natural subjectivity.

Thus it is the question concerning the subjectivity appropriate to initiating the constitution of nature that holds the two parts of the work together. It is this question which dominates the first half of the work and which now dictates the transition to the second half.

Spirit is essentially formative of society. It binds persons together to form a community (in all forms of simultaneity and history). Spirit also makes possible for the first time a genuine encounter between subject and object, that is, one which is no longer a real relatedness of the one to the other but a free intentional relation (and this in all forms of activity and passivity, the latter including affectivity and receptivity). Just as real relatedness of subject to object is causal, so is the intentional relatedness exclusively the relatedness of motivation: the object motivates spirit, particularly with regard to the specification of its (active and passive) behavior. Motivation appears in a series of forms (rational motivation, association, experiential motivation, etc.) and constitutes the basic lawfulness of spiritual life: where there is motivation there is spirit. The constitution of the spiritual world is first made possible on the basis of this situation, and on this basis alone. And this in clear analogy to the constitution of the world of animate nature. Animate nature is psychic nature; it is constituted in the apprehension of the psyche's inwardness, so that, in addition to material bodies, bodies with the psyches which belong to them are thinkable (i.e., through "empathy"); finally, this also includes myself as being one among the thus constituted members of the world of living beings. The world of the spirit is a world singled out by motivation; *meaning* (as inwardness guided by motives) becomes visible in its members as pervading them throughout, as permeating them and "ensouling" them, meaning which allows itself to be understood by me (both as the meaning of things as well as the meaning of spiritual being, i.e., man). Comprehension here corresponds to appresentation (comprehension as the understanding of meaning, be this the understanding of "spiritualized" things or the understanding of beings who possess spirit). It is through comprehension that spirit and spiritual persons are originally capable of being thought by me; it is through comprehension that the world of spirits and the spiritual world are originally constituted; and finally it is through comprehension that my own ego is also constituted as a member of the spiritual and personal world within the unity of beings of like nature.

Three moments reach their conclusion in the constitution of the spiritual world: the constitution of nature, the constitution of the world, and the constitution of myself as a human being. As regards the constitution of nature: nature at first was only a nature "for me alone," a pure world of appearances without true objectivity. Subsequently, in the constitution of psychic beings, other living beings arose within nature who were similar to myself, that is, real natural subjects, and hence for the first time the thought of a relationship of world and nature not simply to myself but also to the endless plurality of other natural beings like myself could originate and the theme of the intersubjectivity of world and nature could be introduced. This theme of a "nature and world for everyone" (and hence the theme of an objective nature and world in-itself) could be first carried out, however, only in the constitution of the spiritual world, for here the relationship could be transformed into a form no longer simply causal or real, but into the form of a free intentional relationship. True intersubjectivity can occur only in this form and only now can nature be thought of as being objective. As a correlate, only now does the thought of an "objective" *science* of nature receive its proper foundation: only in dependency upon the personal-spiritual world does the thought of nature fully constitute itself as the thought of an objective nature, that is, as the possible object of the natural sciences. As regards the constitution of the *world:* with the constitution of the spiritual world and the constitution of nature not only are both spheres of the real world each constituted in their own right, but they are also constituted in the unity of their implications and mutual relationships. This means that they are constituted as the *one* real world which is structured in this manner. Spirit here is fundamental to this relation of implications and correlations and to this extent it may be designated as the absolute in contrast to nature, the field of thorough and universal relativity. Finally, with respect to the constitution of *myself* as a human being: at first I was simply a pure ego within my body. With the constitution of living nature there also arose my own self-understanding as a truly real and natural being composed of body and psyche. Finally, after the constitution of the spiritual world, I can conceive of myself as also being a real person, a complete human being endowed with spirit and thus a member of the world of mankind.

With the constitution of the spiritual world, constitution itself has reached its conclusion. But it should be noted that it has not thereby reached its beginning or its source. This would be *pure, transcendental* subjectivity (as the pure ego and, implied therein, the pure "We"). This has remained concealed throughout the entire course of constitution. That which stands at the end of this whole, the ego as person and spirit and the "We" as a personal and spiritual community, is not the ego and the implicit We which stood as the theme of the *Cartesian Meditations.* The ego and the We, being constitutive *as such*, are different from the ego and the We which, to be sure, are constitutive of the thoughts concerning nature but which nevertheless are themselves constituted: spirit and the spirits in the world.

Again not quite so important and scarcely one-third as extensive as the second volume of the *Ideas* is *Ideas III*. This volume does not contain what Husserl had originally planned for it (an essay on the "Idea of Philosophy"); rather is it composed of scientific-theoretical investigations

Husserl's Posthumous Writings

(which again were originally to have belonged to the second volume of the *Ideas*). Husserl's reflections here take "essential differences between objectivities" as their point of departure, differences which can and must furnish principles for differentiating the various areas of science. The most basic of these distinctions are those between the simply material thing, the body, and the psyche (or psychical ego); corresponding to these distinctions are the divisions of physics, somatology, and psychology. Somatology is marked off from physics to the extent that the separation of bodily sensitivity and bodily sensations follows successfully from the very fabric of nature. There now arises, however, the problem concerning the possibility of distinguishing psychology from somatology, for what supposedly serves to establish the unique character of somatology—sensations—is no less also the object of psychology. Therefore, if somatology and psychology are to represent a real or final division, there must be a basic difference with respect to the manner in which somatology and psychology observe sensations. Husserl views this difference as follows: in the somatological interpretation, sensations are natural events, and that means that they are produced causally. By contrast, in the psychological interpretation, sensations are something original; they are simply the *given* material, which is taken as a point of departure and which stands in certain functional relationships. No questions as to cause are addressed to them from the psychological point of view. A second group of questions concerns the relation between ontologies and the empirical sciences mentioned above. Thing, body, and psyche prove to be regional concepts. This provides Husserl with the occasion for once again taking up (and this time quite adequately) the theme of regional concepts and their transcendental genesis from a respectively unique type of experience of reality. In advancing through the foundational relationship between the basic types of our experience of reality, there also emerges a foundational relationship from one level to another between these regional concepts and various regions of objects (material thing, aestheological thing, psyche or human being). The regional concepts prescribe what must be necessarily attributed to a thing in the appropriate region, that is, its regional and *a priori* essence. These form the themes of the different (regional) ontologies. A specific and valuable word is devoted to the difference between the relation of physics and psychology to their respective ontologies. The immediate occasion for this discussion is the equivocal term "description" (description of nature, descriptive psychology, essential description). In physics description is not a basis for validity, but it is such in psychology. The reason for this is that the role of phenomena ("appearances") is quite different in psychology and in physics. The appearances of material nature are held by the physicist to be *simply* appearances, appearances of some other true nature, an invisible and inexperienceable nature, and therefore an objective nature. Physics eliminates the relation of material nature to the human psychophysical constitution and organization, and indeed also eliminates its relation to the "normal" psychophysical constitution. The phenomena described in psychology, however, are *not* the appearances of something else; rather they are the psychic itself, and hence already constitute the object of psychology. Also to be distinguished is "essential description": it leads to a rational psychology (as the ontology of the psychic).

The last problem concerns the relation of the regional ontologies to (transcendental) phenomenology. All ontologies prove to be dogmatic: even though they are situated within the eidetic attitude and are directed toward the eidetic (fundamental) essence of their objects, they are nevertheless simply directed to actual beings in a straightforward manner. Phenomenology's object, however, is transcendental consciousness together with all the events which take place within it (specifically within the twofold form of the noesis-noema correlation). All talk of beings receives its meaning and basis within this consciousness alone. Hence only through phenomenology do these ontologies experience a clarification of the meaning and basis for all that they think and say. Phenomenology's theme is the idea of a complete and ultimate establishing of all knowledge in terms of purely intuitive sources. All knowledge: this first of all means all ontologies and, second, all empirical sciences. Four appendices are attached to *Ideas III;* of these the first is the most important and is to be strongly recommended for study.

Also of greater importance (and the last work to be reviewed here) are the investigations concerning a genealogy of logic which L. Landgrebe has edited under the title: *Experience and Judgment.* The genealogy of logic has as its central interest the genealogy of the central element in all *logos:* judgment. Genealogy is to be understood as transcendental: as essential clarification through the return to grounds and to the ultimate ground, and, correlatively, as the following of the development from grounds and the ultimate ground. It consequently asks the question: how and from what ground does the evidence of predicative judgment proceed? The Husserlian question retains its clarity only when the Husserlian conception of thinking, knowing, and judging has been taken into account. According to this conception, all thinking and judging presupposes pregiven objects as that which all possible thinking and judging is about. Therefore, the evidence pertaining to judgments presupposes evidence of objects, the evident givenness of what is to be judged: prepredicative evidence. The genealogy of predicative judgment will therefore designate pursuing the development of the evidence pertaining to judgment from the prepredicative stage through all mediating stages. The title "prepredicative evidence" is hereby taken in a radical sense: all mathematical-logical (i.e., exact) idealizations (which are today accepted as self-evident) are to be withdrawn, and we are to go back to the point where the given has not yet taken on the sense of an objective world existing for everyone; hence we are to go back to the pure life-world (*Lebenswelt*), the purely passively presented basis of experience. The work does not set itself the task of carrying out a universal and complete genealogy of the logical; it treats only one, although perhaps the most important, theme of such a genealogy: the development of categorial judgment on the basis of a perception which is posited as having been already constituted. The only path it pursues, therefore, is the path leading from perceptual evidence to the evidence which pertains to judgment (this latter, however, is pursued up to the evidence pertaining to the higher, multilayered, constituted judgments). The first section presents an analysis of prepredicative or receptive experience. This section distinguishes the pure passivity and associational structure of the pregiven from "affection," attention, and the "turning of the ego's interest towards . . ."; next, the observing perception is distinguished from explication (originating in the explicative synthesis are the categories of substratum and determination, the primordial categories for all possibilities of judging), and distinguished from this in turn is the grasping of relations, specifically in terms of its being established in passivity (as necessary connections between the objects of perception which are given upon the basis of the one time which presents the form of all sensibility). The second section gives an analysis of predicative thought and, as a correlate to this, an analysis of the objectivities belonging to the understanding which can be construed as the accomplishments of predicative thought. Here it is primarily a question of seeing how and through what moments of receptivity the different accomplishments and forms of judgment emerge. Thus, for example, judgments expressing a serial arrangement of consecutive determinations have their origin in explications which are simply continued, or the attributive (adjectival) form of judgment, which has its origin in a nonuniformly distributed interest. Analyzed next is the origin of an affair-complex as a new type of object (reached by means of substantializing a simple judgment), which can then become the substratum for predication in a higher, founded judgment. Thus the affair-complex (*Sachverhalt*) is the primordial type of all (categorial or syntactical) objectivities of the understanding. All objectivities of the understanding are characterized by unreality: their temporal form is that of "all times." A specific chapter is devoted to the origin of the modalities of judgment. The third section investigates the constitution of universal objectivities ("all X's are . . .";

203

"X in general is . . .") and raises the question: how are such universal judgments possible? And, since the possibility of comprehending the individual rests within the relation of the individual to the universal, investigating the constitution of universal objectivities ultimately signifies an investigation into the constitution of comprehending thought: how is comprehension, this highest *telos* of logical activity, possible? Husserl clearly distinguishes the empirical universal from the pure universal (or the universality of essence). Both reveal themselves to be not only different in the logical sense, but also different with respect to their constitution. Pure universality emerges from the method of essence-intuition. Perhaps the most satisfying and compelling discussions of this theme in the entirety of Husserl's work are to be found here (free variation, the role of examples taken as the point of departure, the necessity for conceptually retaining the entire manifold of variations for the purpose of intuiting an essence, the meaning of intuition, the meaning of speaking about the explicit disconnection of all existence-positings for the purpose of grasping a pure universal). A few comments are also given (which are again of great importance) concerning the theme of obtaining the highest and ultimate universals, that is, the regions (or categories). The last chapter treats that highest spontaneous accomplishment for which the constitution of universal objectivities forms the logical presupposition: the constitution of general predication itself or that of judgments "in general."

3. The Concept of the Reduction

The concept of the reduction is the key to Husserl's philosophy; it opens the way for understanding all other basic concepts connected with this philosophy. The reduction leads to transcendental subjectivity (the ego and the "We"); it first makes philosophical knowledge of the world possible in that it serves to expose the various domains of the world's constitution; it is the fundamental condition for elaborating the theme of a universal critique of reason (the problem of reason and nonreason). Hence our first analytical and critical work must be aimed at this concept of the reduction.

Philosophy begins with the reduction; what lies before the reduction is the naive possession of the world, the naive belief in the world, whether this occurs in the manner of everyday existence or in the manner of the sciences. Naiveté has no suspicions concerning what takes place within the unfathomable; it speaks without suspicion of the world, of man, and of his consciousness; it lives without suspicion in the world. Should it become thoughtful it would say: in all that we call everyday knowledge and science the only thing which is unfathomable is that there is a world and that we who are within this world with our familiar and favorable capabilities come more or less and little by little to know ourselves and this world. This naiveté would come to an end if it should be asked: what does it mean to say that *there is* (a world, that we are within it, that we have our familiar capabilities)? What does this mean: I know, I am certain, it is perfectly clear to me that these (above-mentioned) things are? It means this: even though all this may be given without my or our doing, there is nothing for me and for us without my and our accomplishment. Our simplest possession of the world as well as our highest science is there thanks to my and our accomplishment. To have no suspicion is to say that something is, without reflecting upon what it is which makes this belief, this knowing, this self-evidence, possible.

The reduction brings an end to this naiveté and its lack of suspicion and points toward the unfathomable from which all that is there for me and for us emerges: my and our conscious activity, my and our life of consciousness within which all that is there for me and for us is constituted. As a correlate, it is the accomplishment of the reduction to make the world of the world-accomplishing consciousness (next to the world which is given to me and to us only upon the basis of my and our accomplishments) capable and in need of investigation. This, therefore, is the thematic made possible by the reduction and made urgently required: I and We as the ones who accomplish (as subject); the world as the totality of what there is for me and for us as that which has been accomplished by myself and ourselves (as object). Since now in this sense the world and all that belongs to it is not to be understood as existing in itself but as a "phenomenon," this reduction is characterized more precisely as "phenomenological" (Ia 58 ff.; 116; Ib 15f; II 6; 12 ff.) [12]

The reduction thus leads to the subject, to the accomplishing life of consciousness. If the subject epitomizes immanence, and if the world epitomizes transcendence, all possession of the world is the arising of transcendence in immanence. The question concerning how transcendence can possibly arise in this way is termed the "transcendental question." This question can be answered only if immanence, in part or in its entirety, is absolutely certain: if it is characterized by apodictic evidence (Ia 61 f.), if it possesses a universally apodictic structure of experience (67). All transcendence emerges from this immanence; not as if the former would or could in some sense be an actual part of the subject, or as if the latter actually extended itself to include the former; much rather does transcendence emerge from immanence with precisely that same meaning which it has always had: its being-in-itself. It emerges out from and is included within immanence as nonreal (Ia 65). Immanence, the subject, is not itself a part of the world (163 ff.; 116); it is something which "*is*" *not* so that it can thereby be the *source* of all "that is." It is therefore certainly not the real human psyche, the factual consciousness. It is not a mundane quantity (B 127). It is not the empirical subject, but the transcendental subject; it is not a worldly being which accidentally possesses the ability to know; rather is it unworldly, and its very essence is to be capable of intending (*zudenken*) its transcendence for what is transcendent, and therefore capable of allowing what it is not to be what it is and of giving this what it already possesses (this is indeed the very essence of *transcendere*). Once again, it is definitely not a factual but a pure subject: the reduction, as phenomenological, leads out of the world. Insofar as it leads to the pure essence of the subject in general, to essential laws, essential possibilities, and essential kinds of accomplishing consciousness, it leaves all facticity behind as something which is only secondary (as something, namely, which has its ground in the eidos, as something which presents a single instance of the eidos) and is at the same time an eidetic reduction (Ia 103 ff.; Ib 28; II 8; VI 141 ff.).

The reduction leads beyond the world when it leads to the transcendental subject; it leads to something which *is not* but which is the ground for everything "that is." It leads away from facts to something which is not fact but essence. The subject is neither mundane nor factual: it is transcendental and pure. As such, it is to begin with the pure *ego, my* pure ego. But in the experiencing study of my pure ego I discover myself to be an ego which, in its pure (transcendental-phenomenological) ego-experience, differentiates itself from other egos, therewith distinguishing its own ego-accomplishments from the ego-accomplishments of others. I therefore rightly and necessarily divide the sphere of pure and transcendental subjectivity into a sphere which uniquely belongs to me and a sphere of the others. Here my own sphere is more fundamental: in it alone can and must other subjectivities (the spheres of others who, like myself, are genuine subjects) be constituted, and furthermore in such a way that these other subjects, together with myself, present the first complete presentation of subjectivity, and hence that subjectivity whose accomplishment it is that the world which is, is there for me and the others. The truly pure and transcendental subject is therefore not simply myself alone, or simply "We," but both together. This insight arises from that distinction which must be necessarily made within my pure ego-experience in virtue of which the We arose from within myself when I reduced myself to my ownmost sphere.

The reduction makes an end to naiveté by enlightening us with respect to the unfathomable out from which all possession of the world originates; it makes knowledge of the world and reflection upon the world philosophical. It places the immediate world at a distance and brings subjectivity with its accomplishments into view. Its final purpose is thereby to base all knowledge of the world and reflection upon the world upon their ultimate and absolute ground: this subjectivity. This final purpose is identical with the idea of an absolute or genuinely scientific truth (Ia 52 f.); with the idea of an ultimate foundation for knowledge (66); with the clarification of the problem of reason and nonreason (Ia 91/2; Ib 24 and 30; III 313 to end).

It is important, however, to see exactly how Husserl means this. He is not simply concerned with the problem of validity and objectivity "like Descartes" (Ib 15) and classical Idealism (especially Kantian and NeoKantian Idealism), but rather with traversing all regions and levels of the entire life of consciousness. He will "pursue the constant flow of cognitive life and being, view all that is to be seen, explain and penetrate it, and grasp it descriptively in concepts and judgments . . ." (Ib 14).

For classical Idealism, transcendental reflection stands at the beginning of philosophy; for phenomenology it is the reduction. With the step taken by reflection, classical Idealism departs from the world and enters the sphere of pure validity, an ideal sphere, a sphere of principles. By contrast, with the step taken by the reduction phenomenological idealism enters a sphere which is, to be sure, pure, nonmundane, and which possesses the character of being foundational, but a sphere which nevertheless is a sphere of new *experience,* the sphere of pure experience (Ia 68; Ib 12; V 141 ff.). In Husserl's sense, therefore, pure subjectivity possesses a structure such that experience corresponds with it as the means of gaining access to it; it is describable (first factually and then eidetically); it is life, although a pure and foundational life. It does not possess the quite differently structured character of a sphere composed of principles. The reduction makes possible a "science of concrete transcendental subjectivity as given in real and possible transcendental experience" (Ia 68).

We must now pass on to the criticism of this Husserlian thought of the reduction. This criticism cannot begin other than with a vigorous approval of this thought as such. Not only because it agrees with thoughts which, although in different form, have been held in approval for a long period of time: but in certain essential respects it also goes beyond them—and in this Husserl has not deceived himself—to something more basic.

I shall arrange the first part of our criticism so that I can at the same time clear up the old question of "idealism" as it pertains to Husserl. The reduction leads from naiveté to knowledge of that consciousness which, in all possession of the world, is already and constantly an actively accomplishing consciousness. The world which we already possess and within which we believingly and knowingly exist is something that has already been achieved. The reduction leads back from what has been achieved to the accomplishing, from that which is grounded to the ground, from the sphere of the conditioned to the sphere of conditions. I am to have knowledge of the world—which is not, however, the accomplishment of consciousness. But whatever I know and believe with respect to the world, whatever it might be accepted as being in all speaking of the world, is all the accomplishment of subjectivity. I perform the *epoché* in order to distinguish between world and "world," and with this I introduce the reduction: establishing a ground for this world out of the accomplishments of the streaming life of consciousness. The *terminus a quo* of the reduction is the "world," its *terminus ad quem* is the accomplishing ground for this world. The reduction is the passage between two spheres which are related to each other as ground and grounded, as condition and conditioned. The basic schema of the reduction is that of the relation between two spheres, and as such is not different from the basic schema of all idealistic two-world theories (from Plato to Rickert and Bauch)—nor is it better or worse.

Now, however, for Husserl's *radical* purpose. He is not simply concerned with installing the accomplishing subjectivity as the reason why the "world" and its parts are the way they are. The world still exists: it exists in-itself, and the fact *that* it is and *what* it is, is independent of all your, my, and our opinions about it. Quite naturally. Everyday consciousness and the "realists" are justified in this conviction. And yet, shall this conviction, no matter how correct, remain groundless, incapable of being grounded, or in no need of a ground? Shall we remain content with this pure assurance, whose intensity alone is subject to variation? If not, then we must show: (a) what accomplishments of subjectivity make it possible to attribute to the world what it properly possesses (it is one thing to say that something exists, but it is an entirely different matter to say that we can think of it adequately; certainly this latter statement requires its own adequate basis), and (b) the reason why this conviction is truly valid and the source for this "self-evidence" possessing its unshakable justification. It is just this that Husserl sets himself as the ultimate and definitive foundational task. He does not offer an emphatic but empty "realistic" assurance: he carries out what the "realists" omit. With respect to phenomenological idealism, Husserl states: "Its sole task and accomplishment is to clarify the meaning of this world, precisely that meaning in which it is accepted as actually existing by everyone and with real justification. That the world exists . . . is completely doubtless. It is quite another question to understand this indubitability which sustains life and the positive sciences and to clarify the basis for its justification" (*Postscript* to the *Ideas;* V 152/53).[13] The reduction culminates in this accomplishment. Husserlian idealism and "realism" maintain the same thesis, only the first also offers the foundation for this assertion and thereby becomes a genuine philosophy.[14]

The reduction leads beyond the entire world to a pure subjectivity which is no longer a part of the world. For this also Husserl cannot be sufficiently praised. The subjectivity which must be sought naturally has to fulfill the conditions which must be attributed to the *subjectum veritatis*, the ὑποκείμενον, the sustaining and accomplishing ground of truth—of all truth, the entire and ultimate truth. It must be the absolute ground of all truth of the world as the totality of all beings whatsoever. It can be absolute only if it does not itself belong to the world. If (as with Hartmann) the subject of truth is one being among others, it is a part of the world and all truth is thrown away and lost: that which is conditioned cannot accomplish something unconditioned. Subjectivity is to be thought of as being outside of the world: it is not any kind of being (*Seiendes*). From the point of view of beings and the world it is nothing (and Nothingness). Since truth cannot exist without a ground, however, subjectivity, as this indispensable absolute ground, is Being and Idea. Being and Idea "are" not, but they are the absolute ground for all "that is," that is, for the beingness of beings and the truth of what is true.

The insight that the true subject cannot be a being, a part of the world, is part of the ancient heritage of classical Idealism. Husserl had known how to make this insight fruitful. In classical Idealism (especially Neo-Kantianism) true subjectivity and my (your, our) subjectivity remained externally opposed to each other as the normative and that which is subject to the normative, as rule and that which is regulated. My (your, our) subjectivity is not the ground of truth but is merely empirical and factual: true subjectivity remains standing over and against us. What true subjectivity is, is what I am not, and what I am not is what true subjectivity is. Husserl understands that these terms, which are certainly to be distinguished from each other, are to be connected in a positive way: in the reduction, I, on my own ground, disclose myself as true, pure subjectivity, or, as a member of this subjectivity. I *am* (or, we *are*) this pure subjectivity. And therefore, I, also on the basis of my own ground, am not simply something which also "is," not simply a part of the world. I myself am that principle and rule which, according to Neo-Kantianism, remains simply external and opposed to me: the absolute ground for the truth of what is true, for the validity of what is valid.

This departure from classical Idealism is decisive for all evaluation of Husserl; it is also decisive for determining the relationship between Husserl and Heidegger. What is it that occasions and necessitates this departure? It is the difference between the Husserlian and the classical-Idealistic way of "returning back," that is, the difference between the phenomenological-eidetic reduction and classical transcendental reflection. The departure thus rests upon the difference in philosophical method. We must now turn our attention to this difference.

Classical transcendental reflection is theoretical reflection. As reflection it is no longer concerned with beings directly but only *modo obliquo;* it goes immediately to the noema which has emerged out of the "pure-directedness toward-being." It tests this noema for its objective validity (its truth); this occurs through the regressive building up of the noema out of those principles which constitute it in its validity. What therefore comes to light in this reflection are solely principles, and indeed principles constitutive of the validity of the noema. Though they are unquestionably principles of objectivity, they are not objects; they themselves are not beings. Their totality is the idea of the absolute ground of all truth. This reflection does not question *how* the noema comes to be constituted (it does not inquire after the noesis of which the noema is the result); such a question is held to be irrelevant to validity and therefore would be "merely empirical," a question of "psychology."

The phenomenological reduction does not directly pass over to the investigation of validity. It also turns toward the noema and searches for its grounds, but it does not search for those principles which constitute it with respect to its validity, but rather searches for the manifold of specific noeses out from which the noema, together with its simple or multilayered structure, emerges. This reduction discovers the manifold of the accomplishing life of consciousness; this is the ground sought for in the reduction. What is disclosed in the reduction is a new field of experience and not simply a sphere of principles; it is a pure sphere of grounds, not of principles; a sphere of pure noeses, not of noema-principles. The reduction is a search for the how and whereby of the noema's coming-to-be; it is a search for the accomplishing noesis. Yet this is no "merely empirical" or "merely psychological" investigation. All accomplishing life of consciousness, all such noeses, are not mundane, do not belong to the world, and therefore do not belong to the psyche. Husserl is the first to have seen and to have established that the question of the "how," the question of the noesis, has a transcendental and pure meaning.

All this can be granted: but how shall this sort of "returning back" also accomplish the task of investigating validity? How can it replace the transcendental reflection of classical idealism, that is, how can it also accomplish what the latter alone was able to accomplish? Obviously it can do this only if validity can be discovered in disclosing the sought-after noeses. And this is the presupposition which Husserl actually views as being fulfilled. According to him, there are noeses from which validity is inseparable, noeses in which validity is unquestionably present and in which it can be seen, witnessed, experienced. Just as what is unique to the Husserlian notion of pure subjectivity is dependent upon the unique nature of the reduction, so also is the reduction's adequacy to the task of establishing a universal foundation dependent upon the theory of distinguished evidences. Further on it will become our task also to examine this theory.

The reduction does not lead to principles, yet it does lead beyond the world. It leads to noeses, the life of acts, the stream of experience, but to pure and transcendental noeses, and so on. This is the ground for all acceptance of the world and its parts. It is an experienceable ground (principles could not be experienced). And yet only a being can be experienced, and thus for Husserl nothing else remains but to think of this nonmundane ground of all validity, the pure and transcendental subjectivity, this sphere of foundations and conditions, as a kind of being (*Seienden*). To be sure, it alone (that is, over and against the world and all its parts) has the meaning of absolute being (V 153), but precisely for this reason does it first come to have the character of being (*Seinscharakter*) and the meaning of being (*Seinssinn*). It is nonrelative being; everything else, however, is relative to it as its ground. The relationship is therefore not reciprocal, nor is it even a relationship of mutual implication.

With this the two-sphere theory takes on the worst imaginable (i.e., philosophically quite impossible) form: the spheres stand opposed to each other in a way which ground and consequent, condition and conditioned, could never be opposed. At this point Husserl remains uninstructed by Plato, Kant, Fichte, and Hegel. And hence this exceptional and in so many individual respects splendid thought of the phenomenological reduction, a thought which in some places brings with it an enormous advance, finally terminates in a philosophical (i.e., in principle and in theory) impossibility.

The speculative fault which thus burdens Husserl's thought of the reduction is a considerable one. To be sure, there are places where it is to some extent made tolerable, at least with respect to the factual procedure itself which Husserl exercises. At the beginning of the *Fourth Meditation* we find the statement "that the transcendental ego . . . is what it is only in relation to intentional objectivities" (Ia 99); this would in principle constitute suspending the absoluteness and irrelativity of the foundational sphere. But only in principle; on the whole and *de facto* this speculative

211

fault remains to the end. In such circumstances it is understandable that Heidegger should drop Husserl's thought of the reduction and replace its particular moments with something else.

Do therefore only fragments of Husserl's thought remain? And must we on the whole simply go back to the classical form of the absolute "returning back," to transcendental reflection? And would we be compelled once more to allow true subjectivity to be opposed in the externality of a purely normative relation to that "empirical" subjectivity which we ourselves are?

The work of Richard Hönigswald gives an answer to this situation. It contains an attempt to solve both problems within the context of classical Idealism and with its proven means: the problem of the relation of both spheres and that of the relation between the pure and factual subjectivities. In both cases the relation of pure opposition is replaced by a relation (which, speculatively, is the only one possible) of reciprocal implication. With respect to the second problem this signifies an advance which goes beyond whatever Neo-Kantianism (and any similar theory) might call for. Objectivity, givenness, and presence successively conjoin with each other as principles in a continual and reciprocal implication; with the latter (i.e., presence) subjectivity (always understood as a *principle*), or the monad, receives a fundamental concreteness and facticity characterized by an original temporality.

To discuss the reduction further is to speak of Heidegger and Hönigsweld rather than Husserl. And this, finally, is no longer to speak of the work that Husserl has accomplished but rather of the work which we, in considering Husserl, Heidegger, and Hönigswald, must ourselves accomplish.

4. The Principle of Pure Subjectivity

Husserl had explicitly indicated many times in what sense and with what divergencies he had attached his thought to Descartes. He continually praised the Cartesian point of departure from the ego as the primordial source of all *cogitationes,* and correlatively, of all *cogitata,* that is, as the primordial source of all accomplishing of the world. He continually censured Descartes' immediate relapse into the mundane understanding of this ego.

This censure certainly has its justification, only it is not radical enough, and this betrays a deep fault in Husserl's own deliberations. Let us analyze for a moment the decisive passage in the second half of Descartes' *Third Meditation.* Descartes asks "whether I myself, possessing this idea of God, could exist if God did not exist?" He also asks how it is possible for myself together with my idea of God to exist. He seeks the cause which produces myself and my idea of God. The "I" is meant in the sense of its formal reality; the idea of God is meant in the sense of its objective reality, and both are meant in terms of their respective "beingness," and, understood in this way, both—taken individually and together—require a corresponding cause, one which is itself existent. Of decisive importance is the fact that the idea of God (and along with it *all* "ideas," *cogitationes, noemata*) is interpreted *ontically* (i.e., as a being which requires an existent cause for its beingness), and this equally insofar as it is simply a question of its intentional character, of its objective content. This is certainly what is meant by the terms *realitas objectiva, esse objective* (which Descartes took over from the scholastic tradition). Thus Descartes understands intentionality to be thoroughly ontic. He interprets thinking, even with respect to its noematic aspect (with reference to the meaning of its objective validity), along the lines of being. And only for this reason does he have in mind both the possibility and necessity of permitting "myself and my thinking" to emerge from a correspondingly existent cause.

Husserl criticizes the persistent mundaneness of the *ego cogito*. He does not criticize the beinglike character of pure intentionality, pure thought, and pure subjectivity. He does not criticize this because he himself retains it uncritically and unreflectingly. And yet it is quite inconceivable how one is to escape Descartes' metaphysics once thought and subjectivity are understood in ontic terms.

As is well known, after Descartes discovered his point of departure (the *ego,* the *cogitare,* and the implied *esse*), he restricted himself to take from it simply his universal criterion and rule (the first paragraph of the *Third Meditation*). He does not draw out what *must* be present in this point of departure if it is to serve as the true point of departure leading to the *subjectum* of all truth and certainty (this is first accomplished by German Idealism): he does not draw out the *principles* for all truth and certainty. In place of declaring what all true judgments bring with them by virtue of their being true, he simply indicates the kind of judgments of which one can be certain.

Husserl does not find fault with this because he too remains attached to criteria and rules, and does not arrive at the rigorous thought of principles. And yet only this thought leads beyond all ontic interpretations of thought and subjectivity, for the principles that constitute the truth of thought and which bring noemata into the truth are certainly not beings, either relative beings or nonrelative. It is only this thought which permits us to avoid Descartes' metaphysics; only this thought is sufficiently radical to make a real "beginning" toward discovering the ground of all truth.

One must have thoroughly grasped these fundamental considerations if one is sincerely to evaluate Husserl's theory of pure and transcendental subjectivity. This subjectivity is indeed pure, transcendental, and extramundane, but it remains understood ontically. The Husserlian theory is indeed transcendental philosophy, transcendental idealism; but it is the Ontic of a singular being, a nonrelative and absolute being termed pure subjectivity.

Against the background of this theory, which is satisfactory from a speculative point of view in other respects, several very significant accomplishments emerge with respect to the philosophical theory of the subject: they signify in part something totally and principally new. Husserl succeeded in admitting certain moments to the concept of the one true subjectivity which no idealism before him had attempted to incorporate (apart from a few modest beginnings, known and studied by Husserl, made by Natorp). Here it is a question of certain moments which had always been thought of in connection with empirical subjectivity and which had therefore remained apportioned to psychology (hence the earlier talk of Husserl's having fallen back into psychologism). Insofar as Husserl had gathered up these moments, he succeeded in expanding the concept of pure subjectivity and significantly limited the competency of psychology.

Fortunately, Husserl did not share the bias which is the death of all authentic investigation of subjectivity: to speak of subjectivity is to speak simply of myself, yourself, and ourselves, thereby committing the double mistake of saying that everything within us is subjectivity and that subjectivity is only what we ourselves are. Husserl understood from the beginning that the question of subjectivity is the search for the *subjectum veritatis*, for the accomplishing and supporting ground of the truth of all true thoughts (noemata). Hence the question: what must be and what must hold if all these thoughts are to be and be true? Raising the question in this way, and in this way alone, Husserl also inquires into what I am, what the other and others are, what we are. All "disclosure" of subjectivity, all exploration of the pure life of consciousness, is to be understood in this way and in this way alone. It is the disclosure of the indispensable ground, be it capable of being experienced or concealed, be it given or something which is simply required.

The most striking, difficult, and fundamental moment of pure subjectivity was worked out rather early by Husserl: its primordial *temporality*. The posthumous writings, at least up to this point, present us with nothing new in this respect. Here we need only mention what is essential.

Husserl's Posthumous Writings

Pure subjectivity is structured temporally (and this is new for Idealism); not in the mundane sense of possessing a temporal structure and, therein, change and duration, but in the transcendental sense of first constituting time: temporality, together with all change and all duration in what is meant as such, is the unique accomplishment of subjectivity itself. Pure subjectivity is itself this primordial flow, is this temporality, is this primordial time-consciousness; it constitutes itself therein and at the same time it constitutes the possibility of temporal processes, change, duration, and so on.

I encounter some degree of confusion when I attempt to criticize this part of Husserl's theory. It is one of the better accomplishments of recent philosophy, as fruitful as it is sound. And yet in spite of this I must hold it to be not entirely adequate in certain theoretical respects. Of particular importance is the crucial distinction between constituted and constitutive temporality and the thought that constitutive temporality is to be connected with the essence of pure subjectivity. Inadequate, however (indeed, impossible), is the situating of the ultimate essence of pure subjectivity directly within this constitutive temporality. For if this latter is to be truly something ultimate it must possess the character of being a genuine principle, that is, it must stand in a reciprocally implicative συμπλοκή with subjectivity itself. Then, however, subjectivity can indeed be thought of as being temporality, but is not (no matter in how sublime or obscure a sense) to be thought of as being itself temporal. Principles are not objects. They establish temporality and historicity, but do not in themselves possess these characteristics. Consequently, the constitutive temporality of immanent time-consciousness cannot be the one single ultimate; much rather is it one of the many moments of pure subjectivity which reciprocally imply each other. To wish to discover pure subjectivity's absolute and basic essence in this temporality or in this historicity is to misconceive this temporality and the historicity rooted within it as existent properties of an ontic quantity. Constitutive historicism is, as a final word, also a theoretical mistake.

Next to primordial temporality stands the *concreteness* of pure subjectivity. Concretion, the full concretion of subjectivity within the pure and transcendental sphere, is again something new in idealistic philosophy. It was Husserl who first came upon this thought and knew how to carry it through. Concretion is of fundamental importance, for only upon this basis can we discover those elements which lead to the third essential (and, once again, new) moment of pure subjectivity: the double-structure of the pure "I" and the pure "We." Only within the concreteness of the pure ego can the pure "We" emerge.

215

Hans Wagner

Let us first consider the structure of the pure ego itself, its self-structuring to the point of full concretion. When I perform the *epoché*, thereby passing over to the reduction, there lies before me the (no longer transcendent and therefore incomprehensible world, but) "world" as the totality of my pure accomplishments, the "world" as the totality of my noemata. I, together with the manifold of my accomplishings (noeses), am the ground of this "world." "World" as consequent and pure ego as ground stand over and against each other as two poles and at first *only* as two poles. In relation to every single noema, one can at first say only this of the pure ego: it is the ground for this and that noema (Ia 100; IV 97 ff.). This cannot satisfy us. Tracing a manifold back to something singular remains senseless as long as this singularity (which is, to be sure, the unity of a manifold) does not serve to clarify the internal differentiation of this manifold as well (i.e., the difference between the various members of this manifold). Hence this identical singularity—as the sufficient ground for the "world" as a manifold of experience (the different noemata)—must accordingly itself be capable of an unfolding, and this means that it must be capable of being explicated to the point of its full concretion. (This thought of Husserl's is entirely free from objections; Heidegger was not forced to change it in any way.) "World," each "worldly" object, and every type of "worldly" objects (i.e., every one of the various and different kinds of noemata) thus become specific clues for accomplishing a transition to the accomplishing ground and to the manifold of specific noetic accomplishments. The latter is disclosed by the analysis of the noemata. Just as the "world" is an open and endless manifold of objects (or noemata), so also is their ground, the pure ego, an open and endless manifold. To disclose the pure ego in its concretion and with the entire manifold of its accomplishments signifies setting about a task which is itself endless. Hence the task implies all the characteristics of an endless task, above all the characteristic that it can be accomplished only in terms of an anticipatory regulative idea (Ia 87, 89, 90; Ib 21 f.; D 49, 52).

The first element of concretion is the habituality of the pure ego. The pure ego does not immediately forget its accomplishments but preserves them; it remembers them and they become and remain (until some future cancellation or until they are eventually disavowed) its own. The conviction which the pure ego has won remains and lives on in the ego's future. It stands by the resolutions it has formed and will from now on live in subordination to them. In preserving what it has achieved the pure ego gains the continuity of a persisting and in the widest (and naturally non-mundane) sense "personal" ego which adheres to its own identity. All this is the ownmost active accomplishment of the pure ego (Ia 100 f.; Ib 26; IV 111 ff., esp. 116). And every such active accomplishment is the primordial establishing of an attribute which persists throughout immanent time.

To this first element of concretion, an active universal principle of the pure genesis which is constitutive of the ego, is added a passive principle, a principle of the passive genesis of habitualities which equally serves as a foundation. Thanks to this principle the world and objects within the world are already familiar and known to me. Correlatively: thanks to this principle I already have at my disposal a foreknowledge of whatever I may encounter, whether what I encounter is of benefit or disadvantage to my history. Husserl terms this second element of the pure ego's concretion "association." It is a fundamental moment "without which an ego as such is unthinkable" (Ia 114, 111 ff., 141 ff.; IV 222 ff.; D 44 f.). All preacquaintedness and all expectation rests upon this association as the pure ego's primordial history and forms an *a priori* realm.

The pure ego advances along its way step by step within its primordial history and is determined by it. In modal terms, this means *necessarily:* within this history the circle of its possibilities becomes more and more limited and determinate. The sphere of the pure ego is not distinguished by free-floating pure possibilities, for nothing is arbitrarily compossible in this concrete ego. Its possibilities always depend upon what it has succeeded in accomplishing in its (active) history and upon what has happened to it in its passive history (Ia 107 ff.). Furthermore, all that Husserl had often and extensively dealt with under the title of "horizons" or under the title of the relation between the actualities and potentialities of the pure *ego cogito* lies within the primordial history of the pure ego (Ia 81-85, 95, 100; 18 f.; III *passim;* IV 26 ff.; D 42 ff.).

"Pure" and "transcendental" indicate a being that is both nonmundane and a ground. Pure subjectivity is distinguished by temporality and concretion, but it belongs to the world by virtue of neither of these two characteristics; these are also to be understood as pure, transcendental, primordial, and constitutive. If one takes these characteristics in their mundane sense, the pure ego is to be characterized as "unchangeable" and as having no "primordial and acquired characteristics, no capacities, dispositions, etc." (IV 104). In order to have knowledge of myself as a mundane being I must enter into the infinity of my self-experience, its manifold, and its problematic. In order to have knowledge of the pure ego "no great amassing of self-experience can instruct me better than the single experience of an individual and simple *cogito*" (*ibid.*). In every noesis the pure ego "is given in absolute selfness and in its nonperspectival unity, (and) is to be adequately apprehended in the reflective viewpoint" (105). The possibility of adequate apprehension, the highest level of evidence, is granted to the pure ego alone as the ground of all accomplishment. Only for this reason can (and must) all grounding of knowledge be established in the form of disclosing the pure ego which can be given in this way. At this point the *ego* takes on a privileged position in opposition to everything which can be designated as "being" ("*seiend*") (IV 101). It must be noted, however, that this absolute and adequate evidence is granted only to the pure ego as such and not to the entire manifold of its temporal and historical life. At a given moment only one part of transcendental experience is truly experienced in an adequate way, that is, its current presence to itself, and *not* everything which is implied in this moment with respect to the self's *pastness*, habitualities, capacities, and so on, all of which is perhaps "meant" along with it but is not authentically experienced or given along with it. Hence surrounding this select "part" lies a horizon of presumed, indeterminate, and self-concealed parts, a horizon which, quite unlike the first select part, is not "open" to being apprehended adequately and which therefore presents a field of possible doubt and error (Ia 62).

The situation here is very critical. On the one hand, there is adequate evidence, but it concerns only the pure ego as the present center of the ego's functions and only within the boundaries of current self-presence. On the other hand, there is the experience of the full concretion of this pure ego, a concretion which is of decisive importance but which is not given with adequate evidence. Now the ownmost essence of pure subjectivity rests upon this full concretion, and upon this essence rests the subjectivity of the other ego; pure and transcendental intersubjectivity, the surmounting of solipsism, and gaining the world as one which is intersubjective, objective, and existing within itself rests in turn upon that; in other words, everything which is of decisive importance is based upon this full concretion and the certainty of our experience of it. All preparation would come to nothing if this difficulty were not resolved, for we should not reach our goal.

Husserl is the master of this critical situation. Indubitable evidence extends further than the simple identity of the "I am." Even though particulars in the realm of concretion may still be subject to doubt and error, what is of decisive importance is indubitable evidence within the realm of full concretion: the universal and essential fundamental structure of this concrete pure ego, and this is an apodictic structure of experience (an example of which is constitutive temporality). Thus it is true that we have adequate evidence of the pure "I am"; we furthermore have apodictic evidence of the fundamental structure of the concrete pure ego: within this structure the ego is indubitably manifested as being necessarily concrete, living with a unique and individual content of experiences, habitualities, and capacities. We furthermore have simple (i.e., nonexceptional) experiential evidence for all the unique particulars built upon the basis of the universal fundamental-structure of the individual ego, an experiential evidence which refers to an open infinity in which errors and improvements have a place, but which yet remains directed and regulated by evidence which is both of an exceptional kind and apodictic.

In other words, what the individual pure ego is within the context of its concretion is not given with absolute evidence, but the structures which it necessarily possesses in order to be a determinate and fully concrete pure ego *are* given with absolute evidence. And this apodictic evidence directs and regulates all disclosure of the concrete pure ego in its full concretion (Ia 66 f.). The difficulty is thereby resolved: the concretion is given in terms of an adequate kind of evidence. What must be built upon this concretion can be carried out without difficulty.

This is primarily the separation of what is my own from that which is not my own within the concrete pure ego's field of experience. With the separation of these two spheres this pure ego first reaches its full concretion and becomes a monad in the transcendental sense of this word. At the same time this separation is the first in the series of steps with which the primary task approaches its fulfillment: namely, to understand the world as it is groundlessly, although emphatically, understood by everyday consciousness and the so-called realists, only now with a ground for this understanding and with insight into this ground: the world as intersubjective, objective, genuinely transcendent, existing in-itself. Much of this already hinges upon the first of these steps. For this reason, and also to assure ourselves as to the full superiority of the Husserlian undertaking, we shall now analyze the transcendental reduction to the sphere of ownness.

When we consider the world as it is we discover that it is transcendent and that it exists in-itself, and as such it requires that it be thought of by all in terms of these determinations. It also contains an open infinity of beings who, like myself, are thinking world-possessing subjects and who are related to this one world just as I. All these subjects are objects for me. As subjects, they accomplish something (for this is contained in the very notion of subjectivity); indeed, they accomplish something similar and akin to what I accomplish. If I am world-forming, they certainly are also: I, therefore, am surely not world-constituting alone. And just as I constitute them as subjects within myself, they constitute me within themselves. The constitution of the world is therefore an intersubjective constitution, an accomplishment of a pure community of subjects.

In order for me to be able to think of the world as objective I must surely constitute it within myself (otherwise I would know absolutely nothing about it), but I must constitute it as a world which is not only constituted by me, but by me in association with all other subjects. On

219

the one hand, I must therefore constitute these co-constitutive others as such within myself, and, on the other hand, I must think of myself as one who knows himself to be simply a member of this constitutive community. Both are the accomplishments of the pure ego and both lie within it, but the one lies within the pure ego as that which I must attribute to others—as the sphere of otherness—and the other lies within the pure ego as that which I attribute to myself—as the sphere of ownness. Thus what is my own and what is not my own draw apart. What is my own belongs to the pure ego itself in an absolute sense: it is its own concrete essence and is in no way separable from it. What is not my own is constituted within, by means of, and on the basis of what is my own and represents that component of pure subjectivity which is required above and beyond what is my own in order to bring about with full justification the sense of an objective world and its distinct being-in-itself which is independent of other subjects who, like myself, are constitutive and who, in terms of their being and accomplishment, are independent of me.

This means that *within* what is its own the pure ego has, and must have, the possibility of transcending itself to a being which is other than itself and to be in touch with it. What is my own is precisely the basis—the point of departure and ground—for all transcendence. Yet being which is other than myself (other subjects and the world) cannot yet receive the complete sense of objectivity, for it can receive no intersubjective validity as long as there is only one subjectivity (I myself in the sphere of my ownness). There can be no sense of genuine transcendence apart from what is my own; nor can there be this sense with it alone. The sphere of ownness simply achieves a primordial transcendence, and yet without this there could not possibly be a true and full transcendence.

In order to be able to think of the objectivity of the world I must first be able to think of its intersubjectivity, and for this the thought of a community of all subjects is required which once again presupposes a plurality of subjects. The next step must therefore be the constitution of a genuinely other subject and other subjects. If, however, I should constitute such subjects, they will be as accomplishing and as constitutive as myself (for this is the pure essence of subjectivity). It is therefore inevitable that I thereby come to be markedly influenced in the meaning of my own being. In the constitution of other subjects through the pure ego the meaning of this concrete and pure ego's being, the concrete character of its subjectivity, must be appreciably modified.

Transcendence is already there in the sphere of ownness, for this sphere is the basis of all transcendence. Therefore others and other beings are already present in the sphere of ownness. But the transcendence which is there is only a primordial transcendence: the others do not yet possess the meaning of genuine subjects (world-forming beings like myself), and consequently what is other does not yet possess the meaning of intersubjective validity. In order that others can receive the meaning of being genuine subjects I must attribute something to them, something which is not "within" or "upon" them like the reading off of an attribute. I must attribute to them what I myself essentially am and what they essentially should be, a meaning of being which I can only know and experience within myself. If, therefore, I am to attribute this meaning to them, I can do so only by way of transferring it to them (the mundane analogy for this would be as follows: I see others only as bodies; however, I necessarily attribute life, psyche, and spirit to them so that I may think of them as being similar to myself which, as all of my transactions with them inform me, they certainly are). The meaning of the other's subjectivity is not given to me from the outside and in its original presence. I do not think of them upon the basis of some primordial presence of themselves to me, but rather do I think of them through an appresentation achieved by me with good reason (Ia 137 ff.; Ib 34 f.). It is the insertion of what is my own into the other, who was primordially constituted simply as a physical part of the world, and in such a way that what I have attributed to him in return constitutes what is his own. Thus another monad (who exists as autonomously as I and who achieves the same things as I) is appresentationally constituted within my pure monad (Ia 144).

In this way a plurality of pure concrete subjects emerges for the first time, a plurality-structure in the concept of concrete and pure subjectivity as such. One particular feature of the way in which this plurality-structure emerges should be noted. From the very start other beings and subjects had already emerged upon the basis of the primordial transcendence as parts and members of the world, and hence upon the basis of the world as already and primordially constituted. The appresentationally constituted subjectivity of the other is one which likewise refers to this primordial world and which belongs to this world within which it lives and achieves. And this precisely in terms of its transcendental and pure being. All this, however, for the following reason: the other's subjectivity receives its meaning through the insertion of what is my own into other physical entities (or bodies). With the plurality of such bodies there necessarily emerges a plurality of subjects, each in every case belonging to and possessing its body. And thus corporeality itself also belongs to the notion of pure and concrete subjectivity. Its plurality-structure hinges primarily upon this. But also more than this: pure and concrete subjectivity is the subjectivity of bodies; since these bodies, however, are to be met with at various places within the primordial world and since

221

Hans Wagner

they are consequently different from the world and every part of the world, they accordingly experience the world and parts of the world differently: no two of the many pure and embodied subjects experience the one world and all self-identical parts of this world as being the same. No two of these subjects can have the same "world-picture" of the one identical world. I know that every other subject must see and hear the same part of the world differently than I, for I am here, another subject is there, another over there, and so on. Our "pictures of the world" do not and cannot coincide: they are different perspectives on the one identical world, and no one of them, including mine, is privileged with respect to any other.

Both the plurality and diversity of these "pictures" of the one world hinge upon the corporeality of the pure and concrete subjectivity.

If we had to conclude with this diversity of "world-pictures," that is, the systems of appearances of the one world, how and with what ground could they be understood as different pictures of *one and the same* world? How in general is it possible for the thought of an identical world (in contrast to the diversity of pictures which alone are experienced) to emerge and with what ground?

Obviously it is only possible, and then necessarily so, when the appearance-systems truly prove to be a system of appearances, for then something appears in them which is necessarily to be distinguished from them. An adequate and convincing ground for the manifold of these systems can be given, and this is precisely the diverse "situations" of the pure, concrete, and embodied subjects (its "situation" in the world in its entirety and its "situation" over and against each individual part of the world). Finally, the problem of the manifold of systems can be resolved by means of the free convertibility of the diverse situations among themselves (for example, I "could" at some time go over there and then the system of my appearances would be identical with that belonging to the individual who is found there). The systems of appearances thus prove to be variable in accordance with rules and as capable in principle of being harmonized, indeed, identified, with each other. The world appears in them as one and the same world, diverse according to certain rules, capable of being harmonized and identified according to other rules, and knowable by all as the same world by following other rules. This means that the world is ultimately intersubjective and objective.

I am therefore not a privileged member in terms of what is my own over and against the others with respect to what is their own: we are alike. Each of us has only a conditioned and limited "picture of the world." In order to complete each of these pictures, in order to remove their conditioned and limited character, all of the others are required. The accomplishments of everyone, of each individual, is required. Thus a communal accomplishment, that is, communal subjectivity, the community of monads and intersubjectivity, is required. True and pure subjectivity is the transcendental "We." It is this subjectivity which first achieves the meaning which the world already possesses; the pure ego alone does not suffice.

Along the path leading to the constitution of the other subject we have seen that corporeality belongs to the essence of pure subjectivity and therefore to my own essence as pure ego. Corporeality is as constitutive of me as I (within the context of primordial transcendence) am constitutive of it. If, however, corporeality is constitutive, the primordial world is also constitutive. Hence primordial worldliness is constitutive of my subjectivity. The world is constitutive of me to the same degree as it is constituted by myself and others.

This means that all world-constitution achieved by me is a constitution such that within it the world is in return also constituted by me as being itself constitutive of me. This finally means that the meaning of the world's being is not exhausted in its being constituted by me. It contains more than this: the world is (*seiend*) in such a way that it in turn is the ground for something of what I am.

"Solipsism" is thus truly overcome and the "transcendence" of the world is actually reached. I am not alone: with me are the others. I also possess a body; I am in the world and I have always and already been in the world which I constitute precisely as world-constituting. I recognize, as Merleau-Ponty states, "my belongingness to a 'pre-constituted' world" (E 105).

When one considers what the world means, then one understands that the task which had been set before us is actually fulfilled. The world now encompasses everything which can have the meaning of being-in-itself, objectivity, and intersubjectivity: the pure and the animate world of nature, the world of psyches and spirits, the world of culture, the world of ideal objects. Now all talk of the world, of world-belongingness, of being-in-itself, of objectivity, and of transcendence finally has meaning, and now it is also finally in possession of its justification.

The theory of pure and concrete subjectivity is one of the best elements in Husserl's entire philosophy. The works of Husserl now available to us reveal this theory in its full significance. In view of Husserl's tremendous accomplishment it is therefore difficult even at this point to bring forward those objections which one cannot refrain from raising.

Apart from the difficulties already noted with respect to the thought of temporality, our objections here concern only a few individual points. Even though they relate to clear theoretical, that is, speculative, flaws,

223

they are not such as to call into question the entire theory of subjectivity. Before presenting them I shall therefore cite the reasons why they cannot be of such weight as to compel us to forsake Husserl's entire theory of subjectivity.

Actually Husserl's reflections constantly menace and not seldom confuse the ontic of pure subjectivity. In the "Postscript" to the *Ideas* the ego is still referred to as "being absolutely in-itself and for-itself" (V 146), and is accepted as an absolute, nonrelative being (V 153, 154). If one took only such statements seriously and if one did not adequately note what Husserl—above all in the *Cartesian Meditations*—truly accomplishes, one indeed would still not be able to say (as do Ingarden, Celms, Hartmann, and Pos) that Husserl had not set himself the task of demonstrating genuine transcendence, but one could necessarily conclude that he had not achieved such a proof and that he had quite frankly thwarted his own aims. Namely, if the ego is truly absolute—and this in some existent (*seiende*) fashion—then another genuine being-in-itself, a real transcendence, is in fact impossible.

If, however, one pays sufficient attention to what Husserl (at least in the *Cartesian Meditations*) truly and finally accomplishes, one must say that the pure ontic is avoided and that the test of the real and decisive speculative *experimentum crucis* is passed. The concluding interpretation of the relation between pure subjectivity and the objectivity of the transcendent fulfills the basic principle-theoretical condition for this relation in an exceptional manner. It is a characteristic of all naive opinion that being-in-itself and transcendence appear all the more assured and known the more subject and object are and remain opposed to each other. And yet thought and being, subjectivity and objectivity, both understood as principles, cannot be thought of as being abstractly and analytically opposed without losing the ability to define them. Of course, just as little does the relation of a pure, that is, abstract and analytical, identity hold between them. The truth is that they—like all ultimates—are to be thought of in terms of a synthetic identity, that is, they are absolutely indeterminable in their unity and are first capable of being determined only within the context of their inner συμπλοκή, and then certainly as different and opposable members, or, as we might also say, they can be thought of only in terms of reciprocal implication. Only in this kind of synthetic identity and reciprocal implication with subjectivity does transcendence and being-in-itself receive its proper meaning.

Certainly Husserl's version of the speculative requirement is remarkably adequate: just as it is certain that pure and concrete subjectivity is constitutive of all transcendence, so is it equally certain that the latter (as both concrete alter ego and as world) is in return constitutive of the final meaning of pure and concrete subjectivity. Transcendence, precisely insofar as it is related to subjectivity by way of implication, is in general now first capable of being thought of in a determinate way in accordance with the meaning of its being. What rightfully belongs to the transcendent can now be attributed to it.

Had Husserl not grounded and secured the meaning of the being of transcendence in this unobjectionable way the faults which are to be discussed now would be so important that they would ruin this entire theory of subjectivity from the ground up, and the ultimate meaning of this theory could not be defended against the charge of its setting forth an untenable idealism.

Husserl introduces intersubjectivity in order to reach full transcendence: the simply pure ego extends only to primordial transcendence and not to true being-in-itself, true objectivity. After he has introduced and grounded intersubjectivity he is satisfied. To Husserl it appears that with the introduction of intersubjectivity full transcendence and objectivity are *eo ipso* reached. Clearly this is justified only on the condition that intersubjectivity implies objectivity (and being-in-itself and transcendence) and that it therefore presents the foundation for this same objectivity. Hence the question arises as to the relation between these two. Now this relation is not quite so simple. Philosophical tradition states that objectivity is "more" than intersubjectivity. The "more" is the moment of truth (the intersubjective is not necessarily true). Truth, however, is either the individual unconcealedness of the individual being or the unconcealedness in principle of beings in general (and thus the truth of Being). To the notion of truth always belongs relatedness to an object (in the first case this relatedness exhausts the essence of truth; in the second case it is its foundation and gift). In the moment of relatedness (indeed, of *valid* relatedness) to an object, therefore, objectivity would be more than intersubjectivity. Thus with the addition of the moment of valid object-relatedness it appears (and this is the conviction of the philosophical tradition) that objectivity stands outside of intersubjectivity. Yet this cannot be so. Much rather does intersubjectivity itself already include object-relatedness: only with reference to the identical object and the object which is to be identically determined do subjects first come together. All intersubjectivity is intersubjectivity with respect to something. Object-relatedness is therefore "earlier" than intersubjectivity. It is required in order to think of the latter.

Husserl's sequence is thereby justified: primordial transcendence—intersubjectivity. Is the equating of intersubjectivity with objectivity also justified? Does the world truly have the meaning of objectivity if it has the meaning of "being true for everyone"? Intersubjectivity is intersubjective object-relatedness: objectivity is valid object-relatedness. Intersubjectivity is nothing if it is not *valid* intersubjective object-relatedness. Like Husserl, one can take intersubjectivity to mean objectivity only when one has already presupposed the validity of the first. And this is clearly what Husserl has done—tacitly, without any principle-theoretical foundation, and thus without justification.

If, however, validity is presupposed, so is objectivity, for validity is validity with respect to objects, and this is identical with objectivity. The equating of intersubjectivity and objectivity proves to be an illusion. In truth, both object-relatedness and objectivity precede, by implication, intersubjectivity.

If objectivity is presupposed, however, transcendence and (in some sense) the world are also necessarily presupposed. Unfortunately, not simply acknowledged, but presupposed. This speculative obscurity thus entails lack of radicality. On this point one must admit the justice of Thevenaz's claim that there is a lack of radicality in Husserl (E 11 ff.; 28 f.). There is in fact something which is simply presupposed with respect to the relation of intersubjectivity and objectivity (transcendence or world). Of course on the other hand one cannot grant Thevenaz's further claim that transcendentalism must always and necessarily lack ultimate radicality (he names Kant and Heidegger as examples: E 29). Just as Husserlian idealism is not idealism as such, so also Husserlian transcendentalism is not transcendentalism as such. One can say of neither Hönigswald, the last major representative of Kantian Idealism, nor of Heidegger that radical endeavor is lacking in their treatment of the problematic of principles connected with objectivity. Or perhaps with changed titles and features one no longer recognizes the identity of the problem?

Thus we see that if Husserl had not satisfactorily grounded the meaning of transcendence in the way first analyzed, he would not have been able to ground it with his partly defective theory of principles. One could not construct a metaphysics (be this either a metaphysics in general or a metaphysics of subjectivity) in terms of that part of Husserl's theory just analyzed.

5. *The Theme of World-Constitution*

Pure subjectivity is the ultimate ground of all constitution and hence is also the ground of the constitution of the world and the major world-regions: nature, psyche, and spirit. Husserl's investigations (particularly those in the second volume of the *Ideas*) pursue the course of this constitution with penetration and in detail. They claim thoughtful study and are worth detailed analysis and evaluation. In the present context there is space only for a critical examination of those basic thoughts which serve to articulate Husserl's principal aim.

Dominating and guiding the entirety of these investigations is of course the idea of transcendental thought itself. If it is certain that there is a nature, a world of nature (and who can doubt this?), transcendental thought *secures* this surety lest it simply remain an assertion. Transcendental thought cannot remain with the "report" of the threefold division of the world into nature, psyche, and spirit, but seeks the ground of this triadic manifold and also the ground for the unity of this manifold as one world, for here as everywhere unity and manifold are not accidental and therefore require reflection.

Various philosophies accept two things as self-evident which (reverently or not) must be allowed to stand as ultimate facts which speak for themselves. The first is that there is just one nature (and fortunately the human intellect can come to know something like this). The second is that there are two sources of knowledge: sensibility and understanding (and fortunately they appear to complete each other). In truth, however, both of these "facts" are very difficult to comprehend.

The first requires that nature and spirit be distinguished from and opposed to each other while still granting to the one term, which certainly does not itself have to be the other, the capacity for knowing the other (as if that were less difficult). The second requires that one part of nature, sensibility—which as every part of nature is substantially conditioned through and through—be required to contribute to unconditioned truth.

In my opinion one of Husserl's great merits is not only *not* to have forgotten the philosophical task with respect to both of these "facts," but equally to have made this task easier through valuable clarifications.

The human body (and at first it cannot appear otherwise) is a part of nature and nothing else. Even as a body with a psyche it is nothing else, for psychic reality, like reality itself, is constituted through psychophysical dependencies (cf. IV 138). As a part of nature, however, it is conditioned to an incalculable extent in all respects, causally determined in its processes, and characterized by what Husserl terms a "dependency upon circumstances" (IV 41 ff.). What holds for the body in its totality also holds for sensibility. At first it also can only be a complex of natural processes, a part of nature, and therefore it also cannot at first be thought of other than as something thoroughly conditioned, as something dependent upon natural factors in all of its individual processes. Yet how is it possible for something of this kind to be in a position of becoming a coaccomplishing ground of that Unconditioned we call truth?

227

Hans Wagner

Sensibility is therefore required to be a source of knowledge, and this means that it is required to be a coaccomplishing ground of valid knowing, that it be capable of becoming a condition (instead of something merely conditioned), and that in addition to being substantially and naturally conditioned it be capable of appearing within another dimension as a member of a conditioning complex: that of valid knowledge. That is: the body and sensibility cannot be thought of simply as parts of nature, but rather must be thought of as indispensable conditions for the knowledge of nature. Body and sensibility must belong to the whole of that which is the ground of the knowledge of nature. If, on the one hand, they assuredly are certain objects among others for the knowledge of nature, they must on the other hand also belong to the conditions for there being objects of such knowledge, that is, to the *complete subject* of the knowledge of nature. The body and sensibility are to be included in complete subjectivity.

Abstract idealism is entirely correct when it locates truth in thought. For there can be no doubt that sensibility can become a source of truth only when it is criticized, that is, only to the extent that it is tested in accordance with the principles of our knowledge of objects. Sensibility possesses no epistemological dignity outside of its justification by thought. This only means, however, that sensibility itself is not an unconditioned condition, but a conditioned one. Nevertheless, as such it belongs to the totality of conditions: thought constitutes complete subjectivity only in conjunction with sensibility. Knowing preserves concreteness only to the extent that the understanding has entered into sensibility: it does this in order to organize sensibility as a source of knowledge, and therefore it rightly makes up its organization. Concreteness of the understanding and the organized character of sensibility reciprocally imply each other, and they first form the true and entire ground of the knowledge of nature within this implication. The failure of abstract idealism consists in its overlooking this reciprocal implication and in taking into account pure thought alone.

Therefore, there is nothing to be changed in the fact that Husserl's reflections upon the constitution of nature center around the constitution of the body, for in this they are fully justified: the body must be capable of being a condition in order to be a source of knowledge. The body conjoins the nature which is to be known with the subjectivity which is to know it insofar as there is a real sense in which the body is a thoroughly conditioned part of nature and is at the same time and in a transcendental sense a condition outside of nature. The body belongs to both dimensions. Since, however, it belongs to the former by itself and to the latter purely on the basis of the thoroughly organized character of its sensibility effected by thought (its belonging to subjectivity thus subject to its being conditioned by thought), and since it is furthermore equally certain that the constitution of nature cannot as yet have reached its conclusion in the constitution of the body, Husserl therefore, and again with total justification, moves beyond the constitution of the body and requires an additional condition for the constitution of nature: the constitution of spirit and the world of spirit.

Corporeality can be a condition in the above-mentioned sense only insofar as it is itself bound up with the principles of thought. This occurs solely in the criticism to which the data of sensibility must be continually submitted, a criticism which contradicts "sensible appearances" as often as it endorses the "testimony of the senses." Thus as a real element of nature sensibility requires criticism from the start, for it is simply subordinate to the laws of nature and not to the *telos* of truth. It is irrevocably a part of nature: its processes are dependent upon external circumstances and are constrained and thoroughly conditioned. If the condition which sensibility is to be is itself within the world, and if it is to possess this character of being a condition *as something worldly*, corporeality and sensibility simply cannot be what is required. What is actually required, therefore, is the transition to some element (certainly related to the body but yet distinct from it) which is characterized just by the fact that it, too, is in the world, but which, as *worldly*, is not causally determined but ideally motivated; not thoroughly determined within the context of nature but free with respect to it. What the real conditions (corporeality and sensibility) of the knowledge of nature have hitherto lacked is essentially possessed by spirit: motivation and freedom (IV 188 ff.; 211 ff.; 257 ff.). Hence spirit is speculatively necessary and not simply theoretically accidental.

Finally, that all constitution of the subject can find its conclusion only along the path leading to the constitution of the corresponding intersubjectivity is a basic thought which once again deserves frank approval.

Man can only constitute himself as an entirely natural subject (a living being with a body and a psyche) when the bodily *solus ipse* is transcended and other natural subjects are constituted appresentationally in their full meaning (IV 90; 161; 162 ff.). The complete and full unity "man" is primordially constituted first in appresentation and empathy. I too unfold my own full natural subjectivity insofar as this unity can be and is carried over to myself. In addition, the individual spiritual subject is first constituted as full *spiritual* subject (and thus as a person) to the extent that he is included in the intersubjectivity of the spiritual world (i.e., the *community* of persons). With intersubjectivity the discrepancy in content between the various individual "pictures of the world" emerges as a theme which needs to be worked out in the task of doing away with these discrepancies in terms of an intersubjectively valid and objective knowledge of the one world (IV 208).

Thus "objectivity as such" becomes a comprehensible task for the individual subject. The subject truly becomes subject for the first time in this task of objectivity, for to be subject clearly means to be the subject of objectivity, the ground of truth.

The approval due this last basic thought is rooted in the fact that it stands under the universal speculative law of the reciprocal implication of all principles. It is a convincing and fruitful exposition of the reciprocally implicative relationship between subject and truth.

In conclusion, we can say that the basic ideas contained in the theme of the constitution of the world are justified beyond any doubt. Even though deficiencies and weaknesses can be discovered here and there in individual details, they concern neither what is central nor the basic outline. On the other hand, this theme is neither so fundamental nor so unfathomable as the theme of pure subjectivity or the theme which we shall consider now.

6. The Problem of Reason as the Idea of a Universal Critique of Reason

The theme of Husserl's philosophy we shall consider under this title was the object of much criticism from the very start, wherein the critics, each from his own point of view, were of course not entirely united with respect to the real points of weakness. One is compelled to consider seriously the particular details of this earlier phase of criticism, but one must look for a new point of departure for critical considerations with respect to the whole, and this all the more since this theme to some extent takes on a modified, more profound, and also improved form in Husserl's later work.

I must certainly confess that with all my attempts to turn the various parts of this theme this way and that in order to find their most adequate internal relation, the final form of this theme appears to me to be deeply inadequate. So much so that, remembering the remarkable accomplishments of Husserl within the range of problems already discussed, I must constantly ask myself whether I have done Husserl an injustice. Therefore, when I express my criticism in what follows I do so not so much with a claim to finality as with a desire to provide a useful incentive for an earnest new appraisal by delineating as clear a position as possible.

Husserl's Posthumous Writings

As a corollary to the theme of being and nonbeing, the theme of reason and nonreason is a universal theme of phenomenology (Ia 91) and is concerned with the issue of truth and falsehood.

Reason is therefore not understood as an accidental fact, but as a universal and essential form of transcendental subjectivity in general (92). Upon reason depend the ideas of rational demonstrability, of providing with a ground, of direct seeing or mediate insight (III 333), of verifications carried through to their ultimate conclusion (Ia 53), the idea of a transcendental grounding of knowledge (66), that of the validity or form of being (both as absolute; 52), and finally, since according to Husserl all validity is grounded in evidence, the idea of evidence itself.

For Husserl, the entire theme of the problematic of reason falls into two stages of research (Ia 68): an exploration of the enormous realm of transcendental self-experience, and, related to this, a critique of this experience and a critique of transcendental experience in general which is to be carried out upon the basis of ultimate and apodictic principles, a critique which is at the same time a self-critique of transcendental experience (Ia 78).

Quite different from the earlier beginnings, which actually remained only assertions whose criticism (such as, perhaps, Hönigswald's) was relatively easy, the Husserlian theme is placed before us today in a well-developed form. It now carries with it those essential features without which no question can be termed philosophical, and clearly not the least of which is the character of being unlimited and ideal (*Ideencharakter*). The question of reason is also intended to be absolutely radical. It is still addressed to the logical (Ia 53, 179) for the purpose of exhibiting the origin of the formal-logical (Ia 94 ff.; *Formal and Transcendental Logic; Experience and Judgment*). And with its unlimited and radical character explicitly emphasized, the question finally achieves its idealistic meaning and once again assumes its necessary relation to the goal of a true, concrete, and universal ontology as the systematic unfolding of the universal *logos* of all conceivable being (Ia 181).

I would not know what faults are to be found either in the question itself, in the manner of its determination, or in the manner of its formulation. In my opinion, possible objections first arise in connection with the nature and direction of the answer found in Husserl. Here two features strike us: first, with respect to both of the above-mentioned tasks (Ia 68), Husserl (at least in the works now available) has clearly executed only the first; he has not reached the point of carrying out the critique of transcendental knowledge.

At the end (Section 63) of the *Cartesian Meditations* Husserl consoles us with the thought that from the hints he gives us we should nevertheless

231

be able to gain some idea of the nature of the critique which is to be carried out. He also consoles us with the assurance that no particular problems or difficulties stand in the way of such a critique (perhaps, for example, in the form of an infinite regress) (Ia 178). Yet neither this thought nor this assurance can take the place of the critique itself, nor can they serve to dispel completely conceivable doubts concerning its possibility.

Second, the contention that the radical question of reason must unconditionally lead to the idea of evidence and to ultimate evidences, that in other words all ultimate grounding can and must have its innermost key in the problem of evidence, is so uncertain that it must be repeatedly called into question.

Let us first consider the theme of evidence in order subsequently to focus our attention upon what—in spite of all the assurances Husserl gives us—is possibly concealed by the absence of a real critique of reason.

Husserl constantly reworked the theme of evidence. One of the most important expositions is found in *Ideas I* in the chapter concerning the phenomenology of reason (III 333 ff.).[15] All considerations must start with what is stated there.

The text outlines basic distinctions between immediate and mediate, original and nonoriginal, adequate and inadequate, assertoric and apodictic evidence, and the referral of all rational theses back to the idea of original and adequate givenness. "Idea" is explicitly meant in the Kantian sense of a predelineated infinity (351).[16]

The kind of evidence decisive for philosophy's task of establishing an absolute ground is apodictic evidence. Such evidence is granted to the principles of all grounding as their unique characteristic. All apodictic grounding takes place as a *return* to these principles, principles to which apodicticity originally belongs.

Now all these theorems concerning evidence are well and good, but can evidence thus characterized, evidence in general, be thought of as something which can give an ultimate ground? The phenomenological concept of evidence was subjected to various attacks quite early. These attacks were directed almost exclusively against three points: against the attribute-character which evidence as the self-givenness of a being seemed to have, against the criteriological character granted it, and against the belief that evidence could only emerge in an isolated element of meaning. These three points are internally related, as can be seen at once when one pays attention to what the critics set over and against this theory. An ultimate grounding must have the structure of a complex of implications. An interweaving of relations in thus decisive in ultimate grounding. If evidence is a property of an evident object-noema, it lacks the requisite relational character. If this character is lacking it cannot serve as a criterion for a relational structure is required for the concept of a criterion. All grounding and verification is a relation of one element to another: if there is to be something like verifying or grounding evidence, it must once again be the relationship of one element of meaning to another. Thus an isolated element of meaning must lack every possibility of verification.

Were these attacks justified at the time? And, if they were, are we today allowed to repeat these earlier critical objections? At the very latest, from the *Ideas I* on the area subject to attack has been largely withdrawn. From the *Ideas I* on Husserl begins ever more rigorously and decisively to work out in a positive manner the thoroughly and universally relational character of evidence as this is understood phenomenologically. He does this in frankly stressing its universally synthetic character.

In *Ideas I* the adequate evidence for the simple idea of a thing already rests upon the harmonious character of its unlimited and continuous determinations (III 366 ff.)[17] and, furthermore, each of its components has the character of being an idea which from its side also implies a demand for an internally harmonious continuation of determinations (368).[18] This continuation stands under a rule for the advance itself, a rule which predelineates an entirely determinate and determinately ordered series of appearances which are internally coherent (370).[19] In the *Meditations* synthesis is recognized in a very classical fashion as constituting the primordial form of all consciousness (Ia 77 ff.; Ib 17 f.). It is recognized as such with respect to the meaning of both objective and subjective accomplishments: as the all-encompassing inner time-consciousness which first makes all particular syntheses of consciousness possible (Ia 81), and as the universal cogitatum, the totality of life and world (*ibid.*; Ib 21). *This* evidence, now actually understood as a universal constitutive synthesis, is now the "synthesis of evident verification" (Ia 9). The error of an isolating perception is no more an error which would in fact be disastrous (Kynast, Hartmann etc.). Husserl himself explicitly states that individual evidence cannot provide us with enduring being, that evidence in his sense is not a "fact of experience" but the synthetic and limitless unity of those intentions and their verificational connections which are related to one and the same thing (Ia 96). A perfect experience of evidence, not only for the world as a totality in itself but also for every individual part of the world, requires this prior idea of a whole, that is, the idea of an endless, unconcluded, and yet thoroughly harmonious connection of all experiences, of all noemata (Ia 97).

Thus for the later Husserl those attacks which would reproach Husserl's concept of evidence with lacking a many-sided relationality and a universal implicational character are doubtless wide of their mark. Husserl himself demands that every particular evidence belong to a totality, to a limitless total evidence (Ia 98), and he doubtless understands this belongingness as one in accordance with rules for harmonious interrelatedness.

If the apparently debatable elements in Husserl's concept of evidence disappear in this way, it then appears that all specific criticisms disappear with them and that the rest can be only verbal dispute. Is this actually the case? Does this concept of evidence accomplish what is required of it? Does it seriously accomplish the task of an ultimate grounding and can it truly ground *itself* as well as *everything else?*

In order to answer this new and final question our considerations require a new point of departure. None better offers itself than the one contained in the thought of the transcendental genesis and the stratalike arrangement of all evidence.

I will begin by citing a particular instance which exemplifies Husserl's general and fundamental thought on this topic. In *Ideas II* Husserl reflects upon the point of departure required for passing over to the investigation of the essence of the psyche. He rejects beginning with any sort of interpretation or theory (i.e., any kind of mediate thinking) and requires a point of departure which begins with the "most primordial presuppositions" for such theoretical and mediating thought. Of what do these most primordial presuppositions consist? They consist of "what above all originally giving perceptions (in our case, experience) have posited in a direct manner as being (*Seiendes*) and thereby as being a determinate 'content' or meaning." This particular object-meaning, obtained from original intuition and experience, cannot be invalidated by any theory. Much rather does it predelineate "an absolutely binding rule" to all theoretical endeavor. Theory can wish to accomplish nothing other than a "predicative determination through mediate thinking" of this originally given, intuited, and experienced meaning. It is and remains the norm to which predication, thought, and theory are rationally bound (IV 90, 91).

As a consequence, theory and predication are dependent upon the pretheoretical and the prepredicative for their content in general and for the validity of their content in particular. For the theme of evidence this means that with reference to content and content-validity all theoretical and all predicative evidence is dependent upon and grounded in pretheoretical and prepredicative evidence.

Even though it is limited to a particular problem (the most important problem, however, which arises in this connection), *Experience and Judgment*, edited by L. Landgrebe, presents an exhaustive working out of this

Husserl's Posthumous Writings

idea. It is explicitly developed several times in the "Introduction" (VI, especially 11 ff.).

How, in terms of this idea, is the dependent and founded nature of the predicative determined with respect to judgment? A phenomenological clarification of the origins of the logical not only shows that logical accomplishment is already present in strata which lie below predicative strata, but also shows above all that precisely in these lower strata "are to be found the hidden presuppositions on the basis of which the meaning and justification (!) for the logician's higher-leveled evidences can ultimately be made intelligible" (VI 3). Thus the field of predicative judgment does not constitute what is *originally* logical: the ground of its meaning and justification lies outside of it in the prepredicative. The final and most primordial ground from which the entire field of the logical originates is a passive primordial belief (*Urdoxa*), a passive certainty of being, a preconstitution of objects. Upon this is constructed the authentic constitution of objects: the already active accomplishment of the ego and the constitution of an identical something in terms of its identity. Above these strata lie the true strata of established and fixed knowledge: predicative judgments (VI 64). To be sure, this prepredicative constitution of objects (as in perceptual consciousness where the object is meant as being real) is in the broad sense of the word already a judging, even though it is not predicative (VI 62/3). Logical elements are thus inherent in predicative as well as nonpredicative judging, and are also already inherent in the passive primordial belief. Judging is not necessarily predicative from the very start. What the judging of the primordial belief presupposes is only the activity of the ego and the full meaning of "object"; what predication possesses over and against the nonpredicative is only explicitness and the sense of having ascertained something (the formation of an authentic possession of knowledge). On the other hand, the higher levels cannot excel the lower in point of logical content itself and as such, and this also with respect to their meaning and justification; the higher levels are to be inviolably bound to the lowest with respect to logical content: founded in and dependent upon it.

Let us also include explicit reference to the situation with respect to the theoretical. Wherever we are confronted with purely theoretical objects which are the results of purely theoretical acts, the principle holds that these objects must have been consciously constituted *prior to* these theoretical acts through certain pretheoretical intentional experiences, for the nature of the theoretical is such that those objects which first become theoretical objects are in a certain manner *there prior to* the theoretical. Thus one necessarily returns to the pregiven objects which did not originate in theoretical acts. These pretheoretical objects, which function for

235

all theories as primordial objects, are, with reference to nature, meaning-objects. An entirely pretheoretical and precategorial "aesthetic synthesis" is at work in them. This is the most basic object-formation, serving to found all others (IV 4; 6; 7; 17; 18 ff.).

Now what does all of this mean? What meaning is common to all such referring of the predicative to the prepredicative, of the judgmental to the prejudgmental, of the theoretical to the pretheoretical? In what sort of dimension do all variations of this referring back come together?

The transcendental-genetic investigation "not only shows that logical accomplishment already lies in strata where the tradition had not seen it and that the traditional logic-problematic first starts with a relatively high stage, but it shows in particular that it is precisely in these lower strata that the hidden presuppositions are to be found on the basis of which the meaning and justification of all the logician's higher-level evidences ultimately become intelligible" (VI 3). Hence it is a question of proving that the logical is already at work in the foundations and roots of what the tradition otherwise understands by "the logical." One *logos* encompasses both. It is least developed in the former, but for this very reason it is also all the more fundamental. Thus the dimension which is called into play is the dimension of the developed and the undeveloped, where the undeveloped is fundamental and the developed is dependent. It is the dimension of a stratification of the logical from the lower to the higher and which is not only genetic but which is ordered in terms of meaning and justification.

Thus arises our first critical question: are we not without any doubt presented here with a positivism of the logical, a positivism established in an intuitionistic manner and sublimely carried out? Yet does it constitute a positivism of the logical to say, as Husserl does, that what is to have true logical and theoretical value must be cogiven in pure givenness, that it is to be read off from and reported in terms of pure givenness, and that whatever does not fulfill this condition is valueless, theoretical-logical "trimming"? And is not this just what Husserl asserts when he allows all the predicative and theoretical to be dependent upon what is given prior and along with prepredicative and pretheoretical evidence for its meaning and justification? Clearly this question can be decided only when we closely observe *what* is added from stage to stage in this ascending stratification and development and remain attentive to the truly unique nature of the "plus" in each case. It is always the same: an advance in the constitution of objects toward full objectness and objectivity. This is already true in the aesthetic synthesis. From the mere conditions of sensation and in the synthesis of the sensorial data something like an object is discovered for the first time, something identical throughout various sensorial manifolds. Or in the transition from the passive primordial belief to perceptual experience: this advance encompasses more than the merely passively pregiven unity of identity, namely, the *objective* identity which is comprehended and retained *as such* (VI 60). As far as strata of predication is concerned, this not only brings a general advance in objectness (as "confirmation"; VI 64 f.), but also a new type of object: the categorial object or the object of the understanding. If this ascending stratification and development in each case bring a "plus" in objectness, this doubtlessly signifies that they bring *new principles* of objectness, objectivity, and validity into play from one stage to another. And this is indeed already assured from what we have been able to make clear with respect to the thought of a universal constitution on the part of pure subjectivity on the one hand and from what we have been able to make clear with respect to the synthetic character of all true evidence (through harmony, regulative structure, etc.) on the other. Finally, there is no doubt that Husserl held all supervening additions to be absolutely legitimate and to be proven in their legitimacy. With the postulation of such legitimate moments of objectness and objectivity, moments which are not yet given along with what is primordially pregiven, Husserl's position distinguishes itself radically from all positivism of the logical.

What does this dependency of the theoretical and the predicative truly signify? It does not mean that in and with this dependency nothing legitimately new can emerge over and against the pretheoretical and prepredicative; it only means that there is a dependency of the new and "in itself" legitimate in a certain respect: everything lower is the *condicio sine qua non* for everything higher, and nothing more than this. Everything fallacious in Husserl's position, however, therewith appears to have been actually eliminated. Is this really so? No, for there still remains a very important and specific point of criticism. Whatever legitimately new factor appears in a stratification certainly does not have its legitimation within that field of experience from which the pregivenness of the pregiven itself stems (for example, not in sensory data or perception) but in some other field of experience. But then, however, the law of the origin of all evidence once again holds: it, too, stems from an original (even though certainly not sensory) apprehension, from original self-givenness. Original givenness, the prepredicative evidence for any highly synthetic, ideal, and categorical object of the corresponding judgmental synthesis, is continually presupposed. Phenomenologically speaking, to every region of possible objects there corresponds a basic kind of originally-giving consciousness and a basic type of original evidence which belongs to it (III 340).

237

Thus the specific problem of Husserl's position does not lie in the closely defined and certainly not mistaken dependency of the theoretical and the predicative upon a pretheoretical and prepredicative evidence mentioned above. It first comes into view with the thesis that *everything having the nature of a principle* must also be capable of possessing the ground for its legitimacy in nothing other than prepredicative and pretheoretical evidence. The debatable character of this thesis lies in the certainly questionable consequence that it then becomes speculatively difficult, if not entirely impossible, in general, simply and legitimately to distinguish the principle from that which is subject to principles. For where can one derive a differentiation and contrast which itself belongs to them if not from their different relations to some ultimate ground? And it is just at this point that they are completely equated; the ground of justification enters in the same way for the one as for the other: prepredicative and pretheoretical evidence. This may indeed be adequate for establishing their mutual correlativity, but it is certainly not adequate for distinguishing between them. Husserl must, however, distinguish them, for only distinguishable moments can be correlated with each other.

If ultimate grounding is attributed to evidence, principles cannot be truly and essentially distinguished from that which is subject to principles. It is possible that evidence is adequate for justifying principles as the *condicio sine qua non,* but then it is precisely not *their* true and sufficient ground. The Husserlian theory of evidence obstructs and conceals the true thought of principles, and hence for this theory the problem of the "essence of the ground" becomes particularly acute.

This criticism, which in effect touches upon Husserl's entire theory of reason and, implicitly, his entire position, cuts so deep that it might seem to gain assurance when it is found to be in agreement with other central points of critical analysis.

These are certainly not lacking. (a) The transcendental reduction is one which is eidetic as well. It leads to the eidetic. No matter to how great an extent the eidos has the *a priori* function of regulating what is factual and of prescribing an essential structure for it, it itself is not something which is ultimate: there are still principles inherent in it. These would first be what is truly ultimate. Here also principles (that which is ultimately constitutive) do not come into view *as such.* (b) The transcendental reduction leads to a *pure* field of experience, but to a field of experience nevertheless; it leads to the pure accomplishments of transcendental subjectivity which can be experienced in their purity. True principles, however, cannot be experienced in pure experience. The transcendental reduction does not lead to true principles from this point of view either. (c) We have seen (section 4) that Husserl does not object to

Descartes' satisfaction with criteria and rules. Husserl also contents himself with the universal features of criteria and rules rather than with principles. Descartes' clarity and distinctness in this respect correspond exactly to Husserlian evidence as an exceptional mode of intentionality in general. (d) If all truly ultimate principle-theoretical grounding has the structure of implication and correlation, a structure which holds to the very end, then by contrast Husserl's ultimate ground, transcendental subjectivity, proves to be a nonrelative, absolute being. All συμπλοκή-structure which the ultimate ground must *possess in itself* for the purpose of making all forms of objective synthesis possible so that it can *give* such syntheses is excluded from this absolute and nonrelative being.

If our critical discussion is correct, we must admit that Husserl has made important contributions toward clarifying what it is that achieves all validity and truth and how it achieves this. He has also made important contributions to the further question as to how and in what ways validity and truth are achieved by pure subjectivity. Husserl's attempt to establish an ultimate ground, however; remains unsatisfactory with respect to this final question: by *what means and from what ground* can validity and truth be achieved along the ways indicated by the subjectivity which is characterized in this manner?

The object of this question must necessarily contain within itself (1) the presupposition which makes all accomplishments of this pure subjectivity possible (all constitution, self-reduction, evidence, etc.) and (2) the presupposition which makes the philosophical *theory* of this pure subjectivity and its accomplishments possible. In other words, it must be that final principle-complex for all objects of phenomenology as well as for phenomenology itself. As is well-known, Husserl has simply given us assurance with respect to the problematic of this self-critique of phenomenology (Ia 178), the assurance that we could at least frame some provisional idea of the internal structure of this self-critique, especially with regard to its freedom from a bad infinite regress. If our conclusion is correct, we can no longer have confidence in this assurance. Certainly a well-founded ultimate ground is free from a bad infinite regress, but this is only an implicit definition of a well-founded ultimate ground itself. Only through working to establish an ultimate ground exclusively in terms of genuine and rigorous principles can an infinite regress be adequately avoided. Doubtless a critique of the critique could have been achieved by Husserl only if he had made the transition to a true idea of principles. What Husserl has submitted in this respect does not even give us a "provisional" idea of such an explicit rigorous working out in principle of a critique of this critique. Thus it is certainly not an accident that it is lacking.

239

Hans Wagner

In this respect Husserl has considerably fallen behind what contemporary Neo-Kantianism, in particular those representatives who have also attempted to come to critical terms with Hegel, has achieved. The result is that clear speculative weakness in Husserl's position to which Fink has lately referred (E 53 ff.).[20]

On the other hand, Husserl has certainly surpassed the Neo-Kantianism of that period in several important respects. He succeeded in mastering that distressing externality within which the empirical and the pure (transcendental) subjectivity had to be opposed to each other. He also succeeded in extracting a pure transcendental meaning from the question concerning the "how" of subjectivity's knowing accomplishments, and this in a measure and radicality which far surpasses the modest beginnings made by Natorp. In both of these points I see something of the most enduring elements in Husserl's work.

But Husserl has not only forced philosophical thought beyond Neo-Kantianism, but his own thought of the living quality of pure subjectivity necessarily forced philosophical thought to go beyond Husserl himself. And the necessity for this lies precisely in the defect we have worked out in this section: the lack of a completely adequate ground that finally clarified *the basis upon which* pure subjectivity can, with evidence, accomplish that evidence in all things which is to include all things and provide them with a ground. Thus from Husserl himself comes the necessity for inquiring once again into the essence of the ground: what must this accomplishing already be in its own ground with respect to reason and truth if we are to make intelligible how it can accomplish what it is to accomplish? A new dimension of questioning must be directly opened if we are to inquire in this way after the *mode of being* of the "subject" which is to present us with the ontological ground for all exceptional or nonexceptional intentionality.

It can by no means be my task here to conclude by speaking of Heidegger in place of Husserl, and perhaps to justify Heidegger's way. Apart from this, however, at least this much is certain: all determinations which are to be granted to the mode of being which belongs to the being which we ourselves are (from being-in-the-world to transcendence, ek-sistence, and in-stance) fall into one and the same dimension of the final ground "for the reason that man can render beings as such present and can be conscious of what has been rendered present." For "to and from where and in what free dimension is all intentionality of consciousness to move if man did not already possess his essence in the in-stance (*Inständigkeit*)?"

Clearly, therefore, Husserl's phenomenology leads at the very least to this transcendental, indeed, transcendental-*ontological* question and requires it by virtue of its own defect.

It seems to me, however, that it also leads to a new dimension of the old transcendental-*logical* question. According to Heidegger, the τὸ αυτό in Parmenides signifies the unity of thought and being. Certainly not a unity in the externality of a groundless falling apart and accidental occurring together. Thought and being belong together in the well-defined sense of synthetic identity and reciprocal implication; they belong together because they reciprocally require as well as reciprocally presuppose each other. And therefore the transcendental-"ontological" and the transcendental-"logical" questions continually and necessarily require each other. If the one enters a new dimension, it is necessary that the other do likewise. Hence the old transcendental-logical question also truly poses itself to us anew.

In this respect Husserl also remains the point of departure and therein proves his philosophical greatness. For the greatness of a philosopher lies in the fact that his accomplishment has brought it about that from now on philosophical truth can no longer be discovered behind him but only through him and in the direction of his own advance.

NOTES

1. Many additional volumes of the *Collected Works* have been published since this article appeared.—ED.
2. Friedrich Kreis, *Phänomenologie und Kritzismus* (Tübingen: 1930); Rudolf Zocher, *Husserl's Phänomenologie und Schuppes Logik* (Munchen: 1932).
3. Eugen Fink "Die phänomenologische Philosophie Edmund Husserls in der gegenwärtigen Kritik," *Kant-Studien* XXXVIII (1933), 319 ff. (Included in this volume, pp. 69 ff.—ED.)
4. *Philosophia*, vol. I.
5. Oskar Becker, "Die Philosophie Edmund Husserls," *Kant-Studien* XXXV, 119 ff. (Included in this volume, pp. 38 ff.—ED.)
6. Eugen Fink, *Das Problem der Phänomenologie Husserls*, 1938.
7. Ludwig Landgrebe, *Phänomenologie und Metaphysik* (*Hamburg:* 1949).
8. *Kant-Studien* XXXVIII (1933), 206 ff.
9. *Ibid*, pp. 209 ff. [A detailed analysis of this work is available in Paul Ricoeur, *Husserl: An Analysis of His Phenomenology* (Evanston: Northwestern University Press 1967), pp. 82-142.—ED.]
10. Cf. Fr. J. Brecht, *Bewusstsein und Existenz* (Bremen: 1948) (written in 1932).
11. There follows a summary of the addresses given at the *International Phenomenological Colloquium* held at Brussels in April, 1951. Wagner offers this summary as partial documentation for the "changed situation" with respect to the guiding themes of the

scholarly interest in Husserl, a change evidenced by renewed critical interest in "internal" phenomenological problems. In addition, Wagner maintains that Husserl's phenomenology should be set over and against Richard Hönigswald's form of Neo-Kantianism, a form which, in Wagner's opinion, does away with several of the inadequacies present in the Neo-Kantianism of the Marburg school.—ED.

12. References to texts and to quotations will be abbreviated as follows (—ED.):
   I = *Husserliana*, vol. 1.
   Ia = *Cartesian Meditations* (German text).
   Ib = *The Paris Lectures* (held in February, 1929).
   II = *Husserliana*, vol. 2: *The Idea of Phenomenology*.
   III = *Husserliana*, vol. 3: *Ideas I*
   IV = *Husserliana*, vol. 4: *Ideas II*.
   V = *Husserliana*, vol. 5: *Ideas III*.
   VI = Husserl-Landgrebe: *Experience and Judgment*.
   A = 0skar Becker. (Page references will refer to the translation of Becker's article included in this volume.—ED.)
   B = Eugen Fink. (Page references will refer to the translation of Fink's article included in this volume.—ED.)
   C = Helmut Kuhn's review of the *Cartesian Meditations* in *Kant-Studien* XXXVIII (1933).
   D = L. Landgrebe, *Phänomenologie und Metaphysik*.
   E = *Problmèmes actuels de la Phénoménologie* (Paris: Desclée de Brower, 1952)

13. In Gibson's translation of the *Ideas (New* York: Macmillan, 1931), the "Author's Preface to the English Edition," p. 21.—ED.

14. All those who see in Husserl a repudiation or weakening of the "realistic" or "ontological" thesis are mistaken: Ingarden, Celms, Nicolai Hartmann, etc. I myself under the influence of the literature, judged falsely in my first publication (*Apriorität und Idealität*).

15. Gibson's translation of the *Ideas*, pp. 379 ff.—ED.

16. *Ibid.*, p. 397—ED.

17. *Ibid.*, p. 413—ED.

18. *Ibid.*, p. 415—ED.

19. *Ibid.*, p. 417—ED.

20. Eugen Fink discusses "Intentional Analysis and the Problem of Speculative Thought": hence the question concerning the justification and limits of phenomenology. Phenomenology claims to be anti-speculative. Fink questions whether or not phenomenology is correct in so doing. Does it do what it claims to do? Fink answers both questions negatively and shows how the central concepts of phenomenology require a speculative foundation: a speculative foundation for the "affair itself" in opposition to the layers of meaning which have become affixed to it through history, for concepts and their conceivable relations to something which is possibly prelogical, for the reductive method, for prepredicative being, and for the appearance or phenomenon.

Husserl's Departure from Cartesianism

Ludwig Landgrebe

1. The Significance of the Lectures on "First Philosophy"

THE SECOND part of Husserl's lectures on *First Philosophy*,[1] given in 1923-24 and published as the eighth volume of *Husserliana*, has a character quite different from his previously published works. While the texts which have been made public to date were either published by Husserl himself or aimed at and brought to the point of being ready for publication, this does not hold true of the text of the *First Philosophy*, particularly with respect to its systematic second part. To be sure, Husserl had given these lectures in the winter semester of 1923-24 with the aim of preparing them for publication, but this project, which occupied him until 1930, was dropped for reasons we shall discuss below. In spite of this, however, the first and historical part of these lectures, together with its supplementary appendices, presents a self-contained whole containing everything Husserl achieved through his lectures and exercises in the history of philosophy since his Göttingen period in coming to terms with the historical tradition and in preparing a historical foundation for the necessity of phenomenology, so that this project of the lectures is based upon long and extensive preparatory work and therefore achieves a great measure of internal resolution. It is quite different with the second part of the lectures which we are to discuss here. This part not only presents long-cherished thoughts which are brought together for didactic purposes, but also has the character of a first draft which is worked out from hour to hour and conveyed in lectures. It is the path of an experimenting adventurer in thought whose successes are constantly thrown into question in the reflections which accompany the lectures[2] and whose goal is not fixed from the start so that it actually leads elsewhere than initially foreseen. It was of course Husserl's purpose in these lectures to present a way to phenomenology which would take into account all the advances made by his thought since the appearance of the *Ideas* (1913), advances in terms of which phenomenology would be established once and for all with respect to its historical and systematic necessity. But it is the paradoxical result of this attempt (the full significance of which was only gradually seen by Husserl himself) that this way and this foundation is in general not workable, with the result that in the later work of the *Crisis*[3] an entirely different way will finally be taken. Hence this work has a significance for understanding the historical development of Husserl's thought comparable to that possessed by Hegel's *Phenomenology of Mind* for the development of Hegel's system, and the history of this work's origin, which is the history of an ever further pursued improvisation, is also comparable to the origin of the Hegelian phenomenology. Of course Hegel had authorized his *Phenomenology* by publishing it himself, whereas Husserl, after intensive efforts in the years following these lectures, had finally left this project behind as incomplete and as incapable of ever being finished. Thus the history of the origin of the text before us is the history of a shipwreck. If it was simply a question of the shipwreck of a new attempt to introduce phenomenology, however, one must view the undertaking of publishing such a text as highly questionable. But this shipwreck—and this could be clear to neither Husserl himself nor to those who heard the lectures at that time—is more than an author's accidental misfortune. It is not the sign of a failing systematic creativity; it is rather the case that in no other of his writings is Husserl's radicalism concerning the continually new "presuppositionless" beginning and the questioning of all that had so far been achieved so visibly confirmed. In no other work has Husserl exposed himself to the "force of the absolute" (Hegel) to such an extent, so that this basic feature of his thought is manifested here to a unique degree, a thought which does not aim at a will to mastery through system, but one which advances toward the "affair" (*Sache*) with restless abandon. A retrospective glance from the historical distance we have now achieved permits us to understand that there occurs within this text a departure from those traditions which are determinative for modern thought and a breaking into a new basis for reflection. It is a reluctant departure insofar as Husserl had wished to complete and fulfill this tradition without knowing to what extent his attempt served to break up this tradition. It is therefore a moving document of an unprecedented struggle to express a content within the terminology of the traditions of modern thought that already forsakes this tradition and its alternatives and perspectives.

The risk of publishing this problematic text is thereby splendidly justified. Not only because it is the key for understanding the development of Husserl's phenomenology; for the problems that emerge here first make it possible to situate correctly Husserl's later work within the course of this development and to relate it properly to his earlier work, so that within this context it is comprehensible why in the later *Crisis* Husserl found himself forced to strike out on a new path (whose novelty is once again partially obscured by the self-interpretation he gave it); but because, in addition to its significance for the interpretation of phenomenology itself here, before the eyes of the reader, occurs the shipwreck of transcendental subjectivism, as both a nonhistorical *apriorism* and as the consummation of modern rationalism. Today, primarily as a result of Heidegger's work, the "end of metaphysics" is spoken of as if with a certain obviousness. We shall first properly understand the sense of such language if we follow closely how, in this work, metaphysics takes its departure behind Husserl's back. One can state quite frankly that this work *is* the end of metaphysics in the sense that after it any further advance along the concepts and paths of thought from which metaphysics seeks forcefully to extract the most extreme possibilities is no longer possible. To be sure, neither Husserl nor those who were his students at that time were explicitly aware of this, and it will still require a long and intensive struggle of interpretation and continuing thoughtful deliberation until we have experienced everything that here comes to an end. From this, new light will also be cast upon Heidegger's relation to phenomenology. Heidegger knew the thoughts affecting Husserl at this time from his first stay at Freiburg and from his many conversations with Husserl, and had therefore also experienced the shipwreck of this attempt through his own observations and had drawn the proper consequences in attempting, from that point on, to take his leave of the language of metaphysics which Husserl himself still employed.

The effort required to penetrate this work's almost inextricable train of thought, which, continually interrupted by excursions and the reinterpretations of themes already executed, laboriously draws itself forward with constantly new beginnings, will therefore be richly rewarded. To be sure, its study places severe demands upon the reader, who has no clear and surveyable train of thought to follow as a clue and who can only penetrate the sense of what takes place by drawing upon the appendices (which compose three-fifths of this large volume) added to the main text, by looking ahead to Husserl's later work, and by glancing back to his earlier work.

The editor of this volume has already indicated its unique character in his very important and instructive introduction and this character justifies his editorial procedure in every way. It is proper that the main text of the lectures is reproduced without any attempted gloss (the temptation to proceed in this way could well have been suggested by Husserl's own later critical comments on the text) and that all of Husserl's self-critical reflections appear only in the notes and appendices. These are so aptly chosen from the vast abundance of manuscripts belonging to the domain of the text's problem that one cannot exclude any of them from his attention if he desires to obtain a just picture of the entire problematic. The same exemplary care predominates in the critical textual apparatus as in the previous volumes of the collected works, although here the editor saw difficulties before him greater than in previous volumes and the manner in which he overcame them deserves the highest praise.

From these introductory remarks it follows that the evaluation of this work within the framework we have presented here must limit itself to emphasizing basic thoughts and their relationship for the purpose of attaching critical-interpretative considerations to them, considerations which, at least at some points and in a quite provisional fashion, shall serve to fix what has already been generally indicated concerning the work's significance. For the more detailed analysis of the train of thought, its turnings, breaks, and later corrections, one must refer once and for all to the editor's introduction. To add to it would require a critical commentary accompanying the entire text. One must also refer to this introduction with respect to the occurrence of the title, *First Philosophy,* and the meaning its employment has in the development of Husserl's thought. Here we need only remark that after the completion of these lectures this title recedes more and more into the background and appears only in passing in the *Cartesian Meditations,*[4] and only once again in quotation marks in the *Crisis.* When the editor remarks that it is replaced by the more general expression "transcendental philosophy," this could be made more precise by remarking that it is not simply a modification of a term designating one and the same subject matter. Husserl saw that he was compelled to abandon the subject matter itself, and that means that the guiding thought of the basic discipline of phenomenology designated by the title *First Philosophy* is to be abandoned as incapable of realization.

2. *The Guiding Thought of the "First Philosophy" and Its Problematic*

We must first seek the guiding thought of the work designated by the title. In a somewhat earlier essay[5] Husserl speaks of *First Philosophy* as the "science of method in general, of knowledge in general and of possible goals of knowledge in general, i.e., of possible knowledge in general in which all *a priori* sciences that have disconnected all types of the contingent (and also the contingent and material *a priori*) show themselves to be branches which have developed from one and the same science. A *mathesis universalis* stands above all sciences . . . as a mathematics of knowledge-achievements. . . . This highest logic, illuminated by absolute intelligibility . . . moves within exceptional forms of pure subjectivity and requires the study of pure subjectivity in its entirety. . . ." This, therefore, is nothing other than the idea of the phenomenological transcendental philosophy, which was required in the *Ideas* as the "first of all philosophies"[6] in the form of a basic science of transcendental subjectivity and its constitutive achievements. In opposition to all constituted being it is a "region" of absolute being, since everything which we can in general speak of as "being" (*Seiendem*) is being (*Sein*) for consciousness and must permit the justification for its being posited as "being" to be exhibited in consciousness.

By contrast, according to the lectures of 1923-24, *First Philosophy* not only has the task of systematically presenting this idea, but also includes within itself as equally belonging to its systematic content those meditations and preparatory meditations upon the way which leads to this idea and its absolute beginning.[7] With reference to an absolute beginning, *First Philosophy* is itself a universal science which establishes an absolute ground. It is that science "which 'in itself,' that is, in terms of inner and essential grounds, is first."[8] "The name 'First Philosophy' would then indicate a scientific discipline of beginnings." "The beginning of *First Philosophy* would itself therefore be the beginning of all philosophy in general."[9] As such, it is a philosophy which is absolutely self-justifying in every step of its thought. In this way Husserl continually points to the exemplary Cartesian quest for the *fundamentum absolutum et inconcussum* which is to be found in the indubitable evidence of the *ego cogito.* It is the idea of a first science which issues from a firm, indubitable, and, in this sense, apodictic, evidence, and whose every additional step is built upon it in a similar manner and is derived from and justified by it. With its performance of the phenomenological reduction to the transcendental ego as the dimension of an ultimate and absolute foundation it is to accomplish what Descartes strove to achieve with his beginning but had failed to accomplish in carrying through this beginning.

The introduction of this guiding idea in the first three lectures[10] already permits us to discern the path traversed by Husserl since the presentation and introduction of the phenomenological reduction in the *Ideas.* After pointing out the "general thesis of the natural attitude," the belief in the world which all thought and action already carries with it, he introduced the reduction as an "affair of our perfect freedom," [11] that is, as the result of a free resolve whose necessity was not established by any additional grounds. The transition to the reduction simply follows the presentation of the natural attitude with the words: "instead of remaining within this attitude, we shall radically alter it."[12] Now, however, this "naiveté" is to be surmounted by meditations upon the situation with respect to the motivation of the "beginning philosopher." Establishing the necessity for this step must emerge from these meditations. Thus the Cartesian principle of starting from the "I am" is concretized into "I, the beginning philosopher."

The philosopher "necessarily requires an individual resolve which, originally and as such, makes him a philosopher, an original self-causation, as it were, which is an original act of self-creation. No one can simply fall into philosophy."[13] This resolve to effect the phenomenological reduction to the dimension of an absolute and ultimate foundation signifies a "radical world denial" as the means necessary for "viewing an ultimate and true reality, and, therewith, for living an ultimately true life."[14] No exemplar for such a resolve can be pointed out in life as it is lived upon the basis of the "natural attitude," or a life lived in "kinship with the world."[15] This life is content with attaining the closest and most limited goals and is satisfied with clarity concerning the presently given limited situation. This also holds for an involvement with philosophical borderline problems within the individual sciences, problems which are then pursued to a point seemingly required for the solution of paradoxes and difficulties in method belonging to a determinate problem.

"In fact, therefore, it is a question of an entirely 'unnatural' attitude and an entirely unnatural way of contemplating life and the world. Natural life is carried out as an entirely primordial and thoroughly necessary surrender to the world and as a being lost in the world. Unnatural life is the life of radical and pure self-reflection upon the pure 'I am,' upon the pure life of the ego and upon the ways in which something gives itself within this life as being in some sense objective, and how it achieves just this sense and this manner of acceptance as something objective solely through the inner and ownmost achievement of this life itself."[16]

If, therefore, no exemplar for the resolve of the "beginning philosopher" can be found in the natural life in the world, its possibility is nevertheless already found here (although not at all apprehended as such) "in the motivation of the scientist in general," and this means that it is found in the fact of striving for knowledge as such. For this striving, in accordance with its very essence, aims at a steadfast truth, and therefore not only aims at knowledge, but at knowledge which has also been established upon the basis of some ground,[17] so that this striving already contains the tendency to surmount "naiveté concerning the attainment of knowledge."[18] Not only the striving for knowledge, however, but also all striving in general belonging to the natural life demands justification and vindication. Thus the striving after scientific truth is here already viewed with reference to the question concerning the vindication of all striving, with reference to its "meaning which encompasses all pure cultures."[19] For the truth of all man's striving after the good, the true, and the beautiful is ultimately vindicated by the knowledge of the justness of the norms from which it is derived, so that "in the knowledge-forms of theoretical truth all other truth, and hence every truth concerning values (what we term true and genuine values) and every practical truth, is expressed and determined in predicative forms of knowledge and takes on forms of being knowingly established. The authenticity of values and the truth of striving are ultimately vindicated in knowledge."[20] Therefore the striving after knowledge is essentially directed toward universality, toward "omniscience,"[21] and in this sense is directed toward "universal science." These expressions, however, have no quantitative meaning but refer solely to the fact that no isolated knowledge can have the character of an absolute foundation and that such a character can be obtained only within the universe of all possible knowledge in general, for knowing reason is one and universality does not signify that the totality of knowledge is actually attainable, but only signifies the idea of the correlativity of all possible knowledge in general and its organization within the unity of reason. As far as quantitative universality is concerned, philosophy as absolute science is an "idea situated in the infinite."

Hence the resolve of the beginning philosopher is the resolve to pursue earnestly the striving already present in human life, the resolve for a "universal critique of life,"[22] and "thus the idea of philosophy itself includes a kind of finality and a sort of radicalism in finality"[23] which presuppose nothing less than "some sort of break with all naive knowledge-values and science-values . . . in knowledge . . . and the necessity for a completely new beginning and a completely new kind of science."[24]

But this striving for an ultimate vindication of knowledge does not only have meaning for the reflections of the individual. He is always a member of the community. "The self-responsibility of the individual who knows himself to be a member and functionary of the community also includes responsibility for this kind of practical life and accordingly includes responsibility for the community."[25] "On the other hand, to bring others to responsibility belongs to my self-responsibility within this actual and possible union."[26] In this way the idea of a "highest axiological form of community" emerges "which would enact this absolute valuation as the idea of a goal which consciously guides the progress of the community."[27]

Thus it is the idea of the philosopher's human responsibility not only to himself but also to mankind that is involved when, with the philosopher, there emerges the idea of a striving after a rational and no longer traditional foundation for his existence, an idea which Husserl had developed several years earlier[28] and which is now taken up in the course of the meditations concerning philosophy's absolute beginning. Of course here it sounds as if once this beginning were carried out by the philosopher it would be established with compelling evidence once and for all and could be performed again by anyone else with the same evidence. Yet even in the historical part of the lectures, where phenomenology was to have been established as the secret longing of all Western-European thought, thereby receiving a historical foundation for its necessity, a problematic arises in the absolute beginning which is attempted here of which Husserl gradually becomes aware and which finally compels him to surrender the attempt to establish philosophy upon a *fundamentum absolutum et inconcusum* in the spirit of Descartes. How this becomes visible in the further course of the lectures and in the accompanying reflections and how it finally leads to the new way of the later works will be indicated in what follows.

This idea of the goal of life's absolute philosophical self-vindication and self-justification is guided by the experience of evidence as a "having of the thing itself," as the consciousness of the actual presence (*Selbst-Dasein*) of what is meant: "In the various forms of the activity of striving, the knowing subject is conscious of the fact that he has now reached the very goal of his striving. He knowingly views the 'truth,' that is, what he had striven for, the 'thing itself that belongs to the judgmental intending"[29] and which is opposed to a "mere," "empty" opinion. Hence there are two sides to the requirement of an absolute justification: the knowledge in question is to be an "ultimate" knowledge, for the positing of the goal is guided by the idea of a steadfast and ultimate truth, a truth obtained as an ultimate truth; and, on the other hand, it is to be a truth which is evident "in every respect."[30]

"That which is known is not to possess essential determinations which are excluded from the sight of my otherwise perfect evidence and which, by virtue of their not being known, bring with them initial unclarities, puzzlement, and doubt."[31] Such evidence "is also termed adequate evidence."[32] "In any case, we only know that it is this kind of evidence by means of a second, reflective, evidence, which must once again be adequate."[33] This characteristic of adequate evidence "stands out in the test of passing through doubt and negation."[34] Similarly, it includes insight into the impossibility of not-being and not-being-so and is in this sense apodictic evidence.[35] Husserl here[36] refers to the fact that this is nothing other than the Cartesian maxim of indubitability construed as the principle of perfect justification. Here "apodictic" and "adequate" are equated with each other and we shall for the moment disregard the fact that Husserl later on distinguishes between them.[37] In what follows, it is only a question of seeking adequate evidences, and the task of criticizing the adequate evidences which have been won with respect to their apodicticity is indicated as a later task which is not taken up in these lectures.[38]

Let us now inquire more closely into the problematic encountered by Husserl in this explication of phenomenology, an explication which is carried out under the idea of a science established upon an absolute basis. This clarification will for the first time present us with the possibility of grasping the later train of thought of these lectures. The explication of the guiding idea of the First Philosophy is at first attached to the argument of the first four lectures (38-41). In order to understand the problematic of these lectures we must also take into account Husserl's later reflections, reflections which are in part already recorded in the continually backward-glancing reinterpretations of the lectures' progress that are found later on. Briefly, this problematic can be indicated in the following way. What is sought is a field of apodictic evidences which can serve as the basis for absolute justification and vindication, and which includes insight into not-being-able-to-be-otherwise (*Nicht-anders-sein-können*). If there were only subjective opinions "which stood firm only occasionally and approximately," there would be no "absolute norms for all correspondingly directed opinions—and then all talk of a truth valid in itself and all striving after truth would have lost its meaning."[39] Hence the sought-after apodicticity must possess the character of essential insight which had already been discussed in the *Ideas*; namely, insight into unconditioned universality and necessity. Now, however, apodicticity in the sense of apodictic evidence is also defined as "having the thing itself," as consciousness of the actual presence of what is meant, and, in this sense, is defined as an immediacy, as an immediate standing-in-front-of-the-affair.

The outcome of the initial meditations was this: "At the very start . . . there must be an immediate knowledge, possibly a field, coindicated by immediate knowledge, of entirely accessible and therefore itself immediate knowledge, and these immediacies must be certain in an immediate fashion."[40]

But such immediate certainty can be nothing other than the certainty of experience. Hence later on it is stated that the investigation leads "to transcendental subjectivity as the sole source of apodictic immediacies, of absolute and indubitable experiential givenness."[41] This thought is developed further in a reflection originating from approximately the same period: all experience is ultimately referable to intuition, for only intuition is consciousness of the sought-after immediacy: "absolute justification thus presupposes absolute intuition."[42] The phenomenological reduction

251

to the transcendental ego therefore opens up "the possibility of an absolute experience and an absolute science of experience,"[43] and the question then becomes "where such immediate intuitions and therefore absolute experiences" are to be found.

"If there are absolute experiences, they must be such that I, while I am originally enacting them, 'cannot possibly imagine' that what is experienced could be something which does not exist, or is doubtful, or is only possible."[44]

Here "experience" must be understood quite literally. It must not be misconceived as having the sense of the traditional notions of an "intuition of an idea" (*Ideenschau*) or an intellectual intuition. The radical break with the convictions of traditional metaphysics which follows later is thereby already indicated, for among the basic presuppositions of traditional metaphysics belongs the assumption that insight into unconditioned necessity and universality, and therefore insight into "eternal" and "necessary" truths, can never be derived from experience, which always has to do with the factual and in this sense with the contingent. In the light of this tradition, an absolute experience which guarantees apodicticity would be an absurdity. Numerous reflections accompanying the lectures continually raise the question whether the goal of an apodictic foundation can in general be reached, or rather whether it must be abandoned, and indicate that Husserl was fully aware of these difficulties. This is most visible where he speaks of the "normative force of original self-givenness."[45] When, namely, all self-givenness ultimately refers back to absolute experience, nothing other than the positivistic principle of the "normative force of the factual" is expressed, a principle with which every possibility of subordinating the factually given to the apodicticity of eternal truths is annulled. Positivism's hidden meaning as a protest against the suppression of facticity by metaphysical thought is hereby clearly visible, and hence we stand at the point to which Husserl seeks to return beyond positivism (a meaningful alternative only upon the basis of metaphysical thought) or beyond empiricism and rationalism.

Of course this break with the tradition does not occur here for the first time. It had already been initiated in an earlier (1908) and persistently maintained definition of metaphysics as the theory of facts, and in the expositions of the first part of these lectures.[46]

In fact, Husserl, in all essentials, had already left the Cartesian way of establishing a foundation behind insofar as he conceived the Cartesian "apodictic" evidence of the "I am" together with all of the content included within it as an absolute experience, indeed, as an entire realm of experience. Results secured in a similar manner could only be achieved by Descartes by means of the doctrine of innate ideas and their force which was guaranteed by the existence of God—a way which is not open to Husserl because it can give information concerning the origin of innate ideas only by means of metaphysical argumentation and not by returning to absolute experiences. But for this way such experiences must also be capable of being exhibited as constitutive achievements belonging to the transcendental subject if its claim to truth is to be provided with a foundation. Kant's "regressive" return to the dimension of ultimate foundations from the fact of the "I think" and its experience to the "conditions for its possibility," which cannot in turn become the "object" of an experience because it first makes all experience possible, is closed to Husserl for similar reasons. Both ways fail to conform to the requirement of making-evident, of bringing something to immediate intuition

Neither is there a simple intuiting of the "eternal truths" as things existing in themselves—a Platonizing aspect which is still at work in the *Logical Investigations* concept of categorial intuition—and therefore no Platonic θιγειν of Ideas and Idea-relations, for then transcendence as something in itself would stand over and against the evidence of subjectivity. Talk of this sort of "something in itself" can be permitted only when its sense is exhibited by returning to its origin within subjectivity's constitutive experience-achievements. The sense of talking about truths existing in themselves holds only in correlation with the subjectivity which can experience them, and this does not mean in correlation with their being experienced by some possible consciousness-in-general but with subjectivity's factual primordial experience. Thus possibility does not precede actuality; much rather do all considerations of possibility serve only to illuminate the facticity of transcendental experience,[47] so "that in general a real and an ideal being which passes beyond total transcendental subjectivity is an absurdity and is to be understood as such."[48] For these reasons Husserl criticizes Kant for having both unquestioningly accepted and presupposed logic and logical evidence, and later, in the *Formal and Transcendental Logic*, he will attempt to lead the question concerning the origin of logic and logical evidence within the achievements of subjectivity to its conclusion. From this we can also understand that Husserl, in his historical observations, places Hume and his questioning of origins higher than Kant as a precursor of phenomenology.

It would extend far beyond the scope of this essay if we were to draw out what consequences this has for resolving the difficulties[49] involved in the concept of a dimension of ultimate foundations which is not to be a dimension of preceding *a priori* acceptances but one of absolute experience. Here we can only point out that the question concerning the meaning of the *a priori's* "priority" hereby takes on a new form.[50]

Ludwig Landgrebe

Keeping all this in view, we can understand to what extent the problem of apodicticity not only shows the inadequacy of the Cartesian way, but also shows the inadequacy of all further developments of the question concerning the principles of an ultimate foundation from the problematic of "innate ideas" to that of "synthetic judgments *a priori*," and how the scope of this problematic in modern philosophy is thereby transcended. Thus, beginning with these lectures, the problem of the way or ways leading to the dimension of an ultimate foundation retains that centrality which is the reason for Husserl's repeatedly devoting new reflections to this problem in the following years, of which only a small selection are presented in the published "appendices." This problem of the way leading to the dimension of an ultimate foundation is therefore not simply a problem relating to the presentation and a correct didactic introduction to phenomenology; rather (as we have noted above) does it belong to the "systematic content" of phenomenology itself. Naturally this holds only as long as we adhere to the assumption that there is an absolute and apodictically establishable beginning which, once discovered to be a firm truth, must remain fixed "once and for all." Even though this assumption already begins to appear problematic to Husserl himself in these lectures and in the chain of reflections affixed to them, it nevertheless remains effective in the following years as a motivating force and only gradually fades into the background with the eclipse of the guiding idea of the First Philosophy, whereby the question concerning the number of ways and their relation to each other also loses importance.

3. Transcendental Subjectivity as a Field of Absolute Experience and the Problem of the Ways Leading to Its Disclosure

It is not possible here to discuss in greater detail the problem of differentiating the various ways leading to phenomenology and their relation to each other in terms of the text at hand.[51] Rather do we intend to point out the problem which stands as the driving force behind this question concerning the ways into phenomenology. By means of these ways transcendental subjectivity is to be disclosed as the "field" of absolute transcendental experience and therewith a threefold question is to be answered:
1. In what sense can we speak here of experience?
2. How is the subject of this experience to be defined?
3. What is the province or "field" of this experience?

Obviously we are concerned here with three aspects of one and the same question that cannot be separated from each other; but it is also a question which, depending upon which aspect is emphasized, also permits of being answered in different ways. If we attempt to distinguish these three aspects, we must point out that this differentiation does not entirely coincide with Husserl's attempts to distinguish these ways. The attentive reader of the appendices will discover that in many respects these attempts contradict and partly cancel each other, so that on the basis of the texts presented in this volume we cannot come to any confident conclusion as to how many ways Husserl himself had distinguished precisely because he had not reached any final differentiation. Rather is it a question of discovering a clue which can expose the inner logic of Husserl's inconclusive attempt to differentiate these ways and the reason for its failure, and which can also indicate that we are dealing with a basic problem in phenomenology which, despite this failure, cannot be passed over precisely because it is here that the problem resides. Only in this way can we succeed in clarifying the lectures' argument, an argument which is exceptionally difficult and internally disunified with respect to this issue.

The question as to the sense in which we can here speak of experience was already treated by Husserl in the conclusion to the preparatory meditations (Part I), and is then given particular treatment in the first two chapters of the second part[52] where this concept of experience is set apart from the customary and familiar one. Experience, according to the latter concept, is always understood as the experience of beings in the world, and as the experience of the world itself as the totality of everything that can be experienced. But such experience cannot measure up to the criterion of apodicticity: it is always presumptive, correcting itself as its course develops, unmasking and negating something supposedly already experienced as being only an appearance; indeed, in general there is no apodictic certainty that it will proceed further in a continuous way as the experience of the world, and it is possible that in place of such a continual advance the continuous consciousness of experience, together with all of its presumptions' corrections, and negations, will dissolve into a "tumult of sensations."[53] If this experience rests upon the "general thesis of the natural attitude,"[54] and this means that it rests upon the belief in the thoroughly real character of the experienced world, this belief is not one which could be apodictically justified and established. Consequently, the belief that the experienced world *is* contains no apodictic certainty which could serve as a point of departure for a way leading to an absolute foundation. The experience of the world is not the sought-after basis of absolute experience. The belief in the world's reality cannot, therefore, be coenacted, but rather must be included in the absolute overthrow of all previously held convictions.[55] The true being of the world is nothing other than the idea of a nondissolving course of perceptions whose further development is one which is harmonious.[56] The world's being is contingent and for this reason is not to be established as a necessity. Belief in the world is therefore the "universal prejudice of positivity,"[57] and "world" is nothing other than a title for facticity whose questions belong to metaphysics but not to the beginning absolute science.

Of what sort, then, is an experience which conforms to the requirement of absoluteness? It can be nothing other than the reflective self-experience of the "I am." The proposition "I am" is "the true principle of all principles."[58] Hence this "first" way to the dimension of absolute experience we are seeking passes through the "critique of mundane experience" (the title of the second part of the lectures). It signifies the attempt to develop the Cartesian point of departure without Descartes' metaphysical substructures and is therefore also termed the "Cartesian way."

2. How can the subject of this experience be defined more precisely? It is not an ego in general, such as belongs to all thinking subjects, for talk of other thinking subjects already presupposes the being of the world, a being which must be included within the absolute overthrow of all previous opinions. For this reason the meditations concerning First Philosophy can only be formulated in the first person.[59] Other egos are given to me only as subjects in the world and in a way such that I perceive their bodies along with other things in the world and "place" a consciousness in these bodies. Perception of the other's being is perception through "interpretation,"[60] and his being as grounded in my perception of his body is just as apodictically certain as all worldly beings and the world itself, and therefore must be included in the overthrow. The sphere of experience which is apodictically certain is the sphere of the "I am" which is thought of as the *solus ipse*.[61] Transcendental phenomenology can therefore only begin as egology: one's own life has the privilege of being a first and original givenness.[62]

This critique of the experience of others is at first only hinted at in connection with the critique of mundane experience and is then discussed in greater detail in the concluding part of the lectures,[63] which is a glance back at the results which have been achieved.[64]

After this reduction to egology the question is raised whether or not this amounts to an epistemological circle. In simplified form, this question can be understood as follows.[65] The acceptance of mundane experience is disconnected because it does not withstand the critique of apodicticity.[66] But I have won the reflective knowing of myself and the "I am" only as reflecting upon myself, the one who experiences, or presumably experiences, the world, and who maintains that at least this certainty is apodictically secured. Yet I have reached this certainty only because I had previously had this experience, or presumed experience, of the world and

256

worldly beings. Is it not therefore a "naive assumption" to suppose that I could have obtained an apodictically secured basis in this way? Has not the world been indirectly presupposed here? For in general do I not have the possibility of reflectively turning back upon myself and my consciousness in this manner only as an ego within the world?

The resolution of this apparent circle follows from distinguishing two senses of the ego: the human ego and the transcendental ego.

"In a concrete sense, I am an ensouled body, a psychological reality belonging to the world and to the totality of realities. I am an object of mundane experience among other such objects. Must I not separate from this that ego which here is the subject of this experience: the ego which is the subject for the ego-object? More precisely: I, the ego who actively lives through a continuing world-experience, find myself confronted by this manifold and unified world, and thus as a world-encountering subject I am most assuredly the subject for all objects, the subject for the entirety of the world. I also encounter myself as being situated within this world, i.e., I encounter myself as object, as this human ego together with the entirety of its psychical life."[67]

This equivocation is of course not accidental, but is grounded in the fact "that I, the subject of experience, (am) identical with the ego which has become objective in man."[68] Thus I can at any time "return from the reflective experience of the subject-ego to the objective and mundane experience of the human-ego."[69] I have not indirectly presupposed the being of the world and have therefore not argued in a circle when I claim a higher and eventually apodictic certainty for this subject-ego. Much rather is it the case that "if the created world, the object of my experience, is annihilated, I, the pure ego of experience, am not annihilated, nor is this experience itself annihilated."[70] "The epistemological contingency which the world has by virtue of the essence of my mundane experience together with everything which results from this contingency concerns neither my ego nor the life of my ego in their purity."[71] Thus the critique of mundane experience has the function "of making the previously concealed transcendental subjectivity and its transcendental life visible . . . as a sphere of being which is separable from the world—and yet not separate from it in any natural sense, as if it were a question of a realm of being existing severed from the world. Transcendental being is fully self-enclosed, and yet, thanks to the unique sense of mundane experience (an achievement carried out within the transcendental ego), it can be experienced as the ensoulment of a body."[72] This method leads, therefore, to the knowledge "that I, in my own ultimate and true reality, live an absolutely enclosed life of my own, a life of constant objectifying achievement, a life which shapes mundane experiences, which shapes an objective world within itself as its phenomenon, and therefore as a phenomenon within this ultimate subjectivity."[73]

Therewith the sought-after subject of absolute experience is first defined and a further insight into the unique character of its experience is won. It is a reflective experience, but as such it is to be distinguished fundamentally from the traditional sense of "inner experience." For, as Husserl continually emphasizes, this latter would have identified the experiencing subject with the human ego, with the ego of man in the world, and thereby would have occasioned all of the epistemological aporiae which dominate modern thought. This reflective self-experience of the transcendental ego, the "primordial ego" (*Ur-ich*), is to be distinguished fundamentally from the psychological reflective experience which never discards the character of being mundane.[74] This objection is not only directed at a specifically psychological analysis and theory of consciousness (in particular, the psychology first made autonomous and free from philosophy in the nineteenth century). Rather it also extends to the entire modern problematic of consciousness, and not only to the theory of consciousness and the theory of the human psyche, but also to every questioning of man's essence which intends to elevate man or "humanity" to the level of being the principle of an ultimate foundation.[75] Correctly understood, it is thus directed against the entire movement of anthropologism which, beginning with Feuerbach, dominated modern thought to a degree which for a long time had not been fully recognized. Kant also had not been able to free himself from this "anthropologism,"[76] and his transcendental philosophy could be nothing other than a transcendental psychology.[77] Of course a coming to terms with apparently similar distinctions present in the various systems of German Idealism is lacking in Husserl.[78] But these indications already make it clear that the distinction between psychological and phenomenological reflection and analysis of consciousness, which is viewed as something foreign, indeed, even superfluous, by many phenomenologists, is of central importance for understanding Husserl's phenomenology. It is for this reason that in the years following these lectures Husserl paid unceasing attention to this distinction.

Here we can only point out that the difficulties involved in this distinction are already indicated by the fact, which is constantly emphasized by Husserl, that a purely psychological description and analysis—when it does not presuppose any theory concerning psychophysical connections as its basis, but simply limits itself to what is consciously known *purely as* it is consciously known—must lead to the same results as a phenomenological description and analysis of individual and different modes of consciousness and of different kinds of acts, so that such psychological

Husserl's Departure from Cartesianism

analysis can be "read" as being phenomenological merely by an "advance notice" that they are to be treated in this way. The first part of the *Ideas*[79] had already referred to this relation, although there the difference between psychology and phenomenology was understood as the difference between an inductive factual science on the one hand, and an essential science on the other[80]—even though the possibility of a correctly understood "rational psychology," that is, of an essential science of the psychical, was left open in the third volume of the *Ideas*.[81] The problem becomes more acute after the phenomenologically reduced subjectivity is presented as a field of transcendental experience, and after the eidetic science of transcendental consciousness is characterized as an instrument for the transcendental science of facts,[82] a science resting precisely upon the basis of "absolute experiences." By contrast, the possibility of such a transcendental phenomenological science of experience was explicitly denied in the *Ideas I*.[83] We are now compelled no longer to distinguish psychology as an inductive science of experience from phenomenology as an eidetic science, for there must be both a psychological and a phenomenological factual science as well as a psychological and a phenomenological eidetic science, and the relation between these two directions of inquiry must be determined. We cannot discuss here how this problem adds further complications to the question concerning the various ways leading to phenomenology.[84]

In fact, a problem is hereby touched upon which also concerns most of the current projections of a philosophical anthropology. On the one hand, they claim universal validity for their assertions about man, his difference from animals, his realm of inwardness and the genesis of this inwardness, and so forth, and on the other hand (and with justice), they base their assertions upon the results of partly empirical and partly experimental research. As long as these generalities are not established by metaphysical reference to a theory of values and a realm of values, it remains completely indeterminate as to whether their character is that of an empirical and presumptive generality or that of an unconditioned, and therefore *a priori*, generality. This becomes clear in an exemplary fashion in the anthropology of Gehlen, with its richness of important material. Understanding the dimension of an ultimate foundation as one comprised of "absolute experience" will first be capable of eliminating this difficulty by revising the alternatives of "empirical" and "*a priori*."

259

Ludwig Landgrebe

4. The Extent of the Field of Transcendental Experience: The Consciousness of Horizons and Its Importance

The distinction between transcendental and psychological subjectivity has only been touched upon in the development of the "first way" leading to transcendental subjectivity discussed so far, and has not yet been treated in detail. It requires a more precise differentiation between phenomenological and psychological description on the one hand, and a theory of reflection on the other. First, however, there follows an observation[85] which is to serve as a kind of "survey" of the realm of transcendental experience. It presents the central theme of the lectures and is later retrospectively designated as a phenomenology of the phenomenological reduction.[86] It introduces a treatment of both of these other two problems: a discussion of the difference between phenomenological and psychological analysis (within the context of an anticipatory view of and a retrospective glance over the entire course of the lectures),[87] and a discussion of the theory of the phenomenological reflection in a chapter[88] which Husserl later characterized as an excursus.

We shall first set aside both of these problems and proceed to sketch the basic features of this "survey" of the realm of transcendental experience. This observation applies to the problem mentioned under the third heading of this essay, namely, the question concerning the extent to which the absolute sphere of being of the "I am" can be viewed as a self-enclosed field of transcendental experience. The first way into phenomenology, the "Cartesian way," does not provide an adequate answer to this question. It only establishes a reference to the sought-after dimension of the absolute foundation (which remains entirely empty) by leading back to the indubitable evidence of the "I am" through the critique of mundane experience and the overthrow of the belief in the world's existence. This way does not grant us insight into everything that has been overthrown with the discarding of this belief, nor does it grant us insight into what still remains with this evidence of the "I am," that is, how this momentary point of certitude with respect to my own existence as the indubitable ego already includes further evidences which are equally assured, evidences with which a "transcendental field of experience" can be disclosed.

Initially, this part is introduced only as an observation serving to give "a more precise view of transcendental subjectivity." Only in a later reflection is it first designated as a new "second way" into phenomenology, a way which, entirely apart from the previous "Cartesian way" of disconnecting the belief in the world, exemplifies the performance of the reduction upon individual kinds of acts and shows how the full

260

Husserl's Departure from Cartesianism

transcendental field of experience can be disclosed in terms of these acts.[89] It is first shown retrospectively that the different kinds of acts analyzed in this connection are not arbitrarily chosen examples. These acts reveal how the entire transcendental field of experience is already implied in all actual moments of the "I am" and its performance of this or that act. Hence it presents this text's development of the theory of intentional implications.[90]

This theory is of central importance, not only because it is here that the concept of the world in the Husserlian sense is first clarified, but also because it shows that, as the locus of ultimate foundations, transcendental subjectivity is not exhausted by the "present actuality" of consciousness[91] and that all constituted "sense" and "meaning' cannot be traced back to this aspect of consciousness.

The systematic significance of this part rests in the following: it was at first maintained that after the critique of mundane experience and after the reduction to the "apodictic" evidence of the "I am" there remains not merely an empty point of consciousness, but also a consciousness that "I am, and that I am experiencing this experience of the world."[92] We must therefore show how in the current act of experience, which, as an experience of worldly beings, is primarily a perception, not only this and that particular being is now currently perceived, but also how in this perception, actual at this moment as the rendering present of some being, the experience of the world is already implied by this being's "actual presence" in its sensory givenness. The present perception is known as constituting one moment within the stream of perceiving experience. It is both consciousness of what has just been perceived and the anticipation of what is immediately to come—a connection which was first presented in detail in the lectures concerning the consciousness of time.[93]

There it was already shown that the domain of synthesis in consciousness extends much further than was seen by the tradition and that this domain does not concern the bond between the succession of acts in the course of consciousness alone. The decisive difference between Husserl and Kant must already be understood from this point, the discussion of which would of course be the task of a separate investigation. Here we can only point out that with this analysis Husserl succeeds in penetrating into a dimension of consciousness and in answering questions of which Kant stated: "How this should be possible we are as little capable of explaining further as we are of accounting for our being able to think the abiding in time, the coexistence of which with the changing generates the concept of alteration."[94] In itself, therefore, actual consciousness as a rendering present already implies re-presentation (*Vergegenwärtigung*) which on its side can at any time be transformed into a present act of

261

remembering or into an imaginative depicting by way of anticipation. Thus in every present *ego cogito* I already "know of my transcendental being or life in both past and future."[95] This "knowing" is already included in every presentifying consciousness, and the fact of alleged remembrance or ability-to-remember belongs to its phenomenologically reduced (reduced to its pure meaning, disconnecting its claim to validity) and secured content. This is the presupposition for the fact that we can inquire whether and to what extent memory deceives and can be corrected. Upon this re-presentifying mode of consciousness rests the fact that the evidence of the "I am" is not limited to the momentary now-presentifying consciousness, but that it continually includes consciousness of an experiential bond extended into the past and into the future, so that there is consciousness of a presumably experienced real world in this extendedness.

There are, however, not only such acts of real and presumably perceiving consciousness together with the rememberances and anticipations which belong to them. They, as positional acts, are to be distinguished from quasi-positional acts,[96] acts of anticipation and the delineation of possibilities which are bound up with real perception, or acts of pure fantasy. Consciousness is not only consciousness of real objects in the existing world, but is also consciousness of ideal objects and ideal relations (logical and mathematical objects and relations, etc.), and is so always upon the basis of its consciousness of the world, for the ideal worlds of science, art, and so on, together with their creations, all belong to our world. If we now consider that this not only relates to consciousness of what is factual, but that it also relates to consciousness of pure possibilities, and, if we consider that essential insights can be gained by a free variation of what is factually given in presentifying experience and that in the light of such generality (which in some way or another is always already understood) this worldly being is grasped as "a man," "an animal," and so forth, the significance of this analysis of re-presentifying acts and the extent to which re-presentification and fantasy belong to the constitution of worldly reality become clear. These elements, already implied at any given time by actual consciousness as the consciousness-of-backgrounds evidenced "when I advance in such-and-such a manner in my experience . . . ," are responsible for the fact that this consciousness of the "I am" as experiencing implies the consciousness: "this, my world, is." But even more: to this stream of my experience there also belongs the experience of others, an experience which, according to Husserl's exposition, is nonpresentifying. Only the bodies of others are given through presentifying perception and a consciousness "like mine" is indicated within these bodies which are also directed toward and which also experience the same world that I experience. This knowledge of the other is therefore the achievement of a special group of nonpresentifying (but re-presentifying) acts on the basis of which the world experienced by me is accepted by me as not only my world, but as the public world. The experience of the world implies the experience of mankind as an encompassing personal community.[97] The result of this survey of the field of transcendental experience is this: it is indeed a field and its correlate is the world as it is intended by consciousness. Also disclosed is the fact that the reductive analysis of the individual act-consciousness cannot remain with these individual acts, but leads to the consciousness of horizons which is already implied by every consciousness of acts. If, therefore, the true phenomenological reduction is to be performed (in which all presupposed objectivity is set out of action), it cannot limit itself to the individual acts but must include that consciousness of horizons implied in every consciousness of acts, a consciousness which is ultimately consciousness of the world as the total horizon. First of all, therefore, it must annul the acceptance of the world's being which is concealed and implied by individual acts.[98] And therefore the analysis of the consciousness of individual kinds of acts requires an analysis of the consciousness of horizons.[99] With this result the domain of transcendental experience is accessible in its full extent.[100] It is also shown that the attempt (with which this part of the lectures began) to perform the reduction upon individual acts can only be viewed as a way leading to the field of transcendental experience when not only the positing of the object as existing is set out of action, but when its entire horizon, the being of the world, is also "bracketed." Hence this way, carried through to its end, leads to the same result as the first way, only that with this way questions can be answered which were left unanswered by the first.

Of course in the present text the train of thought does not proceed in this unbroken manner. The necessity of bracketing horizons in order to reach the transcendental field of experience by departing from individual acts is only afterwards shown to be the result of this train of thought and is at first motivated by a consideration (later withdrawn) as to whether the attempted reduction of individual acts together with their being-thesis and its correlates is not just simply the psychological reduction and by the question how this reduction is to be distinguished from the transcendental-phenomenological reduction.[101] We cannot touch upon this issue here.

This analysis of the consciousness of horizons and the insight into the necessity of including this consciousness (in its widest extent) within the overthrow effected by the reduction—which Husserl himself viewed as one of the most important discoveries in these lectures—is of significance in many respects. It is the basis for the assertion that it is the world and not merely beings in the world that is actually experienced. Of course the world is not experienced nor is it capable of being experienced as one object among others; neither is it the totality of experienced objects and objects which could possibly be experienced (as such it is an "idea"), but it is constantly experienced as something the existence of which is believed in as the uncontested horizon of the "and so forth" of our experience. In fact, with this theory of the implication of the total-horizon within every single actual consciousness an essential advance has been made beyond the entire tradition of the modern theory of consciousness which permits us to understand the limits of this tradition's position and the aporiae which result from its limitations.

From this the following emerges as being of particular importance for the evaluation of phenomenology's relationship to Kantian transcendental philosophy: experience is not only the "discursive" apperceiving which runs through individual elements and gathers them together and reaches a totality of experience only as a limiting concept of reason. Experience is already involved with the whole of experience as the horizon of the world *before* all discursiveness in individual experiences, a horizon which not only accompanies every act of consciousness as the potentiality of being able to advance further and to go back further into the past through memory but which also directs every act of consciousness. The more exact analysis of the consciousness of horizons cannot be discussed here. This horizon is known to be open in terms of an indeterminate openness, "without real boundaries and yet bounded and with variable boundaries,"[102] an openness therefore which for the immediate having of the world cannot be designated as the consciousness of either a finite or an infinite openness, so that the concept of the world as an open horizon does not fall under the antinomy of the concepts of "finite" and "infinite" that arises from reflection

On the other hand, this discovery signifies a motive which is of great importance for the further development of Husserl's thought in the later works. Although here this discovery is carried out in terms of the consciousness of perception and the re-presentifying consciousness which is essentially implied by it, nevertheless we shall soon see that the horizon of the world is not only the horizon of what actually is and can be perceived, but also as the horizon of a common world it implies in itself all of the opinions, "prejudices," and schemata for understanding and regulating our experience, which refers to its historical-communal evolution, and which no less refers to the evolution of those perspectives and problem-directions of the sciences which are already decisive in this

Husserl's Departure from Cartesianism

historical-communal world, and which themselves therefore belong to the horizon of this world through which this world is already understood in a determinate way. This insight thus motivates a twofold inquiry that is first taken up by Husserl in the later works:[103] on the one hand, there is the return to the "life-world," the return from the scientifically interpreted world-horizon to the conditions for its formation in terms of subjectivity's prescientific and extrascientific encounter of its world; on the other hand, there is the question concerning the conditions of this becoming as a *historical* becoming.

If, therefore, this horizon is one of absolute experience and is as such the horizon of my own ego, the analysis of the horizon-consciousness cannot limit itself to exposing the general structures of this horizon in terms of its significance for the constitution of the world in all of its levels—from the prescientific to the scientific interpretation of the world—but is intensified by the question concerning this determinate historical ego in its determinate historical origin, and this means that it is intensified by the question concerning the historical horizon of this "I am" which can set before itself the goal of an apodictic foundation and justification and hence orient itself within the horizon of Western science, philosophy, and world-certitude. These are of course perspectives first worked out by Husserl in his later years and which are announced only in his consciousness of the incompleteness of the way leading to phenomenology in these lectures.

In glancing back over the course of the lectures up to this point,[104] Husserl observes that with the requirement of disconnecting each objectivity and extending the reduction to include the hidden objectifying opinions and convictions which are only darkly at work as a horizon, the goal of an apodictic foundation for transcendental subjectivity as a field of absolute experience is not yet reached: rather does the task of an apodictic critique of transcendental experience still remain to be achieved. Husserl had in fact nowhere carried out this critique for the simple reason that once and for all it cannot be carried out in the traditional sense as the establishing of a beginning. Husserl had of course first reached full clarity concerning this in connection with his work in the *Crisis*. In an important reflection written in 1935 we read: "Philosophy as science, as earnest, rigorous, indeed, apodictically rigorous science—the dream is spent."[105] These words relate to a text which is concerned with the question: "how is history a requirement" for the radical philosophical reflection? Here we see how the dismissal of the guiding idea of an apodictic science goes hand in hand with the decisive turning toward establishing the way of phenomenological reflection historically (including the history of philosophy). This is not a break with Husserl's earlier beginnings but is rather the consequence of a program dedicated to an ultimate establishing of philosophical truth upon "absolute experience." The way leading to this consequence was first opened by the analysis of the consciousness of horizons which, as consciousness of the world, inseparably belongs to every act performed by the ego, and by the conviction that this, too, must be included in the "overthrow" effected by the reductive bracketing; for the overthrow of all self-evident convictions which draw their effectiveness from this horizon and which had been uncritically accepted previously must indeed also question the self-evidence of the belief in necessarily starting with the evidence of the "I am" and must also justify it. But this is not possible by having recourse to a general essence of consciousness, or to its intentional achieving and world-formation—a way which is inaccessible to Husserl at the very moment when the requirement that every justification is to be based upon absolute experience and upon the subject of absolute experience is advanced to a primary position. Therefore the foundation in the *Crisis* work follows an entirely different way by reflecting upon the earlier history of this requirement in European science and philosophy in order to demonstrate that this requirement is the *telos* of this history.[106] Hence one can say that the historical-philosophical establishing of phenomenology in the *Crisis* work fills in the place left empty in the lectures by the failure to fulfill the requirement of an apodictic critique. This occurs as the consequence of Husserl's return to "absolute experience" and not by way of turning to something new. It is therefore no overstatement to maintain that in this return to absolute experience, as it is followed out for the first time in the *First Philosophy,* lies the motive whose consequences lead to the destruction of the framework which sustained the metaphysical thought of the tradition (in particular, its Cartesian form). Husserl himself was of course never entirely aware of the full extent of this break with the tradition. Beginning with the *First Philosophy*, it is played out behind his back in his incessant endeavor to establish phenomenology.

The following must be mentioned for understanding the importance of this development in Husserl's thought and in order to reflect further upon the consequences inherent within it. The historical foundation obviously can no longer be apodictic in the traditional sense; it cannot be derived from eternal truths and rational necessities. Rather it is a foundation resting upon a historical fact and upon a willingness to affirm and to grasp the "resolve" of the philosopher and the possibility it offers. Although Husserl had not worked this out, one would misunderstand his historical-teleological establishing of phenomenology if one desired to interpret this as a "dogmatic" and theoretically established thesis concerning the course of history. It is much rather a "regulative" principle determinative for

Husserl's Departure from Cartesianism

man's activity and behavior. For, as the resolve of the "beginning philosopher," the resolve to enact the reduction is an act of will and in this sense signifies an "entirely personal conversion." This teleology of history is discovered only when it is taken up by the will of the one who reflects and who thereby takes upon himself this datum which serves to establish his own existence. To this extent this teleology is an idea, but not one which is to be viewed in some absolute realm; rather it is a task posed to the beginning philosopher by his own history and grasped in resolve so that the resolve to accept this task as one which is given starts anew at every moment with a free will. From this it follows that the "absolute experience" upon which all of life's justification and responsibility rests is an historical experience. Its absoluteness and finality does not rest upon the knowledge of some truth in itself, or upon the grasping or conquering of an "eternal truth," but is absolute in the sense of the philosopher's being placed before an insurmountable facticity which can only be accepted. The foundation is final in the sense that the resolve for its acceptance ("it shall be so") is the settlement of deliberation. This alone can be the sense of an absolute foundation after the ideal of its apodicticity proves to be unrealizable.

To the possible objection that drawing out these consequences does violence to Husserl's work, it can be answered that this interpretation alone makes it possible to grasp the continuity and internal logic of the development of Husserl's thought beginning with the *Ideas*, progressing through the *First Philosophy*, and concluding in the later work of the *Crisis*. The way leading to a historical foundation for phenomenology was prepared quite early in the importance granted by Husserl to the considerations of the history of philosophy, considerations which he often called his "tale" (and later on his "poem") "of the history of philosophy"[107] in which phenomenology was to have proved itself to be the "secret longing" of the earlier beginnings of European philosophy. But this observation is not only given in his occasional lectures on the history of philosophy, but is also given in the historical part of the *First Philosophy*, preeminently within the framework of a pure history of philosophy. It is in the *Crisis*, with its genealogy of "objectivism" as the fundamental attitude of the modern period, that the establishing of phenomenology's necessity first follows from an encompassing world-historical and cultural-critical perspective. The theoretical-scientific foundation, which was of central importance for Husserl in the *Ideas* and during the years after the first World War, is here systematically included within the problem of the "renewal of European Man" for the first time. Certainly Husserl's coming to terms with Heidegger's *Being and Time* was not without its influence for this "existential" turning point, but it cannot be understood solely in these terms. The theme had already been treated earlier in the above-mentioned essays, even though its treatment was very general. Naturally this last step of Husserl's does not follow as a consequence of pure reflection—only the possibility of such a step was disclosed by the problematic of the *First Philosophy*. It was above all the historical experience of the thirties which demonstrated to Husserl that the "collapse" signified more than a crisis in the foundations of the sciences and that it was to be understood in the context of the historical collapse of "European Man." And where is the great thinker who has not received his last and hidden force from such historical experiences?

Let us now turn back from the view of the perspectives disclosed by the discovery of the horizon-structure of consciousness to the text of the lectures itself. In this context the indication of the horizon-structure served to demonstrate that the basis (the "I am") won by the reduction not only concerned the momentary evidence of the act just performed by the ego but that along with this act a field of transcendental experience was also won. This means that the requirement of extending the reductive bracketing to include the consciousness of the world implied in the horizon of every single act signifies not only retaining the momentary now of the "I am," but also retaining the world which is cogiven in the horizon-consciousness as something which is also intended. What remains is the "I am" together with its consciousness of the intended world, this stream of its intended world-experience—no matter how it might stand with respect to the true being of the intended world. The phenomenological reflective experience is now directed toward this stream of experience, an experience which is therefore not simply the experience of the world but the reflective experience of the world-experience, the reflective experience of the constitution of the intended world within the achievements of my experience. This remains as something absolutely given after the reduction has been performed. Only by viewing these achievements can we decide and justify the sense, possibility, and limits of every truth of beings which is to be gained.

Understood in this way the transcendental subjectivity won by the reduction can no longer be called "subjectivity" in the traditional sense. Transcendental subjectivity is nothing else than the inseparable unity of world-experience and its intentional correlate, the intended world experienced within it, upon which the possibility of the traditional distinction between "subjective" and "objective," "inner" and "outer," is based. Hence what remains after the reduction is not only the certainty of individual acts performed in the living present, the present life which alone is immediately given,[108] but also certainty of the total-horizon as the already cointended world just as it is intended and, in this sense, certainty of the "entirety of an endless continuity of life."[109]

Thus in the reduction "I survey my life . . . and at one with this and in a correlative turn: I survey the world, the world which is continually formed and reformed in the manifold modifications of content in my intentionality, my judgmental certainties and probabilities, my positings of value, and my actions."[110] Clearly it is not a question of "an actual view, an actual reproduction of past life within a continuity of explicit remembrances . . . and of an explicit depiction of the likelihoods and possibilities of my future life."[111] Rather it is a question of the universal essential structures of this achieving, world-formative life. In particular, we are concerned with the "essentially unique feature of my life that in every present phase it has and continually produces anew—even though it be empty—a consciousness of distance, a consciousness of horizons."[112] In this way "I gain the pure universal life, and the worldly universe is transformed into universal intentional objectivity as such."[113] In this way the reduction discloses a "new realm of experience."[114]

The central portion of the lectures ends with this result. It only remains to note briefly its conclusion.[115] It is presented as a retrospective glance over the results which have been attained and chiefly strengthens the necessity for the egological character of the considerations up to this point by continuing the analysis of the perception of the other, where the other is never "there himself" and whose presence is indicated solely by its bodily character as an object in the world. We do not, however, hereby end with solipsism, for solipsism is only a methodological "passageway." Precisely when we inquire with the criterion of "actual presence" after the truth of the being of all presumably existing things, and when the other *qua* other fails to measure up to this criterion, this is reference to the fact that here something exists which is genuinely transcendent over and against my own subjective continuity and which has its own manner of being confirmed with the apperception of the "other" enduring through the course of experience.[116] "Absolute being," therefore, and this means transcendental subjectivity as the basis for the ultimate foundation of absolute experience, is not exhausted by my own subjectivity which, together with its world-constituting achievements, is disclosed in phenomenological reflection; absolute being is the universe of transcendental subjects, the "transcendental totality of egos."

"The sole absolute being, however, is the being of the subject as it is originally constituted for itself, and absolute being in its entirety is the universe of transcendental subjects which stand in actual and possible community with each other. Thus phenomenology leads to the monadology anticipated by Leibniz with ingenious insight."[117]

Ludwig Landgrebe

5. The Problematic of the Absoluteness of Transcendental Subjectivity and of Establishing This Absoluteness by Means of the Theory of the Phenomenological Reflection

Does not phenomenology thereby lead to a spiritualistic metaphysics and hence to the consummation of modern rationalism (even though Husserl had criticized the "dogmatism" of the Leibnizian philosophy),[118] and how is this compatible with the assertion that it is precisely in these lectures that the shipwreck of this metaphysics takes place? Husserl had in fact never revoked the thesis that transcendental subjectivity is absolute being, a thesis already advanced in the *Ideas* and maintained in the *Cartesian Meditations* of 1930. It was this thesis, however, which, after the appearance of the *Ideas*, evoked disagreement on the part of Husserl's Göttingen students who refused to go along with this step toward "idealism." Although in many cases this resistance was based upon inadequate arguments taken from the arsenal of epistemological "realism," it contains nevertheless the legitimate question whether this step was the end to which the phenomenological point of departure necessarily leads. Therefore a critical inquiry into the foundation for this thesis would have at the same time the task of exposing the justifiable elements in this question. Its point of departure must be taken from the contradiction residing in the fact that the argument of the *First Philosophy* contains just those above-mentioned moments which result in questioning the thesis that transcendental subjectivity is absolute being. Husserl himself had not drawn this consequence, so that his departure from metaphysics had not reached its conclusion. This is the reason for all difficulties encountered by the interpretation of Husserl's thought: the character of the absoluteness of transcendental subjectivity as well as the meaning of the foundation-laying "operative" concepts derived from this character (concepts such as constitution, achievement, transcendental life, etc.) are left incomplete and require self-contradictory interpretations.[119] Therefore, the adoption of a critical stand must strive to uncover the basis for these obscurities, a basis which must permit itself to be pointed out in the course of Husserl's analysis itself, so that it is not forced to require an argumentative critique drawn from the outside.

We must therefore first ask where in these lectures is the foundation for the thesis concerning the absolute being of transcendental subjectivity to be found. The indication of the consciousness of horizons has led to the insight that the immediate evidence of the "I am" is not just evidence for the act (and the act's intentional correlate) which has just been performed, but that it already implies consciousness of the intended world, and that therefore subjectivity is disclosed by the reduction as a *field* of phenomenological experience. From this, however, it does not yet follow that this field of transcendental experience is a field of absolute being. Rather is this thesis rooted in Husserl's interpretation of the essence and achievement of phenomenological reflection. If it can be shown that this interpretation cannot stand up to criticism, it seems to me that the thesis affirming absolute being of transcendental subjectivity becomes untenable. Husserl's theory of reflection is inserted into the crucial portion of the lectures as an excursion.[120] The discussion of this theory has been delayed until now so that we could give an uninterrupted presentation of the entire train of thought of the lectures. Now we must take up this discussion so that we can gain the point of departure required for our critical observations. For this reason we shall briefly outline the basic thoughts of this theory.

A first consideration concerns the general structure of reflection, which is again presented in terms of the "simple" example of external perception. In perceiving I am directed toward what is perceived. The perceiving ego is thereby in a state of "self-forgetfulness," or as Husserl rephrases it: the ego is latent. Insofar as it continues to perceive, however, it can at any time turn back upon its perceiving of which it is still retentionally aware as "having-just-perceived." Thereby the ego enacts the explicitly reflective consciousness "I perceive," wherein the previously latent ego of perception becomes evident. Reflection is therefore a "becoming-subsequently-aware."[121] It consists of the fact "that the reflecting ego is performing an act which makes the previously latent ego an intentional object, i.e., the object of an act of reflection." Now the reflecting ego is latent in its turn and can become evident in a higher-level reflection. Essential here, however, is the fact that the performing ego always remains latent in performing its acts. For example, in the living presence of the course of a perception we have "in coexistence a twofold (*verdoppelte*) ego and a twofold ego-act: the ego which now continually observes the house, and the ego which performs the act: 'I am now aware of this'."[122] This, however, does not lead to an infinite regress of reflections from which the performing ego would constantly escape. Because the performing ego, the "subject-ego," knows itself to be identical with the "object-ego," or the object of its reflection, it follows that this possible infinite reiteration can remain ignored because it leads to nothing new; it continually leads to the same self-identical ego which is aware of its identity. Thus we can say "that the plurality of act-poles are in themselves evidently the same ego, or that one and the same ego makes its appearance in all of these acts . . . (and) that the life of the ego in its activity is from beginning to end nothing else than a continual dividing-of-itself-in-its-active-behavior."[123] Reflection is thus presented as the making of the previously latent ego into an intentional object. The ego-subject thereby becomes the intentional object of its own observation.

So much for the structure of reflection in general. Now what distinguishes the natural, mundane reflection from phenomenological reflection is this: at all times mundane reflection follows from an interest in the being of the object[124] toward which the ego was previously straightforwardly directed; for example, in perception I seek to assure myself of the being and character of what I have presumably perceived by reflectively considering "what I have really seen," and so forth. Perception thereby posits its intentional object as something which is real. It is positional consciousness and thereby rests upon the basis of the "general thesis" of the belief in the world; it enacts this belief along with its perception and thereby serves the aims of worldly experience. It is content when it has provided itself with a certainty regarding what it has experienced adequate to its objectives. By contrast, phenomenological reflection has already set this belief out of play; it lives with an interest solely for the subjective course of the intending and the intended as such, that is, as the correlate of the intending, without coperforming the positional act which belongs to this intending. For this reflection "only the purely subjective exists, and my theoretical interest is occupied with observing and determining this pure subjectivity and its entirely immanent contents."[125] We need not reemphasize the sense in which "subjectivity" and "subjective" are used here; namely, as the indissoluble correlation of world-experience and its intentional correlate, the "world."

In the light of the specific interest which guides phenomenological reflection, an interest which is essentially different from all worldly interests coenacted within the natural attitude and within natural reflection, there emerges the possibility "of conceiving of a broadest possible concept of a 'sympathizing' or 'nonsympathizing' ego, or rather of a denying-all sympathy-with-itself reflecting ego, and of conceiving thereby the idea . . . of an entirely general and disinterested theoretical self-observer and self-knower."[126] Free from all worldly interests, this self-knower establishes himself as the "impartial observer" of the mundane ego and its involvement with worldly interests. When Husserl designates his interest as "theoretical," what is meant is this moment of detachment, of not cosympathizing with mundane interests. Therefore the ego's theoretical theme in performing phenomenological reflection is the reflective experience of the play of mundane interests as a "subjective" play which can be discovered in universal phenomenological reflection. Its interest "is a pure interest in subjective being,"[127] the "pure experience of subjective acts." These latter are defined "as what can be posited in experience and what at any time can be posited and known when I, as reflecting, disconnect everything that is straightforwardly accepted."[128] In an appendix Husserl adds: "Prior to this, transcendental subjectivity is not only there unnoticed, but it is nonthematic and absolutely anonymous to itself; only the worldly ego, including the human ego, the ego as a 'child of the world,' is already given, experienced, evident."[129] According to this observation, therefore, one must distinguish the latency of the mundane ego, which can be made evident in mundane reflection and which is already there even though it is unnoticed and nonthematic, from the absolute anonymity of the transcendental ego which cannot be simply removed by the possibility of thematically turning toward it at any time. The mundane ego is at any time also "copresent" in being "straightforwardly" directed toward its objects and can be made thematic in reflection. For this reason Husserl also modified "self-forgetfulness," the expression for this copresence, into the expression "latent." Disclosure of the transcendental ego requires a unique resolve. It is the resolve of the "beginning philosopher" for absolute justification and responsibility.

This distinction contains the problematic of this theory of phenomenological reflection wherein the basis for the thesis affirming absolute being of transcendental subjectivity must be sought. We must ask whether it is actually in a position to accept the role of establishing this thesis. For this reason we must take our point of departure from the problem which provides the context for developing this theory of phenomenological reflection. This problem is the question concerning the unique motivation, not found in any worldly condition, for this striving after freedom from cosympathizing with the interests of the mundane ego. At the very outset Husserl indicates that no model is to be found in the natural life for this striving.[130] It is "an entirely 'unnatural' attitude and an entirely unnatural observation of the world and of the self."[131] To be sure, we already find in natural life (at least insofar as it is guided by a striving after scientific truth) a striving to establish some foundation and to attain some established truth, and also a striving to establish knowingly a basis for norms determinative of practical life and its interests. But this striving is content when it has reached grounds which appear to be adequate to its current interests and does not mount toward an absolute (and therefore universal) foundation, justification, and responsibility, toward a "universal critique of life." The resolve to achieve this does not find its motivation in the natural life. Rather does it rest in an act of freedom: "I can in my freedom renounce this natural cobelief of reflection."[132] "Only through the free act of holding back judgment, of willfully-freeing-myself from this primordial cointerest, can that attitude of the disinterested observer come into being." In addition, however, "a particular motivation must release me from this sympathy."[133] Thus the

273

question arises: "What can serve here as a motive?"[134] But this question remains unanswered in the remaining portions of the text. In an appendix Husserl indeed attempts to answer this question: "The motive is clear: I come to know and to deepen my knowledge that all knowing and intending of the world stem from my own experience."[135] Therewith is meant not only the epistemological argument from the "principle of consciousness," but also the insight that everything which holds for me as my world, together with those interests contained in this world and which determine my life, is not something which is purely given and which must simply be accepted, but that it holds for me only upon the strength of my affirmation, recognition, and "position"; that I not only accept my given world and agree to its requirements, but also that I am responsible for the world's being the way it is. But this insight is nothing other than consciousness of myself as a free ego, an ego not subordinate to any mundane complex of conditions or interests; and this, and nothing else, is the "transcendental ego." It is the ethical ego which passes judgment upon all of its worldly interests.

But the free ego is not simply free as the ego of an "act": it is the subject of absolute experience, and this primarily as *my own* subjectivity, *my* consciousness. It is not, as in Hegel's *Phenomenology of Mind*, the self-experience of absolute spirit which in the course of its experience comes to know what it already was in-itself, thereby ascending from being-in-itself to being-for-itself and to being-in-and-for-itself. Much rather does the facticity of the absolute experience of the transcendental ego precede every possibility which is first constituted within it as such,[136] and therefore the interpretation of the absolute nature of subjectivity in the sense of absolute idealism is excluded. Understood in this way, it would not be an experience of the "streaming transcendental life" with its indeterminate and open horizon of experience. Upon this openness is based the possibility of its freedom to be responsible for what is experienced.

Nevertheless, it remains undecided as to how the absoluteness of absolute subjectivity is to be understood positively. The reason why Husserl leaves its character indeterminate can be discovered by a critical analysis of his theory of the phenomenological reflection. We must ask the question how this ego, conscious of its freedom, can be "entirely anonymous" before the reduction. Is not this consciousness of its freedom already presupposed by the possibility of resolving to enact the reduction? The resolve for absolute responsibility and justification cannot be motivated by the insight that the world as it is for me is what it is upon the strength of my freely taking up a position; rather is consciousness of the necessity of responsibility and justification the presupposition for

Husserl's Departure from Cartesianism

reaching this insight. It is therefore not accidental that all of Husserl's attempts to discover the motivation for the phenomenological reduction, in particular those which the appendices to these lectures also reveal, could not achieve satisfactory results. His theory of the phenomenological reflection, and the thesis concerning the absolute being of transcendental subjectivity which it serves to found, is itself an obstacle to the answer that had been sought. This is shown when one asks why Husserl must stress the absolute anonymity of transcendental subjectivity before the discovery of the reductive procedure. Only in this way does he gain the criterion for distinguishing transcendental subjectivity as a unique and absolute realm of being from mundane subjectivity or the human ego, which, although for the most part latent, already knows itself to be an ego before the phenomenological reduction takes place. And the thesis affirming this absolute anonymity has its basis precisely in the theory of phenomenological reflection. We must now show how it follows from this theory.

The temporal structure of reflection is that of a "subsequent awareness." Continuing with the example of an external perception, the reflecting ego directs itself toward the retentionally alive "having-just-perceived," and thereby becomes aware of itself as the same ego that has just perceived and which now reflectively directs itself toward this having-perceived. It becomes aware of itself in this identity as a being which constitutes itself as temporal, or as a self-endurance of the ego in its temporalization. With this, the step is already taken which leads from what at first appears to be the momentary evidence of the "I am" to the I am as the "stream of experience" which, in its experience and world-constituting achieving, becomes the field of transcendental experience. "That which is actually perceived in the streaming now, whose pure content has been reached by the reduction, is an absolute self"[137] to which, however, there inseparably belongs the horizon of temporality, so that the "pure ego extends much further than one at first understands."[138] "The concrete streaming present, the immanent as enduring and as giving itself with changing content in a unified manner in streaming continuation . . . is given in its absolute originality as continuing and as developing in such and such a manner."[139] The transcendental ego, which constitutes itself in its temporalization, "is absolutely present for itself" within this consciousness of its identity, and is the sole being which exists for itself absolutely in the "sense of an absolute being which presents itself in an absolute manner."[140] Its self-presentation is essentially different from the self-presentation of a perceptual object, whose variation through appearances is always presumptive, thereby leaving open the possibility of deception and of being "canceled" (i.e., the possibility of its nonbeing) in the further course

275

of perception.[141] By contrast, the appearance of the ego as identical in the temporal succession of its acts is an absolute self-presentation, that is, it is a presentation of itself which excludes all possibility of nonbeing. It is in this sense that we are to understand Husserl when he speaks of transcendental subjectivity as an absolute realm of being which, as such, can become a field for description. It not only exposes the ego's achievements in the constitution of things and their horizon (the world), but also the "achievements" of temporalization through which the ego constitutes itself as identical in every now.

This self-constitution of the ego, upon which basis it exists for itself in an absolute manner, is thus presented in accordance with that basic (and, for Husserl, authoritative) model of all constitution as the constitution of objective unity throughout a manifold of modes of givenness. The transcendental ego becomes thematic in phenomenological reflection, and this means that it becomes objective (*gegenständlich*) as the unity which constantly maintains itself throughout all of its acts, or as the ego which is always copresent, even—although for the most part latent and "self-forgetful"—in its natural worldly life where it is directly addressed to objects. All talk of the anonymity of the transcendental ego before the performance of the phenomenological reduction must therefore refer to this constant copresence, for in natural reflection the ego is aware of its copresence before this reduction only occasionally and only in the service of limited mundane interests. Through the phenomenological reduction and its pointing out the constancy of this copresence, all possible "excuses" are taken away from the ego and it now stands placed before the universality of its responsibility for everything that holds for it as its world.

Understood in this way, all trace of an idle "theoretical" inquisitiveness is removed from our speaking of the "impartial observing" of the phenomenologically reflecting ego. This universal reflection proves itself to be the way along which the requirement placed upon the ego for a "radical critique of life" and its own absolute self-responsibility can now be established in its necessity. This is possible only by "escaping from a kinship with the world" and a "world-denial," which means an escape from simply accepting and coenacting all given interests, practical considerations, and worldly ties. Hence the phenomenological reduction signifies the act in which the ego becomes aware of its freedom for absolute self-responsibility. Only because phenomenological reflection is an impartial observing in this sense (namely, as becoming aware of oneself as the absolute "performing-ego" which is not permitted to accept either the world or worldly interests simply as something given) can Husserl later state in the *Crisis* that such reflection can lead to a "complete personal transformation" of man. It thereby loses the appearance of being merely in the service of a restful satisfaction with searching out and analyzing the infinitely rich play of subjective intentional achievements. Husserl can with justice repeatedly quote St. Augustine's "go back into yourself, for truth dwells in the inner man,"[142] for this way of reflection serves the same end.

We must now, however, show how this simple state of affairs is once again obscured from another side insofar as the constant copresence of the transcendental ego (discovered by the reduction) is, in an idealistically sounding turn, presented as an objective (*gegenständlich*) field of absolute being. This is a consequence of the already often noted fact that for Husserl being (*Sein*) primarily signifies being-an-object (*Gegenstand-sein*) for an act of consciousness which presents it. Only for this reason is it possible for Husserl to conceive of the temporalizing self-constitution of the ego in accordance with his basic model for all constitution; that is, as the constitution of objective unity through the manifold of its modes of givenness. The absolute self-existence of the transcendental ego can therefore mean only existence as the object (*Objekt*)—which holds firm and establishes itself in its continuing continuity—for the ego which is reflectively directed toward this existence. The truth of its absolute being therefore means that it has established itself and can establish itself in acts of identification. It is nothing other than its continuance as the performer in all of the acts which it performs, and which becomes objective in phenomenological reflection. Since for Husserl truth primarily signifies the self-establishing objective continuance of self-existence, Husserl can view the achievement of phenomenological reflection as consisting of its discovery of the performing ego within the previously anonymous continuance of its copresence and constitutive achieving as a domain of absolute being, and therewith as a field for descriptive analysis.

Yet, is this absolute subjectivity actually present to itself in its self-temporalization in such a way that, in terms of its absolute existence-for-itself, it can become the object of a reflective presentifying re-presentation? If the world is universally exhibited by the phenomenological reduction as something formed out of intentional achievements and as something for which I, as formative subject, am responsible, can this freeing of the ego for its absolute responsibility take place by disclosing a domain of absolute being as a new field of experience? May we not find moments in Husserl's analysis of the temporal self-constitution of the ego which make this questionable? In the lectures on time-consciousness,[143] it was already established that absolute subjectivity is an "absolute flux"—Husserl speaks in a later manuscript of a "Heraclitean flux"—for whose constitutive elements "we are totally lacking a name," since all names are

277

only the names for the worldly and objectified being which comes to be constituted within this flux. Nothing of objective continuance or endurance can be found within this flux. Rather, this is first discovered in a "subsequent awareness," and upon the basis of a retrospective reflection upon the unity and identity of the ego (which have always been already "constituted" within this flux) which, recollecting itself in all of the previous phases of the "stream of experience" that have run their course, discovers itself as being the same ego. If this continuance and endurance are to be understood as belonging to absolute being, is it not thereby presupposed that the "performing ego" is completely incarnate in what the subsequent awareness of presentifying and objectifying reflection has been able to establish with respect to the already enacted achievements and their results? If this is correct, the ego would first constitute itself in its absolute identity only through its retentionally established "having-been" (*Gewesen-sein*), which is then to be objectified reflectively in recollection. It apprehends itself only as what it has been until now. Opposed to this, however, is the fact that belonging to the consciousness of the ego as a constituent of its identity within its "living presence" is not only what has been retentionally retained, but also the future-oriented protentions whereby it directs itself toward what is to be directly expected and experienced, while knowing itself to be identical in this self-directedness with the ego which is subsequently known in reflection. It is precisely this protentional directedness toward "what is to come" and what is temporally "immanent" that grounds the possibility of openness for new experience and for factual responsibility for this experience.

It is clearly no accident that the structure of protention is only briefly treated in the lectures on time-consciousness.[144] Its further consideration would have served to question the theory that the self-constitution of the ego is accomplished by its past experience and that the winning of its objective identity as the identity of a continuing field of absolute being is discovered by a "subsequent awareness" and retrospective reflection. Thus the Husserlian theory of the identity of the absolute ego cannot render intelligible how this identity, which comes to consciousness in reflecting upon the constitutive achievements which have already been enacted, is one which can establish an identity with the presently active ego, and that means the ego which is extended beyond itself into the "future." Thus the performing ego is not, in its identity, completely incarnate in what the subsequent presentifying and objectifying reflection can establish as its accomplished performances. Rather is it the case that its self-knowing identity is already presupposed by the possibility of such subsequent awareness and retrospective reflection. It must therefore already possess some kind of self-knowledge in the very performance of its acts, one

Husserl's Departure from Cartesianism

which is clearly not entirely identical with the knowledge of its performances gained by reflection. For this reason, Scheler had already emphasized that the essence of acts "can only be experienced in their performance," and that reflection "is to be distinguished from all presentifying acts as such."[145] The ego's self-knowledge won by objectifying reflection is only a knowledge of what it has already enacted, that is, acts with their respectively determinate intentional direction wherein the ego constitutes an objective unity for itself. This way of reflection permits the ego to experience itself only in the results of the achievements it has already performed and not in their actual performance. Its ownmost identity, which includes both of these moments, can never become an object for it, but is already there prior to all objectification and can never be overtaken by objectifying reflection. It is always more than what it knows itself to be in reflection and is never present to itself in reflection, for it is always ahead of itself. It has, however, a knowledge of itself prior to all reflection, for which reason Sartre has made the attempt to differentiate a prereflective *cogito* and a reflective *cogito*. The self-identity of the performing ego is therefore not one that can become objective and cannot be described by concepts referring to objective being; it can be grasped only as the "dialectical" relationship of " being-identical-in-being-other."[146] As such, the transcendental ego is of course anonymous when measured in terms of absolute existence-for-itself as absolute self-presentation. But this anonymity cannot be removed by any objectifying reflection. It is that by virtue of which the ego is already ahead of its present, and in this "being ahead of itself" it is open for new experience and for responsibility for this experience. But this unique character of the ego's unity cannot be conceived of by Husserl because he equates being with objective identity, even though his analysis of time-consciousness could have offered him the occasion to recognize this character. For this reason alone, Husserl can present transcendental subjectivity as a field of being which can only be disclosed by means of the reduction.

Further consideration of Husserl's analysis of the temporal self-constitution of the ego also forces us to surrender this thesis. It falls victim to Kant's criticism of the paralogism implied by the doctrine of the soul which has its roots precisely in applying the category of substance to the concept of the ego—and this is just what Husserl's concept of a "unity becoming objectively present" amounts to. Because Husserl, despite his criticism of Descartes, remains implicitly bound to the modern metaphysical concept of substance, his analysis of self-consciousness, and therewith the departure from metaphysics, remain incomplete.

279

This confirms our previous assertion that, on the basis of the guiding concept of true being as a self-verifying identity capable of being presented in an objective manner, what Husserl had correctly seen under the title of transcendental subjectivity and its absoluteness becomes so obscured that he was not able to arrive at an unequivocal determination of this concept. In terms of this concept of truth, transcendental subjectivity, as the basis of absolute foundation and justification, must be an absolute being, and the theory of phenomenological reflection is meant to confirm this. But as free subjectivity this is just what it is not—and only as free can it find within itself the motive for absolute self-responsibility and set out upon the path of the reductive removal of its "anonymity." For this reason as well, Husserl can find no adequate answer to the question concerning the motive for the "radical critique of life," for this motive is none other than its freedom and openness for absolute experience, and just this excludes its subsumption under a concept of being as continuing objectivity. Thus the concept of absolute subjectivity vacillates between the concept of a free ego, open to absolute experience and responsibility in its "being-ahead-of-itself," and the idealistic concept of an absolute being which assures itself of this being in its theoretical and disinterested self-contemplation. The question concerning the motive for this striving after absolute justification and for the reduction as the way leading to this justification cannot be answered if the self-responsible and self-justifying ego is presented as an absolute foundation of being. Husserl's self-critical observations published in the appendices show that Husserl himself found continually new difficulties on this point. That is, he did not succeed in adequately establishing the connection between the "theoretical" ego, which is directed toward the ultimate foundation of knowledge, and the "practical" ego, the free ethical ego, although his efforts aim in this direction. A further indication of this lack is found in Husserl's mention of the phenomenon of conscience as a "passional-reflective attitude,"[147] which is indeed mentioned under the mode of reflection, but which surprisingly is not related to the question concerning the motive for the striving for justification by which the reductive procedure is guided.

Since Husserl cannot penetrate to the ultimate ground of the ego's absolute self-certainty as a ground which does not reveal itself to objectifying reflection, not only does the concept of transcendental subjectivity remain "in suspense," but also all other "operative" concepts,[148] such as "constitution," "achievement," and "transcendental life," with which the essence of transcendental subjectivity is to be interpreted.

Husserl's Departure from Cartesianism

6. The Result of This Critical Analysis

The result of this critical analysis can be indicated only in brief. It has shown that Husserl's term "transcendental subjectivity" is not unequivocal, but that two different elements must be distinguished within it:

1. The subject as free and as called to its responsibility, a call which it experiences in inwardness as its own self. In this sense, transcendental subjectivity is the "subjectivity" of the subject, or, to speak with Kant, the "intelligible character" of man. As such, however, it cannot be reflectively objectified and cannot be a "field" for description.

2. The indissoluble correlation of world-constituting achievement and what is achieved within it, which can no longer be designated as "subjectivity" in the traditional sense. The presentation of this correlation is actually that great task of phenomenological analysis which can be achieved by the reductive method: herein lies the "field" of phenomenological analysis. If this analysis is to result in the insight that this achievement constitutes the essence of transcendental "life" as the life of a transcendental community, a transcendental "We" or the transcendental "totality of egos," this means that what we call the "world" is nothing other than the interpretation of something experienced and about which, "in-itself," nothing could be possibly said apart from this correlation with the experiencing and "entering-into-community" consciousness. In this respect Husserl is entirely correct in naming phenomenology "transcendental phenomenology," and indeed "transcendental" in Kant's critical sense, even though it is to be distinguished from Kant's transcendental philosophy with respect to method and range. "World" in this context is the result, constantly changing throughout the history of man, of constitution as an interpretation, an expounding of something which, before and apart from this expounding, is nameless and unspeakable.

When the attempt is made, however, to raise this play (*Spiel*) between the correlation of world (always formed by interpretation beforehand) and constitutive world-forming as the "holding sway" (*Walten*) of the world itself to the level of something absolute,[149] then it appears to us that in this understanding its "holding sway" is lost, for the world in its "holding sway" is nothing other than the free play (*Spielraum*) of transcendental subjectivity in the first sense, transcendental subjectivity as an experience which is free and which is therewith open for an advance and a history for which it is responsible. When understood in the first sense, the being of transcendental subjectivity breaks away from the immanence of a self-enclosed "holding sway" of the world. That is, the experience of the absolute subject as a free subject not only consists of its experience of the world and worldly beings in taking up a position for which it bears

281

responsibility, but equally consists of its absolute certainty of itself as free and as called to absolute responsibility, a certainty in which it experiences its relation to the "absolute" in the true (Hegelian) sense, that is, its relation to the source of the possibility of a responsibility which is free from all worldly interests and conditions. Therefore the world in its "holding sway" cannot be the absolute. This certainty with respect to its ground which is included in the free subject's absolute self-certainty, and which, like the certainty of its freedom, can neither be objectified nor brought under concepts of objective being, is therefore the certainty of a transcendence in the sense of something nonworldly which, however, does not stand opposed to it as a distinct and separate object, but which announces itself in it as a free subjectivity. Thus transcendental subjectivity in this sense, as a subject which is aware of its freedom, is not itself the absolute but the place where the absolute is experienced—whereby experience is here clearly spoken of in a radically different sense than as experience of the world and worldly beings, a sense which is in harmony with Husserl's requirement that every transcendence, if it is not to be an empty thought, must have a manner of showing itself and announcing itself to consciousness which is appropriate to it.

Subjectivity in its "anonymity" as free before all reflection is always absolutely certain of itself beforehand. Because Husserl, however, believed that the "performing-ego," the "ego which takes up a position," could be brought completely within the grasp of the "subsequently aware" objectifying reflection he was unable to discover this immediate "being-within-itself" as the ground for the possibility of both reflection and responsibility. To be sure, Husserl was somehow aware of this under the title of a "deeper ground of intentionality" ("*Untergrund der Intentionalität*"), but the attempt to determine more precisely the relation of this "deeper ground" to the explicit subjective-thematizing reflection finally leads to the difficulty understood contention that the ego, as long as it performs no acts of reflection, is not at all aware of its own subjectivity,[150] precisely because the concept of "consciousness" is oriented from the very start along the lines of the objectifying consciousness which makes something into its intentional object.

We cannot here explicate further how this revision of the concept of absolute subjectivity also presents us with the possibility of giving a more precise meaning to other of Husserl's basic operative concepts that interpret this subjectivity. A separate investigation would also be required in order to show how this immediate prereflective "knowledge" of itself is not that of a "pure" subjectivity, whose purity is just that of the universal and theoretical reflective observation and objectification, and how it possesses the ground of its possibility in its worldliness, a worldliness to

Husserl's Departure from Cartesianism

which its bodily nature belongs, so that its body is not simply a constituted, although exceptional, "thing"—as it first appears to objectifying reflection—but which itself, in the immediacy with which it is experienced,[151] belongs among the constituents of its subjectivity which is known to be free and capable of acting. From this follows the revision of Husserl's inadequate analysis of the "Other"[152] and the impossibility of the egological point of departure for the phenomenological analysis of the constitution of the "world," as well as a modification of the meaning of distinguishing transcendental and psychological subjectivity.

This, as already indicated, is of lasting significance for the critique of modern "anthropologism." But this critique and its intended distinction can no longer be interpreted as a description disclosing two realms of being and an eidetic which is to be based upon this description, whereby the problem of the parallelism between the psychological and phenomenological analyses disappears, a problem with which Husserl had unceasingly struggled. There remains the distinction between "transcendental subjectivity" in the first-mentioned sense as the dimension of "absolute" or "ultimately foundational" experience, but which is not, however, a "field" of objectifying description and eidetic, and "transcendental subjectivity" in the sense of that indissoluble correlation of constitutive world-formation as the process of advancing history and the presently already constituted world as the horizon of this advance. This latter is actually the field of phenomenological experience, but this is an experience into which all the results of psychological and anthropological empirical investigation continually enter. It need not be said that the methodological grounding of the possibility that the empirical can provide access to "absolute experience" occasions a revision of the distinction between "empirical" and "*a priori*," a distinction whose character as an exhaustive alternative has already become questionable from the side of researches into the foundations of logic.

All this is said here only to indicate how this project of the *First Philosophy*, whose own aims had failed, is, in this failure, not an end, but a beginning which signifies the disclosure of a great wealth of problems which not only concern the understanding of Husserl's work and its unity, but which also concern the horizon of those questions which, with the end of modern metaphysics, become inescapable with the prospect of a way leading to their resolution.

Ludwig Landgrebe

NOTES

1. Edmund Husserl, *Erste Philosophie: Erster Teil* (Den Haag: Martinus Nijhoff, 1956). See D. Henrich's review of this work in *Philosophische Rundschau* (1958), 1 ff.
2. For example, *Husserliana*, VIII, 354 ff.
3. Edmund Husserl, *Die Krisis der europäischen Wissenschaften und die transzendentale Phänomenologie* (Den Haag: Martinus Nijhoff, 1954) (*Husserliana*, VI).
4. *Husserliana*, I, 47 (*Cartesian Meditations,* trans. Dorion Cairns, p. 5.—ED.).
5. About 1921; cf. VIII, 249.
6. III, 8 (cf. Gibson's translation of the first book of the *Ideas*, p. 46.—ED.).
7. VIII, 5.
8. VII, 4.
9. *Ibid.*, p. 5.
10. VIII, 3-25.
11. III, 65 (Gibson, p. 109).
12. VIII, 63.
13. *Ibid.*, p. 19.
14. *Ibid.*, p. 166.
15. *Ibid.*, p. 123.
16. *Ibid.*, p. 121.
17. Cf. the appendix: "The Principle of Sufficient Reason for All Scientific Knowledge," III, 329 ff.
18. *Ibid.*, p. 19.
19. *Ibid.*, p. 23.
20. *Ibid.*, p. 25.
21. *Ibid.*, pp. 196, 344.
22. *Ibid.*, p. 154.
23. *Ibid.*, p. 21.
24. *Ibid.*
25. *Ibid.*, pp. 197 ff.
26. *Ibid.*
27. *Ibid.*, p. 200.
28. "The Idea of a Philosophical Culture," *Deutsch-japanische Zeitschtift* 1923; reprinted in *The Kaizo* (Tokyo: 1923). The portion of this article which is important for this problem is taken up by Husserl in the text of *Husserliana*, VII, 8-17.
29. VIII, 8.
30. *Ibid.*, p. 31; cf. also pp. 9, 48, 366 f.
31. *Ibid.*
32. *Ibid.*, p. 33.
33. *Ibid.*
34. *Ibid.*, p. 35.
35. *Ibid.*, p. 380.
36. *Ibid.*, p. 125.
37. *Ibid.*, p. 310; *Husserliana,* I, 55 (*Cartesian Meditations*, trans. Cairns, p. 14.—ED.).
38. *Husserliana*, VIII, 169, 380.
39. *Ibid.*, p. 366.
40. *Ibid.*, p. 40.
41. *Ibid.*, p. 41.
42. *Ibid.*, p. 367.
43. *Ibid.*, p. 362.

44. *Ibid.*, p. 368.
45. *Ibid.*, p. 452.
46. *Husserliana*, VII, 258.
47. Cf. VII, 258.
48. VIII, 482.
49. Henrich, *Philosophische Rundschau*, and Wagner, "Critical Observations concerning Husserl's Posthumous Writings." (See pp. 192-242 in this collection.—ED.)
50. Cf. VII, 358, 363.
51. Cf. the editor's introduction to *Erste Philosophie: Zweiter Teil.*
52. VIII, 37-64.
53. *Ibid.*, p. 49.
54. *Ideas* I, p. 62 (Gibson, p. 105—ED.).
55. VIII, 68.
56. *Ibid.*, p. 52.
57. *Ibid.*, p. 461.
58. *Ibid.*, p. 42.
59. *Ibid.*, p. 59
60. *Ibid.*, p. 63.
61. *Ibid.*, p. 66.
62. *Ibid.*, p. 174.
63. *Ibid.*, pp. 174 ff.
64. Husserl had already given a first presentation of the reduction of "intersubjectivity" in a lecture given in 1910. It is not treated in the *Ideas* and the inclusive presentation of this topic first occurs in the *Cartesian Meditations* of 1930.
65. Cf. VIII, 70 ff.
66. *Ibid.*, p. 69.
67. *Ibid.*, p. 71.
68. *Ibid.*
69. *Ibid.*, p. 72.
70. *Ibid.*, p. 73.
71. *Ibid.*, p. 74.
72. *Ibid.*, pp. 76 ff.
73. *Ibid.*, p. 78.
74. *Ibid.*, p. 79.
75. Cf. the postscript to the *Ideas*, V, 140.
76. Cf. VII, 354 ff., 357 ff.
77. *Ibid.*, p. 401.
78. Cf. Henrich, *Philosophische Rundschau*, p. 17.
79. *Ideen I*, p. 175 (Gibson, p. 213.—ED.).
80. *Ibid.*, pp. 193 ff., 220 f. (Gibson, pp. 231 ff., 260 f.—ED.).
81. V, 73 ff.
82. VII, 258.
83. *Ideen I*, p. 149, note (Gibson, pp. 183 f.—ED.).
84. See the appendices to VIII, 443 ff.
85. *Ibid.*, pp. 81-163.
86. *Ibid.*, p. 164.
87. *Ibid.*, pp. 120-130, 139-146.
88. *Ibid.*, pp. 87-111.
89. *Ibid.*, p. 127.
90. *Ibid.*, p. 153.
91. Cf. Henrich, *Philosophische Rundschau*, p. 20.

92. VII, 81.
93. Edmund Husserl, *On the Phenomenology of the Consciousness of Internal Time*, trans. John Barnett Brough (Dordrecht: Kluwer Academic Publishers, 1991).
94. *Critique of Pure Reason,* note to B. xli (Kemp-Smith translation, p. 36—ED.).
95. VIII, 84.
96. *Ibid.,* p. 115.
97. *Ibid.,* p. 127.
98. *Ibid.,* p. 153.
99. *Ibid.,* pp. 146-164.
100. *Ibid.,* p. 146.
101. *Ibid.,* p. 142.
102. *Ibid.,* p. 467.
103. On the interpretation of the later works see A. Gurwitsch: "The Last Work of Edmund Husserl," *Philosophy and Phenomenological Research* (1956), 380 ff. [reprinted in Aron Gurwitsch, *Studies in Phenomenology and Psychology* (Evanston: Northwestern University Press, 1966), pp. 397-447.—ED.].
104. VIII, 169.
105. VI, 508.
106. Cf. Stephan Strasser, "Des Gottesproblem in der Spätphilosophie Edmund Husserls," *Philosophisches Jahrbuch* 67, 130 ff.
107. VI, 513.
108. VIII, 175.
109. *Ibid.,* p. 153.
110. *Ibid.,* p. 157.
111. *Ibid.,* p. 155.
112. *Ibid.,* p. 161.
113. *Ibid.,* p. 162.
114. *Ibid.,* p. 163.
115. *Ibid.,* pp. 164 ff.
116. Cf. *Ibid.,* p. 495.
117. *Ibid.,* p. 190, also pp. 482 ff.
118. VII, 366.
119. Eugen Fink, "Operative Begriffe in Husserls Phänomenologie," *Zeitschrift für philosophische Forschung* (1957), pp. 321 ff.
120. VIII, 87-111; the analysis is carried on further in the Kant essay from 1924, VII 259 ff.
121. *Ibid.,* p. 89.
122. *Ibid.*
123. *Ibid.,* p. 91.
124. *Ibid.,* p. 95.
125. *Ibid.,* p. 97.
126. *Ibid.,* p. 99.
127. *Ibid.,* p. 108.
128. *Ibid.,* p. 110.
129. *Ibid.,* p. 417.
130. Cf. above, p. 264.
131. VIII, 121.
132. *Ibid.,* p. 92.
133. *Ibid.,* p. 98.
134. *Ibid.*
135. *Ibid.,* p. 416

136. Cf. above, p. 270.
137. VIII, 466.
138. *Ibid.*, p. 477.
139. *Ibid.*, p. 467.
140. *Ibid.*
141. *Ibid.*, p. 466.
142. As quoted by Husserl at the end of the *Cartesian Meditations.*—ED.
143. *Internal Time Consciousness*, pp. 23-24.
144. Ibid., pp. 410 f.
145. Max Seheler, *Der Formalismus in der Ethik und die materiale Wertethik*, 5th ed. (Bern: Franke Verlag, 1966), pp. 46, 385.
146. Cf. Landgrebe, "Des Problem der Dialektik," in *Marxismusstudien* III (1960), 11 ff.
147. VIII, 105. (Here Husserl refers to acts of "reflection" which need not be "intellectual," and which can have an emotional tone. As an example Husserl cites a possible "reflection" upon the fact that "I love," a reflection in which I can be joyous or displeased and self-reproachful.—ED.)
148. A reference to Eugen Fink's notion of concepts which are not thematically "fixed" but which are employed as "intellectual schemes" whereby "thematic" concepts receive objective determination. They compose a "conceptual milieu," a conceptual "horizon," in terms of which other conceptual moments which are essential to a philosophical position can be ordered and explicated. Cf. Eugen Fink, "Les Concepts opératoires dans la phénoménologie de Husserl," *Husserl: Cahiers de Royaumont, Philosophie III*, p. 218.—ED
149. Cf. Eugen Fink, *Sein, Wahrheit, Welt* (Den Haag: Martinus Nijhoff, 1958).
150. This is found in what for this problematic is a very important section— "Natural and Transcendental Reflection and the Deeper Ground of Intentionality"—of the Kant essay (VII, 259 ff., esp. 266).
151. Cf. VIII, 61.
152. Concerning the difficulties encountered by this analysis see A. Schütz, "Das Problem der Intersubjectivität bei Husserl," *Philosophische Rundschau* (1957), pp. 81 ff. [In the *Collected Papers I* (The Hague: Martinus Nijhoff, 1962), Schütz states: "Nevertheless, Sartre's statement that Husserl has not succeeded in explaining the problem of intersubjectivity in terms of a relationship between transcendental subjectivities seems to be correct. The appresenting term of the coupling is not my transcendental ego but my own self-given life as a psychophysical I within my primordial sphere, that is, as a modification of my mundane I within the world. And what is appresented by this 'pairing' is first the object in the outer world interpreted as the body of another human being, which, as such, indicates the mental life of the Other—the Other, however, still as a mundane psychophysical unity within the world, as a fellow-man, therefore, and not as a transcendental Alter Ego. Husserl, so it seems, has shown in a masterful way how within the mundane sphere man and fellow-man are compossible and coexistent, how within this sphere the Other becomes manifest, how within it concordant behavior, communication, etc., occur. Yet he has not shown the possibility of a coexisting transcendental ego. This, however, would be necessary in order to overcome the solipsistic argument in the transcendental sphere" (*ibid.*, p. 197). It is interesting to compare this evaluation of the problem of intersubjectivity in Husserl with Wagner's evaluation (cf. above, esp. pp. 238ff.).—ED.]

NOESIS PRESS PAPERBACKS

Classics in Phenomenology
R. O. Elveton (ed.): *The Phenomenology of Husserl.* Selected Critical Readings. (CP 1)   ISBN 0-9701679-0-3

Klaus Held. *The Living Present.* (CP 2)

Contemporary Phenomenological Thought
Damian Byers. *Intentionality and Transcendence: Closure and Openness in Husserl's Phenomenology.* (CT 1)

CONNECTING FORWARD